ON THE
GROUND

ON THE
GROUND

The Black Panther Party
in Communities across America

Edited by Judson L. Jeffries

UNIVERSITY PRESS OF MISSISSIPPI • JACKSON

www.upress.state.ms.us

The University Press of Mississippi is a member of the Association of American University Presses.

Copyright © 2010 by University Press of Mississippi
All rights reserved
Manufactured in the United States of America

∞

Library of Congress Cataloging-in-Publication Data

On the ground : the Black Panther Party in communities across America / edited by Judson L. Jeffries.
   p. cm.
   Includes index.
   ISBN 978-1-60473-492-8 (cloth : alk. paper) — ISBN 978-1-60473-493-5 (ebook) 1. Black Panther Party—History. 2. African Americans—Politics and government—20th century. 3. African Americans—Civil rights—History—20th century. 4. African Americans—Services for—History—20th century. 5. Poor—Services for—United States—History—20th century. 6. Civil rights movements—United States—History—20th century. 7. United States—Race relations—History—20th century. 8. United States—History, Local. I. Jeffries, J. L. (Judson L.), 1965–
   E185.615.O57 2010
   322.4'20973—dc22   2009047230

British Library Cataloging-in-Publication Data available

This book is dedicated to Michael Jackson,
a revolutionary in his own right.

CONTENTS

INTRODUCTION
The Second Installment

Judson L. Jeffries and Ryan Nissim-Sabat

The Black Power movement, compared to its predecessor, the modern civil rights movement, was comprised of fewer organizations and members. Simply put, there were many more card-carrying civil rights activists than there were advocates of Black Power. Arguably, the four most prominent civil rights organizations—the National Association for the Advancement of Colored People (NAACP), the Congress of Racial Equality (CORE), the Southern Christian Leadership Conference (SCLC), and the Urban League—had hundreds of chapters across the country, with massive membership rolls in the thousands, perhaps hundreds of thousands, of people. For example, in the 1950s the NAACP had over 500 chapters and hundreds of thousands of members. While certainly not as impressive as the NAACP, the SCLC, the CORE, and the Urban League also boasted scores of chapters as well as members. It is likely that no Black Power organization had more than fifty chapters or a membership equal to that of any of the major civil rights organizations. The Black Panther Party (BPP), with its reported forty branches and chapters and estimated (but never substantiated) 5,000 members at its apex, was perhaps the largest of the Black Power organizations.[1]

In recent years, some scholars have incredulously lamented that a comprehensive and exhaustive study of the BPP has yet to be done. Although true, the same can be said of most organizations of any era, including those that comprised the Black Power movement. Writing a comprehensive and exhaustive study (if there is such a thing) of any organization is a daunting, one might even say a nearly impossible task, for obvious reasons. Having said that, though, of all the Vietnam War–era organizations, the BPP is most in need of serious, systematic, invasive, and rigorous scholarly examination. We can think of no organization that was or is more maligned, misrepresented, or misconstrued than the BPP. The party suffers from a distorted and warped image that was largely framed by both the print (including the Panthers' own newspaper) and television media, which, for the most part, reduced the entire organization to the Bay Area (the Panthers' birthplace) and a few high-profile personalities. Consequently, for some, the Panthers are known more for their histrionics and showdowns with police than their community survival programs. We venture to say that the image that many academics and laypersons have of the party is a sensational one that does not mesh with reality.

While we philosophically do not believe that a comprehensive and exhaustive history of any organization can be written, we do believe that it is possible and indeed imperative to fill gaps in knowledge by investigating the events and activities in various branches and chapters of this particular organization. Fortunately for scholars, the BPP had a relatively short life span, purportedly consisting of no more than forty branches and chapters during its existence. Because of its relative small size, writing a history of the BPP via its local branches and chapters is, on its face, manageable, at least theoretically—hence, the purpose of this long-term project: the second installment on the local history of the BPP. The first volume, *Comrades: A Local History of the Black Panther Party* (2007), studied the goings-on in seven cities where Panther branches and chapters were established—Baltimore; Winston-Salem, North Carolina; Cleveland; Milwaukee; Indianapolis; Philadelphia; and Los Angeles—with the expressed purpose of painting a more complete portrait of this organization than has heretofore been done.[2]

This second volume examines Panther activity in Seattle; Detroit; Kansas City, Missouri; New Orleans; Houston; and Des Moines, Iowa. To our chagrin, the decision to embark on this long-range project was made after *Comrades* went to press. Had the decision been made with a modicum of foresight, perhaps the volumes would have been arranged according to region, year, or some other theme. It should be noted, however, that scholars who elect to undertake the BPP as a research project start at a disadvantage. Given the depths to which the BPP was reportedly infiltrated, many former Panthers are suspicious (and rightly so) of those whom they do not know, and thus are reluctant to share their stories with many outside of their circle of friends. Additionally, many former Panthers are difficult to track down for a whole host of obvious and not so obvious reasons. Consequently, the direction of one's research is sometimes influenced and guided by one's access to human capital.

Nevertheless, as stated in *Comrades*, in order to delineate and chronicle the rich history of the BPP, one has to examine local Panther activities throughout the United States. For whatever reason, this approach has been to a large degree overlooked when the history of the BPP is told. Again, Oakland is the lens through which the party is most often studied, which is problematic, if for no other reason, because the Oakland/Bay Area experience is not representative of the entire organization. Moreover, what is written tends to focus on dramatic events, such as confrontations with police officers, Huey P. Newton's legal troubles, the execution of Fred Hampton and Mark Clark, or the murder of other prominent Panther leaders. For this reason, we believe it is important to take a substantively different approach when studying the BPP. This local case-studies approach is one that is rigorously invasive and features the voices of people who served on the ground—those who staffed the offices and kept things in order, escorted the elderly around town, administered sickle cell anemia tests, set up health clinics, and launched free clothing drives. Members of the BPP were responding to the basic needs of local black communities throughout the country. As Bobby Seale described, the Panthers wanted to establish "a broad, massive, people's type of political machinery" that served the needs of their respective communities.[3] Indeed, in some cities where Panther offices existed, these programs were both wide-ranging and far-reaching. At the same time, the Panthers maintained that it was important to understand the larger context of their struggle. From the Panthers' standpoint, the liberation of black people in the United States was inextricably linked to the global self-determination struggles of all oppressed people, especially people of color.[4]

Through its community survival programs, the BPP sought to improve black people's lot. Just as important, through these endeavors the BPP hoped to raise the consciousness of the people it served. The party's survival programs were not handouts devoid of political messages, but were considered the foundation upon which the impending revolution would be built. As was noted in *Comrades*, most historical accounts of the BPP have tended to gloss over the party's important community initiatives.[5] Newspapers that published photos of Panther men and women with scowls on their faces and shotguns in their hands rarely printed images of these same Panthers handing out bags of groceries, doing blood pressure screenings, or hovered over a hot stove preparing breakfasts (on frigid wintry mornings in places like Detroit and Kansas City) for children before they headed off to school. When reporters covered the Panthers' community survival programs, they often condemned them as a tool of indoctrination because the Panthers used these opportunities to teach children about black history, black pride, and community uplift.

Complicit in this superfluous depiction of the BPP is the academy, which has to some extent framed the BPP around its early emphasis on armed resistance and Panther standoffs with some of the nation's most notorious law enforcement agencies. This has contributed to a selective documentation of the party on the national level, disregarding the experiences of the rank and file throughout the country. Recently, the emergence of a new body of Panther scholarship has created greater space for interrogating the intricacies of the BPP on the local level.

The local chapters and branches of the BPP were dependent upon specific local circumstances that defined their community and their access to resources. Each Panther outpost had a particular context that initiated a unique application of the BPP's Ten Point Program and Platform. Documenting such stories accomplishes a key research goal described by Bruce C. Berg in his book *Qualitative Research Methods for the Social Sciences*, which is to "assure that the real-life experiences and memories of people cannot be so easily omitted, edited, shredded, or swept away."[6] Most of the Panthers to whom we have spoken over the years were, on the whole, not mentioned in the *New York Times, Los Angeles Times*, or *Washington Post*, nor were they the subjects of nightly news telecasts or featured in documentaries of the period. For every Huey P. Newton or Elaine Brown there were tens of Panthers whose names and deeds have heretofore gone unnoticed by academics and laypersons alike. In this volume, like the previous one, ordinary Panthers' names and works are highlighted, along with their stories. Oral history provides increased understanding and living content to the otherwise one-dimensional information frequently offered by documents alone. With the use of interviews, we give voice to the forgotten and the unknown. Having said that, since some of the material in this volume is based upon individual memories spanning some forty years—and it is reasonable to expect less than 100 percent recall—there undoubtedly are statements made with more vigor than coherence and with conflicting interpretations. We therefore feel obligated to provide the reader with accurate and unbiased historical facts that serve as a kind of gyroscopic beacon for keeping this volume in perspective. This was made possible with the use of government documents, credible newspapers (both mainstream and alternative), personal diaries and memoirs, and archival material of certain branches and chapters of the BPP.

Books written about the BPP in the last fifteen years fall mainly within these categories: memoirs by former members, ideologically driven works by Panther critics, studies of event-centered episodes that garnered national and/or international press, works that highlight the sensational aspects of the party, edited books comprised of topics that are as eclectic as their authors, and finally single authored/coauthored scholarly volumes. Only a few of these studies focus on local, grassroots Panther activity. Interest in the BPP was rekindled in the early 1990s after the untimely and tragic death of Huey P. Newton. A quarter of the nearly two dozen books that have since been written were published by the mid-1990s. Earl Anthony's hair-raising and tell-all *Spitting in the Wind* was the first such published, hitting the stands in 1990.[7] Given the outrageousness of some of Anthony's claims, one can understand why some have difficulty taking Anthony's work seriously.

Moreover, of the nearly two dozen books published by reputable presses since Anthony's book, eleven were penned by former Panthers, nine of whom were West Coast Panthers. Only three non–West Coast Panthers—Afeni Shakur, Mumia Abu-Jamal, Evan Hopkins, and Steve McCutchen—have offered books of their own, presenting illuminating portraits of their experiences in New York; Philadelphia; Winston-Salem, North Carolina; and Baltimore, respectively.[8] While valuable contributions to the literature, all four are memoirs, which typically lack the kind of detachment and objectivity for which scholarly studies are known. The only other book-length treatments that highlight Black Panther activity on the local level are Andrew Witt's *Black Panthers in the Midwest*; Yohuru Williams's work on New Haven, Connecticut; and J. F. Rice's 1983 booklet, *Up on Madison and Down on 75th*. To be sure, more works on the local level are needed. Other scholars have paid some attention to local Panther activity,[9] but none of them rival the investment of the works listed above.[10]

Why is this type of case-study research significant? In other words, what difference will this research make? Unless in-depth studies of local branches and chapters are conducted, there are a number of fundamental, yet substantive, questions that cannot and perhaps will never be answered in any meaningful way—questions that will give students of history greater insight into the organization's complexities, seeming contradictions, and nuances. Contrary to what some have been led to believe, members of the BPP were not monolithic in their composition, beliefs, or approach to alleviate local oppression. Those who joined the BPP ranged from high school dropouts to runaways to graduates of doctoral programs; however, the only way to document this claim scientifically is to engage in a branch by branch, chapter by chapter study of the BPP. In order to answer such questions as what forces produced the Panthers, for example, in Seattle versus Phoenix or in Detroit and not Columbus, Ohio, one has to be presented with a more complete portrait of the BPP and the unique situational factors that produced local branches in some places and not in others. Moreover, in order to understand such matters as the motivation of its members, the organization's growth or lack thereof, its accomplishments, its failures, its ideological shifts, and the impact of its community survival programs on America's poor residents, it is necessary to examine as many of the Panther branches and chapters as possible.

Were Panthers in other cities as visible, brazen, and steadfast in their commitment as those in the Bay Area seemingly were? Did the level of local, state, and federal government repression vary across city and chapter; if so, in what ways? Did it matter which political party controlled city hall and/or state government? Did it matter whether the police chief or mayor was white or a person of color? Specifically, did the Panthers, under black mayoral rule, experience lesser or greater government repression than did Panthers in cities governed by white mayors? To what degree was Panther posturing related to government repression? To what degree were the Panthers able to garner community support in one city vis-à-vis another? Was the government more likely to repress local branches and chapters that had strong community ties and less likely to repress chapters that suffered from minimal community support? What were women's contributions, and how vital were these contributions to the chapters' day-to-day operations? The answers to questions such as these can only be gleaned by conducting a local, grassroots examination of the BPP. Anecdotal accounts of police repression and of the role of women in the BPP, for example, can be suggestive and even compelling pieces of evidence, but suggestive and compelling evidence does not allow one to generalize about the extent of such practices and beliefs. This project seeks to lay the groundwork for a broader and, at the same time, more detailed understanding of the BPP.

Again, while it is possible to write a general history of the BPP, it is imperative to note that such an exercise cannot be done without recognizing the importance of understanding the distinctive qualities across branches and chapters. The absence of this kind of well-rounded and intricate history leaves us with a relatively segmented understanding of the BPP. Only by detailed comparative studies of all of the organization's branches and chapters in all their human variety can we hope to understand any one of them. While each essay in this volume offers a fair amount of detail about each Panther charter, one should not expect that each writer will cover every single event or activity that occurred on a given day in the branch's history, nor should one expect an exhaustive treatment of the history, conditions, and precipitating events in the cities in which these Panther branches were launched. While due consideration will be given to these matters, one should keep in mind that this volume consists of essays, not book-length treatments of each branch. It is our hope that this volume will inspire others to embark on book-length studies of the branches and chapters examined in this book. It should also be noted that these essays are written in the prose typical of a scholarly work. In other words, these works are intended to inform, to enlighten, and to spark intellectual discourse, not to entertain or tantalize in the way a novel might.

Each writer has his or her own style. One writer might feature prominently the voices of the persons whom he or she interviewed, while another may background the voices of former Panthers. Some chapters are longer than others, but one should not assume a thirty-page essay to be less substantial than a sixty-page essay. Numerous factors account for this. Some Panther chapters functioned longer than others. Some chapters had a more eventful history than others. Some chapters boasted members who were more colorful than others. Some chapters had a richer history than others.

This work will, among other things, undoubtedly shed new light on the BPP, thereby urging some to reevaluate the BPP's legacy, for better or for worse. Moreover, this project may help disabuse some of the pejorative Panther images that have, for the most part, been etched in the annals of history. Painting a more complete portrait of this much maligned organization may perhaps enable students of history to render more informed judgments about the Panthers' place in American cultural and political history. Just as important, this volume will give voice to those unsung Panthers whose valiant efforts have heretofore either gone unnoticed, unheard, or ignored.

Notes

1. While the BPP, at one time, may have had forty branches and/or chapters, not all of them were what we consider substantive and/or substantial branches and chapters. Substantive chapters are those that meet the following criteria: have an actual office, were in operation for at least one year, offered a breakfast program for at least one year, and had a record of selling the *Black Panther* newspaper. Having a record of hawking the newspaper means that there should be, on the part of longtime residents of that particular community, some memory of the newspaper being sold on a regular basis by members of the BPP.
2. Judson L. Jeffries, ed., *Comrades: A Local History of the Black Panther Party* (Bloomington: Indiana University Press, 2007).
3. Bobby Seale, *Seize the Time: The Story of the Black Panther Party and Huey P. Newton* (New York: Random House, 1970), 412.
4. The words "black" and "African American" are used interchangeably according to sound and context.
5. For an exception to this rule, see Paul Alkebulan, *Surviving Pending Revolution: The History of the Black Panther Party* (Tuscaloosa: University of Alabama Press, 2007); Andrew Witt, *The Black Panthers in the Midwest: The Community Programs and Services of the Black Panther Party in Milwaukee, 1966–1977* (New York: Routledge, 2007).
6. Bruce C. Berg, *Qualitative Research Methods for the Social Sciences* (New York: Simon and Schuster, 1995).
7. Earl Anthony, *Spitting in the Wind* (Los Angeles: Roundtable, 1990).
8. Jasmine Guy [Afeni Shakur], *Evolution of a Revolutionary* (New York: Simon and Schuster, 2004); Mumia Abu-Jamal, *We Want Freedom: A Life in the Black Panther Party* (Boston: South End Press, 2004); Evan D. Hopkins, *Life After Life: A Story of Rage and Redemption* (New York: Free Press, 2005); Steve D. McCutchen, *We Were Free for a While: Back to Back in the Black Panther Party* (Baltimore: PublishAmerica, 2008). Steve McCutchen joined the BPP in Baltimore but later went to Oakland in the early 1970s when many of the branches around the country were shut down.
9. Yohuru Williams and Jama Lazerow, eds., *Liberated Territory: Untold Local Perspectives on the Black Panther Party* (Durham, N.C.: Duke University Press, 2008); Reynaldo Anderson, "Practical Internationalists: The Story of the Des Moines, Iowa, Black Panther Party," in *Groundwork: Local Black Freedom Movements in America*, ed. Jeanne Theoharis and Komozi Woodard (New York: New York University Press, 2005), 282–299.
10. Curtis Austin, *Up Against the Wall: Violence in the Making and Unmaking of the Black Panther Party* (Fayette: University of Arkansas Press, 2006); Laura Pulido, *Black, Brown, Yellow and Left: Radicalism Activism in Los Angeles* (Berkeley and Los Angeles: University of California

Press, 2006); Jeffrey O. G. Ogbar, *Black Power: Radical Politics and African American Identity* (Baltimore: Johns Hopkins University Press, 2004); Jack Olsen and Elmer Pratt, *Last Man Standing* (New York: Anchor, 2000).

ON THE
GROUND

ARM YOURSELF OR HARM YOURSELF

People's Party II and the Black Panther Party in Houston, Texas

Charles E. Jones

If you're ever in Houston: go down Dowling Street.
—LESTER "WINTERTIME BLUES" WILLIAMS

By 1970 the Black Panther Party (BPP) mushroomed from a locally based California group into an international phenomenon with official units in twenty-eight states and the District of Columbia. In addition, the BPP operated an international chapter initially under the leadership of Eldridge Cleaver in Algiers, Algeria. While the epicenter of the Panther movement remained in Oakland, California, during the group's sixteen-year (1966–1982) history, the organization's official links extended to local black communities throughout the nation. African Americans quickly established BPP chapters in many of America's large urban centers. Panther affiliates also formed in sparsely black-populated cities such as Des Moines, Iowa, and Seattle, Washington. Moreover, BPP units penetrated the terrain of the southern-based nonviolent civil rights movement.[1]

Among those southern communities with a BPP outpost was Houston, Texas. Panther activism in the city occurred in three different waves between 1968 and 1974. Black Houstonians organized the initial BPP formation during the spring of 1968, which lasted until November 1968. After nearly a year-and-a-half absence of a Panther presence in Houston, Carl Hampton founded People's Party II (PP II), modeled on the BPP, during the spring of 1970. The third wave began in October 1971 when PP II members received authorization from central headquarters in Oakland to establish the Houston branch of the BPP. The final Panther formation existed for approximately three years. The Houston Panthers ceased operations in August 1974 after the national BPP leadership ordered Houston party members to relocate to Oakland.

This essay examines the origins, nature of membership, leadership, activities, and government response to the three Panther iterations in Houston. This study contributes to a growing body of scholarship on the BPP at the local level. I have long maintained that very little is known about local Panther activity throughout the United States. As was referenced in Judson L. Jeffries's earlier work, *Comrades: A Local History of the Black Panther Party,* looking at the BPP at the local level gives us a much richer perspective, thus providing "a more complete portrait" of the inner workings and activities of the BPP.[2] An essay by Reynaldo Anderson on the Des Moines, Iowa, BPP chapter, which appears in the Jeanne Theoharis and Komozi Woodard anthology *Groundwork: Local Black Freedom Movements in America,* and one by Jon Rice on the Chicago BPP chapter, published in Theoharis and Woodard's *Freedom North: Black Freedom Struggles Outside the South, 1940–1980,* underscore the aforementioned observation. Similarly, the research of Judson L. Jeffries and his colleagues in *Comrades: A Local History of the Black Panther Party,* which examines seven BPP units, offers critical insight on the varied experiences of Panther chapters. Finally, the recent edited volume *Liberated Territory: Untold Local Perspectives on the Black Panther Party,* by Yohuru Williams and Jama Lazerow, enhances our knowledge about Panther politics on the local level in such places as Omaha, Nebraska, and New Bedford, Massachusetts. These four anthologies as well as Yohuru Williams's study of the New Haven, Connecticut, Panthers and Andrew Witt's analysis of the survival programs sponsored by the Milwaukee, Wisconsin, BPP chapter contribute to developing a fuller understanding and greater appreciation of the history of the BPP. This scholarship moves Panther historiography beyond the preponderance of the Oakland-centric analyses of the party.[3]

Although the BPP has received substantial scholarly attention during the past decade (1998–2008), the Panther experience in the South remains largely unexplored.[4] Notable exceptions to this omission in Panther historiography include Benjamin Friedman's research on the BPP in Winston Salem, North Carolina, arguably the most effective chapter in the South, and Orissa Arend's oral history of the New Orleans Panthers.[5] This chapter partially fills a void in the extant BPP literature by analyzing Panther dynamics in the southern locality of Houston, Texas, from 1968 to 1974. This chapter also underscores the broad geographical appeal of the Black Power concept, which moves scholarly discourse beyond a static and artificial North-South fault line. The essay proceeds with an examination of the Houston sociopolitical landscape. It then identifies black protest antecedents to Panther activism in the city. Subsequent sections of the study analyze the attributes of the three Houston BPP formations. Finally, the chapter concludes with a discussion of the legacy of the BPP in Houston.

Houston's Sociopolitical Context

Black presence in Spanish Texas predates the origins of Houston, founded in 1836 by A. C. and K. C. Allen, brothers and New York real estate speculators. Three centuries earlier, Africans were members of the Spanish expeditions that conquered the indigenous people of South America. Under Spanish and later Mexican rule, Africans enjoyed the status of a free person, which enhanced the territory's attraction to runaway enslaved Africans from New Orleans. From Houston's onset, people of African descent have been an integral component of the city. Enslaved Africans developed the Houston site by cleaning swampland designated for the new city. Notwithstanding its Spanish Texas origin and "cowboy symbolism," to overlook the city's southern predilections would obscure an understanding of African American insurgency in Houston. A paramount feature of Houston's southern-derived political culture has been an enduring history and legacy of racial segregation. For example, three years after the enslaved Africans and Mexican prisoners of war cleared Houston's swampland, the city council enacted laws restricting the individual liberties of free black residents.[6]

Segregation and white supremacy circumscribed black life in Houston. Black Houstonians experienced restricted access to public education, employment, transportation, and places of public accommodation. While segregation certainly appeared in Houston, historian David McComb notes that "no comprehensive black code to regulate rigidly the behavior of races existed."[7] It appears then that Houston offered a less rigid system of segregation than in, for example, Birmingham, Alabama, or Jackson, Mississippi. Students of southern politics differentiate between the political dynamics of race in peripheral southern states such as Texas and those of the Deep South. In Houston, political and economic elites granted concessions, albeit minor, to desegregation demands when many of their southern counterparts remained recalcitrant. As early as 1954, Houston abolished segregation at its golf courses and libraries. Segregation on city buses ended a year before the historic 1955–1956 Montgomery bus boycott. In 1962 a mayoral proclamation by Lewis Cutrer ended de jure segregation in all city-owned buildings. More important, the local terrain of Houston was largely devoid of white terrorism prevalent in many other southern settings. While the Ku Klux Klan reigned supreme in the city during the 1920s, the city's only two documented African American lynching victims distinguish Houston from most southern municipalities. However, Houston's relative racially tolerant environment did not mean that African American residents were immune from acts of racial subordination and police abuse.[8]

Historically, Houston has been among the top southern cities with a large concentration of African Americans. On the eve of the Civil War (1860), enslaved Africans comprised 22.2 percent of all Houstonians. After emancipation,

Houston became a magnet for newly freed Africans, who swelled the ranks of the black population to nearly 40 percent. In 1920 the black population experienced a decline, which continued until it reached an all-time low of 21 percent in 1950. From 1960 to 1970, the black community in Houston, similar to the city as whole, experienced rapid growth. Over 100,000 black people migrated to Houston for economic opportunities during the 1960s, thereby increasing the black percentage to 25.7 percent of the total population.[9] In contrast to other southern cities, however, Houston has always included a significant Mexican American presence. In 1970 Mexican Americans comprised approximately 12 percent of Houston's total population. Although not legally sanctioned, social custom mandated residential segregation, which relegated African American residents to designated areas of the city. In 1970, 93 percent of black Houstonians resided in the Third, Fourth, and Fifth wards. In his political-economic analysis of Houston, *Free Enterprise City*, Joe Feagin notes that "for many decades most minority residential areas have had poor public services, including one or more of the following: inadequate sewage treatment plants and lines, inadequate water lines, inferior water and sewer systems, poor storm drainage, problematic public transportation and segregated schools."[10]

City officials' failure to respond adequately to racial inequities confronting black residents was not surprising in light of Houston's political milieu. The city's political culture reflected a probusiness, free-enterprise, conservative orientation undergirded by a laissez-faire governmental role. Rugged individualism, anti-Communist sentiment, white supremacy, and opposition to redistributive politics constituted highly prized core values. In the 1950s, Houstonians voted to limit public housing, and the school board rejected federal aid for subsidized lunches well into the late 1960s. Tatcho Mindiola, Yolanda F. Niemann, and Nestor Rodriguez also note that Houston was "a hotbed of right-wing extremism in the 1950s which culminated in the city becoming a major center of McCarthyism which created a large and active network of anticommunist groups who considered any change in the established social order subversive. For many members of these groups, including Houston's power elite, communism, labor unions, and the civil rights movement were seen as the same threat."[11] The mayoral administrations of Louis Welch (1964–1974) coincided with Panther activism in Houston. Closely aligned with the city's powerful business elites, Welch appointed Herman Short, the hard-line, nineteen-year police veteran, to head the Houston Police Department. In the seminal study *Biracial Politics: Conflict and Coalition in the Metropolitan South*, sociologist Chandler Davidson described Short as "distinctly a conservative on both civil rights and civil liberties."[12]

Short's administration continued a long tradition of pervasive police abuse and mistreatment of black Houstonians. Indeed, two of the city's most egregious acts of police brutality—the 1966 Lucky Hill incident and the 1970 stomping death of Bobby Joe Conner at the Galena Park police station—occurred while Short was police chief. The Criminal Intelligence Division (CID), initially established during World War II to counter political subversive activities, assumed a prominent role in his administration. Short first expanded the authority and scope of the CID to combat organized crime and then later redirected its antisyndicate focus to monitor and derail political activists in the city. He resigned as police chief in 1973 rather than serve under the newly elected mayor Fred Hofheinz, a liberal politician by Houston's standards. Reflecting upon the Houston Police Department under Short's supervision, Hofheinz remarked that it "was militaristic. It was very heavy-handed. It was largely a white police department without any ambition to be otherwise."[13]

In 1975 the Houston local American Civil Liberties Union (ACLU) filed a $55 million class action suit against the Houston Police Department on behalf of Gertrude Barnstone and Larry Sauer. The two local white activists claimed that during Short's tenure as police chief, the CID illegally wiretapped, spied, and kept surveillance files on local political activists and other Houston citizens. Carol M. Lynn, who succeeded Short as police chief, testified before a subcommittee of the Judiciary Committee in the House of Representatives of the U.S. Congress that before he became chief, "Houston policemen routinely engaged in illegal wiretapping, housebreaking, falsifying of evidence, and the keeping of illegal files on un-accused private citizens."[14]

Houston's repressive police apparatus, in conjunction with an entrenched conservative political culture, subdued black activism in the city. As one scholar noted, "there was less activism in Houston than in most comparable cities, southern or northern."[15] Feagin also reported that Houston had "fewer instances of urban protest movements appear than in other major cities; for example, there have been no ghetto riots comparable to those in the northern cities during the 1960s and 1970s."[16] The lack of a strong tradition of black activism in Houston may also be attributed to the city's economic prosperity, which offered improved opportunities for black Houstonians. In 1970 the black unemployment rate in the city was half the nationwide average for black Americans. Moreover, "Houston's black median family income ($19,908) was nearly 77 percent of the nation's white family income median."[17] Simply put, black Houstonians may have been reluctant to risk their economic foothold by challenging racial inequities.

Finally, Houston's black leadership's proclivity toward sustaining the status quo also stifled African American insurgency. In the absence of political representation, a church-based leadership predominated in the Houston black community. Judson Robinson Jr., the first African American to serve on the city council, was not elected until 1971. Sociologist Robert Bullard explained, "The minister-leader exhibited a great deal of power and influence in the black community. The Houston Baptist Ministerial Alliance, for example, was an influential organization in the 1950s and 1960s."[18] Unfortunately, this leadership group, as well as mainstream civil rights organizations, tended to thwart rather than facilitate black activism. For instance, L. H. Simpson, the prominent minister of Pleasant Hill Baptist Church, the largest black church in Houston at that time, opposed the early direct action tactics in the city, while the local Houston chapter of the National Association for the Advancement of Colored People (NAACP) during the 1960s "was more successful in preventing civil rights militants from demonstrating than influencing white officials."[19]

Suffice it to say, prior to the 1960s collective black armed resistance in Houston was rare. The 1917 race riot involving black soldiers stationed at Camp Logan near Houston represents the lone exception. During the evening of August 23, 1917, nearly 100 soldiers of the all-black Twenty-fourth Infantry rebelled against the town's white police officers and white residents in response to pervasive racial abuse and conflict. Black soldiers seized rifles and ammunition from the army base in response to rumors that the Houston police murdered two of their comrades. While both soldiers were definitely beaten by white law enforcement officials, they remained alive. However, rumors of their alleged murders took on a life of their own due to past incidents of police brutality. Armed black soldiers from Camp Logan marched toward downtown Houston through the city's Fourth Ward and killed fourteen white townspeople, including four police officers, by the time the National Guard quelled the racial disturbance. Four months later, in December, thirteen soldiers were court-martialed and found guilty of murder and hanged for their participation in the melee. Several other participants received a life sentence in prison.[20] Notwithstanding the paucity of black urban rebellions in Houston, a preoccupation with violent civil unrest risks overlooking important precursors to Panther activism in the city.

Antecedents to Panther Activism

While there is a general consensus among scholars that Houston lacks a rich tradition of black collective activism, black Houstonians—grassroots leaders, activist ministers, race men and women, students, as well as ordinary laypersons—did in fact dare to challenge racial oppression. At the turn of the twentieth century, black Houstonians, similar to their African American southern counterparts, resisted the emergence of de jure segregation. Black residents launched a two-year (1903–1905) streetcar boycott to protest a segregated seating ordinance. The boycott eventually failed to overturn the statute regulating separate seating for black and white riders, but nonetheless remained an important example of black unity. The vast majority of the traditional civil rights organizations were largely absent from the Houston landscape. For example, the Urban League did not appear in Houston until 1968, and the Congress of Racial Equality (CORE) never operated in the city. However, Houston was among the early southern localities to form a local chapter of the NAACP during an era when white government officials considered it a subversive organization.[21]

Chandler Davidson noted that Houston's "local chapter of the NAACP," founded in 1912, "is by far the oldest and most respected of the Houston civil rights organizations."[22] During the 1930s and 1940s, the Houston NAACP branch, led by Clifton F. Richardson Sr., owner and managing editor of the *Houston Informer*, and Albert Lucas, the minister of Good Hope Baptist Church, one of the leading black religious institutions in the city, spearheaded racial resistance. Lula B. White, the wife of a prominent businessman, served as executive secretary of the civil rights affiliate from 1942 to 1949. The Houston NAACP chapter often pursued an aggressive litigation strategy to expand voting rights and educational opportunities for black citizens. Beginning in 1924, the local NAACP affiliate initiated a series of lawsuits culminating in *Smith v. Allwright*, a 1944 ruling by the U.S. Supreme Court that declared the white primary unconstitutional. It also launched the 1950 groundbreaking case *Sweat v. Painter*, which established an important legal precedent of the intangible effects of segregation for the landmark *Brown v. Board of Education of Topeka, Kansas* judicial ruling in 1954. These two notable Supreme Court rulings bolstered the stature of the Houston NAACP. During the early 1950s, it became one of the largest affiliates in the country, with approximately 9,000 members.[23]

Two factors undermined the surge in black activism in the 1950s. First, sociologist Robert Fisher has noted that "the Cold War ideology and repression that soon followed in Houston and the nation put an end to this era of black activism."[24] Second, a strategy shift from litigation to direct action tactics in the civil rights movement minimized the effectiveness of both the local and national NAACP. Several black advocacy and protest groups in the city competed to fill the leadership void created by the growing irrelevance of the Houston NAACP. Those organizations included the Harris County Council of Organizations (HCCO), the Progressive Youth Association (PYA), Hope Development Incorporated, African Americans for Black Liberation (AABL), and the Organization of Black Student Unity (OBSU). Among these groups, only the HCCO predated 1960s activism. Founded in 1949, the HCCO possessed an impressive membership of sixty churches as well as civic and political groups. However, the HCCO failed to capitalize on its broad coalition to achieve leadership ascendancy. HCCO's church-based leadership and electoral orientation ran counter to the emerging black insurgency Houston.[25]

During the 1960s, black protest in Houston was steeped in student activism. The sit-in movement in Greensboro, North Carolina, which ignited challenges to segregation across the South, did not escape Houston. In March, a month after the February 1, 1960, sit-in by four students from North Carolina A&T University, Texas Southern University (TSU) students targeted Weingarten Drug Store near the campus in the Third Ward. During a sixteen-month period, March 1960 to July 1961, TSU students and the PYA, headed by Eldrewky Stearnes, waged a successful sit-in campaign that desegregated lunch counters and a host of city facilities. Notwithstanding the mass arrests and substantial bail and fines, the sit-in activists in Houston experienced less white resistance than black protesters in other southern settings. Nevertheless, the sit-in victories did not alter systemic policy concerns of the black community such as police brutality, school desegregation, and poor municipal services, which stimulated black activism.[26]

The campuses of TSU and the University of Houston became incubators of black militancy. During the spring of 1967, campus protest at TSU merged with activism in the broader black community in Houston to trigger the decade's most explosive incident of racial unrest, the so-called TSU riot, which occurred May 16–17, 1967. Prior to the disturbance, pockets of student dissent permeated the TSU campus. Students protested a major thoroughfare that divided the campus; they also expressed dissatisfaction with an administration policy of reporting the names of draft-eligible students to the local draft board. Moreover, the emergence of a campus formation called the Friends of SNCC (Student Nonviolent Coordinating Committee)—led by F. D. Kirkpatrick, Millard Lowe, and Lee Otis Johnson—which sought campus recognition as an official student organization, further fueled student dissent. Fearing the repercussions of housing the Black Power student group on campus, the university administration was reluctant to recognize the Friends of SNCC as a student group. In March the university suspended the Friends of SNCC group from campus and terminated the contract of its faculty adviser, political scientist Mack H. Jones, because of an anti–police brutality rally organized by the militant student organization.[27]

TSU students initiated a flurry of acts of civil disobedience, including selective class boycotts and a lie-down-in campaign that impeded traffic on Wheeler Avenue. Student activists launched a second wave of direct action tactics in April that led to the arrest of the Friends of SNCC leadership, further exacerbating the conflict with the administration. On May 16 campus activism spilled over into the larger community when TSU students participated in the protest at Northwood Junior High School and the Holmes Road dump. Black activists opposed the discipline disparity between black and white participants in a racial melee at Northwood. School officials expelled the black students, while the white combatants only received a three-day suspension. After a drowning death of a black youth at the Holmes Road dump, the dump continued to be a long-standing site of contestation among black community activists. The Reverend Bill Lawson of Wheeler Avenue Baptist Church noted that "the police really got rough with the protesters at both sites."[28] TSU student protesters were among the arrested activists at Northwood and the Holmes Road dump.

Later that night, students held an impromptu rally expressing discontent with events stemming from the earlier demonstrations. During the rally, a student activist, Douglas W. Waller, allegedly threw a watermelon rind at a police officer. During Waller's arrest, the police discovered a concealed pistol and charged him with possession of a weapon and loitering. The Houston police's high profile on and proximity to campus inflamed the situation. Historian Dwight Watson, in his superb study *Race and the Houston Police Department, 1930–1990*, noted: "In a provocative move, Short placed patrol units on the periphery of the campus and ordered them to drive through the campus at regular intervals. They had been on campus long enough to understand what type of reaction their presence would cause."[29] Incensed students threw rocks and other debris at the law enforcement officers. Sniper fire from Lanier Hall, a male campus dormitory, wounded police officer Robert G. Blaylock, a member of the CID, in the leg, which escalated the unrest.

On the alleged order of Mayor Louie Welch to "Let's go in and clean 'em out," approximately 200 Houston police officers and Harris County Sheriff deputies stormed the campus and fired over 4,000 rounds in a forty-minute barrage of gunfire. During the police assault on the TSU campus, a second police officer, Dale Dugger, was wounded, and a ricochet bullet from a police weapon struck a third officer, Louis Kuba, between the eyes and killed him.[30] Thirty years after the campus unrest, Carol Vance, the Harris County district attorney at the time, commented on the likelihood that a ricochet bullet caused the death of Officer Kuba: "As I recall, it was a .44 or .45 bullet that hit the officer, and the guns the police found in the dorm were all .22s."[31]

After seizing control of the campus, the police arrested 488 students and ransacked dormitory rooms. According to a *New York Times* reporter, "Screens on television sets had been broken. Radios were thrown against the wall and smashed. A watch on one table had been hit with some object. Clothes were torn and ripped."[32] While nearly all the students detained during the mass arrest were released, five student leaders—Charles Freeman, Trazawell Franklin Jr., Floyd Nichols, John Parker, and Douglas Waller—were charged with inciting a riot. Freeman's trial was moved to Victoria, Texas; it was the only adjudicated case among the so-called TSU Five and ended in a mistrial. Criminal charges were eventually dropped against the other four students.

Although the university administration banned the Friends of SNCC from campus, the group remained a magnet for politically conscious students awakened by the winds of black power. After his military discharge in 1967, Ester King, a longtime Houston activist, returned to the city seeking to become active in the local black liberation struggle. King made several inquiries about movement activities in Houston when a childhood friend eventually introduced him to Lee Otis Johnson of the Friends of SNCC in June 1967. King recalled that "I have always been in an organization since that day."[33]

Born in 1943 in Jasper, Texas, King moved with his family to Houston, where he was raised in Acres Homes, a North Houston neighborhood. Although King attended Bishop College in Dallas in 1964 during the crucible of the civil rights struggle, he was admittedly apolitical. King remarked, "While I recalled the freedom rides, we didn't discuss them. We used to think Malcolm X was crazy." King attributed his political awakening to a tour in the military. First, he noted that his military experience "shattered illusions about white people being smarter than blacks," which in turn shattered the notion of black inferiority as a justification for de jure segregation. Second, military service exposed King to racially conscious black soldiers from across the nation. King remembered, "I was having discussions with brothers from all over the country and some of these brothers were very advanced. I really didn't know anything about the history of black folks. I had been to college yet I knew nothing of Africa, I was what the Nation of Islam called the 'dead.'" The crystallizing event of King's political awakening occurred in September 1966 during his leave in Copenhagen, Denmark. He recounted:

I came out of the hotel and there was this crowd of people reading the newspaper about the assassination of the South African Prime Minister, Hendrik Verwoerd. When they saw me, they ran to me and wanted my opinion. They wanted to hear from a black man. I didn't know what the hell they were talking about. I didn't know there were white people in South Africa. I was very embarrassed because I had sense to know that this is something I should have known since they expected me to know. I am nodding and agreeing and I am saying to myself, I'm going to correct this. I am not going to get caught like this again. I got back to the post [military base]. I went to the library. It wasn't a very large library and I wound up reading every book with black, colored, or Negro in the title. It was like someone had exploded a grenade in my head because all of this I did not know and I'm a grown man. I thought slavery was about someone picking cotton and that was about it. So now I'm digesting all of this information; I'm filtering it through and I'm having a reality check with the racism in the military, and the whole thing with Muhammad Ali. Then I read the *Autobiography of Malcolm X*. Someone sent it to a friend of mine. By now I don't think Malcolm is crazy. He had been assassinated. When I first used to hear those sound bites and I thought he was crazy. I read it and the book answered questions that I did not know that I was supposed to ask.[34]

King further explained: "At that point I made up my mind that if they cut orders for me to go to Vietnam, I was going to Sweden. By then I was not going to die or kill for an oppressor. Fortunately, I didn't get tested on that, I rotated back to the States. I promise myself that I was coming back and devote my life to the movement." King joined the Friends of SNCC when he returned to Houston during the summer of 1967. Upon enrolling at TSU in the fall, he became a member of the OBSU, a student organization modeled on Malcolm X's Organization of Afro American Unity. King later joined the AABL, led by Omowale Luthuli (Dwight Allen) and Gene Locke. Initially formed in 1966 as the Committee of Better Race Relations to ensure the inclusion of black students in the mainstream of campus life at the University of Houston, the AABL eventually shifted its focus to community issues. Both the OBSU and the AABL proved critical to the formation of the first official BPP chapter in Houston.[35]

First Panther Formation: May–November 1968

Willie "Iceman" Rudd, a twenty-nine–year-old native of Houston and graduate of Phyllis Wheatley High School, founded the first Panther formation in Houston during the spring of 1968. Rudd, who drove an ice truck for nine years, worked as a Teamsters union steward and driver with a national trucking firm when he formed the initial Houston chapter of the BPP. Rudd's union organizing job allowed him to travel extensively and paid him a lucrative salary of $12,000 a year. He frequently donated money to local civil rights organizations. Rudd explained: "I am from the ghetto. I know the language. I know the people and I know the problems, and my lot in life is to do something about the conditions of the ghetto. We were so poor, I was afraid to come home at night because I knew there wouldn't be anything to eat there. I would stay out all night hustling until I had $7 or $8 to give my mother to help feed my brothers and sisters."[36] Rudd, a onetime member of the Nation of Islam, once was fired from his job for participating in a demonstration organized by Rev. Ralph Abernathy of the Southern Christian Leadership Conference (SCLC). During his travels to Oakland, California, Rudd met the leadership of the BPP, who inquired about the 1967 "TSU riot." Rudd's friendship with the wife of Lee Otis Johnson, who frequently visited Oakland, provided entrée to the BPP hierarchy.

In spring 1968 Rudd received authorization from the Panther leadership to establish a BPP affiliate in Houston. Rudd soon contacted the OBSU to gauge the membership's interest in forming a local Panther unit in the city. While the OBSU members expressed their surprise that Rudd actually secured permission to form a BPP chapter, they eagerly agreed to join. Similar to the Boston BPP chapter, the membership of the first Panther affiliate in Houston was largely comprised of students. Members of the OBSU provided the chapter's rank and file. The first headquarters of the Rudd-led Panthers was located on Dowling and Francis streets. Charlotte Phelps, a local college professor and white radical activist, paid the first month's rent. The original Panther cohort consisted of fifteen to twenty individuals, which included such members as Ester King, Stan Wright, Floyd "Preacher" Nichols, Jack Hunter, Barbara Fitzgerald, and Larry Jackson.

During its very brief existence, Houston's initial Panther formation sponsored limited programs. The group held political education classes and operated a liberation school.[37] The paucity of community programs was largely due to the chapter's short-lived existence. Almost immediately upon the founding of the chapter, several members of the local Panther affiliate suspected that Willie "Iceman" Rudd, the founder and leader of the group, was a police informant. BPP members raised questions about Rudd's ownership of flashy cars, such as a convertible Corvette, and his absence from work due to frequent out-of-town trips. Local Panthers also raised concerns about organizational procedures that required individuals to document their attendance at meetings. Ester King recalled that "every time we met we had to fill out a sign-in sheet. I asked one of my comrades don't you think that's strange?"[38] Brother Raheem, another early party member, remarked: "I always believed that he [Rudd] was a plant, a couple of times he tried to isolate me to get me to do things with him. Everybody was saying 'Iceman' is the law."[39] Within two months of the inception of the BPP chapter in Houston, rumors surrounding Rudd led many of the original members to leave the local Panther affiliate. Their departure left the Houston BPP unit largely defunct. However, the chapter was not officially closed until November 1968 when Bobby Seale, chairman of the BPP, visited Houston.[40]

The AABL invited Seale to town to give campus and community lectures. AABL members contacted the OBSU to provide security during Seale's speaking engagement. Omowale Luthuli explained: "We brought Bobby Seale at the University of Houston to speak. We also wanted him to give a community based speech. We acquired a local church for Bobby Seale to give the community based speech." However, during Seale's speech at the church, a fight erupted between two factions within the OBSU. Luthuli complained that the fight "left a bad taste in our mouths because we went out of our way to get a progressive church. I had to apologize for the fracas."[41] Afterward, Seale publicly disbanded the Houston BPP chapter.

PP II: April 1970–September 1971

During 1969, the BPP did not exist in Houston. On the national level, the party confronted intensive government repression. In January the covert actions of the Federal Bureau of Investigation's (FBI) Counter Intelligence Program (COINTELPRO) exacerbated organizational conflict between the Panthers and members of the cultural black nationalist group US, which resulted in the death of Alprentice "Bunchy" Carter and John Huggins during a gun battle on the campus of UCLA. As the year closed, Chicago Panther leader Fred Hampton and Mark Clark, captain of the Peoria, Illinois, branch of the BPP, were killed in the infamous December 4 police raid. Four days later, on December 8, the Los Angeles police SWAT unit raided the local party headquarters on Central Avenue.

Over the course of the year, the FBI and local law enforcement officials frequently raided BPP offices across the nation. The leadership of the New York Panthers was decimated by fabricated conspiracy charges, and the party's co-founder, Bobby Seale, faced murder charges along with Ericka Huggins and thirteen members of the New Haven, Connecticut, branch of the BPP in the torture and murder of Alex Rackley, a suspected Panther police informant. Six party comrades lost their lives in police altercations, and four other Panthers died in conflicts with US members in 1969. The ACLU declared in a December 29 press release that "the record of police actions across the country against the Black Panther Party forms a prima facie case for the conclusion that law enforcement officials are waging a drive against the black militant organization resulting in serious civil liberties violations."[42]

Despite this onslaught of government repression, black youth throughout the country clamored to join the BPP, and Houston was not an exception. At least three different individuals sought to establish a BPP outpost in the city. Ayanna Ade (Gwen Johnson), a member of the first Panther formation as well as the OBSU, recalled that "we had, prior to People's Party, tried to form a Houston chapter of the party while I was at Texas Southern and for many reasons, many variables, that did not come to fruition. So, I was always attracted to the philosophy of the Black Panther Party and I always wanted to on some level become actively involved in what was going on with the party in terms of their day to day activity."[43] Ade would later join the third Panther formation in Houston. She relocated to Oakland with some of her Houston comrades, where she taught at the party's Oakland Community School.[44]

Charles "Boko" Freeman, a native Houstonian from the city's Sunnyside neighborhood, also had similar intentions. At the behest of his aunt, who recognized his artistic abilities, Freeman relocated to New York in 1968 to finish high school. While attending Andrew Jackson High School in Queens, New York,

Freeman became acquainted with the BPP. After several visits to the Queens' office, Freeman announced his intentions of returning to Houston to establish a BPP chapter. To assist Freeman, the officer of the day gave him a box of Panther propaganda materials—posters, newspapers, buttons, and literature. "I planned to return to Houston to start a Black Panther chapter. I went to Texas Southern and met some people in the Black Student Union and told them my intentions. They told me that there was a brother already here by the name of Carl Hampton who was organizing a chapter of the Black Panther Party that they call People's Party II."[45]

Carl Hampton, the founder of PP II, the city's second BPP formation (April 1970–September 1971), was raised in the Pleasantville area of East Houston. The twenty-one-year-old charismatic Hampton was a talented athlete and musician at Phyllis Wheatley High School. He pitched for the Wheatley Wildcats and played flute in the marching band. Steve Edwards, a childhood friend since elementary school, remembered that, at an early age, Carl Hampton displayed leadership qualities: "When we played baseball, Carl would coach us. He positioned the players and would scout the other team." Edwards remembered Hampton as "charming, articulate, very intelligent young man that people gravitated toward." Hampton quit high school and traveled with a soul band. Edwards explained that "a segregated school like Phyllis Wheatley could not offer anything to a person with an intellect like Carl's."[46]

While touring with the band in the Oakland Bay Area, Hampton looked for the national office of the BPP. In *Surviving Pending Revolution: The History of the Black Panther Party*, historian Paul Alkebulan wrote that he "met Carl Hampton in 1969 when he stopped me on the street and asked directions to BPP national headquarters in Berkeley."[47] By late 1969, in order to minimize government repression, the party leadership closed ranks and did not admit new members to the organization. Undeterred, Hampton volunteered at the national headquarters, where "he attended PE [political education] classes and sold papers before returning to Houston to found an organization called People's Party II."[48]

Upon returning to Houston during the winter of 1970, Hampton reached out to the city's black activists. Hampton, like Rudd did earlier, attended an OBSU meeting to seek the members' support in forming a Panther chapter in Houston. Hampton's attempt to build a core Panther membership among militant college students was largely ignored. According to Ester King, OBSU members sharply rebuffed Hampton when someone "phoned Oakland who reported that Hampton was not authorized to start a BPP chapter." King lamented that "the way they handled it was abusive."[49]

Instead of relying on militant students, Hampton turned to the black youth in his old Pleasantville neighborhood to recruit members for his new organization. Among the first PP II recruits were Steve Edwards and James Aaron, a friend of the Hamptons' and Edwards's families. Claude "Chilly" Frost, a youngster from the nearby Clinton Park neighborhood, also became an early member of the organization. The initial cohort of PP II members also included Stan Wright, one of the few OBSU members to join Hampton. Wright was a former member of the city's first BPP formation. These members were later joined by Charles Freeman, a Sunnyside resident who returned to Houston from New York City, and Floyd "Preacher" Nichols, one of the "TSU Five." Notwithstanding the presence of Nichols and Wright, the early PP II membership (six to ten individuals) was decidedly young, male, and undereducated. Both Hampton and Edwards were slightly older, at twenty-one years of age, than Aaron, Frost, and Freeman, all of whom had recently turned eighteen years of age. One member, David Hines, was only sixteen years of age. Women were absent from the first wave of PP II members. The group also lacked formal education, as Steve Edwards recalled that he "had the most education, the others were largely high school dropouts."[50]

In short, Hampton's early core members were primarily drawn from the so-called black lumpen proletariat. Arguably, the PP II's initial lumpen membership base, rather than the college students of the OBSU, better reflected Hampton's political orientation:

When the black people start picking up their guns they start developing military power. When they see that black people can organize themselves like they and the Panther Party; this begins a threat to the establishment of this country because they realize that niggers of the street hustlers, pimps and prisoners can organize themselves into a military army. They know that if black people do it all across the country, organize, then we will have political power; we can send representatives to the political arena and can get our desired objectives.[51]

While the PP II did not have official ties to Oakland, it adopted the BPP's platform and advocacy of armed resistance. PP II members sold the *Black Panther: Black Community News Service* (the BPP newspaper), held political education classes, implemented survival programs, and participated in multiracial coalition politics, a staple of Panther praxis. Finally, the Hampton-led group, similar to BPP comrades elsewhere, encountered pervasive police repression.

The PP II first appeared on the Houston landscape during the spring of 1970. Initially, the members operated out of Carl Hampton's home on Isabella Street, where they held political education classes. The group's other early activities included participating in community protest rallies, collecting clothes for a future free-clothing program, and developing a multiracial coalition with the city's progressive organizations. Hampton was introduced to the rainbow politics concept by Robert E. Lee Jr., a Houston transplant and former Chicago Panther. Both Lee and Harold "Poison" Gaddis spearheaded Chicago's multiracial coalition between the party young patriots, Students for a Democratic Society (SDS), and the Young Lords. Robinson Block reports that "Hampton and Lee met at the apartment of Mickey Leland, a black activist and friend of Hampton, who later became a Democratic congressman for Houston. They watched the film *American Revolution 2*, which documented the establishment of the Rainbow Coalition in Chicago."[52] Influenced by the Chicago Panthers' rainbow coalition, Hampton replicated the multiracial tactic in Houston by building alliances with the John Brown Revolutionary League (JBRL), a white leftist formation, and the Mexican American Youth Organization (MAYO), a recently formed Chicano nationalist organization.

Members of the JBRL, led by Roy Bartee Haile, a former SDS leader at Southern Methodist University, opposed the Vietnam War and white racism; they were frequently armed. JBRL "did not have a permanent headquarters building like the PP II, out of fear of police raids."[53] MAYO was founded during the late summer of 1967 by five Mexican American student activists affiliated with St. Mary's University in San Antonio, Texas. The Chicano grassroots organization engaged in direct action confrontation politics as well as fostered Chicano nationalist consciousness. After its participation in the Volunteers in Service to America (VISTA) Minority Mobilization Project, Ignacio García, a political scientist, writes that "MAYO grew from one chapter in San Antonio to nearly fifty chapters—of a few members each—in South Texas in one year."[54] Young Mexican American activists also formed a MAYO chapter in Houston.

The sphere of the rainbow coalition also extended beyond Houston's city jurisdiction. State and regional white leftist groups such as the SDS chapter in Austin, Texas, and the Red Panthers cadre, an antiracist, anti-imperialist, pro–women's liberation collective based in New Orleans, also coalesced with members of the Houston rainbow coalition. Roxanne Dunbar-Ortiz, a leader of the radical cadre, which relocated to New Orleans from Cambridge, Massachusetts, explained, "We had close ties with leftists throughout the South in Birmingham, Atlanta, but especially Houston since it was the home of the John Brown Committee."[55] The Red Panthers worked with the Republic of New Africa (RNA) and the Southern Female Rights Union (SFRU) in New Orleans, as well as other groups in the South. Dunbar-Ortiz remembered Hampton speaking at a rainbow gathering; he impressed her since he "wanted to see unity with Mexicans, whites and whomever."[56] Carl Hampton explained PP II's philosophy on coalition politics to a reporter of the *Voice of Hope*:

We considered ourselves revolutionaries. We feel the Government and the whole country is controlled by criminals. Our organization will work with others to take the power from the criminals and give power back to the people. We have formed a coalition with a white group known as the John Brown Revolutionary League and a Mexican-American organization known as MAYO (Mexican American Youth Organization). We will work to weed out the racism in Houston's society. It is a known fact that racism is used to keep the working class of people divided so that the establishment can maintain control. We don't hate white people or any other group of people, we judge them by what they are doing.[57]

Claude Frost remembered that early rainbow coalition activities mainly included "speaking at each other's rallies and things like that."[58]

During the first week of July, the PP II moved to its first headquarters at 2828 Dowling Street. Freeman recalled that "it used to be an old donut shop that we converted to our headquarters. We found an old door that we used as a sign on which I painted People's Party II Information Center."[59] The Dowling Street location placed the PP II's headquarters on the central artery of Houston's Third Ward, the home of TSU, John Yates High School, and several of the city's major African American cultural and economic institutions, such as Emancipation Park and the Standard Saving Association, the state's sole black-owned savings-and-loan business. The once-vibrant thoroughfare and hub of the Third Ward included a broad swath of businesses—legitimate and illegitimate—nightclubs, bars, as well as prominent black religious institutions. The Dowling Street headquarters, in conjunction with the members' provocative display of weapons, dramatically increased the PP II's visibility. Veteran black activist Omowale Luthuli recounted that his "earliest recollection of People's Party II was early summer 1970 because I remember going on Dowling Street with some of the people I knew watching them walk around with rifles and things in broad daylight."[60] Steve Edwards recalled the looks of astonishment he and his fellow PP II members received while attending an anti–Vietnam War rally at Emancipation Park armed with weapons.[61]

The elevation of the profile of the self-avowed black revolutionary organization undoubtedly attracted the attention of both local and national law enforcement officials. Members of the Houston Police Department's CID and the FBI closely monitored PP II activities. Reflecting on the constant harassment endured by the PP II membership, Edwards remarked, "It was a stressful time." He recounted an incident in which he and Carl Hampton were stopped by Bel-Air (a Houston suburb) police while driving to a meeting with MAYO members. Police officers aimed shotguns directly at his and Hampton's faces while threatening to shoot them. Ultimately, the pervasive repression caused Edwards to leave the organization in early July. He lamented that "I was embarrassed. I felt I let Carl down. He told me that I would come back."[62]

Dowling Street Shoot-out

Within a month of moving into the PP II's new office on Dowling Street, Carl Hampton and his comrades were embroiled in an incident reminiscent of the legendary armed standoffs between Huey P. Newton and the Oakland police during the party's early Panther police alert patrols. Bobby Seale recounts one such incident in *Seize the Time*:

The pigs kept trying to move the people, saying, "you're gonna get under arrest." So Huey just went over and opened the door to the Panther office and said, "Come on in here. They can't move you out." He took his key, opened the door, and let the people go in. "Now, observe all you want to!" The pig said, "What are you going to do with that gun?"

"What are you going to do with *your* gun?" Huey said. "Because if you try to shoot at me, or if you try to take this gun, I'm going to shoot back at you, swine."[63]

On the afternoon of July 17, a Houston police patrol car made a U-turn near the PP II's headquarters to interrogate David Hines, a young PP II member who was selling copies of the *Black Panther*. While the police officers warned Hines to stay out of the street selling the paper, an armed Carl Hampton, who had a .45 pistol in a shoulder holster, arrived in a car driven by Floyd "Preacher" Nichols. Hampton explained that "many have said that I came out of the office with guns pointing at the police officers. I was getting out of the car from home, 1310 Isabella Street, that's why I was carrying a pistol because I was transferring money from one office to the other."[64] As Hampton approached the police car to inquire about the interrogation of Hines, he was joined by Charles "Boko" Freeman and Claude "Chilly" Frost, who grabbed their weapons and joined an armed Hampton after observing the situation from the headquarters. One of the stunned police officers quickly asked Hampton what he was doing carrying a .45 pistol, to which Hampton replied that it was his constitutional right to have the pistol. Hampton recalled that one of the police officers "jumped out of the car and started to approach me. I asked him to stop. I didn't pull a gun on him. I asked him to stop approaching me. I hadn't broken any law. And then at this point the officer drew for his gun. When he drew for his gun I drew for mine. And I was coming from the shoulder he was coming from the side and I beat him to the draw and we were at a standoff both of us with our weapons drawn."[65]

As the second officer radioed for police reinforcements, Hampton, flanked by his armed comrades Freeman and Frost, retreated into the PP II office. Soon afterward, approximately thirty heavily armed police officers with riot shotguns surrounded the headquarters. In the interim, black sympathizers with weapons flocked to the PP II Dowling Street headquarters. Many of these armed supporters, young black male lumpen proletariats from across the city who abhorred the racist actions of Houston police officers, would become full-time PP II members. Among the groundswell of new PP II recruits were Johnny "Shotgun" Coward, Fred Sparkman, Robert "Picadilly" Wallace, Clifford Fagan, and Kenneth Butler.[66] Many of these individuals personally experienced police brutality. Johnny Coward, known as a "street" hustler in Houston's Third Ward, lost his right eye in one such incident after being kicked and beaten by two Houston police officers. Other black Houstonians gathered and refused to allow the police to attack the organization's headquarters. Freeman remembered that "they [community residents] told the Houston Police Department they weren't going to shoot unless they shot through them."[67] Fortunately for Hampton and his comrades, after forty minutes the police withdrew from the area. The PP II members had significantly less firepower than the police, and their headquarters lacked sufficient fortification to withstand an assault by the heavily armed police. Unlike many BPP offices across the country, which had been fortified with sandbags and metal doors, PP II activists secured positions behind a barricade of metal folding chairs and clothes collected from a Catholic church.[68]

During the next ten days, PP II members and their allies, armed with weapons, secured the one-block area in the vicinity of their headquarters in order to prevent the police from apprehending Carl Hampton, who had been charged with assault with intent to murder a police officer in the July 17 incident. Members of the burgeoning rainbow coalition, radicals of the JBRL, and activists from MAYO lent armed assistance. In fact, Claude Frost remarked the JBRL "was the group that gave us most of the guns we had down there."[69] Black activists from the AABL and OBSU also provided armed security. Omowale Luthuli recalled: "We would set-up patrols. My shift was from 2 a.m. to 5 a.m. to watch the headquarters."[70] The tense ten–day confrontation—exacerbated by inflammatory newspaper headlines and the violent rhetoric espoused by Ovidle Duncantell, a local black activist, at a July 22 city council meeting—exploded on July 26, 1970. Duncantell, the chairman of the Central Committee for the Protection of Poor People, told members of the city council that "People's Party II had secured the area around its headquarters and will fight until we're all dead to keep the police out."[71]

Late Sunday night, on July 26, after a week of intense negotiations for Carl Hampton's surrender to legal authorities, the prolonged standoff erupted into gunfire between the police and the PP II. Prior to the shooting, Hampton and his allies held an impromptu rally to raise funds for two allies arrested by the police earlier that evening. Charles Freeman remembered that shortly after the rally, three women passed the headquarters and "shouted that there were white men on top of the rooftop of the church."[72] Five members of the CID of the Houston Police Department armed with .308 rifles had secured a position on the rooftop of St. John Baptist Church on the corner of Dowling and Dennis, which was adjacent to the PP II Dowling Street headquarters. Among the police snipers was Robert G. Blaylock, a CID police officer wounded in the "TSU riot." After being informed that there were white men on the roof of the church, Roy Bartee Haile later explained to a KPFT-FM reporter, "I quickly was able to assure the people that these weren't John Brown members since those would be the only whites who would have business there."[73]

Carl Hampton grabbed his M-1 carbine rifle and went to investigate the situation. As soon as Hampton approached the corner of Dowling and Dennis to observe the church rooftop, gunfire erupted, wounding him twice in the abdomen, and he was taken to Ben Taub Hospital. Roxanne Dunbar-Ortiz and her Red Panther comrades of New Orleans had intended to participate in the demonstration against the police; however, by the time they arrived in Houston, they were asked to rush to the hospital to see about Hampton. During the early morning of Monday, July 26, Hampton died as a result of his gunshot wounds. In her autobiography, *Outlaw Woman: A Memoir of the War Years, 1960–1975*, Dunbar-Ortiz writes: "We managed to make our way to the hallway outside the operating room where Carl Hampton lay dying. We stood in the hall with his mother and younger brother as Carl was pronounced dead, five minutes after we arrived." Dunbar-Ortiz and her comrades comforted Carl's mother before returning to New Orleans "in silence" as they "drove home against the wind."[74] During the ensuing gun battle, "nearly 100 shots were exchanged between steel-helmeted police and armed groups who poured into the street."[75] Four additional individuals were wounded, and fifty-two people were arrested as approximately 100 to 150 police raided the nonfortified PP II headquarters and secured the surrounding area. Among the wounded was JBRL leader Roy Bartee Haile. Two recent PP II recruits, Fred Sparkman and Johnny "Shotgun" Coward, also suffered gunshot wounds.

In the aftermath of the Dowling Street gun battle, the PP II was in a state of disarray. The police had ransacked the organization's headquarters and killed the founder and charismatic leader of the upstart group. Moreover, a host of PP II members and supporters had been arrested on a variety of criminal charges related to the shoot-out. The day after the police assault on the PP II headquarters, Charles Freeman and James Aaron met and talked about going forward. Freeman assumed the position of minister of culture, and Aaron replaced Carl Hampton as the leader and chairman of PP II.[76] The new leaders of the beleaguered organization faced isolation and nonsupport from the city's mainstream black political establishment. The group's revolutionary language and advocacy of armed resistance did not endear the PP II to Houston's conservative black community. The Reverend E. E. Coates, the pastor of Wesley Chapel AME Church, proclaimed: "They started carrying guns around in the street. I said from the pulpit that I didn't approve of that. It's not good for the community. I don't approve of brutality by the police either. But there are ways to correct wrongs."[77] Although a "Black Coalition" emerged demanding the resignation of Chief Herman Short by calling for an economic boycott, its demands largely went unheeded by black Houstonians. In fact, the local NAACP and several prominent black ministries opposed the boycott.[78]

PP II Organizational Dynamics

Unexpectedly, the PP II benefited from an influx of new members as a result of Carl Hampton's shooting death by Houston CID police officers. Alan Wolfe contends that acts of government repression, such as Hampton's death, are intended to neutralize activism and deter others from challenging the existing political order. However, an unanticipated yet fortuitous outcome of the Hampton death was a surge in activism by outraged black youth in Houston. Steve Edwards, a former member who resigned earlier due to police harassment, returned to the organization. Ruby Morgan, a twenty-year-old Houstonian and one of the first women to join the PP II, became a member after Hampton was killed. Both Morgan and Maggie Hicks, Carl Hampton's girlfriend, had recently delivered their babies at the same hospital shortly before the Dowling Street incident. Hicks befriended Morgan, and they both often stopped by the PP II office. Morgan explained, "I joined People's Party II right after Carl Hampton got killed. I didn't like the way that they killed him. The night that they killed Carl is when I went down to Dowling Street and that's what really prompted me to join."[79]

Morgan's membership in the PP II served as a precursor to female presence in the organization. Prior to the shoot-out, women were absent from the PP II. During its nearly year-and-a-half existence, approximately six women joined the PP II. Women who became members after Ruby Morgan included Annie Harris, Veronica Campbell, Loretta Freeman, Tanganyika Hill, and Carolyn Cooper. In most instances, these women were girlfriends of the males in the organization such as the couples of Charles Freeman and Annie Harris as well as Claude Frost and Tanganyika Hill. This feature of women's participation in PP II does not negate the dedication and commitment exhibited by the organization's female members. Ruby Morgan, who ascended to the highest leadership position among the women, regularly served as officer of the day. Veronica Campbell, one of the top newspaper salespersons among the party comrades, frequently spoke at PP II rallies. Several of the women would become longtime veterans of the BPP. Charles Freeman and other members maintain that the PP II's commit-ment to the revolutionary principle of gender equality produced an organization in which "men and women in the party participated equally in party activities."[80] Ruby Morgan echoed the sentiment when she remarked: "We did not have any problems of gender issues. We did not have those kinds of problems. They knew that I could deal with anything. We were like equal yoke."[81]

Over the next few months of its relatively short existence as PP II, the members devoted their energies to combating police brutality, mobilizing le-gal defense campaigns, and implementing survival programs. Police mistreat-ment was a long-standing concern of Houston's black residents. PP II mem-bers shared the BPP's conception of the police as an occupying army within the black community. They combated police brutality by publicizing incidents of police misconduct, organizing rallies, and advocating armed self-defense. While PP II members in Houston never operated armed police patrols, as the Panthers did in Oakland, they openly displayed weapons. During its brief ten-ure, the PP II sponsored approximately half a dozen anti–police brutality ral-lies, which provided venues of solidarity between the PP II and community residents.[82] On April 4, 1971, the PP II organized the first-year anniversary rally of the death of Bobby Joe Conner, killed by police officers at the Galena Park police station. Charles Freeman expressed solidarity when he spoke at the well-attended rally: "Today we come out in memory of a brother who was brutally stomped to death by the police department. This brother was handcuffed when he was beaten to death. . . . I didn't know him, but we are both Black and what affected him affected me."[83]

The PP II also devoted critical resources to legal defense campaign efforts to exonerate arrested members. Two PP II members faced criminal charges as-sociated with the Dowling Street gun battle, which required legal defense cam-paigns. James Aaron, who succeeded Hampton as chairman of the PP II, was indicted on aggravated assault on a police officer stemming from his participa-tion in the July 17 armed standoff that triggered the so-called Dowling shoot-out. Aaron eventually received a two-year sentence in the county jail after a guilty verdict in September 1971. Newcomer Johnny "Shotgun" Coward also faced charges of assault with intent to murder a police officer for his involve-ment in the July 26 shoot-out.

Throughout the PP II's existence, the organization confronted intensive po-litical repression. Several PP II members were arrested on multiple occasions. Houston police officers closely monitored the black militant group, often tar-geting its leadership primarily by relying on legalistic repression, which Alan Wolfe defines as "the use of laws and/or the legal system for the purpose of sti-fling dissent," rather than overt repression entailing police raids and shoot-outs to thwart PP II activism.[84]

More than sixteen warrants were issued for the arrest of PP II members. Legal indictments ranged from repairing an automobile on a public street to assault with intent to murder a police officer. While the preponderance of the police actions taken against the PP II were largely within the legalistic category, the Houston police did not abandon acts of overt repression. On two occasions police officers raided PP II dwellings. On June 8 law enforcement officials raided the PP II's headquarters for a second time in less than six months. Twenty-five heavily armed police officers wearing bulletproof jackets, with the support of a hovering helicopter, stormed the headquarters at 2720 Dowling Street, arresting nine PP II members and confiscating eight weapons, a large ammunition cache, and two gas masks. Police officials explained they "were acting on information that a rifle taken in a May 24th burglary was in the building."[85]

On February 9, 1971, Charles "Boko" Freeman and his two comrades, Claude Frost and Kenneth Butler, were charged with violating a seldom enforced city ordinance prohibiting making car repairs on a public street. Although the police thoroughly searched the three activists before transporting them to the police station for detainment, a matchbox of marijuana was later found on Freeman, which had been planted on him by the police. Thus Freeman's arrest on a minor charge was seriously escalated with the additional felony marijuana charge. Black activists were keenly aware of the thirty-year sentence Lee Otis Johnson, a local black militant, received for allegedly giving a police informant two marijuana cigarettes. In October an all-white jury acquitted Freeman. Nevertheless, the false arrest minimized Freeman's political activism due to the necessity of mounting a legal defense to secure his freedom.[86]

PP II members' frequent arrests exacted a major toll on the organization's small, hardcore (ten to fifteen individuals) membership. Numerous legal indictments against the members drained limited resources and diverted critical attention from mobilizing community support. Six months after the Dowling Street gun battle, the PP II failed to sponsor a single survival program. Notwithstanding their dedication and perseverance, the young, inexperienced black militants were unable to cultivate strong pockets of support among Houston's black populace. Meager organizational resources, weak community support, and intensive police repression minimized the effectiveness of PP II. In a November 30, 1970, COINTELPRO memorandum, an FBI official wrote: "Because of the lack of organizational know-how, the lack of money and the apparent animosity between various PP II members, the disorientation and state of semi-chaos continues to exist and, with the effective utilization of informants, it is anticipated that the PP II will continue to be neutralized in the Houston area."[87] The aforementioned factors all contributed to the organization's inability to launch a free health clinic.

The failure to launch a free health clinic in tribute of the life and legacy of their fallen leader was particularly disappointing for PP II comrades. Before his death, Carl Hampton sought to establish a health clinic to serve impoverished black Houstonians. Panthers across the nation often memorialized fallen comrades by establishing health clinics and other survival programs in their honor. For example, in October 1969 BPP members in Kansas City, Missouri, opened the Bobby Hutton Free Health Clinic. Chicago party members founded the Spurgeon "Jake" Winters People's Medical Center in 1970, while Black Panthers in Philadelphia named their health facility the Mark Clark People's Free Medical Clinic in tribute to the leader of the BPP chapter in Peoria, Illinois. All three health clinics were named in honor of Panthers slain in altercations with law enforcement officials.

On December 6, 1970, the PP II sponsored a rally at Emancipation Park to announce its future plans to open the Carl Hampton Free Health and Medical Center. During the rally, PP II leaders and supporters urged the attendees to make Hampton's dream a reality. Charles Freeman declared that the rally "was called to cite the inadequate medical facilities for blacks. We felt it best to help set up a free medical clinic in the black community."[88] TSU student activist Mickey Leland, a friend of Carl Hampton's and future member of the U.S. Congress, remarked, "The Carl Hampton Free Health Clinic will act as a referral clinic and provide some much needed assistance in getting sick residents admitted to Ben Taub and other hospitals."[89] PP II members rented a two-story brick building to house the clinic. However, they could not complete the plumbing and other repairs needed to pass city building inspections. Police harassment furthered hampered PP II efforts to establish a free health clinic. White leftist supporters from the Harriet Tubman Brigade and the Health Coalition often confronted police harassment when they visited the building of the proposed health clinic. Tanganyika Hill, a PP II member, was also arrested on vagrancy charges while working to establish the clinic. In late December 1970 targeted activists complained to the city council about the police harassment; however, the issue was tabled until the submission of a police report on the matter.

At the onset of the new year, money woes continued to plague the organization. PP II members were unable to raise $250 to purchase an allotment of BPP newspapers.[90] In addition to serving as the voice of the BPP, the *Black Panther* also operated as a major source of income for rank-and-file members, who sold the paper for twenty-five cents a copy and were permitted to keep ten cents from the sale of each paper. In May 1971 Harris County sheriffs evicted the PP II from the building of the proposed health clinic for failure to pay three months' rent. In August, after locating another building for the health clinic in the Fifth Ward, the PP II secured a promise of assistance from the Minority Contractors Consortium (MCC), an association of thirty-five minority contractors. After a passionate plea from James Aaron, the MCC "pledged building materials, advisors, and tradesmen to help members of the party renovate a fifth ward building."[91] Unfortunately, the MCC failed to honor its pledge to the PP II. Years later Freeman lamented, "They never came through. It was just rhetoric."[92]

In summer 1971, approximately a year after the death of Carl Hampton, the fledging organization offered its first and only outreach initiative—a free pest control program. PP II chairman James Aaron initially proposed the idea to offer free extermination services to the elderly residents in the Third Ward. Unlike sponsoring a health clinic or breakfast program, the free pest control program did not require substantial resources to implement. PP II members made inquiries at a local pest control supplier and purchased the necessary chemicals and equipment needed to exterminate pests from homes. They advertised the free pest control program in local black newspapers such as the *Forward Times* and distributed flyers throughout the community. Steve Edwards also remembers a public service announcement of the outreach program on KDIA, a local Houston radio station. The free extermination program was well received and much appreciated by the elderly residents in the Third Ward.[93]

Nearly forty years later two extermination cases still resonate with Charles Freeman. In one instance, he recalled, "We first set-off a 'bomb', and it just agitated the roaches. The place was saturated with roaches. We then sprayed the canisters, and I remembered pulling back the wallpaper and the whole wall was covered with a layer of roaches." On another occasion, Freeman was stunned by the abject poverty of an elderly couple who resided in "a cardboard house with a dirt floor." He remembered thinking, "I did not know that people lived like that."[94] According to Freeman, the house was infected with fleas due to a dead animal in the couple's backyard. Freeman and his colleagues were bitten several times before finally ridding the dwelling of fleas. The dedication and commitment to "serving the people" as demonstrated by the members' implementation of the free pest control program ultimately won the PP II official status from the national BPP leadership in Oakland. Apparently, the FBI declared the Black Power organization's demise premature in a COINTELPRO memorandum that concluded: "Due to the actions of the HPD [Houston Police Department], their Intelligence Division and informants of the Houston Division, the PP II will never again become a formidable black nationalist group in the Houston area."[95]

Houston Chapter of the BPP: October 1971–August 1974

During the late summer of 1971, the PP II gained the addition of a key member who proved instrumental to the group's eventual formal linkage to the BPP.

John "Bunchy" Crear, a native Houstonian who lived in Los Angeles with his mother, joined the PP II upon returning to Houston to attend his grandmother's funeral in August 1971. Crear's introduction to the BPP occurred when his high school photography teacher suspended the class lecture and permitted the students to listen to a live radio broadcast of the December 8, 1969, police raid of the party's headquarters on Central Avenue. As a student enrolled at California State University at Northridge, Crear attended BPP political education classes and did community work at the Central Avenue office. Crear's association with the BPP prompted a visit from the FBI. He recalled:

I had been doing community work with the party in Los Angeles. I was not an active member. I will never forget, my mother came into my room and said there are two gentlemen in the living room that want to talk to you. They're from the FBI. I am like, you got to be kidding. So they come in and introduced themselves and ask why I was a member of the Black Panther Party. You know I wasn't a member of the Black Panther Party. I just sold papers on weekends. So they go on and what really made me proud of my mother was that in the middle of the conversation she said, "Wait a minute. Look, I read that J. Edgar Hoover said the Black Panther Party was the most violent organization in the history of country." She said, "What about the mafia?"[96]

While in Houston to attend his grandmother's funeral, Crear decided to find the PP II office. Crear remembered: "I came by the office and was struck by one thing that they were struggling and they worked hard. James [Aaron] was in the leadership position, and he worked as hard as everybody else." According to Crear, unprovoked police harassment crystallized his decision to remain in Houston and become a member of the PP II. One evening during a visit to the office, Crear and other PP II members left in Crear's car and were stopped by the Houston police. Although Crear showed his California driver's license to the police officer, he was nevertheless arrested for failing to have a Texas driver's license. Crear recalled that "when the rest of my family was going back to California, I already made a decision to stay with these brothers and sisters of the People's Party II."[97]

Shortly after joining the PP II, Crear and his new comrades sought permission from the national headquarters in Oakland to operate as an official chapter of the BPP. Crear's grandmother bequeathed him an automobile, which he, Charles Freeman, and Johnny "Shotgun" Coward drove to Oakland to secure authorization from the BPP national leadership. Crear remarked: "We get to Oakland; it was late at night when we got there. So, we just parked in front of their offices and slept in the car. So they get up the next morning, who the hell is this out here in front of our office? So, they kind of chastise us, why didn't y'all just tell us? You could have come and stayed inside."[98] During their stay in Oakland, the three Houston activists met Ericka Huggins and other national party leaders. Coward also participated on the picket line at Bill Boyette's liquor store. Impressed by Coward's fearlessness of the police, Huey P. Newton went to the boycott site to personally meet Coward.[99]

Thus began the third and final Panther formation in Houston. It constituted the most effective period—October 1971 to August 1974—of BPP activism in the city. The newfound status derived from the official recognition as the Houston chapter of the BPP emboldened the Houston activists. First, it validated the original goal of their slain founder, Carl Hampton, to establish a Panther affiliate in Houston. Second, it formally linked them to a national movement, which reaffirmed their prior activism. Houston's small hardcore chapter experienced its largest membership—between twenty and twenty-five individuals during the third BPP formation (see Table 1).[100]

Table 1. Houston Branch of the Black Panther Party 1970–1974

1. James Aaron	17. Tanganyika Hill
2. Ayanna Ade	18. David Hines
3. Veron "Sensei" Benton	19. Willie Jones
4. Kenneth Butler	20. Charles Martin
5. Veronica Campbell	21. Ruby Morgan
6. Lavaugh Castilow	22. Fred "Preacher" Nichols
7. Johnny "Shotgun" Coward	23. Bobby Reed
8. John "Bunchy" Crear	24. Ikles James Roberts
9. Steve Edwards	25. Joy Smith
10. Clifford "Buddha" Fagan	26. Fred Sparkman
11. Charles "Boko" Freeman	27. Aliya Sutton
12. Loretta Freeman	28. Harry Taylor
13. Claude "Chilly" Frost	29. Shirley Taylor
14. Carl Hampton	30. Robert Wallace
15. Annie Harris	31. Kenneth Williams
16. Ronald Hatton	32. Stan Wright

During this period, Ayanna Ade once again became a member of the BPP in Houston. As a youngster, she joined the first BPP formation in the city. Ade knew James Aaron, who was in high school while she attended TSU and participated in the OBSU. Aaron used to come by her apartment to view her posters and books as well as engage her about the movement. Carl Hampton previously consulted with Ade about starting a free clothing program.[101]

Ade started working with Steve Edwards, the leader of the third BPP formation. She spent time at the party's headquarters before becoming a member.
Ade recalled, "I quit school with about half a semester left." She poignantly
remembered the primacy of the lumpen proletariat in the organization:

I came at the end. These brothers and sisters had been there for a while. It was
a struggle to fit in, to get in to the mix. I saw some things one way, and some of
the comrades saw things in a different way. I was trying to make things mesh.
When I came in as a matter of fact, I had a son with Steve Edwards and so that
male/female kinda thing existed. Some of the women had pressure on them or
whatever. Some of the sisters had issues with me because I was in college. One
sister told me, "The focus was one that the lumpen was going to be the vanguard of the people and basically you were intellectually masturbating if you
went to college." That was the perception. I had to prove myself a little bit.[102]

Joy Smith and Lavaugh Campbell were other women who also became members of the local Panther chapter during its final period. They were joined by
Willie Jones and Vernon "Sensei" Benton.

During the third phase of Panther activism in Houston, the local party de-
emphasized the advocacy of armed resistance in favor of electoral politics and
litigation in accordance with the new stance of the national BPP leadership.
In 1972 three local Houston Panthers won elections to serve on community
boards of directors representing residents of the Fourth Ward. John Crear held
a seat on the Harris County Community Action Association Board, while
Loretta Freeman served on the Model Neighborhood Residents Commission.
Party member Charles Martin was elected to the board of the Houston Legal
Aid Foundation. Late in 1974 the party endorsed and campaigned on behalf
of Frederick L. Kay, a candidate for the Houston County Clerk position. Steve
Edwards, information minister of the local Panther chapter, declared that the
party "has placed the full weight of its organization and prestige behind the
candidacy of Brother Frederick L. Kay, a 26–year-old African American deputy
clerk in the Harris County Clerk's office."[103] Reminiscent of the local NAACP
chapter of the 1930s and 1940s, the Houston Panthers employed the litigation
strategy to expand their influence. The BPP chapter in Houston participated
in a suit filed by Kay and Shirley A. Mitchell seeking an audit of county books
and records to identify any potential fiscal discrepancies among the unaudited
county monies.

In September 1973 representatives of the Senior Citizen Task Force requested
the assistance of the Houston Panthers after two failed attempts to persuade the
city council to reduce the bus fare from forty cents to fifteen cents for senior citizens. Houston's party members joined with the task force to collect over 10,000

signatures on a petition to lower the bus fare for senior citizens. Edwards noted that "we've been working about four months on this particular project."[104] Party members lent critical assistance to the petition drive when Edwards secured monies from the Menil Foundation to pay for a full-page advertisement in the *Houston Chronicle*. Edwards recalled that he pleaded with Dominique de Menil, who was reluctant to make a donation. He told her that "these are people your age; they are not rich. They are poor elderly people. You don't have to give the party the money you can pay the newspaper directly."[105] The initiative garnered the endorsement of the League of Woman Voters, State Representative Mickey Leland, the Houston Metropolitan Ministers Association, and the SCLC. Leaders of the coalition presented the petition to the city council without success.

Nevertheless, the party's shift from revolutionary posturing to pragmatic activism improved the fortunes of the organization, as evident by its new survival programs.[106] Three additional community outreach programs were added to the free pest control project. The new survival programs included a free breakfast program for children, free food giveaways, and sickle cell anemia and other health preventive testing. After several unsuccessful attempts, in March 1973 the Houston BPP finally launched its free breakfast program. Due to a lack of support from area churches, the Houston Panthers sponsored their first free breakfast program at the Dew Drop Inn, a neighborhood beer joint on Dowling Street. Charles Freeman explained:

At first, the idea of operating a breakfast program from a beer joint took us back too. Ever since we moved our base of operation from Dowling Street to over here on Pierce (in the Fourth Ward), we have been wanting to get active again in the Third Ward because we knew there was a need for our survival programs. However, we must have approached about 20 churches in that area last year as we looked for place to have the breakfast program. We were looking for a place that had a kitchen and that was not occupied during the morning. We found about a dozen, but none of these churches would let us use the place to feed hungry poor children.[107]

Houston's party members fed approximately fifty children between 7:00 and 8:30 a.m. during the school week at the Dowling Street tavern. While the party's breakfast program was a testament to the members' dedication to serve the people, Freeman nonetheless noted that the members "realized that the Dew Drop Inn wasn't a suitable location for children to be coming in, so we moved to Fourth Ward."[108] BPP members in Houston eventually secured the support of Rev. Samuel L. Smith, who permitted them to use the kitchen and cafeteria at his Mt. Horeb Baptist Church in the Fourth Ward. During his remarks given at a testimonial in honor of Bobby Caldwell, a local Houston civil rights attorney, Rev. Smith recalled:

When they [Houston Panthers] left the Third Ward and went to the Fourth Ward nobody wanted to mess with them. It was hands off. This young man here [Charles "Boko" Freeman] was sitting in my study with a Bible in his hand; I didn't notice it at first. He said, "Brother Minister, we want to know if we can use your church to feed the children." And I said yes, and he almost fainted because at that time there were nineteen functioning churches in area and everybody had turned them down.[109]

John "Bunchy" Crear incredulously remarked that the "other ministers accused Reverend Smith of working with the devil for allowing us to use his church for the free breakfast program." Party members collected money from community residents and acquired donations from local mom-and-pop stores as well as major grocery stores. The members' mantra was, "If you do business in the community, you should donate to the community."[110]

As late as March 1973, Houston Panthers announced the construction of the Carl Hampton Free Health Clinic at the 2300 block of Gregg Street in the Fifth Ward. However, the health clinic never materialized. Although party members failed to sponsor a free health clinic, they never abandoned their commitment to health care for the black community. The Houston BPP affiliate sponsored a preventive health care program that tested individuals for sickle cell anemia, diabetes, and hypertension. Party members conducted screening for the diseases at shopping centers, community centers, and community events. To assist with the implementation of the testing program, they "organized a medical cadre composed of Texas Southern University students and community workers."[111] Under the supervision of Shirley Mitchell, a licensed medical technician, volunteers received training to screen individuals for the three health maladies.

The party's growing influence during the third wave of Panther activism in the city generated new members and critical additional resources undergirding its free food giveaway program. Houston Panthers sponsored two survival-day rallies in which they gave free groceries to the attendees. In 1972 the local BPP affiliate held a survival-day rally at Emancipation Park. In March 1973 it distributed 500 bags of food at a survival-day rally at the Black Arts Center on Lyon Avenue.[112] Houston Panthers capitalized on their newly acquired legitimacy as an official BPP chapter and the move from their storefront operations on Dowling Street to a residential neighborhood in the Fourth Ward. The new Pierce Street location complied with a Newton directive for Panthers to reside in neighborhood dwellings to minimize police raids. Steve Edwards noted that his organization "gained a source of strength in the Fourth Ward."[113] Party community outreach programs "melted the ice" to help offset negative media portrayals of the Houston Panthers.

A sign of their changing image was reflected by the support of the Menil Foundation. John and Dominique de Menil's foundation donated monies for the party's general operations. Moreover, elderly residents in the Fourth Ward testified to the local Panthers' successful grassroots activism. A senior citizen living in the Fourth Ward proclaimed that "they were my saviors. There're been lots of groups coming into the ward promising to do a lot of things for poor people over here. The Panthers are the only ones who've delivered." Frankie Lee Gipson concurred when she remarked that "the Panthers are like a blessings from God. They're the only ones doing something out here for poor people. And, it don't make no difference if they're Black, white, or Mexicans, those kids help them."[114]

Although the Houston Panthers underwent a strategic shift from armed resistance, the change did not halt the police repression. Within a month of receiving authorization to operate an official BPP chapter, Johnny "Shotgun" Coward was shot yet again by Houston police officers at 2 a.m. on October 9, 1971.[115] This act of overt repression still constituted an exception to the prevalence of legalistic repression levied against the Houston Panthers. Fortunately, party members in the city could rely on Bobby Caldwell, a local civil rights attorney. Born in 1934 in Dallas and a graduate of TSU's Law School, Caldwell was a tireless legal advocate for black activists in Houston. During his forty years of legal activism, Caldwell represented the University of Houston's black student protesters and provided legal counsel for Lee Otis Johnson's successful appeal, which overturned his thirty-year draconian marijuana conviction. Caldwell also successfully represented Houston Panthers on numerous occasions.[116] Despite the repression, the Houston chapter was becoming immersed in local community activism. However, along with their BPP official status came a loss of autonomy. Their local activism was abruptly diverted when the national office ordered all members to move to Oakland.

Conclusion: Long March to Oakland

Panther activism in Houston formally ended in August 1974 when the BPP national leadership ordered the Houston party members to cease local operations and relocate to Oakland. The BPP leadership's decision to transfer Houston Panthers to Oakland was the last vestige of an earlier controversial (1972) strategy to consolidate power in Oakland by closing Panther units across the nation and deploy BPP members to Oakland in order to mount the mayoral and city council campaigns of Bobby Seale and Elaine Brown, respectively. In his seminal essay examining the role of internal factors in the demise of the BPP, political scientist Ollie Johnson writes that "when the membership received the new directive from the Central Committee, many members refused to uproot their lives and move thousands of miles from home. These Panthers simply left the Party. The leaders of the various state chapters expressed misgivings with the Central Committee's directive to close their respective Party units."[117]

This was not the case for the Houston Panthers, who had one of the last BPP affiliates existing outside of Oakland. Although Houston party members enjoyed their largest membership, most extensive network of survival programs, and greatest degree of community support, they primarily greeted the transfer to Oakland with excitement and enthusiasm. Ade stated, "I was excited about going to Oakland because I knew they had a school. I knew that we would be able to benefit from all that they had to give. I knew that they had developed a certain amount of sophistication just by the practice they were involved with on a day-to-day basis. They had been doing it for a much longer time."[118] Charles Freeman recalled that he was also "excited about going to Oakland."[119] Ruby Morgan, on the other hand, was somewhat upset about the impending transfer; she explained: "I didn't want to leave my family, mother and friends. I never been out of Texas." Nonetheless, Morgan went to Oakland because "I loved the party, and I believed what the party stood for."[120] One of the lone dissenters among the Houston comrades was Claude Frost, who remarked, "I always thought that it was a bad move because in my opinion we were doing a lot with our programs."[121]

In the end, nearly all of the members of the Houston BPP chapter went to Oakland. Steve Edwards remembers that when he arrived in Oakland, he "had never seen so many Panthers in one place."[122] However, the excitement of the Houston Panthers quickly dissipated due to the prevalence of violence and authoritarianism in Oakland. Corporal punishment via "mudholing" and dating restrictions for the female party members were alien to the Houston transplants. When Bobby Reed, who joined the party during the PP II era, arrived in Oakland, he remembered being warned "to watch out for the mudholing."[123] As officer of the day of the Houston BPP chapter, Ruby Morgan explained, "Down here in Texas we didn't do violence on each other." She also expressed concerns about the leadership's restrictive dating policy: "I didn't mind the work. It was just too many restrictions. Now it was okay for the brothers to go out there and mess around. Sisters couldn't do that. When we first went to Oakland, you know I was used to doing what I wanted to do. When I went to Oakland sisters weren't allowed to socialize in the community with brothers who weren't in the Party, and I didn't like that." Nevertheless, when Morgan was ordered to leave the party due to a mistake by the leadership, she recalled: "I couldn't understand why they were telling me to leave. I cried like a baby. I couldn't figure out why they were telling me to leave. I didn't want to leave because I loved the kids at the nursery, and I loved the party."[124] Consequently, Houston party members had uneven experiences in Oakland. For example, after a few weeks of life as a Panther in Oakland Charles "Boko" Freeman left the party, citing "growing ideological differences and concerns for his personal safety."[125] Ayanna Ade, on the other hand, was instructed to return to college to complete her undergraduate degree and later taught at the Oakland Community School, an alternative school operated by the BPP.[126]

Panther presence in Houston represented one of the rare moments of sustained black radicalism in the city. While the BPP was not always widely accepted by the city's conservative black community, the perseverance, dedication, and courage of the members are undisputable. They left a legacy of self-defense, multiracial coalition politics, and community empowerment built in the face of rampant police repression. At its height, the small, hardcore Panther formation in Houston sponsored four survival programs—free pest control, free breakfasts for children, free food giveaways, and free medical screening. Most important, these young African American men and women dared to challenge racial oppression and to struggle on behalf of black and other oppressed people.

Notes

1. Charles E. Jones, "Recovering the Legacy of the Black Panther Party through the Photographs of Stephen Shames," in *The Black Panther*, ed. Stephen Shames (New York: Aperture Foundation, 2006), 138–139. For a detailed discussion of the early history (1966–1970) of the BPP, see Bobby Seale, *Seize the Time: The Story of the Black Panther Party and Huey P. Newton* (New York: Random House, 1970). An excellent overview of the BPP from 1966 to 1982 is provided by Mario V. Peebles, Ula Y. Taylor, and J. Tarika Lewis, *Panther: A Pictorial History of the Black Panthers and the Story behind the Film* (New York: New Market Press, 1995), 13–128. See also Paul Alkebulan, *Surviving Pending Revolution: The History of the Black Panther Party* (Tuscaloosa: University of Alabama Press, 2007).

2. Judson L. Jeffries and Ryan Nissim-Sabat, "Painting a More Complete Portrait of the Black Panther Party", in *Comrades: A Local History of the Black Panther Party*, ed. Judson L. Jeffries (Bloomington: Indiana University Press, 2007), 1–12.

3. Reynaldo Anderson, "Practical Internationalists: The Story of the Des Moines, Iowa, Black Panther Party," in *Groundwork: Local Black Freedom Movements in America*, ed. Jeanne Theoharis and Komozi Woodard (New York: New York University Press, 2005), 282–299; Jon Rice "The World of the Illinois Panthers," in *Freedom North: Black Freedom Struggles Outside the South, 1940–1980*, ed. Jeanne Theoharis and Komozi Woodard (New York: Palgrave Macmillan, 2003), 41–64; Jeffries, *Comrades*; Yohuru Williams, *Black Politics/White Power: Civil Rights, Black Power, and the Black Panthers in New Haven* (New York: Brandywine Press, 2000); Yohuru Williams and Jama Lazerow, eds., *Liberated Territory: Untold Local Perspectives on the Black Panther Party* (Durham, N.C.: Duke University Press, 2008); Andrew Witt, *The Black*

Panthers in the Midwest: The Community Programs and Services of the Black Panther Party in Milwaukee, 1966–1977 (New York: Routledge, 2007).

4. David J. Garrow, "Picking Up the Books: The New Historiography of the Black Panther Party," *Reviews in American History* 35 (2007): 650–670.

5. Benjamin R. Friedman, "Picking Up Where Robert F. Williams Left Off: The Winston-Salem Branch of the Black Panther Party," in Jeffries, *Comrades*, 47–88; Orissa Arend, *Showdown in Desire: The Black Panthers Take a Stand in New Orleans* (Fayetteville: University of Arkansas Press, 2009).

6. David G. McComb, *Houston: A History* (Austin: University of Texas Press, 1981); David G. McComb, *Houston: The Bayou City* (Austin: University of Texas Press, 1969).

7. McComb, *Houston: A History*, 110.

8. F. Kenneth Jensen, "The Houston Sit-In Movement of 1960–61," in *Black Dixie: Afro-Texan History and Culture in Houston*, ed. Howard Beeth and Cary D. Wintz (Houston: Texas A&M University Press, 1992), 211–222; David G. McComb, *Houston: A History*, 169–171.

9. Chandler Davidson, *Biracial Politics: Conflict and Coalition in the Metropolitan South* (Baton Rouge: Louisiana State University Press, 1972), 18; Robert D. Bullard, *Invisible Houston: The Black Experience in Boom and Bust* (College Station: Texas A&M University Press, 1987), 14–31.

10. Joe Feagin, *Free Enterprise City: Houston in Political-Economic Perspective* (New Brunswick, N.J.: Rutgers University Press, 1988), 246–247.

11. Tatcho Mindiola, Yolanda F. Niemann, and Nestor Rodriguez, *Black-Brown: Relations and Stereotypes* (Austin: University of Texas Press, 2002), 10.

12. Davidson, *Biracial Politics*, 127.

13. Alan Bernstein, "Former Police Chief Herman Short Dies," *Houston Chronicle*, December 29, 1989. For an account of the Lucky Hill affair, see Davidson, *Biracial Politics*, 31–33. Bobby Joe Conner and Larry Taylor panicked and fled from police officers after running a red light. Upon their arrest, they were taken to the police station, stripped of their clothing, handcuffed, and severely beaten. Conner was stomped to death by two police officers, who were indicted on murder charges but never convicted. See also the following news media accounts of the death of Bobby Joe Conner: "Jury to Hear Tape about Prisoner Death," *Houston Post*, April 8, 1970; "Rookie Says He Saw Officers Beat Prisoners," *Houston Post*, April 7, 1970; "Crowd Forces Officers' Suspension," *Houston Post*, Monday 6, 1970.

14. "Houston Court Ok's Inspection of Police Files," *Black Panther*, April 19, 1975, 9; "Houston Police Chief Pressured to Stop Wiretap Probe: Testifies before House Judiciary Subcommittee," *Black Panther*, June 16, 1975, 8; "Politics Forces Resignation of Houston Police Chief: Federal Probe of Illegal Wiretapping Continues," *Black Panther*, July 21, 1975, 9.

15. Robert Fisher, "Organizing in the Private City: The Case of Houston, Texas," in Beeth and Wintz, *Black Dixie*, 262.

16. Feagin, *Free Enterprise City*, 274–275.

17. Robert Bullard, "Blacks in Heavenly Houston," in *In Search of the New South: The Black Urban Experience in the 1970s and 1980s*, ed. Robert D. Bullard (Tuscaloosa: University of Alabama Press, 1989), 24.

18. Bullard, *Invisible Houston*, 115.

19. Davidson, *Biracial Politics*, 30–33.

20. Robert V. Haynes, "The Houston Mutiny and Riots of 1917," *Southwestern Historical Quarterly* 76 (April 1973): 418–439.

21. Frances Dressman, "'Yes, We Have No Jitneys!': Transportation Issues in Houston's Black Community," in Beeth and Wintz, *Black Dixie*, 118–119.

22. Davidson, *Biracial Politics*, 29.

23. Ibid., 29–33; Jensen, "Houston Sit-In Movement," 211–212.

24. Fisher, "Organizing in the Private City," 261.

25. For an excellent overview of Houston's black protest and civil rights organizations, see Bullard, *Invisible Houston*, 114–137.

26. Jensen, "Houston Sit-In Movement," 221–222.

27. This account of the so-called TSU riot is heavily drawn from Dwight Watson's superb study, *Race and the Houston Police Department, 1930–1990: A Change Did Come* (College State: Texas A&M University Press, 2005), 78–87.

28. Ibid., 83.

29. Ibid., 84.

30. Martin Waldron, "Shot Kills Texas Policeman in Riot at Negro College," *New York Times*, May 18, 1967.

31. John Makeig, "Inches Away from a Major Riot," *Houston Chronicle*, June 19, 1997.

32. Waldron, "Shot Kills Texas Policeman."

33. Ester King, interview by Charles E. Jones, August 5, 2003, Houston.

34. Ibid.

35. Ibid.; Omowale Luthuli (Dwight Allen), interview by Charles E. Jones, August 3, 2003, Houston; "UH Negro Leaders Feel Insulted," *Houston Post*, February 18, 1969; Carol Raeke, "Locke and Allen Trial Near Jury," *Houston Post*, January 14, 1970.

36. Sonny Wells, "Willie Rudd Defends Himself," *Forward Times* (Houston), August 8, 1971; King, interview.

37. King, interview; Brother Raheem, interview by Charles E. Jones, August 10, 2003, Houston.

38. King, interview.

39. Brother Raheem, interview. See also Claude Frost, interview by Charles E. Jones, August 11, 2007, Houston.

40. King, interview; Brother Raheem, interview; Luthuli, interview.

41. Luthuli, interview; King, interview; *Houstonian Year Book Class of 1969* (University of Houston).

42. "American Civil Liberties Union: News Release Issued by the American Civil Liberties Union, December 29, 1969," in *The Black Panthers Speak*, ed. Philip S. Foner (New York: Da Capo Press, 1995), 263. Also see Scot Brown's insightful account of the BPP-US conflict, *Fighting for Us: Maulana Karenga, the US Organization, and Black Cultural Nationalism* (New York: New York University Press, 2003), 91–99, 107–130; Roy Wilkens and Ramsey Clark, *Search and Destroy: A Report by the Commission of Inquiry into the Black Panthers and the Police* (New York: Metropolitan Applied Research Center, 1973); Peter L. Zimroth, *Perversions of Justice: The Prosecution and Acquittal of the Panther 21* (New York: Viking Press, 1974); Donald Freed, *Agony in New Haven: The Trial of Bobby Seale, Ericka Huggins and the Black Panther Party* (New York: Simon and Schuster, 1973).

43. Ayanna Ade, "Roundtable: Black Panther Activism in Houston: The Legacy of Carl Hampton, and People's Party II," Thirtieth Annual Conference, National Council for Black Studies, Houston, March 16, 2006.

44. Charles E. Jones and Jonathan Gayles, "The World Is a Child's Classroom: An Analysis of the Black Panther Party's Oakland Community School," in *Teach Freedom: Education for Liberation in the African-American Tradition*, ed. Charles M. Payne and Carol Sills Strickland (New York: Teachers College Press, 2008), 100–116.

45. Charles "Boko" Freeman, interview by Charles E. Jones, June 25, 2008, Atlanta.

46. Steve Edwards, interview by Charles E. Jones, June 6, 2009, Richmond, Calif.

47. Alkebulan, *Surviving Pending Revolution*, 111.

48. Ibid.

49. King, interview.

50. Edwards, interview.

51. "Space City Blues," 1971 BB 4142, Pacific Tape Library, Los Angeles.

52. Robinson Block, "People's Party II," unpublished paper, University of Houston, December 10, 2008.

53. "Unique/Unusual/One-of-a-Kind: JBRL Meeting Room," http://www.virtualtourist.com/travel/North_America/United_States_of_America/Texas/Houston, accessed June 12, 2008.

54. Ignacio M. García, *Mexican American Youth Organization: Precursors of Change in Texas* (Tucson: University of Arizona, Mexican American Studies and Research Center, 1987), 8; Armando Narvarro, *Mexican American Youth Organization: Avant-Garde of the Chicano Movement Texas* (Austin: University of Texas Press, 1995).

55. Roxanne Dunbar-Ortiz, interview by Charles E. Jones, April 4, 2006, Atlanta.

56. Ibid.

57. Thomas A. Johnson, "Houston Negroes Dispute Police on Fatal Gun Fight," *New York Times*, August 1, 1970.

58. Frost, interview.

59. Freeman, interview, June 25, 2008.

60. Luthuli, interview.

61. Edwards, interview.

62. Ibid.

63. Seale, *Seize the Time*, 89–90.

64. "Space City Blues."

65. Ibid.

66. Freeman, interview, June 25, 2008.

67. Ibid.

68. Ibid

69. Frost, interview.

70. Luthuli, interview.

71. Ovidle Duncantell, interview by Charles E. Jones, August 11, 2003, Houston.

72. Freeman, interview, June 25, 2008.

73. "Space City Blues."

74. Roxanne Dunbar-Ortiz, *Outlaw Woman: A Memoir of the War Years, 1960–1975* (San Francisco: City Lights, 2001), 264.

75. Rosenblast and Singer, "Black Militant Slain on Dowling," 1. See also Duncantell, interview; "Who Fingered Carl Hampton?" *Sepia*, July 1970; Freeman, interview, June 25, 2008; "Space City Blues Who Murdered Carl Hampton," July 26, 1970, KPFT Radio, Pacific Radio Archive.

76. Charles "Boko" Freeman, interview by Charles E. Jones, July 3, 2008, Atlanta.

77. Don Wycliff, "Dowling Ministers Amid Unrest," *Houston Post*, October 3, 1970.

78. "Coalition Asks Chief Ouster, Store Boycott," *Houston Chronicle*, July 29, 1970.

79. Ruby Morgan, interview by Charles E. Jones, August 11, 2007, Houston.

80. Freeman, interview, July 3, 2008.

81. Morgan, interview.

82. "300 Rally to Protest Slaying of Black Militant," *Houston Post*, August 3, 1970; "Rally Staged at Peoples Party II," *Voice of Hope* (Houston), December 12, 1970; Windel E. Culbreath, "No

People at People's Party Rally," *Voice of Hope*, February 13, 1971; W. E. Culbreath, "People's Party II Rally to Protest Conner's Murder," *Voice of Hope*, April 10, 1971; "Welch, Short Are Invited to People's Court' Trail," *Houston Chronicle*, May 6, 1971, Heartman Collection, Texas Southern University.

83. Windel E. Culbreath, "People's Party II Rally to Protest Conner's Murder," *Voice of Hope*, April 10, 1971.

84. Alan Wolfe, *The Seamy Side of Democracy: Repression in America* (New York: David McKay, 1970), 118.

85. "People's Party II Searched," *Houston Post*, June 9, 1971; "People's Party Chairman Gets 2 Years," *Houston Post*, September 22, 1971; "Black Militant Given 2 Years for Police Assault," *Houston Chronicle*, September 22, 1971; Carolyn Raeke, "Grand Jury Gets Dowling Police Shooting Case Involving 2," *Houston Post*, October 8, 1970; Warren Weber, "Jury in Haile Case Resumes Deliberations" *Houston Chronicle*, July 16, 1971.

86. "Freeman Says Marijuana Charge a 'Frame-up,'" *Voice of Hope*, February 27, 1971; Bill Coulter, "Panther Cleared by Jury," *Houston Post*, October 16, 1971; Freeman, interview, July 3, 2008.

87. From: SAC, Houston (157-1210), To: Director, FBI (100-44 2006), Subject: CoIntelPro-Black Extremists, 11–30–70, author's archives.

88. "Rally Staged by Peoples Party II," 3.

89. Ibid.

90. Culbreath, "No People at People's Party Rally."

91. Thomas Wright, "Minority Contractor's Rescue Health Clinic," *Forward Times*, August 14, 1971; Windel E. Culbreath, "Sheriff's Deputies Evict PP II from Carl Hampton Clinic," *Voice of Hope*, May 22, 1971.

92. Freeman, interview, July 3, 2008.

93. John "Bunchy" Crear, interview by Charles E. Jones, August 11, 2007, Houston; Freeman, interview, June 25, 2008; Edwards, interview.

94. Freeman, interview, July 3, 2008.

95. From: SAC, Houston (157-1210), To: Director, FBI (100-44 2006), Subject: CoIntelPro-Black Extremists, 11–30–70.

96. Crear, interview

97. Ibid.

98. Ibid.

99. Ibid.; Freeman, interview, June 25, 2008.

100. Freeman, interview, July 3, 2008.

101. Ayanna Ade (Gwen Johnson), interview by Charles E. Jones, August 10, 2003, Houston.

102. Ibid.

103. "Black Candidate Charges Corruption in Harris County," *Black Panther*, May 4, 1974, 7. For additional information on the election of Houston Panthers to community boards, see "Panthers Won Elections Helping Old Fourth Warders," *Forward Times*, September 30, 1972, Folder: People Party II, Heartman Collection, Texas Southern University.

104. "Petitions for Lower Bus Fares: Black Panthers Seek Aid for the Aged," *Forward Times*, January 5, 1974; "Senior Citizens Seek Reduced Bus Fare," *Black Panther*, April 6, 1974, 3.

105. Edwards, interview.

106. "Breakfast Program in Third Ward Lounge," *Forward Times*, March 10, 1973; "B.P.P. Trains Houstonians for Free Medical Testing Program," *Black Panther*, June 23, 1974, 5.

107. "Breakfast Program in Third Ward Lounge."

108. Ibid.

109. Tribute to attorney Bobby H. Caldwell, Riverside Terrace Café Houston, March 17, 2007, video recording.

110. Crear, interview.

111. "B.P.P. Trains Houstonians," 5.

112. Crear, interview; "Black Panther Survival Rally March 7: Breakfast Program in Third Ward Lounge," *Forward Times*, March 10, 1973.

113. Thomas Wright, "Local Black Panther Chieftain to Go to Prison," *Forward Times*, Folder: People's Party II, Heartman Collection, Texas Southern University.

114. "Panthers War Election Helping Old Fourth Wanders," *Forward Times*, Folder: People's Party II, Heartman Collection, Texas Southern University.

115. "Johnny Coward Shot, as Houston Branch Opens," *Black Panther*, October 23, 1971, 7.

116. Bobby Caldwell, telephone interview by Charles E. Jones, September 17, 2003; Tribute to Attorney Bobby H. Caldwell; Freeman, interview, June 25, 2008.

117. Ollie A. Johnson III, "Explaining the Demise of the Black Panther Party: The Role of Internal Factors," in *The Black Panther Party (Reconsidered)*, ed. Charles E. Jones (Baltimore: Black Classic Press, 1998), 391–416.

118. Ade, interview.

119. Freeman, interview, June 25, 2008.

120. Morgan, interview.

121. Frost, interview.

122. Edwards, interview.

123. Bobby Reed, interview by Charles E. Jones, August 10, 2003, Houston.

124. Morgan, interview.

125. Charles "Boko" Freeman, "Charles 'Boko' Freeman: The Eternal Panther," www.itsaboutmedia.com, accessed June 10, 2008.

126. Ade, interview.

A PANTHER SIGHTING IN THE PACIFIC NORTHWEST

The Seattle Chapter of the Black Panther Party

Jeffrey Zane and Judson L. Jeffries

> Seattle is one of the few cities left in America which can solve its
> racial problem before it becomes unsolvable.
> —REV. DR. JOHN ADAMS

Seattle is an unusual city; it is famous both for its inclement weather and the active outdoor lifestyles of its residents. Although tucked into the farthest corner
of the country, the city has influenced the nation's fashion, music, food, and
technological industries. And while Seattle's population is as racially hetero-
geneous as its many bohemian tastes, African Americans make up less than
10 percent of Seattle's population. Still, they have served as mayor and county
executive, president of the city council and school board, and school district
superintendent. Seattle's image as an enclave for young urban professionals is
featured prominently in the city's marketing campaign, making it somewhat
easy for some to forget that Seattle once had a long history of racial discord.
In response to severe public school segregation during the 1960s, the city voluntarily adopted a busing program (albeit under threat of lawsuit), which was
later disbanded by the school district superintendent.

A casual visitor to the scene in which the July 1968 uprisings and firebombs
occurred will now see an array of large and expensive homes, making it difficult for some to believe that, for ten years, the city was home to the thriving
Seattle chapter of the Black Panther Party (BPP). The Seattle chapter of the BPP
emerged from unique circumstances that distinguish the city's race relations
from those in the rest of the nation. The city that gave rise to such seeming
contradictions informed the experiences of the Seattle BPP as it adapted the organization's teachings to the Northwest, and, as a result, it is difficult to describe
the Seattle chapter outside of the context of the city in which it operated.

A cadre of young activists drove much of Seattle's Black Power movement. These youth led a variety of organizations that would profoundly change Seattle's Central Area, the traditional heart of the city's African American community. The Seattle BPP's unequalled prominence among these organizations makes it an especially interesting organization, and it is made even more fascinating by the experiences of the young activists who embodied national Black Power trends within Seattle's Central Area.

While narrating the Seattle BPP's experiences, this essay will attempt to paint a portrait of the Central Area in 1968 and explain how young activists were motivated to dedicate themselves to forming and maintaining a chapter in Seattle.

From its earliest years, Seattle's Central Area was a diverse neighborhood that housed many of the city's ethnic and economic communities. The neighborhood lies just east of Seattle's downtown and was a natural channel for the flow of newcomers seeking to remain close to the city's ports and budding downtown. Industrial zones and steep hills originally slowed expansion in other directions, so Seattle's Jewish and Italian communities formed in the Central Area neighborhood, where they were soon joined by much of the city's Asian community. Prior to World War II, fewer than 4,000 African Americans lived in Seattle, but that number increased by more than 400 percent between 1940 and 1950. By the turn of the twenty-first century, the city's small African American community concentrated around Madison Avenue in the Central Area and in the red light district around Jackson Street just south of downtown.

During the Second World War, an influx of wartime workers, combined with rising housing discrimination, relegated thousands of incoming African Americans to the Central Area. Postwar segregation ensured that the Central Area became both more concentrated and more African American by the 1950s. The 1960 census reported a black majority in the Central Area for the first time, and the neighborhood's character reflected the newfound majority, becoming inextricably linked to black identity within Seattle.

By 1960 the Central Area had completed its transformation from a diverse neighborhood of Jewish, Italian, Asian, native-born white, and African American residents to a nearly entirely black residential area. Hemmed in by housing and economic segregation, it began to languish in isolation from the rest of the city. Because of this demographic change, the civil rights movement was the most significant event that took place in the Central Area during the second half of the twentieth century. The formation of a movement among Central Area residents to rejoin the greater city community slowly reversed the area's declining economic fortunes and eventually returned the neighborhood to its earlier diversity.

Seattle's civil rights movement occurred later than in other cities, partly as a result of Seattleites' refusal to believe that such racial problems existed. In fact, when word of Dr. Martin Luther King Jr.'s impending visit to Seattle in November 1961 spread throughout the city, some (including certain black leaders) feared that his presence would instigate trouble where there had been none. In response, a few churches refused to rent their sanctuaries for his speech. That some thought King, the apostle of nonviolence, would stir up trouble says something about the mindset of some within the African American community.

Indeed, there were few obvious symptoms to tip one off as to the existence of racial problems. The harsh segregation of the South never took place to any real extent in Seattle, and the African American community never faced lynch mobs or antiblack rioters. One of the first actions of the Washington territorial legislature in 1853 was to ask Congress to give George Washington Bush, a black pioneer, unambiguous ownership of his land. Also, the obvious blight of some major midwestern and northern cities was not present in Seattle, where physical deterioration existed in a much more subtle and relative form along the streets dotted with mature trees and older Victorian homes. Indeed, if Clarence Mitchell, director of the National Association of Colored People's (NAACP's) Washington, D.C., bureau, could visit as late as 1965 and remark that Seattle "rates high" on civil rights, it was easy for average Seattleites to overlook any race problems in their city.[1]

However, such problems did exist and were well summarized by Lewis Watts, executive director of the newly formed Seattle Urban League. He remarked that Washington State possessed the strongest civil rights statutes in the United States, yet de facto equal opportunities in housing simply did not exist for Seattle's minorities.[2] The problem in Seattle was generally not the presence of discriminatory laws, or even a glaring absence of protective laws, but of weak enforcement of the laws already on the books.

Soon after passing the Fair Employment Practices Act, the state legislature created the Washington State Board Against Discrimination (WSBAD) specifically to battle discrimination, and later delegated to it housing enforcement powers. Although these actions were relatively weak, they were the earliest steps of a movement that would sweep the community during the 1960s as awareness of the city's racial ills first spread across the Central Area, and then to the city at large.[3]

The Civil Rights Movement Comes to Seattle

Seattle's civil rights movement did not necessarily follow the pattern described by national historians. In *We Have No Leaders: African Americans in the Post-Civil Rights Era*, Robert C. Smith characterizes the African American struggle in this century as made up of three overlapping phases: lobbying (from the beginning), litigation (1950s), and protest (the 1960s civil rights movement).[4] In Seattle, all three phases concurrently made up and informed the civil rights movement. There was no period during the twentieth century that protests of some form did not take place, be it knocking over tables in a Jim Crow restaurant or protesting the death of a transient at the hands of the police. The same is true of lobbying, which began with William Owen Bush, a black state legislator in the state's first session, and continued through a variety of efforts to place open housing laws on the books in Seattle. Likewise, black Seattleites excelled in the courtroom against discriminatory businesses from the beginning of the twentieth century onward. Although the three phases that Smith describes have continuously made up the civil rights movement, they did not maintain equal or constant roles. Central Area residents chose between each form of resistance to stiffening racial codes throughout the century.

During the civil rights movement, the Central Area's African American community would knock down the most visible and egregious barriers that prevented black access to the rest of the city. However, the removal of these obstacles only cleared a path to greater frustration, as less overt discrimination and economic hardship continued to divide the Central Area from the rest of the city. A combination of more intense activism and heightened expectations led to less patience among Central Area youth with the plodding pace of institutional change. As across the nation, this mixing of activism and intransigent issues proved explosive, and led directly to the Central Area's Black Power movement and activism throughout the next twenty years.

In much the same fashion that the Oakland-based BPP would provide the organizational structure for that city's most prominent Black Power entity, Seattle's civil rights movement owed its impetus to ideas imported from across the country. Arrivals from the South stirred both the community and the city from their slumber, and placed a spotlight upon Central Area problems. Two of the community's most vocal and effective defenders arrived in Seattle in 1958 when Rev. Samuel McKinney and Rev. John Adams stepped off their respective trains. That same year witnessed the founding of the Seattle Urban League, followed by the Congress of Racial Equality (CORE) three years later. Also in 1961 a number of groups formed the Central Area Civil Rights Council (CACRC), perhaps the most effective civil rights organization in that neighborhood. In his study of civil rights in Seattle, Larry Richardson cites four CACRC leaders as the force behind the civil rights movement in the city: Rev. Adams; Edwin Pratt, executive director of the Seattle Urban League; Charles V. Johnson of the NAACP; and Walter Hundley of CORE. The combined membership of all the member groups totaled nearly 3,000. Compounding this clout, Rev. Samuel McKinney, ultimately the pastor of 2,700 parishioners at Mt. Zion Church (voting registration rate: 95 percent), actively supported the CACRC's drives and initiatives.[5] With this move, Richardson quotes Rev. Adams, "The civil rights movement finally crossed the Cascades."[6]

Such numbers, especially in Seattle's still relatively small black community (26,901 in 1960, in a city of 557,087), made unity much easier. Considering the multiethnic membership of many of the city's organizations, the CACRC functioned as a coalition in and of itself. Middle-class, educated, and civic-minded Seattleites of all ethnicities supported either the NAACP or the Urban League, thereby lending at least tacit support to their projects. Indeed, even those outside the city could comment that "Seattle is unique on the West Coast in having a unified front pressing for city-wide racial reform."[7]

The civil rights movement in Seattle was particularly effective not only because it presented this fairly united face but also in that it functioned at the fore of an even broader coalition that included majority-white churches and other organizations. The CACRC achieved its greatest success in open housing, largely because it attracted more allies to this cause than to any other. The influential Greater Seattle Church Council and Mayor Gordon Clinton were key players in the open housing coalition that brought the issue to the city's attention, however temporarily. Also, because the issue affected all of the city's minorities, open housing activists could find allies such as Wing Luke, an Asian American councilman and perhaps the most forceful open housing proponent on the city council until his untimely death in a small airplane crash in 1968.

Such alliances produced several strong victories in improving life in the city's Central Area. However, the failures of even such a unified front—and the issues that were exposed by this front—perhaps led to frustration among young activists, which in turn gave rise to the Seattle BPP. In particular, the CACRC's efforts in battling three forms of segregation in Central Area life would reveal the challenges facing Central Area activists and—to some, at least—the limits of traditional civil rights campaigns in countering these issues.

Housing discrimination was a major problem, even in 1960 Seattle. In a national rating in which 100 denoted complete segregation, Seattle rated a 79.7, well below the national average of 86.2. However, it was a full point above the Pacific Coast average of 78.7, and a significant problem nevertheless.[8] Although state government had addressed the issue earlier, fair housing lost the protection of the law in 1961, when Washington became the first state to declare open housing unconstitutional in *Jones v. O'Meara*.[9]

The campaign for open housing marked the effective beginning of the civil rights movement in Seattle. Until this moment, Seattleites had watched the struggle for racial equality across the South from afar. The NAACP and churches collected donations for their activist brethren in the South, but very little activity occurred on the home front. In 1963, as President John F. Kennedy finally initiated (what some have called, but others disagree with) decisive action in the field of civil rights, the movement gained steam in Seattle.[10]

The *Jones* case proved to be the catalyst to an open housing campaign that took two forms—matching nondiscriminatory homeowners with black buyers outside the Central Area and lobbying for an open housing ordinance. The latter got off to a disappointing start. Several demonstrations and large-scale marches to city hall, including CORE's twenty-four–hour sit-in (the first in Seattle), seemed to have effectively lobbied the city council in July 1963. These actions marked Seattle's first large-scale protest demonstrations, as clerics Mance Jackson and Samuel McKinney led large groups of dissidents to the city's most powerful political institutions.

The CACRC coalition, greatly aided by the work of councilman Wing Luke, eventually generated enough council votes for the ordinance.[11] Yet the council was unable to pass it without public attention, and a petition placed it on the ballot in 1964, where it went down to a dismal defeat by a two-to-one ratio. An open housing supporter commented bitterly afterward that "if we had got a majority to pass the law, we wouldn't have needed the law."[12]

The ordinance proved to be only the opening salvo in the struggle. Prompted by Martin Luther King Jr.'s drive for federal legislation, as well as Mayor Clinton's "humane interest" in the subject, the drive for open housing gained momentum again by mid-decade.[13]

The second form of the struggle, aiding African American homebuyers find housing outside the Central Area, became the strategy of choice in the interim. As it progressed, the issue became one that poised activists and community groups of all colors against at-times reluctant real estate agents.[14] The two largest placement operations, Harmony Homes and the Seattle Urban League's Operation Equality, arranged the sale of over $1 million worth of homes, and new listing services sprouted up across Seattle. Through such efforts of the multiethnic coalition, those willing and able to move "anywhere that's nice," as one African American family put it, found growing opportunities to escape the rundown Central Area and find housing elsewhere in the city. Operation Equality also formed fair housing committees in neighborhoods across the city to welcome these new families, and thus made the idea of "pioneering" less daunting.[15] In addition, community groups across Seattle and its suburbs increasingly sent invitations to Central Area groups, proclaiming their support for fair housing.

This war of attrition against housing discrimination proved a fairly effective strategy, and Quintard Taylor explains that "by the summer of 1965 even the staunchest proponents of the defeated open housing ordinance were slowly conceding that the voluntary approach allowed a growing number of blacks to purchase homes outside the District."[16] That this occurred even before white

Chicagoans would organize against King's efforts in the same field marked the progress Seattle had made in such a short time.

By 1968 the city council unanimously passed the housing ordinance—already made much narrower in scope by national legislation—without much public debate. The concept had achieved credibility among the Seattle citizenry, was strenuously advocated by Washington's Republican governor Daniel Evans, and was now even supported by many real estate agents. Already subject to the federal open housing law in their own field, many real estate agents were anxious to extend open housing legislation to apartment owners and homeowners with the Seattle ordinance.[17]

Yet the housing struggle had an economic side that was intimately tied to the failure of the CACRC leadership to resolve issues of the workplace in Seattle. Without the resources to afford a house, open housing victories could prove depressingly hollow, indeed. Job discrimination in Seattle was rampant, a reality that disproportionately affected the Central Area neighborhood economy, and education within the Central Area left something to be desired. When even the lower-priced sections of the North End were beyond the reach of many Central Area families, the removal of racial restrictions revealed a community largely without the resources to purchase housing.

Accordingly, some organizations under the CACRC umbrella targeted employment discrimination and other economic matters, but these campaigns were less clearly victorious. The specter of hiring quotas has never been without controversy across the American electorate. Also, while denying opportunities to those with the ability to purchase or rent housing seemed wrong enough to most Seattleites, hiring decisions came across as a little more cloudy. Victory in the workplace would not come so easily to African Americans in Seattle.

CORE pursued its own solution in October 1961. Walter Hundley, president of CORE in Seattle, organized a "selective buying" campaign against Bon Marche, a local department store, and soon expanded it to many other department and grocery stores in the area that hired insignificant numbers of blacks. Their direct action tactics included shop-ins, in which activists abandoned shopping carts full of food without paying after ringing up their selections, and shoe-ins, in which CORE activists occupied all the seats in a store and each tried on dozens of pairs of shoes without making a purchase. Safeway conceded first and agreed to hire five black workers at its Central Area grocery store. Others held out until CORE led 1,000 marchers in a downtown protest against Bon Marche in mid-1963. Bon Marche gave in and agreed to hire over fifty African Americans in the next few months. The remaining stores soon agreed to hire varying numbers of African Americans. Nordstrom's, the city's largest store, agreed to recruit, hire, and train African Americans in all staff levels while holding seminars on civil rights issues. In light of these hirings,

Genevieve Hughes of the national office called the campaign "a real model of CORE action."[18]

Yet these campaigns led to a split in the employment coalition between CORE and the NAACP. Certain friction had already risen over the aggressive tactics of CORE. During the shop-ins, exasperated shoppers of all races found themselves highly inconvenienced by the disruption tactics, and perishable items in carts began to spoil during shop-ins. Word of these incidents spread, giving the campaign a radical note that the NAACP hoped to avoid for fear of harming vital citywide support for the campaign. The official break between CORE and the NAACP occurred over CORE's tactics in picketing Picture Floor Plans Realty, a real estate office, for allegedly discriminatory practices. Tensions had risen as the crowd sang, chanted, and jeered outside the firm, and began to push and shove patrons, despite the CACRC's warnings against such physical confrontation. The conflict finally came to a climax in an altercation between an angry salesman and some protesters. CORE suspended the strike, and a court injunction made this decision permanent. Yet the NAACP officially broke ties with CORE in March 1964, creating the first significant fissure within the Seattle movement.[19] Rather than a traditionally portrayed split between the middle class and the working class, or one between separatists and integrationists, this split was more one of tactics and intemperance than anything else. Both sides drew from fairly middle-class memberships, and individual whites and African Americans took part in or condemned militant activities.[20]

Soon after the split, the slow pace of the piecemeal approach to employment frustrated CORE leaders, and they designed the Drive for Equal Employment in Downtown Seattle (DEEDS) project, one of the most ambitious projects of any CORE chapter in the nation. A study revealed that only 2 percent of downtown store workers were black, and that a third of these were janitors. Restaurants were even worse, for 100 percent of their janitors, and none of the waiters, were black. CORE decided to launch a general campaign against Seattle's downtown businesses, and demanded that a little less than a quarter of the projected 5,000 new jobs to be created in coming years go to African Americans.[21]

CORE took on the challenge with little practical help. The boycott began on October 19, 1964, and lasted until mid-January 1965. Braving the typical local rain, CORE members picketed on the bridges over the interstate between the Central Area and the business district, and some black downtown shoppers skirting the boycott found themselves taunted mercilessly. Yet the boycott barely affected the Christmas rush or even regular shopping in January. The federal and city government offices located downtown promised to increase minority hiring, but little changed within the private sector, and the project went down largely as a failure.[22] While bringing job bias to the public's attention, the campaign had also wiped out CORE's budget and energies, and the organization began a period of decline from which it never fully recovered. The drive had not organized a significant coalition of the sort that kept the open housing debate in the city's spotlight. Obtaining a role in the hiring practices of the downtown business establishment without such a broad coalition proved too much for the CORE strategists, and hiring discrimination would remain for another campaign to take on.

The third chief area of segregation lay in the public schools. Nearly all of the city's black students attended crowded and poorly funded Central Area schools, which often provided inadequate education. Such conditions prompted NAACP attorney Philip Burton to begin a suit against the school district's de facto segregation in 1962. To settle the suit, the district agreed to become the nation's first major city to enact a district-wide desegregation plan with the Voluntary Racial Transfer (VRT) program. Under this plan, students could choose to transfer to any school for racial integration purposes. The plan fell far short of expectations, however, and fewer than 250 African American students took advantage of this program to attend North End schools in its first year, with even less reciprocation by white students.[23]

Skeptical of the future success of this program, the CACRC began lobbying to close Central Area schools, so as to force the school board to integrate all Seattle schools with the newly destitute black students. Indeed, the reasoning went, one or two of the aging Central Area schools clearly needed condemning anyway. For its part, the Seattle Urban League proposed a "Triad Plan," which matched white schools with predominantly black schools. According to this plan, elementary schools would be divided into two-year institutions, and the city divided into zones. Students from all neighborhoods within paired zones would attend one school for grades 1–2, another school for grades 3–4, and a third for grades 5–6. Each of these schools would be located within a different neighborhood, providing opportunities for multiethnic education for all students. Presented in March 1965, the Triad Plan was rejected just two weeks later by the Seattle school board. The idea of mandatory busing would not win acceptance its first time around.

Annoyed by the inaction, NAACP attorneys filed a lawsuit against the Seattle school district in March 1966 on behalf of thirty students. The issue escalated, and the NAACP led a boycott of city schools on March 31 and April 1, in which almost half of the Central Area students participated. That almost a third of the boycotting students were white demonstrated the multiracial nature of Central Area activism, even at this early date. However, the protests and plans accomplished very little in the fairly uncharted territory of district-wide desegregation. By 1967 the Central Area schools still housed nearly the entire city's African American students, except for those students who had opted for North End schooling. The voluntary plans had proven almost counterproductive—many of those who left for the North End were excellent students—and the Central Area seemed no closer to enjoying genuinely integrated schools than in 1963.[24]

Despite these setbacks, heading into 1967 Seattle's racial situation still remained remarkably calm, and the upheaval in Watts in Los Angeles and parts farther east from 1965 to 1967 passed largely without comment in Seattle. Although economic problems existed, the Central Area lacked the combination of urban blight, hardcore frustration, and simmering race relations that motivated racial upheaval in the inner cities across the North. Such chaos seemed very far away, despite occasional warnings from local activists. The city even differed from Los Angeles and the Bay Area as far as the small size of the black community and its sheer isolation from heavily black populated centers. Urban problems in Seattle's Central Area certainly existed, but were not acute enough to independently prompt such a movement.

Yet enough problems existed to spawn such a rebellion. The Seattle Urban League detailed the Central Area's dismal conditions in a 1968 report (see Table 2). The African American economic position had seemingly reversed the gains made in the 1950s. Black workers rose from 73 to 76 percent of white median income in Seattle between 1950 and 1960. The Seattle Urban League limited its sample to African American workers in the Central Area only in 1967 and found their incomes just 54 percent that of whites. Although black unemployment actually improved from 14 percent in 1960 to 9 percent in 1968, white unemployment had sunk from 6 percent to 3 percent in the same period.[25] To some, the limits of the CACRC appeared to have been reached.

Table 2. Urban League Report, 1968		
Subject	**Seattle**	**Central Area**
Housing built before 1940	63.4%	87.4%
New building 1950–1960	19.4%	6.8%
Dropout rate, high school	7.84% (city average)	12.96% (Garfield)
Suspension rate	4.93% (city average)	12.96% (Garfield)
Seattle Urban League, "Seattle's Racial Gap: 1968." Seattle Urban League Collection, University of Washington Archives, Manuscripts, and Special Collections.		

In addition, Seattle was not permanently immune to the spirit of youth rebellion that shook the country. The similar timing, economic background, and young age of the founders of both black and white militant groups in Seattle during the period suggest that there is little reason to consider Black Power as entirely isolated from the larger youth movement that swept the nation. Due in part to this movement, an organized and rooted Black Power movement would reach the Central Area just as urban tensions in the neighborhood would finally reach the spillover point.

Finally, the personal experiences of the Seattle Black Panther leadership would inform their view of being black in Seattle. Aaron Dixon recalled his tennis team winning the 1966 citywide league championship at the Lake Washington Tennis Club, yet being prohibited from eating in the club's restaurant or using the swimming pool. Said Dixon, "The winner of the championship game was to have dinner at the restaurant and then go swimming."[26] After the trophy presentation, Dixon's team was told that the restaurant and pool were off-limits to the black members of the team. The same rules did not apply to Dixon's Jewish teammate, the only Caucasian on the team. Instead of enjoying a nice dinner at the exclusive and upscale Lake Washington Club restaurant, club officials brought out hot dogs and French fries for Dixon and his teammates. Dixon noted that "it wasn't like people walked around with hoods burning crosses . . . there were more subtle types of things."[27] Childhood experiences in Seattle would to some extent guide the Seattle BPP's leadership.

Black Power Arises in Seattle

The new generation initially arose from the Black Student Union (BSU) at the University of Washington (UW). The BSU had a leg up on many other Black Power organizations trying to establish themselves at that time in that it catered to young, educated African Americans in a protective, nurturing environment—a university campus. Although it spent its early life addressing mainly university issues, the BSU's greatest single effect upon the Black Power movement in Seattle lay in bringing together under an ideological banner the small cadre of leaders who would head most of the militant movement in Seattle. BSU president E. J. Brisker, vice president Larry Gossett, and officers Aaron Dixon, Elmer Dixon, and Carl Miller formed the nucleus of Black Power in Seattle. Most of this leadership did not immediately adopt Black Power ideology, yet gradually came around to adopt individual versions of it. Although young (between the ages of seventeen and twenty-four), they all had some experience in the civil rights movement and were accustomed to activist action. A Seattle native, Gossett served with Volunteers in Service to America (VISTA) in Central Harlem as a student, and many others had worked for the federal Model Cities program and the Student Nonviolent Coordinating Committee (SNCC).[28]

Other black radical organizations that functioned within the city of Seattle included the Revolutionary Action Movement and the Nation of Islam, neither of which had as strong an impact as was the case in some other cities.

The United Black Front (UBF), founded in 1968, brought together the staff of dozens of Seattle antipoverty agencies and attained certain influence in representing the black poor. This group's lobbying strengthened the development of a separate agenda for the poor, yet the UBF's influence often diminished with the reduced scale of its member programs following budget cuts in the poverty programs. The *Seattle Sun* reported upon the whereabouts of the leadership of groups like UBF in 1976 and found them busy "making payments on a home on the lake, or hustling jobs in the bureaucracy," while Elmer Dixon and others were still "working quietly for survival and change."[29] Similarly, the Central Area committee for Peace and Improvement (CAPI) attracted a variety of black nationalist groups without attaining influence as widespread as the Panther leadership in Seattle. The BSU/Seattle BPP youths' significance to the community lay in their prominence in the public eye, thoughtful leadership, and unshakeable commitment to aiding the Central Area's economically disadvantaged throughout their own lives.[30]

The UW BSU was created in 1967 by the merger of the university's Afro-American Society and the Friends of SNCC, largely in response to the low numbers of black students at the school. Although African Americans had attended the UW since 1890, only 136 of the approximately 30,000 students enrolled were African American. Friends of SNCC had been created initially to support SNCC's southern activities, but evolved with the national party and was responsible for bringing Stokely Carmichael to Seattle. This drift was largely a testament to the impatience of the BSU and SNCC membership. Aaron Dixon was an accomplished athlete and student from the Central Area, raised by an activist-minded father from Chicago and longtime Boeing employee (1958–1978). Aaron and his brother Elmer were inculcated with stories of their parents' struggles against segregation and discrimination, and recalled marching Seattle streets with Martin Luther King Jr. during his 1961 visit. Aaron Dixon saw the BSU and SNCC as opportunities to enact many of the community-oriented beliefs on which he was raised. Larry Gossett, who helped form the organization, was another excellent student, shaped by his experiences as a VISTA worker. They were joined by E. J. Brisker, Carl Miller, and other thoughtful students with an ethic of activism. The BSU was thus created by students who tapped into national militant ideology.[31]

The BSU won its most convincing victory fairly early. On May 20, 1967, the BSU organized picket lines in front of the administration building to call for more African American students and for greater support to those already enrolled. As the protest heated up later that afternoon, the protesters stormed the building during a faculty senate executives' meeting. Failing to come to an immediate agreement with school officials, the protesters refused to leave and barricaded university president Charles Odegaard in his inner office with several aides. After four hours of telephone negotiations, Odegaard agreed to sweeping measures that would increase black clout at the UW. He promised to double black enrollment, recruit minority staff, and create a black studies major, which were virtually all the items the BSU demanded. The BSU had been fortunate to encounter a university president who already agreed with their main points of contention.

As a result of the agreement, the university created the Equal Opportunities Program (EOP) to recruit minority students under a revised admissions policy. The number of black students rose to 465 by the next fall, while the number of black professors increased from one to ten and to fifteen the year after. Also, the BSU obtained an agreement to recruit white graduate students to provide tutoring services for minority students, although most faculty and staff declined to give an hour of their pay to minorities as the protestors requested.[32]

The university and BSU reached this agreement fairly quickly and peacefully, and by the beginning of 1968 the campus paper could still report an absence of uproar at the UW. The university refused to press charges against the protestors, and the BSU remained relatively silent. They had already made the most desired gains, and were busy recruiting black students and handling other aspects of black student life.[33] These events honed the organizational skills of the young men who turned the BSU into a citywide organization, and then split into independent Black Power organizations.

Brisker and Gossett wanted to relate their ideas to the rest of the city as well, and began organizing black student unions at local secondary schools as well as at religious and community colleges. They formed the Seattle Association of Black Student Unions (SABSU) and held weekly meetings to discuss and aid strategies for change. Black history courses, permission to wear hair in the "Afro" style, and specialized counseling for black students generally topped the SABSU agenda.[34]

However, Brisker, Gossett, and other BSU activists faced obvious limitations on what they could accomplish in an organization operating entirely within the confines of academic institutions. Almost inevitably, those espousing the ideas of Black Power would look to organize and implement their ideas outside the schools.

The first local converts to Black Power outside of the classroom were members of CORE, already slightly outside the circle led by those in the NAACP and CACRC. The failure of the DEEDS campaign had ravaged the Seattle CORE and left it demoralized, directionless, and nearly bankrupt. The group's membership steadily declined from a peak of nearly 300 in early 1964. By 1965 it could only attract 65 members to each meeting, and less than half of that number twelve months later. CORE across the nation suffered similar setbacks in various forms. Out of these defeats, internal disagreement often resulted, which defined many chapters after 1964. A new militancy began to arise in CORE, to some extent prompted by Stokely Carmichael. By 1966 Lincoln Lynch, the associate national director of CORE, presented the organization's new platform, which came out in favor of the Black Power ideology of SNCC, black self-defense, and opposition to the Vietnam War. Much of the new platform was a big step away from the tactics of Martin Luther King Jr. and revealed growing impatience with what was considered the civil rights movement's failed promises. By July 1967 the rift with King's Southern Christian Leadership Conference (SCLC) was public, and delegates at that year's national convention in Oakland voted to strike the word "multiracial" from the CORE constitution.[35]

In Seattle, however, the original idea of integration still dominated the chapter. Whites made up 116 of the group's 184 paying members and participated in all activities. John Cornethan, Seattle CORE president, publicly condemned the national decision to the press, and pointed out that all four of Seattle's delegates (three of whom were white) voted against striking the word. He spoke out against the idea of an exclusively black political party, and reminded the membership that Seattle CORE had regularly ignored national directives in the past and would continue to do so now. "There is still a role for white people in CORE," he reassured the media.[36]

Yet a clique of militants had formed within the group and challenged Cornethan's leadership at the next meeting. Cornethan adjourned the meeting after debates got out of hand, and left with his supporters. After his departure, the remaining members, lead by Treasurer Ed Russell, reconvened the meeting and voted to impeach Cornethan. Floyd McKissick, CORE's national director, then assigned an interim government on the grounds that Cornethan had failed to implement national orders. In the new CORE, whites could only work within the white community, and then only under stringent provisions. The white membership quickly left the group, along with many of the group's sixty-eight black members.[37]

Seattle CORE, already in decline, began to disappear. With the drop in membership dues and the ouster of many effective leaders, the group lost its office space and held only infrequent meetings, and soon the weekly newsletter became a partially handwritten affair that pleaded with members to pay back dues. Even the newsletter was discontinued in late 1969. The national CORE so dominated the Seattle group that continued opposition to the CACRC was the only really local item upon its new agenda. Unable to formulate a plausible platform to work its way back into the Seattle community, the group's name only appeared in the newspapers occasionally when the new president, Ron Carson, joined rallies and groups pressing for militant demands. But the days of organizing community-wide campaigns were over. Soon, the group existed in name only. CORE had transformed its opposition to the CACRC into a Black Power ideology, but real Black Power activism came from a new generation of leaders and groups in 1968.[38]

Stokely Carmichael's speech at Garfield High School in September 1967 is the generally ascribed starting point for Seattle's Black Power movement. Had it been up to the principal, Carmichael would have never have given his speech. The principal tried to block Carmichael's visit, but came under intense pressure; he resigned eight months later.

As a leader of SNCC, Carmichael had assumed de facto leadership of Black Power across the nation. His charismatic style was arguably second only to Martin Luther King Jr.'s, to whose nonviolent principles he seemingly began to present a significant challenge. Although SNCC leaders initially styled the organization as direct action troops for King's movement in the South, its members grew frustrated with the slow pace of change, and eventually parted with King and his SCLC. After this schism, SNCC's black nationalist philosophy called for self-defense and an emphasis upon race pride and independence.

Carmichael spoke to about 4,000 students at the UW in the fall of 1967, then made an appearance in front of approximately the same number of people at Garfield High School. While his ideas of black revolution and overturning the power structure sounded exciting to many young listeners, many African Americans of all ages did not buy into the ideas at first. Elmer Dixon recalled, "I didn't agree with anything he said. He used the word 'honky' a lot. My best friend was white and that didn't sit well with me."[39] Other Black Panthers of common middle-class background also recount being cool to the message. Seattle Panther George Newsome at first rejected Carmichael's ideas, and also remembers being distinctly happy upon hearing of the death of Malcolm X in 1965. As a boy raised upon civil rights ideas, he found Black Power's separatist language strange indeed.[40]

Yet Carmichael sowed seeds in thoughtful minds, and many of the youth soon came around to many of his ideas. Those in the crowd raised on the idealism of the local civil rights movement often already thought in terms of helping the community. Now, they also spent time toying with the new ideology to fit it to Seattle's problems. If Carmichael planted the seeds of Black Power ideology, the *Afro American Journal* nurtured and cultivated the minds of those who found Black Power alluring. The *Afro American Journal*, published in Seattle from November 1967 to December 1972, was, according to some, Seattle's most militant weekly newspaper. The paper promoted black self-determination and was critical of the white-controlled school system as well as ineffective black politicians.

At the onset, the Black Power movement in Seattle was often one of middle-class youth, trained for leadership, who took up a newer fight. This struggle differed from the CACRC's in that it shunned the compromises necessary for broad coalition building across business and institutional lines. Rhetorically, at least, black nationalist principles worked against forming broad support outside the community. Practically, this meant Black Power groups challenged the more traditional community institutions, alienating themselves from many within their focus group.

What Seattle historian Dorothy Pieroth terms the "turning point in Central Area politics" occurred unexpectedly on the night of March 6, 1968, at a CACRC meeting at the East Madison Young Men's Christian Association (YMCA).[41] That evening, Rev. John Adams formally presented the CACRC's anticipated plan to cut back or close five Central Area schools, including Garfield High School, a popular neighborhood institution. By closing the Central Area schools, Rev. Adams hoped to force the district to send neighborhood students to the generally better-funded traditionally white schools. After hearing of the plan in advance, BSU members immediately started rallying Central Area opinion against the plan. They portrayed the plan as one from an out-of-touch middle-class leadership that placed its own philosophies above those of the Central Area and its residents, and quietly gathered 1,100 signatures against the plan.[42]

Rev. Adams never stood a chance that night. Carl Miller presented the signatures, and the vast majority of the crowd of 400 surprised Rev. Adams by speaking against the measure. It was the first time the CACRC had encountered major community opposition to one of its plans, and the meeting was a complete rout of the CACRC leadership by the Central Area community. Bereft of Central Area support, the proposal went nowhere. Chastened, the CACRC began a retreat from such public activities, without entirely ceasing to pursue its agenda. However, the BSU had broken CACRC domination of Central Area politics, and from this point onward it was never exactly clear who spoke for the community on any given issue. While Rev. Adams could no longer claim to be a community spokesman, certainly neither Carl Miller nor the BSU reflected a consensus viewpoint either. Adams himself admitted after the meeting that "the Seattle School Board is making a mistake if it thinks it can get a unanimous Central Area position," and that "last night's meeting showed there is a real crisis in the community."[43]

One person's crisis is another's diversity of opinion. Miller and the BSU had astutely sensed disaffection within the Central Area community over the issue of integrated schools. While important to the NAACP, all that the VRT program had accomplished was the removal of several hundred bright students from the Central Area to North End schools. Most Central Area African Americans sought the improvement of the neighborhood and its schools, not their closure. And the issue of integration appeared less important to many Central Area parents than to the CACRC leadership.

Seattle BPP's Formation

The BSU's initial ventures into the Central Area began a string of events that led to Seattle's own "long, hot summer." Events now took place against a backdrop of rising frustration and tension in the Central Area, which approached national levels by 1968. As even Martin Luther King Jr. proved unable to keep protest activity in Memphis, Tennessee, from degenerating into violent turmoil that spring, the Central Area stood poised for a similarly traumatic summer. The first such event occurred at Franklin High School, the alma mater of Larry Gossett and his brother, Richard. A majority-white school on the southern outskirts of the Central Area, Franklin High had gained black students each year since 1957. Despite the increasing numbers of African American students, Aaron Dixon recalls a dearth of black faculty and administrators at the school. Frankly, there were no black faculty at Franklin High School. In late March 1968 the UW BSU organized a demonstration of over 100 people (about two-thirds of whom were students), partly in support of black history courses and the Afro hairstyles that they were not allowed to wear and in response to disparate disciplinary actions meted out to black students. Franklin BSU students were also in attendance.

Apparently, a black student was suspended for his part in a fight with a white student. Details concerning who started the fight were sketchy; what was clear was that the white student was treated more leniently. Larry Gossett, Richard Gossett, Carl Miller, Trolice Favors, and Aaron Dixon attended the rally on Friday, March 29, and participated in the sit-in and forced entry into the principal's office.[44] Aaron Dixon remembers that "some demands were made, but not met."[45] Fearing the situation would spiral out of control, a panicked vice principal released the students early and telephoned the police to take control of the situation. The college BSU members in attendance were arrested for unlawful entry, along with a Franklin senior.[46] They were released the next day, due to no small measure to attorney William Dwyer.

Aaron Dixon would later recall taking a newfound sense of power from the incident, feeling quite victorious over their unexpected impact.[47] Already impatient at the pace of the BSU's efforts, Dixon would begin to search for new organizations and groups that promised faster results. He joined the newly radicalized SNCC, but would find that he "didn't really do much with SNCC beyond reading."[48] Newly emboldened, Dixon sought more opportunities to change his environment. The next Thursday 200 people packed the county courthouse to hear the bail hearings. Richard Gossett was released without posting bond, while the others received an unusually high bail, which was reduced the next day. Although some secondary sources attribute the start of unrest in the Central Area to this court appearance, contemporary news reports and participants tied the resulting violence more to the horrific coincidence of King's assassination in Memphis the same day. Likely, the two events combined to spark several nights of violence, including firebombs and broken windows across the Central Area. While a far cry from the insurrections across the nation, the disturbances were new to Seattle. The events of the week confirmed a growing suspicion in Dixon's mind, he recalled, that peaceful demonstrations would no longer work. "We looked for other ways to get the point across."[49]

Meanwhile, the three BSU members, free until their trial in May, joined Seattle SNCC members and set out for the Bay Area for the second annual West Coast BSU convention at San Francisco State College. The contingent of twenty, which included Aaron Dixon, Elmer Dixon, and Anthony Ware, arrived during the funeral for Bobby Hutton, who had recently been killed at the hands of local police. The Dixon brothers had virtually grown up with Ware, having lived in the same neighborhood and attended the same junior high school (Meany) as well as high school (Garfield). During their visit, they listened to the ideas of the BPP, as well as accounts of run-ins with police of the sort that cost Bobby Hutton his life. Years later Aaron Dixon recalled being especially moved by Bobby Seale's speech at the BSU conference, still describing it as the "one of the most inspiring speeches I have ever heard."[50] The ideas and rhetoric made an impression on the Seattle visitors, as did the sheer number of Panthers in full regalia. The Panthers and their sympathizers, which numbered well over 1,000, were a sight to see. On the other hand, that a group of spry twenty young "brothers and sisters," some of whom were not even in college at the time, would make such a long trip did not go unnoticed by Seale and others. Before the end of the day, they approached Seale about forming a BPP chapter in Seattle.[51] Aaron Dixon recalls that "Bobby and George Murray, the party's minister of education, along with Captain Kenny Denman from the San Diego branch, came to Seattle the following week, April 13 to be exact."[52] Murray was one of the more well known Panthers as he was also a professor at San Francisco State College at the time. As Dixon later stated:

The one thing I'll always remember about George Murray is that he always carried a gigantic brief case around with him. He also had an enthusiasm about him that really stood out. . . . Murray looked like a Panther, talked like a Panther and acted like a Panther. . . . Anyway, all three stayed at my parents' house for two days, meeting with local activists while feasting on my mother's home cooking. On the first night, some of us stayed up all night long talking with Seale, Murray, and Denman about the conditions of black people and ways to eradicate those conditions.[53]

During one of the initial conversations, Dixon said that Seale reminded everyone, matter-of-factly, that membership in the party required that "each person have two weapons and 2000 rounds of ammunition," signaling to everyone present the seriousness of the work that lay ahead.[54] Dixon and others assured Seale that they were committed to joining the party. After a few days, Seale returned to Oakland, but not before authorizing the creation of a BPP chapter in Seattle and making Dixon head. Dixon laughingly recalls that "on the second day Seale asked who was going to be the defense captain, and everyone pointed at me."[55] Dixon would be defense captain of the Seattle chapter of the BPP—the first chapter established (in April 1968) outside the state of California.

Dixon's personality and unique background made him well suited for this important responsibility. His upbringing was atypical of many Panthers who headed chapters and branches across the country. Younger than those who typically headed branches and chapters, he was raised by college-educated parents. His father, a graduate of the Chicago Institute of Art, was an activist himself, and his mother was a nurse's assistant. Both parents were supportive of their children's involvement with the BPP while many parents of Panthers were not. Dixon's father, in particular, had a profound influence on him politically, which may explain why Dixon was undoubtedly a bit more politically mature than his teenage years suggested. Consequently, it is not surprising that everyone pointed at him when Bobby Seale asked who would lead the chapter. Not only did he possess the intellectual temperament, he was enrolled at the UW at the time, and there was a leadership quality about him that shone through even at an early age. In the early 1960s, when Martin Luther King Jr. was invited to Seattle by local leaders to lead a march in protest of the city's segregated school system, Dixon, barely thirteen years old, wanted to join the movement. Dixon never felt so proud marching alongside King. Years later, while at the UW, he emerged as a student leader, helping to organize the BSU there. Dixon's interest in activism and service had been cultivated by his parents, especially his father. While living in Chicago, Dixon's father, a veteran of World War II, had been an admirer of Paul Robeson, serving as a member of the security detail for one of Robeson's youth organizations. Aaron Dixon's interest in politics may have been nurtured by his parents, but his determination to change things was ultimately cemented over the years as he watched the civil rights movement unfold on television. Said Dixon, "Watching the assassination of our political leaders was very profound . . . the first time I saw my father cry was when President Kennedy was assassinated."[56]

Along with Aaron Dixon, among those who formed the founding nucleus of the Seattle BPP were Elmer Dixon, Gary Owens, Anthony Ware, Willie Brazier, Chester Northington, Kathy Halley, Kathy Jones, and John Eichelberger. Several of the newly minted members, including Aaron Dixon, were students at the UW as well as members of the BSU. The Dixons and Brisker initially maintained their positions within the BSU, and were understandably pressed for time as a result. Sharing some of the same leadership, the BSU and BPP often tended to rise and fall inversely with one another. The BPP would spend several months in a state of great activity, then fall relatively silent while the BSU received attention. When the UW Students for a Democratic Society (SDS) took over a building in the fall of 1968 and extended an invitation to the BSU to join with their own demands, the BSU leadership, many of whom who were busy with BPP activities, circulated a letter advising against black participation.[57] Still, the BSU and the BPP assisted one another, and Panthers also would often attend BSU-organized rallies. "They would call on us when they wanted some muscle power," one Panther would relate. "We were part of the BSU planning. . . . Our job was to make sure they didn't get too co-opted."[58]

The Seattle press and police department saw the Dixons, Brisker, and the others almost exclusively as Black Panthers, downplaying their role in the BSU or anything else. The Panthers' black leather jackets, large Afros, and revolutionary berets garnered the attention of local media. The well-reported exploits of Huey Newton and Panthers in other parts of the nation made the local group all the more prominent. Not only did this bring a certain stature to the leaders within certain segments of the Central Area, but these leaders were able to work in the public eye through this group.[59] When the group solicited members, Aaron Dixon reports that, by July, they had been flooded with over 300 applications, a majority of which were accepted. However, he readily admits that the overwhelming majority were "Rally Panthers," a derisive term referring to those who showed up only for rallies—when the television cameras were on. Among the initial recruits were three Asian men, two Japanese and one Filipino. Aaron Dixon remembers that the Asian community had a history of supporting black people's struggles in Seattle, and vice versa; thus it was not surprising that members of that community would want to join the party. By 1970 the Seattle chapter consisted of approximately twenty-five dedicated members, nearly half of whom were women. Says Leon Valentine Hobbs, a New York transplant who joined the party in 1969 after a stint in the U.S. Army, "When the police onslaught came, that number eventually dwindled down to about ten."[60]

In the late spring of 1968 the Seattle BPP took the Central Area by storm. After a mysterious firebombing coaxed a reluctant landlord to lease the space to the BPP in a Thirty-fourth and Union Street storefront, the party was officially under way. Over the next few years the Panthers opened up two community information centers—one on Twentieth and Spruce, the other on Madison. Prior to that time, the Panthers had held meetings at Madrona Presbyterian Church.[61]

For reasons that are unclear, the Seattle Panthers were unable to elicit the support of Seattle's black clergy. "They would not touch us with a ten foot pole.... They would not let us use any of their facilities.... They were afraid that if the police came looking for us they would catch the heat as well," says Hobbs.[62]

Like many Panther offices and centers around the country, the Seattle Panthers fortified their dwellings in the event of a police assault. The group reinforced the office at Twentieth and Spruce with steel, sandbags, and manhole covers to make it impenetrable in case of a raid.

Still smarting from the arrests at Franklin High School, the party made the overly aggressive conduct of Central Area police a primary issue. The topic had become a sore spot to many Central Area residents, and it served the group well. Panther demands for the evacuation of the Central Area by Seattle police meshed well with the already established national party line. By late spring the Seattle members began the Oakland tactic of patrolling the police. Dixon admits that "our patrols were not as organized as those in Oakland.... We did not have tape recorders or cameras."[63] By summer's end the patrols had been shut down on orders from the party's national headquarters. Shadowing the police was nothing new to Seattle—CORE and even the CACRC had done the same in previous years—but the Panthers took advantage of city and state laws and carried unconcealed, usually unloaded weapons in the same manner as their California brethren.[64]

The Panthers took the paramilitary aspects of their organization seriously. Bobby White, Mike Tagawa, and other Vietnam veterans drilled the Panthers several times each week, and the training included visits to target ranges. Public displays were also emphasized, and Aaron Dixon later recalled a particularly fond memory in the summer of 1968, when on a Saturday over 100 uniformed Panthers marched in unison as part of their weekly drills through Madrona Park, as police officers looked on. "The marching stopped traffic.... People came out of their houses, peeked out of their windows as we marched down Thirty-third Avenue to Cherry Street."[65]

The combination of weapons, revolutionary rhetoric, and reputation quickly triggered a police response. Ongoing conflicts with the Seattle Police Department would define the Seattle chapter during its early years. Dixon, for example, stated that the Seattle Police Department made several attempts on his life. The Panther headquarters maintained a constant state of siege, in preparation for police raids. For their part, police officers would relate stories of sniper attacks by Panthers upon police and firefighters, as well as reports of attacks inflicted on citizens who ran afoul of the Panthers. As a result, the party initially found it difficult to move beyond its reputation. Bobby White, an early lieutenant of information, recalled that they engaged in door-to-door sessions and sold Mao Zedong's *Red Book*, but that "a lot of the guys didn't quite understand it. We had a Ten Point Platform, but a lot of people didn't understand that, either. A lot of folks thought we were just into 'kill whitey,' but nothing could be further from the truth."[66]

The reputation lingered. After the three BSU/BPP officers arrested at Franklin High School were sentenced to six months in jail on July 1, the Central Area erupted into violence again.[67] Although the Panthers were soon released on bail for an appeal date in September, firebombs and thrown rocks grew common throughout the month of July in Seattle's "long, hot summer." The uncharacteristic ninety degree weather helped create a tension-filled atmosphere in the Central Area, which worsened on July 19 after twelve Seattle police officers in six squad cars served a warrant to search the Panther headquarters for stolen typewriters. Finding the property, they initially arrested both Aaron Dixon and Curtis Harris. The two were soon freed, but the news of police in riot gear attacking the headquarters threw the neighborhood into more violence for several nights. By August thirty-nine police officers had received medical attention, and over 100 Central Area residents had been arrested.[68]

Still, the scale of Seattle's unrest did not reach that of other major cities across the nation. Disturbances never lasted longer than a matter of hours or repeated themselves more than a couple of nights at a time. Five aspects of the Seattle community combined to help account for this type of subdued uprising. Seattle's small number of blacks is perhaps a partial explanation, although Grand Rapids and Lansing, Michigan, with populations of 23,426 and 12,786 African Americans, respectively, both experienced significantly more unrest. Sacramento, California, was the scene of considerable racial violence in both 1967 and 1968, and its black population almost exactly equaled that of Seattle's. Costly disorders even broke out in the small town of Asbury Park, New Jersey, in which 7,044 of the town's 39,065 citizens were black. Seattle's geographic isolation from other black centers also kept the city out of the streams of discontent that pervaded other parts of the nation. Most important, the Central Area contained neither the usual urban blight that plagued Watts and Detroit nor the sense of hopelessness such conditions usually entail.[69]

Last, although the Dixons sometimes used the threat of upheaval as a bargaining chip, which may have encouraged violence, they did not actively prod Central Area racial tension. Larry Gossett often spoke of massive reform, but in a manner that did not usually invoke the fiery revolutionary edge, and Carl Miller told the crowd at the March 6 CACRC meeting that the public should not "confuse the issue with separatism," which he opposed.[70] Few leaders flooded the community with constant rhetoric calling for violent upheaval, and especially not the destruction of the Central Area.[71] During the early July violence, for example, Miller rescued two whites from a mob armed with lead pipes.

Other Panthers were reported to have roamed the neighborhood to discourage violence and property damage, and later apologized to certain business owners for the more uncontrolled elements of the Central Area.[72] The Panthers themselves were reportedly the targets of several rocks tossed through their headquarters' windows.[73] At the same time, even the commission headed by City Councilman B. Ludlow Kramer that reported on the civil disorders in Seattle cited the restraint shown by police throughout that July. Although it rapped the Seattle Police Department for unnecessarily serving an inflammatory warrant when tensions ran high, it noted that the police force generally comported itself well. Over three dozen police officers required medical attention, and police cars suffered $5,000 worth of damage in July, but not a single shot was reported fired by the police. Still, the BPP did not disown those jailed for violence. After the uprisings, the party organized a peaceful demonstration in front of Seattle Police Department headquarters and attempted to arrange bail for three African Americans jailed for throwing firebombs at police officers. Although the suspects were not party members, for reasons that were unclear, Aaron Dixon offered witnesses who claimed that the men were elsewhere when the bombs were thrown.[74]

The national Peace and Freedom Party convention was held in Seattle that September (1968) amid a string of new incidents that lent credence to those who viewed the Black Panthers as unavoidably violence prone. At the convention, which was held at the Sorrento Hotel, the Seattle Panthers nominated one of their more volatile officers, Curtis Harris, the self-appointed assistant captain of the Seattle chapter, to run for a seat in the state legislature.[75] However, on the day that Harris announced his candidacy, he reportedly threatened a police officer's life while observing a trial, and was arrested in a melee outside of the courtroom doors. Not four weeks later, Seattle police issued a warrant for Harris's arrest on behalf of the Seattle Fire Department, which reported that Harris had tried to run over two firefighters. In addition to those transgressions, it was later discovered that he was also "pulling robberies throughout the city; holding up banks, supermarkets and other businesses in the so-called name of the revolution."[76] He was expelled from the party a year later in early July 1969. E. J. Brisker also ran for Congress under the banner of the Peace and Freedom Party, to no avail. Neither Harris nor Brisker garnered much support. Their candidacies seem to have been more of a symbolic gesture than an actual attempt to win. Dixon recalls that "there was no massive campaign effort to get them elected."[77]

Increasing desegregation of Seattle schools also led to violence early in the school year. Words between two students at Rainier Beach High School led to an interracial fight during the first week of classes. Rainier Beach High School had approximately 2,000 students, of which 100 were African American. On September 4 a sixteen-year-old white student got into a fight with a fourteen-year-old African American student as other students looked on. The white student, already on probation and residing in the custody of juvenile authorities, injured the African American student. The following day, the white student was suspended. Roughhousing continued among the students. Five African American Garfield High School students, dressed in the Panther uniform, came to the school but were asked to leave. Several real Black Panthers gathered in the park across the street. Approximately 100 parents, fearful of impending trouble, withdrew their students from school.

Aaron Dixon was hesitant to get involved. He recalled receiving phone calls from the mothers of several black students, describing a school in which black students were attacked by whites. His reluctance was worn down by the mothers of these students, who implored the Panthers to take some form of action. On Friday, September 5, at about 2:00 p.m., a contingent of armed Panthers arrived at the school and asked to see Principal Donald Means. They demanded to know what kind of school would allow such one-sided racial fights, and were satisfied by what Aaron Dixon describes as the principal's promise to prevent future fights. They originally wanted to recruit inside classrooms, yet were talked out of this and were asked to leave. Parents expressed concerns that openly armed youth were roaming their children's school, and demanded their arrest. Eventually, cooler heads prevailed, and this incident was smoothed over peaceably. At a meeting for parents and students, Police Chief Frank Ramon announced, "I will tell you flatly the armed invasion of any school in Seattle will not happen again!"[78] The incidents remained a chilling indicator of worsening race relations.

Such conflicts took a deadly turn on October 5, when seventeen-year-old Panther Welton "Butch" Armstead was shot and killed by Seattle police officers. As with many clashes between police officers and the Panthers, accounts of the actual events vary. Police officials say that a Seattle patrolman scouring his beat for an auto theft suspect found himself confronted with the rifle-toting Armstead, who had reached for the patrolman's revolver, whereupon he was shot and killed.[79] The shooting was ruled justifiable as a matter of course, but certain nagging questions went unanswered as far as some black residents were concerned. For instance, if Armstead was armed, why did he reach for the officer's gun? An investigation by community residents uncovered an entirely different story. According to Aaron Dixon, police officers went to Armstead's house looking for him. When they arrived, they found his mother outside and began questioning her, reportedly in a hostile manner. Hearing the commotion, Armstead poked his head out of an upstairs window and saw what he believed to be police harassment of his mother. Fearing for her safety, Armstead reportedly grabbed his rifle and ran outside.[80] In a matter of minutes, Armstead was shot and killed.[81]

Certain members of the city's ruling class were concerned with the ease with which some militants were able to obtain guns. Mayor Dorm Braman, publicly looking forward to his term's expiration after the difficult summer, introduced a gun law on September 24 that seriously restricted the ability of the Panthers to carry unconcealed weapons.[82] However, in late February 1969 the state legislature was poised to act against the Panthers' ability to carry arms, prompting party members to leak word that they intended to drive to the state capitol to protest any bill that would in effect disarm them. News of their impending arrival prompted the governor to call out the National Guard in order to patrol the state capitol. Very few groups could have earned such an impromptu audience. The National Guard patrolled the statehouse for nearly a week, then pulled out when it appeared that the Panthers were not going to go through with their protest after all. Unbeknownst to the lawmakers, Michael Dixon, the brother of Aaron and Elmer Dixon, worked at the statehouse as a page and thus had a bird's-eye view of the goings-on. After nearly two weeks, Michael sent word to the Panthers that the National Guard had retreated and that the coast was clear. Upon hearing this, Aaron and several other Panthers hurriedly drove the one-hour trip to the state capitol, where he read a statement to the Ways and Means Committee before heading back to the UW, just in time for a protest.[83]

The Panthers also engaged in running battles with various community figures. Sam Smith, the first African American city councilman, and other influential civil rights leaders bore the lion's share of Panther abuse. Eventually, some Panthers would doubt the wisdom of this policy of provocation, for the CACRC did not take the challenge to their leadership lying down. Both within the community and to the media, the CACRC launched a barrage of rhetoric against the various militant groups and singled out the Black Panthers for special criticism. Civil rights groups had connections within city hall and other private circles to call upon in enacting their own agenda, in comparison to the Black Panthers, who to some appeared merely as a fringe group with no real platform. Smith called them "a headache to all government" and told the press they had "given up on the system" and "turned to violence to bring about change."[84] Leon Valentine Hobbs viewed "Smith and those other civil rights leaders as Uncle Toms," as did various other Panthers.[85] It is not surprising, then, that when Edwin Pratt, the executive director of the Seattle Urban League, was mysteriously shot and killed in 1969, some insinuated that the Panthers were somehow involved. The county sheriff called the murder a "political assassination." Others say Pratt's murder was simply a racially motivated attack. At any rate, the Panthers denied any involvement. The murder remains unsolved.

Needless to say, the rumors linking Panthers to this crime, no matter how unfounded, made for good copy, thus adding to the Panthers' already checkered reputation.

Nevertheless, BPP punches were not the only ones flying throughout the community. Keve Bray and Cliff Hooper's Black Power newspaper the *Afro-American Journal* printed accusations against various individual civil rights and government program leaders of "selling out" the community, including occasional shots at Aaron Dixon and Gossett.

When the Panthers were not trading barbs with the city's "Uncle Toms" and "bootlickers," they were dealing with in-house issues. The Seattle Panthers experienced internal problems of the nature to be expected with such rapid growth. Many "wanted the dignity the uniform gave," recalled Elmer Dixon, "but didn't know how to wear it."[86] Aaron Dixon would write in his memoirs about weekly meetings that "never seemed to get off the ground on a consistent basis," and a central staff that "never functioned as we had envisioned." Indeed, "because so many young people had signed up, discipline was a problem."[87] At the same time, some of the older members proved difficult for the teenage Aaron Dixon to control.[88] Even target practice at the gun ranges sometimes proved troublesome; in 1971 Aaron Dixon was severely wounded when a rifle exploded upon being discharged.[89] The problems inherent with a radical image were typified by the position taken by the Madrona Presbyterian Church, which required certain guarantees from the Panthers before permitting their continued use of the church facilities. In the minds of some, the Panthers were beginning to live up to their billing in many of the local newspapers.

Coalition Building

The Seattle BPP formed at the apex of the national party's fortunes in 1968, but was quickly subjected to the schism that later developed in Oakland. During his imprisonment, national BPP leader Huey Newton developed a doctrine that included an emphasis on service to the masses through a variety of social programs across impoverished neighborhoods. Bobby Seale also supported this notion, which took form in the shape of free breakfast programs, food and clothing banks, and other "community survival programs" aimed at assisting the people whom the party purported to represent. This entailed moving away from the emphasis on guns and entering into a variety of coalitions with groups of all races. Eldridge Cleaver, on the other hand, maintained a focus on armed conflict with the state's agents of oppression. In fact, Cleaver argued for a "Panther Offensive." This power struggle was largely resolved when Newton was released from prison and Cleaver was exiled to Algeria, but only after significant collateral damage to the organization.

This split paralleled an existing divide within the Seattle leadership as well. Aaron and Elmer Dixon had maintained a close personal relationship with Bobby Seale, and increasingly moved toward the philosophy of community survival by 1969. This philosophy also accorded well with the ethos of community service instilled within the Dixon household. Aaron Dixon recalled that he realized "we couldn't go on fighting police and firebombing . . . we had to do more things in our own community. . . . No black churches were willing to let us use their facilities."[90] Indeed, the constant conflict was consuming the party's resources. Furthermore, the city's economic fortunes stood at what would be an all-time low, as Boeing began a series of layoffs that would shrink the aircraft manufacturer's local workforce from 101,000 people in 1968 to 42,000 in March 1971. Although few Central Area workers commuted to Boeing each day, the effects of this massive contraction resounded across the Puget Sound region. The Black Panthers began to emphasize party ideology as well. Although always advocates of the party's political philosophy, including the ideas of Malcolm X, Frantz Fanon, Mao Zedong, and the *Communist Manifesto*, members recalled that the political education during the group's first year "could have been a lot better."[91]

Newton and Seale's philosophy meshed well with existing Seattle Panther ideas. The Seattle Panthers had grown up and attended school with people of other races; thus coalitions were a natural by-product of their personal relationships. The Seattle Panthers had a strong working relationship with a number of organizations. Because the Dixons were predisposed to their father's experience with Paul Robeson, the Panthers worked well with the Communist Party. If nothing else, a coalition with the Communist Party in Seattle was a practical one, for the Communist Party formed an underground railroad of sorts from Seattle to Vancouver, Canada, from 1969 to 1972, which undoubtedly benefited not only Vietnam War resisters but Panthers and other sought-after activists as well.[92] Other groups included the American Indian Movement (AIM); the Seattle Liberation Front, which consisted largely of white college students; the local SDS chapter; and the Chinese Red Guard, to name a few.

Because the Dixons were reared by parents who placed a high value on service, the Seattle Panthers via the Dixon brothers were unavoidably influenced by their mores.[93] The Panthers had responded to certain community requests since the chapter's inception—be it doing chores or running errands for the elderly, compelling a landlord to return a renter's front door, running off abusive boyfriends and drug dealers, or protecting prostitutes from their oft-times violent-prone pimps. Hobbs remembers one story in particular:

We were sponsoring a high school dance. As it began to get dark we started to check the grounds, making sure the area was secure. I noticed a young girl in the backseat of an Electra 225 crying. I approached the car and asked her if she was OK, and she shook her head no. I opened the car door and sat beside her. When I asked her what was wrong, she pointed at the guy in the front seat and replied, "He won't let me go." I then told the sister that there was nothing to be afraid of, and that I would take her home. She responded, "I'm afraid to leave," at which time I took out my blade and began to slash the Zebra upholstery in this pimp's car. This guy was the stereotypical pimp too, with a big loud hat and a suit to match. The whole time I was cutting up his seats he never once turned around to look at me. [When asked why that was so Hobbs chuckled,] because Elmer Dixon had a 9 millimeter pointed at his head.[94]

The Panthers were always doing good deeds. The service aspect of the Panthers' program, though, was officially institutionalized when the chapter created a free breakfast program for disadvantaged children as mandated by the national headquarters. With donations from businesses such as Gay's Bakery, IGA, and Albertson's Supermarket, the breakfast program reportedly served an estimated 300,000 meals from 1969 to 1977. Garry Owens remembers going to Safeway and pointing out to management, "You throw away more food than what we are asking for. . . . Working with the breakfast program gave me a great deal of self-gratification. People depended on us to provide a nutritious meal every single day and we did it. The community came to expect this from us."[95] Rashad Byrdsong, who came to the Seattle chapter after heading up the Tacoma branch, describes how donations were typically solicited: "I would go to a supermarket with a few other Panthers and ask to see the manager. When the manager came out I would introduce myself, explain to him the importance of the free breakfast program, and then ask for a modest contribution. I would point out to the manager that the supermarket was sustained by the members of the community and that it only seemed appropriate that the supermarket put something back into the community. . . . Rarely were our requests rebuffed." When asked about the success rate, Byrdsong estimated that "99 percent of the people we approached for donations complied.[96] "We had a lot of respect and support from members of the community, people gave so freely," says Gayle "Asali" Dickson.[97] "There were some merchants that routinely dropped off food-stuffs at our offices without being asked to; bread, sausage, cookies, you name it, it seemed we were always getting donations," remembers Anthony Ware.[98]

Demand for the breakfast program was so high that by 1970, the Panthers were forced to set up breakfast programs at five different locations: Atlantic Street Youth Community Center in the Central Area of the city; the Highpoint housing project in West Seattle; the Holly Park housing project in the South

End; the Rainier Vista housing project; and the Yestler Terrace housing project, also in the Central Area. It was a known fact that prior to the breakfast program, some of the children from those complexes were going to school on empty stomachs. Vernetta Molson, who at twenty years old dropped out of community college to become the full-time coordinator of the free breakfast program, remembers that "we would fix the kids a hearty breakfast. On some days they would get pancakes and juice, on other days they would get eggs, bacon, sausage, or grits."[99] Anthony Ware adds that "people tend to forget that [at the Atlantic Street office, at least] we also gave the kids cod liver oil to help ward off colds and other ailments. We would line them up and give each a teaspoon of cod liver oil before sending them on their way."[100]

It was expected that residents in these housing complexes would help with the breakfast program by pitching in with the cooking and cleaning. This gave residents a "sense of agency, a sense that they were doing something to empower themselves and their community. . . . The community embraced the program."[101] Having breakfast can make a difference in a child's ability to learn, and the community understood that. When asked how to put that time in her life in perspective, Vernetta Molson quickly responded, "Those were some of the most rewarding years of my life."[102]

The Panthers' free breakfast program did more than just provide children with a free meal. Garry Owens, who helped get the program started at the Atlantic Street office, put it this way: "The breakfast program was a safe haven for kids. . . . I would estimate that 50 to 75 percent of the kids came from homes without fathers, some kids came from abusive homes. . . . We offered a nurturing and loving environment that went beyond food. We showed the kids human compassion. Before sending them off to school we gave the kids a hug and told them that they could be anything they wanted to be."[103]

Unlike perhaps some other Panther free breakfast programs around the country, the breakfast programs in Seattle attracted not only black children but whites and Asians, too. The Atlantic Street office, for example, was located in a neighborhood that some people referred to as Little Italy because of the high number of Italian immigrants who lived there; hence a number of Italian children frequented the program. Since it was run out of the Atlantic Street Youth Community Center, which was operated by Ike Ikeda (an Asian American), quite naturally the parents of Asian American children felt comfortable taking their kids to the center for breakfast. That the program was being run by the Panthers did not matter.

The breakfast program was just one of many services offered by the Panthers. They also held food giveaways to complement the free breakfast program. The Panthers distributed fifty bags of groceries every Wednesday to needy families across the city. For households with several children, these giveaways were a much-needed source of sustenance. Moreover, the food giveaways allowed some to accept help without having to be stripped of their dignity, which was so often the case when seeking assistance from a welfare agency or similar institution. Residents in the Central Area district anxiously looked forward to the weekly food giveaways not only for the reasons mentioned earlier, but also because they did not have to travel far and because the bags of groceries were often more than they could afford; the gesture enabled families to stretch their paychecks a little farther, thus enabling them to purchase other necessities.

While the residents looked forward to the weekly giveaways, once they received their groceries they had to figure out a way to keep them away from the roaches that had occupied their apartments. Apparently many of the units were roach infested, as the Panthers were constantly hearing residents complain about roaches. The residents of Yestler Terrace thought that they were being overrun by them. In response, the Panthers started a pesticide program. Anyone wanting to participate in this effort had to undergo training, which included passing an eight-week course at Paramount Pest Control.[104] Approximately six Panthers completed the training, and in 1974 the program was launched.

For the Panthers, nourishing young minds was just as important as nourishing young bodies. In the spring of 1969 the national organization began developing plans to open "liberation schools" as summer-long supplements to the free breakfast program. Bobby Seale told the *Movement*, an underground newspaper affiliated with the SDS: "We know that the kids in the [public] schools have got to be taught about themselves, about Black history . . . not the same bullshit they get now." He then outlined the curriculum the Panthers intended to implement: "At the high school level we will probably teach more about Revolutionary principles. At the grammar school level we will probably teach more about Black history, about the avaricious pigs. . . . We're going to be talking about downing the class system, cultural nationalists and capitalists, both Black and white, who are the same: exploitative."[105] As for the curriculum, an article in the *Black Panther* outlined the typical week for the Berkeley liberation school: "Monday is Revolutionary History Day, Tuesday is Revolutionary Culture Day, Wednesday is Current Events Day, Thursday is Movie Day, Friday is Field Trip Day."[106] Descriptions of classroom activities implied that teacher-centered instruction in party beliefs was a primary pedagogical focus. At the Vallejo and San Francisco liberation schools, the lesson plan included the origins of the BPP and a discussion of the class struggle.[107]

By 1970 a nationwide survey of urban police departments reported that at least seven national Panther chapters had functioning liberation schools, while ten Panther units implemented schools that had since become inactive.[108] It was in that year that the Seattle Panthers launched their liberation school. There was a fair amount of overlap between the children who participated in the free breakfast program and the liberation school. A number of party members' children were also among the students in the school.[109] The liberation school was held five days a week during the summer months, when most kids were out of school. Having a liberation school during the summer not only enabled the Panthers to cultivate and maintain relationships with the children who participated in the breakfast program but their parents as well. Says Melvin Dickson: "The best way to get families involved in what you are doing is to bring in the children. A few of the parents whose kids were participating in the breakfast program and liberation school ended up becoming volunteers. I believe one or two of them may have even joined the Party."[110]

Whether the curriculum at the Seattle liberation school mirrored that of those in the Bay Area is not entirely clear. Said Anthony Ware, "We focused on reading, writing and discussion."[111] Nearly all of the lessons focused on black history. "Sometimes instructors would use articles from the *Black Panther* newspaper as jumping-off points for discussion while other times discussion would center on current events either locally or nationally."[112] "We were trying to teach them to be critical thinkers," Garry Owens recalled. The liberation school "was like a full-fledged summer school. . . . We started in the morning around 9:00 a.m., fixed lunch for the kids at noon, and ended around 2:30 in the afternoon."[113] There was a heavy emphasis on reading. "Once you get kids reading they enter an entirely different realm," says Dickson.[114] In addition to classroom instruction, the children were also exposed to exercise to keep fit and maintain healthy bodies and minds. And on occasion, students were taken on field trips that were intended to broaden their horizons and enhance their overall learning experience. The school continued until 1972, when many of the chapter's members were summoned to Oakland to work on the mayoral and city council campaigns of Bobby Seale and Elaine Brown, respectively.

For a very short time the Panthers offered a free clothing giveaway in 1970. Anthony Ware recalls that "someone in the community had given them seven gigantic boxes filled with double knit slacks. The pants were considered defects because the zippers were broken. We specifically acquired an empty space on Twentieth and Yesler Way so that we could have someplace to give away those pants. Those who picked them up took them to the cleaners to get repaired."[115] Among the more consistent programs the Panthers provided was a free legal aid clinic, established in 1969. Community residents who could not afford to hire an attorney could go by the office and get legal advice. The clinic was staffed with local attorneys, some of whom were young upstarts who worked full time at the local American Civil Liberties Union (ACLU). Three times a week these lawyers would hold office hours for members of the community. The majority of the clients sought help with tenant/landlord issues and mistreatment by police officers. According to Ron Johnson, while police use of excessive force remained a serious issue, "most of those who sought assistance during the chapter's later years were tenants who had been illegally evicted."[116] John Coughlin, the Panthers' attorney, regularly offered his assistance. One of the more prominent volunteers, though, was attorney William Dwyer, who went on to become a federal judge.

As in several other cities where Panther branches and/or chapters existed, the Seattle chapter launched a free busing to prison program in 1970. Initially, the Panthers used vans and cars to transport loved ones of those incarcerated from the Central Area to state prisons. Later, a thirty-two-passenger bus was donated to the chapter. The Panthers provided transportation to five prisons on a regular basis: Walla Walla State Prison, Monroe State Prison, Purdy Penitentiary (a women's prison), McNeil State Penitentiary, and Shelton State Penitentiary.[117] Said Gayle "Asali" Dickson, "I remember being one of the drivers on one of those trips . . . and I recall being so happy that the people were able to see their family and friends."[118]

Riders were provided lunch, and, on occasion, both riders and inmates were treated to entertainment at the prison. The Panthers secured a number of acts in the form of bands, performing artists, and the like, making a sometimes stressful situation less intolerable. Visiting loved ones and relatives in jail can be a rather trying and emotionally draining experience for all involved. Entertainment was used to lessen the tension-filled atmosphere and to distract visitors and inmates from the sobering reality that is prison.

Unlike perhaps some other Panther branches and chapters, the Seattle chapter was not destitute. The primary and most steady source of revenue came from the sale of the *Black Panther* newspaper. The Panthers were, from time to time, able to secure funds from actors and entertainers with whom they had associations—for example, celebrities such as Greg Morris (*Mission Impossible*), Archie Bell, Buddy Miles, James Brown, Seattle native Jimi Hendrix, legendary blues singer John Lee Hooker, and National Football League Hall of Famer Jim Brown. In fact, the Panthers had developed somewhat of a rapport with Hendrix, providing security for Hendrix's last concert at the Seattle Sick's Stadium in 1970.[119] The Panthers found that more steady donations could be secured by taking large cans to the campus of UW two to three times a week and soliciting donations.[120] In later years, elaborate fund-raisers in the form of cocktail parties and the like were undertaken to help sustain the Panthers' community survival programs. Personalities such as jazz singer Ernestine Anderson helped raise money by performing on occasion. At least one of these later fund-raisers took place at the prestigious Joshua Green Mansion.[121]

While these efforts proved fruitful, the Panthers' newspaper was the group's most consistent source of revenue. Initially, the Panthers relied on the efforts of individual party members to hawk the paper on the streets of Seattle. Party members sold the newspaper on street corners and went door-to-door, which gave them an opportunity to explain the party platform to members of the community. The result: the Seattle Panthers sold approximately 1,000 to 1,500 papers a week. Newspaper sales, however, skyrocketed once Jake Fiddler became the chapter's distribution manager. "Before I came on board we were selling about 1,000 copies on the street weekly.... Heck I put nearly 1,000 papers in stores and businesses alone in every corner of Seattle. You couldn't go in any part of the city and not find our newspaper."[122]

At its height, the chapter sold 2,000 papers a week.[123] Most of the Panthers' customers were black, but many of them included members of the Asian American community as well as white Vietnam War resisters and white students generally. The Panthers were also frequent visitors at the three to four rock festivals that Seattle seemed to host every year. At these festivals, it was not unusual for the Panthers to sell 500 papers in just a few hours. Three places where Panthers experienced the most success hawking their papers were in the UW district, at Seattle University, and downtown Seattle. Said Fiddler, "Students at UW bought copies of our newspaper like it was going out of style." In fact, according to Fiddler, "demand for the newspaper was so high that the national headquarters couldn't fill our orders fast enough."[124]

The Seattle Panthers were especially media savvy and skillfully used both mainstream and alternative media to promote their agenda. In addition to the *Black Panther* newspaper, the Seattle Panthers also passed out their newsletter, the *Ministry of Information Bulletin*, to supplement the party's national newspaper. The *Bulletin* covered local issues and events affecting the black community and was disseminated widely throughout the city. About half a dozen issues were printed during the first year, but the paper fell by the wayside as the community survival programs became the chapter's top priority.

Perhaps the Panthers' most ambitious and laudable effort was their free clinic, the Free Sydney Miller Clinic set up by Leon Valentine Hobbs. Opened in 1970 and named in honor of fallen comrade Sydney Miller, the clinic is usually described as the Panthers' most influential and popular project. Staffed with medical students from the UW and local physicians Dr. John Green (a neurosurgeon also from the UW) and Dr. John Holsemburg, the clinic was equipped with the latest technology. Over the years, the Beckman Medical Corporation donated X-ray machines, stethoscopes, and other pieces of equipment. The clinic offered nearby residents a variety of sorely needed services. Although one could get treated for any number of ailments, the Panthers were vigilant about testing for tuberculosis. They also devoted considerable time and resources to genetic counseling for sickle cell anemia. Leon Valentine Hobbs explains that "genetic counseling was in important component of the clinic. We advised patients and relatives at risk of an inherited disorder of the consequences and nature of the disorder, the probability of developing or transmitting it, and the options available to them in terms of managing and preventing it."[125]

Another important feature was the well-baby clinic, a component within the larger facility. The well-baby clinic started out as a one-night-a-week venture, but due to high demand later was offered five days a week. Says Hobbs: "Parents of newborns could come to the clinic and get diapers, formula, and ointments, for rashes as well as vitamins."[126] Although babies were the Panthers' first priority, adults and children could also go to the clinic and receive vaccinations and prescription medications. Hobbs, who ran the clinic along with Rosetta Hollins, reports that the clinic "screened more than 1,000 people for vaccinations." The clinic also engaged in outreach, testing 278 prisoners in Walla Walla State Prison for sickle cell anemia in 1971.[127] To this day some wonder how the Panthers were able to gain access to Walla Walla State Prison in this capacity. Hobbs tells the story:

I wrote a letter to the warden of the prison seeking permission to provide sickle cell anemia testing on the inmates. I signed the letter Leon Valentine Hobbs III. I then sought the assistance of the assistant state's attorney general who, on our behalf, contacted the warden and secured his cooperation. No one said anything about us being Panthers. When we arrived at the prison the warden was shocked to see that we were black. At that point there was nothing he could do. I guess he thought the name Leon Valentine Hobbs III sounded white.[128]

Although Hobbs is credited with opening the clinic, he is quick to praise Hollins, who "was the glue that held the clinic together. Rosetta came in as a community worker in 1971 and joined the Party shortly thereafter. She did all of the administrative work for the clinic. She was indispensable."[129] The clinic would, in later years, blossom into a full-service family clinic.

This change in the Panthers' direction led to a change in its makeup as well. Curtis Harris and others resisted this evolution and were removed from the Seattle party. In 1969 the Dixons purged members who did not share their discipline or ideological devotion, which proved to be most of the members.[130] The Seattle BPP membership plummeted from nearly 200 to less than a tenth of that within months.[131] Aaron Dixon exclaims, "I had to rebuild the chapter."[132] Much of the remaining membership also remained wary of the new emphasis. When Leon Valentine Hobbs joined after the party purges, he admitted, "I understood we needed coalitions because we are in a predominantly white country. . . . I was not very trusting of white people."[133] Ron Johnson, the chapter's lieutenant of information who joined in 1974, continued as a member despite his strongly held views forged by his experiences in the Watts uprising and the

Nation of Islam. The remaining Panthers formed a vanguard that was able to bring the party to its golden years.[134]

Such works deterred many members but earned the downsized group credibility with mainstream political figures. According to Aaron Dixon, in August 1969 Republican governor Daniel Evans requested a meeting with the Panthers in order to get a sense of the problems that blacks faced in Seattle. It was the only time that a state governor asked to meet with representatives of the BPP anywhere in the country. The Panthers accepted the governor's entreaty and led him on a tour of the Central Area neighborhood. After the tour, the Panthers shared a podium with Evans as he promised to build a government multiservice center in the neighborhood along with various other forms of aid. Aaron Dixon remembers that "the governor came across as sincere, but nothing tangible came of out of the visit."[135] Moreover, such efforts made Gossett and the Dixons occasional targets of the *Afro-American Journal*, but such public relations coups for the Black Power movement legitimized the BPP in the eyes of some neighborhood residents.[136] As Ron Johnson put it, his job was to take the doctrine of the party and "make it palatable to various groups."[137] This explanation of the party's mission often involved debunking myths and correcting preconceptions about the party.

We began to identify ourselves with people so we wouldn't be identified as just some rabblerousing, leather coat–wearing troublemakers. We wanted to be accepted within the community. . . . I had to go into detail and define what we were actually doing, that we're not against white people. . . . We formed alliances with all working poor people, because we fight against oppression, not necessarily racial segregation or racial hatred, although [those were] things we dealt with also. But our main focus was the struggle against this country as we saw it. We felt it was set up that the haves take away from the have-nots.[138]

The party's coalition building reaped dividends when Seattle mayor Wes Uhlman came to office in 1969. Elected in 1969 as the first mayor under the city's new "strong mayor" system, the youngest mayor in Seattle's history launched an effort to eradicate corruption and other problems within the Seattle Police Department. The new city leadership had also reevaluated their strategy in the running fight with the Seattle BPP, and attempted to distinguish actual threats to the city's safety.

In Mayor Uhlman's first year, President Richard Nixon's Department of Justice approached the Seattle Police Department for assistance in an impending raid on the Seattle BPP headquarters by federal Bureau of Alcohol, Tobacco, and Firearms (ATF) agents. Mayor Uhlman was asked for his cooperation, but he supported the police department's refusal to do so. Instead, Uhlman promised only that Seattle police would surround any such operation and would decide on the spot which party acted as the aggressor.[139]

Uhlman would later explain that he thought the Panthers posed no threat to the city by the latter part of 1969. "The police department had placed an undercover agent within the organization, who reported that the group did not engage in criminal activities worthy of a raid," said Uhlman.[140] Even the arms within the Black Panthers' headquarters—fortified in preparation for just such a raid—were reportedly legal, removing any reason for Seattle police to cooperate in a raid. When asked what he thought of Mayor Uhlman's rebuke of the U.S. Justice Department, Aaron Dixon declared: "Uhlman was by no means a champion of civil rights, but he was no fascist either. . . . I suppose he did not want any blood on his hands during his first year as mayor."[141]

Although Uhlman would enter a war of words with Richard Nixon aide John Ehrlichman over the issue, the mayor subscribed to a philosophy about handling the Black Panthers similar to that of Governor Evans.[142] Each young officeholder had maintained that the BPP's membership rolls rose after conflicts with authorities. From this, each had learned to avoid high-profile conflict with the party whenever possible, thus depriving the party of the free publicity that seemed to provide it with fresh recruits. In testimony to the U.S. House of Representatives in 1970 hearings, Seattle Police Sergeant Archie Porter explained that the Black Panthers "were prepared to take full advantage of the publicity that would be gained as a result of any raid on their party headquarters. . . . We do not intend to be stampeded into making martyrs out of any group." Porter continued by noting, "Please don't get me wrong—I am not saying that the Black Panthers are not good Americans," but "we simply feel in Seattle that they are worthy of no extra attention."[143] Porter estimated Panther numbers to hover between eight and twelve by 1970. Officials within the Seattle Police Department reported various illegal activities by Panthers to Congress, but also reported a fairly weak organization incapable of fomenting large-scale unrest at that time. While it was probably true that the Panthers were incapable of instigating large-scale unrest (not that they were interested in doing do anyway), the chapter was far from weak; by most accounts the chapter remained a strong viable unit for nearly ten years.

Uhlman's strategy, however, ultimately proved effective. The Panthers began to drop out of city headlines soon after 1970, and Seattle avoided conflicts of the sort that involved Panthers in Chicago and Los Angeles. There was one notable exception though. In 1970, in an attempt to apprehend Leon Valentine Hobbs, several Panthers and members of the Seattle Police Department engaged in a standoff that began at about 11:00 a.m. and ended around 10:00 p.m. Apparently two police officers spotted Hobbs selling the *Black Panther* newspaper down the street from the Panthers' headquarters on Spruce Street and pulled up alongside him. As they approached, one officer yelled out, "Hey, come over here, I want to talk to you," to which Hobbs replied, "About what?" Irritated at Hobbs's response, the officer screamed out, "Nigger, I said get over here."[144] Hobbs took off running in the opposite direction, with the officers in hot pursuit. Nervous and his adrenaline running high, Hobbs blasted through the front entrance of the party's headquarters, frantically diving over a desk to retrieve a .357 magnum (affectionately nicknamed MLK, because it was, as the Panthers called it, their peacemaker). Just as Hobbs was raising the MLK, the officers lumbered through the front door, only to find themselves in the line of fire. As if in one motion, the officers turned around and scrambled back to the police cruiser, whereupon they called for backup. As additional police arrived on the scene, the media caught wind of the incident and swarmed the area. Police surrounded the Panthers' office. By that time neighbors began to filter out into the street and assemble near the action. As Hobbs recalled, "Some neighbors were armed while others came out with their dogs, German shepherds, Doberman pinschers, and so forth."[145]

The police ordered the Panthers to surrender. Someone inside called the national headquarters in Oakland, whereupon June Hilliard ordered the Panthers to hand Hobbs over to the police. The Panthers briefly discussed it, and finally Aaron Dixon asked for a vote. The result was unanimous: Hobbs stays.[146] Comrades then began preparing for what they thought was inevitable—a shoot-out with the police. Weapons were loaded, flak jackets were put on, and gas masks were pulled off shelves. "Vernetta Molson was then instructed to call the emergency list, which consisted of volunteers and supporters that the Panthers depended on for occasions just like this," said Aaron Dixon.[147] Over the course of the next several hours the situation grew tense, but no shots were fired. At some point, John L. Scott, a deejay for a local radio station, was allowed into the Panthers' headquarters, where he broadcast the standoff between the police and the Panthers. Eventually, a deal was struck between John Coughlin, the Panthers' attorney, and members of the police department; Coughlin would personally escort Hobbs to the police station only if the police backed off. Aaron Dixon remembers that "people in the community were so concerned about our safety that about 100 residents made a circle around the office, positioning themselves between the headquarters and the police officers, causing the police to retreat."[148] Also to the dismay of the police, "members of the Organization of Black Contractors led by Milton Norwood stood behind the police with shotguns in hand."[149] Later, Hobbs, accompanied by Coughlin, went down to the police station in a five-car caravan comprised of armed Panthers and concerned community members. When the entourage walked into the station, they found it nearly empty. Moreover, interest in Hobbs had inexplicably waned: strangely, the police were no longer concerned with apprehending him. Hobbs remembers a police sergeant saying upon his arrival, "There is no lineup." Hobbs, Coughlin, and the others looked at each other and said, "OK, let's go."[150]

Although there would be no other incidents of this magnitude, law enforcement, including the Federal Bureau of Investigation (FBI), would continue to survey Panther activities, reportedly teaming with local utility companies City Light and Pacific Northwest Bell to obtain information.

The Seattle BPP's Golden Years

Arguably, the Seattle BPP's success on the ground lay not entirely in what its members did—other organizations also established food banks, breakfasts, and other poverty programs, without the same flair—but in how they did it, although truth be told, no one organization offered the range of services as did the Panthers. Moreover, the churches could not threaten a store with imminent boycott and disruption to secure donations, as could the Panthers. Nor could the rhetoric of most churches capture the media's imagination in quite the same manner.[151]

The Seattle Panthers developed a political ideology to oppose that of the CACRC. The Panthers had initially adopted the original Oakland ideas and an eclectic Black Power ideology while fighting police brutality. By midsummer of 1969 Seattle's Black Panther leaders had pulled together their vision of where they wanted to take the Central Area community, and that involved a focus on socialism and on economics. Gossett and Elmer Dixon both agreed that "Civil Rights is the right to sit next to a person on a bus; we're talking about human rights—the right to live, right to decent clothing, and such."[152] The ideas involved a clear differentiation between what was loosely generalized as "middle-class" and "lower-class" goals, as Elmer Dixon summarized: "It's not appropriate to look at the Black community as if it is one. Middle-class blacks and working-class black groups may both be black, but have very different goals. We need to understand there are two different groups, each with its own agenda, and then look for common ground. But if you lump them all together, it doesn't work."[153]

Revealing the Marxist theory that Huey Newton had introduced into the party's ideology, the Seattle Panthers phased out much of their racial rhetoric and attacked "capitalists" regardless of race, which was in keeping with the organization's revision of the Ten Point Platform and Program. They described racism as just a capitalist tool to divide and oppress the "lumpen proletariat," and opened their programs to all poor Seattleites. To do otherwise, they argued, would be to join the antiblack racists in a misguided cause. To bring this unity about, the Panthers organized meetings and coalitions with Asian, white, Latinos, and various poverty groups to assist the economically disadvantaged. In broadening their scope, the Panthers recognized the multiethnic nature of Central Area problems, and accordingly prepared for more multiethnic problem solving.

Although generally avoiding the CACRC and similar groups, the Panthers often dubbed themselves spokespersons for the discontented black masses, and opened up dialogue with many other sectors of Seattle's populace. They took some of the first steps toward improving Asian-black relations, which had never prospered in Seattle, through meetings with the Japanese-American League and others. In many small, cooperative ventures to aid the poor through offering job training, food, and medicine, what the Panthers lacked in economic capabilities, they made up for in lending legitimacy in the eyes of many within the Central Area to whatever program they joined. Through both rhetoric and their own actions, the Panthers began attempting to tie the fate of all the economically disadvantaged together, regardless of race.[154]

The Panthers also began to tone down their histrionics. No longer able to tote weapons under new laws, they slowly shed their black leather jackets and berets. The highly visible regalia had served its purpose well in making the group's presence felt to abusive police and a complacent populace. By the 1970s, however, the image interfered with the Panthers' efforts to aid the downtrodden and oppressed. "People were already programmed to be scared of us," Michael Dixon recalled, noting that they found themselves also "scaring the very people we're supposed to help."[155] Although no major conflicts had taken place in several years, constant police surveillance wore on the Panthers. Aaron Dixon alone estimated that he had been arrested around fifty times in his Panther career, although he served real time only once.[156]

After the transition away from open confrontation, Elmer Dixon found that by 1972, he "didn't worry about attacks so much—those days of the Party were over. We could concentrate on Party organizing."[157] Still, this change in focus drove off existing and potential members. Bobby White remembers his sinking feeling that "this is the wrong organization for me. . . . Feeding the kids was cool, it just wasn't for me. I wanted more action."[158]

The Panthers did not limit their partnerships to any particular racial or political group. Panthers worked with doctors and other medical staff from local hospitals, and wrote a successful grant application for funding under the Boeing Good Neighbors program, according to a former Panther.[159]

Meanwhile, work by the BSU declined within the Central Area. The BSU peaked when UW president Odegaard spoke at a Martin Luther King Jr. memorial after the leader's assassination, where he asked white students to "make the extra effort" to help the new black students, and sponsored a Malcolm X memorial soon after in February 1969. E. J. Brisker resigned his post as the group's leader the following month and began to bow out of Seattle's Black Power activities. The elder statesman of the group (at age twenty-six), he left Seattle and went to New York soon after. Larry Gossett succeeded him and initiated another period of activity for the BSU by demanding more African American professors. Revealing the cadre's increasing concern for the disadvantaged, Gossett lobbied successfully to include poor whites under the Equal Opportunity Program (EOP) as well.[160]

After achieving what Gossett considered sufficient strength, the BSU waged its largest campaign in 1970. It demanded that the school sever ties with Brigham Young University (BYU) because of the Mormon school's racial policies, one of which was its policy barring blacks from entering into the priesthood. Athletes throughout the country protested by declining to compete against the school; at the University of Texas, El Paso, Bob Beamon, Olympic gold medalist and world record holder in the long jump, was one such athlete. The UW's administration's reluctance to sever ties led to the takeover of five buildings by as many as 1,000 protesters on March 5. Although the university promised no new athletic contracts with BYU, the BSU demanded an end to current contracts. Also, rumors of cooperation between the two schools on an administrative and research level kept demonstrators on campus and in the corridors. A bomb scare cleared students out of one building after several days, but a lack of progress toward resolution soon prompted the state legislature to investigate the matter and threaten to send in the National Guard.[161] It never reached that point, however, for the BSU canceled several later demonstrations and agreed to work with the administration. The faculty senate backed the BSU, and the UW showed the BSU the contracts with BYU while agreeing to limit future ties. Satisfied, the BSU withdrew three weeks after the protest began, although the demonstrators had evacuated most halls after six or seven days.[162]

Coercing the UW's administration to cut ties with another school was an impressive victory, but it meant little in practical terms to UW student life. It meant even less to the Central Area. The BSU, once an incubator of young leadership for the Central Area, now remained focused on issues with much less relevance to the neighborhood.

After gaining control of the EOP, the black studies program, and certain privileges for African American students, there were few issues left to rally around at the UW. The group had gathered not insignificant strength, yet found few immediately pressing issues over which its members could realistically flex their muscle. The problems of poor academic preparation in underfunded inner-city schools or the dizzying costs of an education were not issues easily addressed by a student organization. When Gossett graduated the following spring, he was replaced by John Gilmore, a business student who organized few of the major ventures that his predecessors had pushed. The BSU spirit of activism faded after 1971, and Gilmore limited his activity to opening a much-needed day-care center and leveling complaints against perceived racism among faculty, with mixed results. In the spring of 1973 the group sent almost forty students to occupy the campus newspaper office after disagreeing with its stance upon BSU issues, but to no avail.[163] The most easily winnable campus battles had already been fought. Opportunities and challenges within the private sector attracted more of the new middle-class generation's attention. As the militant generation graduated, the BSU began to fight its own generation's battles of equal opportunity for educated African Americans. The group lapsed into silence in the local media with this unspectacular new cause.

Meanwhile, the Seattle BPP worked at its survival programs and political education. The array of social services required full-time work by Panthers, who were often exhausted by the end of the day. The Panthers had organized a free legal services clinic by the early 1970s, and expanded the sickle cell anemia testing program. In addition, as the Dixons enforced the reading and ideological training requirements more rigidly, life as a Panther became a very regimented and disciplined existence. Communal living and early mornings and long hours became the dominant features of life, while the more glamorous aspects of being a Panther took a backseat. Such rigor quickly narrowed the membership to single-digit membership. However, the organization also continued to gain credibility within the Central Area. In 1974 the Central Area's newspaper awarded the Seattle BPP its highest award in the Unsung Hero Awards. That any activity by Black Panthers could qualify as "below the radar" was a testament to the increasingly low profile adopted by the party in its later years. The Panthers who remained were not ruffled by their reduced size, and Aaron Dixon recalled the post-1968 survival programs as "probably some of the best times of the Party."[164]

Assessing the Seattle BPP

The Seattle BPP achieved immediate prominence in the Central Area and across Seattle because of its instantly recognizable regalia and ideology.[165] However, such a high-profile character had ultimately proved limiting as well.

Realizing this, the Panthers adopted a multiethnic social service ethic that won respect from residents of the Central Area and later earned praise from national leaders as the "most dynamic and profound" of the Panther chapters.[166] Eventually, this service orientation may have contributed to the Panthers' undoing. While the overt displays of 1968 may have aided the community control movement, and the social work may have earned the respect and goodwill of local residents, it is unclear to what degree the party's proselytizing of its Ten Point Program and Platform or various Marxist ideals caught on with the masses. Instead, the Panthers became one of many entities providing social services while attempting to convert the users of the services—always "politicizing the participants" in their programs.[167] In such fashion, the role that the Panthers took within the community—providers of survival programs—increasingly did not require Panthers to fulfill. The rigid discipline and teachings became difficult to justify in terms of the organization's work within the community, and membership fell accordingly.

The Oakland headquarters began to weaken the Seattle chapter as well. The national party had transferred Aaron Dixon to assist with the mayoral and city council campaigns of Bobby Seale and Elaine Brown, respectively, in 1972, leaving leadership of the Seattle party to Elmer Dixon. Leon Valentine Hobbs was also summoned to Oakland. The reorganization of the party for all intents and purposes gutted the Seattle chapter, leaving behind a skeleton crew to continue the work that took scores of members to do. Other members of the Seattle cadre began to move on as well. Carl Miller left Seattle in 1975, moving to California. Larry Gossett joined the Central Area School Council and held many community-oriented positions. The differences with the national party were becoming stark, recalled Michael Dixon:

It was a completely different socioeconomic setting. The Bay Area is completely different than Seattle. Every chapter was a little different, depending on its topography, but we in the Northwest were a whole lot different. I think we were more successful at building a community network of support, because our approach was more global. . . . We were able to work with Native Americans and Asians. . . . Here, we lived right next to white people and we were intermixing, so our organization was intermixed, so our support organization was really intermixed. . . . We were probably the more innovative chapter. As a matter of fact, I think Oakland probably had concerns from time to time about how to curtail it.[168]

Conflict did not dominate the relationship between the national headquarters and its earliest out-of-state chapter, and Seattle Panthers recall visiting Oakland two or three times each month. Yet tensions arose over petty matters as early as 1969. At this, Michael Dixon recalled wondering if the Northwest chapter should part ways with the Oakland headquarters. Despite the ties between the chapter and its headquarters, the Seattle Panthers turned less to Oakland for support in their social service mission. In 1974 the Panthers closed the Sydney Miller Free Medical Clinic. Said Elmer Dixon: "The facility there simply was not suitable for a clinic: we were not capable of housing a comprehensive family clinic so we decided to shut it down, regroup and launch a much more comprehensive family clinic once we were able to secure the necessary resources. Simply put, we decided that if we couldn't do it right we wouldn't do it at all."[169] In 1977 tensions between the Seattle chapter and the national headquarters resulted in a break between the two. Apparently a rather silly disagreement over the direction of the free breakfast program proved to be the last straw.[170] According to Aaron Dixon, Ericka Huggins was reportedly upset over what the Seattle Panthers served kids for breakfast.[171] According to Ron Johnson, the national headquarters took issue with the chapter's decision to discontinue serving the kids meat. "As we began to learn more about nutrition we began to cut certain meats out, we also started to cook more vegetables," says Johnson.[172] At least one Panther viewed Huggins's behavior as that of a micromanager. Over the next few weeks, plans were put in place by certain members of the national headquarters (which by that time was headed by Elaine Brown) to discipline Elmer Dixon for insubordination. Fortunately, certain forces derailed those plans. Members of the Central Committee maintain that the Seattle chapter did not break from the national headquarters but was expelled. Elmer Dixon says otherwise: "We broke away. . . . If they expelled us, it was after the fact."[173] Whatever the case, Elmer Dixon continued the chapter's important work, retaining the organization's structure and continuing to operate the social services independent of the BPP.

In 1977 the Seattle chapter of the BPP changed its name to the Sydney Miller Community Service Center, and Elmer Dixon became its executive director. Over the next several years, Elmer Dixon and others devoted themselves to bolstering existing and creating new community survival programs. Among the new endeavors was a summer clean-up program. High school students were employed to clean up lots that had become eyesores. Then, of course, there was the summer youth school in which elementary schoolchildren from several schools, including Madrona Elementary, T. T. Minor, and Martin Luther King Jr., attended. Says Elmer Dixon: "There were ten students from UW who served as instructors, and ten students from local high schools who acted as their teaching assistants. There were a couple hundred kids enrolled in the school. Students received rigorous instruction, but also did fun things like go on field trips. We always made sure that learning was made fun for the kids."[174]

The Seattle comrades even set up an advisory board and filed for 501 C 3 status (nonprofit, tax-exempt organization), making their break from the party not only official but legal and permanent.[175] From 1976 to 1980 Elmer and Carolyn Downs worked feverishly at securing the necessary resources in order to relaunch a full-service family clinic. After much planning and groundwork, the clinic was reestablished in 1980. The Panthers secured a spacious facility located at Thirty-fourth Avenue and East Pike Street for a nominal fee. Fortunately, the building was home to a local cable company, which proved fortuitous for the Panthers as they used the rent paid by the cable company to pay for the building.[176] Before the clinic opened its doors, tragedy struck: Carolyn Downs died of cancer. Elmer Dixon remembers Carolyn Downs fondly:

She was a full-time community worker . . . she held no other job. She started by volunteering with the breakfast program. She was only about twenty years old. She was one of my closest confidants. She was a tireless worker . . . she organized many of our cookouts . . . she worked day and night along with me to get the clinic off the ground. I would not have been able to do it without her. When Carolyn died I recommended to the advisory board that the clinic be named in her honor—the Carolyn Downs Family Medical Clinic.[177]

The clinic's grand opening was much anticipated and well received. People of all walks of life flocked to the clinic; some even stopped by, offering to volunteer. The clinic's staff included area youth who were secured through the city's summer youth employment program. These young people were trained to administer free blood pressure screenings as well as conduct sickle cell anemia testing.[178]

Elmer Dixon believes that the community survival programs were richer and more established under the aegis of the Sydney Miller Community Service Center than they were when "we were associated with the Black Panther Party. . . . Our schedule was more consistent, and things operated more smoothly than ever before."[179] "The clinic, for example, had a full staff. We had six or seven examination rooms whereas the first clinic had one. There were four doctors on staff instead of two in the first clinic. . . . We had a physician's assistant and a lab as well as someone who specialized in pediatric care."[180]

In 1982 the Sydney Miller Community Service Center closed its doors. More and more comrades, because of other commitments, drifted away.[181] To compound matters, government funding for social service programs dried up under the Reagan administration. Aaron Dixon later worked with street youth in Oakland, and Elmer Dixon worked for the city Parks Department's hiring program before founding his own diversity consulting firm in Seattle. Most of the leadership cadre continued to work within the community in Seattle, although considerably farther from the local spotlight.[182] And although the Sydney Miller Community Service Center shut down, the Carolyn Downs Family Medical Clinic continued to flourish.

Some have argued that the young activists racked up more tangible accomplishments within the confines of the UW than in the Central Area, within which the Black Panthers functioned. At the university, they increased minority enrollment and hiring and founded the BSU, which would continue long after their graduation. This is not to say that the Panthers' impact on the Central Area community was negligible; far from it. However, one could legitimately argue that the Panthers had a much more far-reaching impact on the campus of the UW than on the streets of Seattle. Arguably one of the most innovative chapters, the Panthers made some inroads in various areas, but were unable to put a dent in the rising Central Area unemployment, poor housing, or poor schooling.[183] They worked tirelessly at the free breakfast and other community survival programs, some of which did not have the kind of long-lasting legacy that many had hoped for; but others did, such as the clinic, which remains open today.

Some have argued that the Seattle BPP operated in relative isolation from the larger Central Area organizations. The evidence suggests otherwise, however. The Panthers formed working relationships with a number of local groups. Indeed, at one time, Ron Carson, the head of CORE, was also a member of the Seattle Black Panthers.[184] The Panthers came out "ready to rumble" with the powers that be and believed they could connect with the community in a way that the CACRC and other traditional community leaders could not.[185] Yet these other political and community leaders had greater sway both within and outside of the Central Area, sway without which the Panthers, BSU, CORE, or any others could scarcely hope to find much success in attacking economic and political problems. In picking fights with the established leadership and their sources of funding and organizational abilities, the Panthers found few effective friends to support their programs. Often the Panthers had only the ability to carp at the CACRC and others, unable to launch their own programs. "They target the Black churches because we have the people that they want," pointed out Rev. Samuel McKinney, adding, "We have the ability to solve the Central Area problems."[186] The role of the critic is a relatively simple one to fill, and the Panthers—despite a formidable background in the writings of socialist thinkers—did not successfully present any realistic, workable plan to solve the community's larger ills. After the March 6 attack upon the CACRC integration plan, Rev. Adams rightly pointed out that "at least we have a plan—nobody else has presented a plan."[187] The Panthers earned (deserved or not) a reputation early as a group long on talk and short on effective action for bigger problems.

But success did not ultimately elude them. Seattle Panthers raised community awareness and helped as much as they could to ameliorate Central Area poverty through their programs. Their struggle against police brutality resulted in an investigation that led to the recruitment of African American police and department-wide "sensitivity training," although the topic would continue to simmer. The influential *Black Panther* newspaper spread their ideology to nearly all corners of the Central Area, through which they presented their critique of the local and national status quo.[188]

The Panthers also scored unintended successes that were not immediately clear, even through their dispute with the CACRC. Herbert Haines made clear in *Black Radicals and the Civil Rights Mainstream, 1954–1970* that the rise of militant black groups actually tended to coincide with an increase in economic support for moderate civil rights groups. Malcolm X, for example, recognized this when he traveled to Selma, Alabama, expressly to scare whites into supporting Martin Luther King Jr.'s efforts.[189] This seemed to be borne out in Seattle by the unanimous passage of the open housing ordinance without protest or comment four years after its ignominious defeat and just four weeks after Central Area unrest began. As the Seattle BPP faded from Seattle in the mid to late 1970s, the NAACP and Seattle Urban League both experienced sharp losses in membership as well.[190]

Similarly, although the Panthers' larger goals went largely unachieved, the group's significance to the Seattle community lay elsewhere. Before the civil rights movement in Seattle, community divisions were clear within the Central Area. The struggle for civil rights in Seattle temporarily united the Central Area under the middle-class leadership through common self-interest. After the civil rights movement achieved most of its initial goals, its leaderships' new goals were simply less inclusive.

Increasingly, the civil rights leadership could appear to place the goal of integration above the day-to-day economic interests of Central Area residents. The hesitation of rank-and-file neighborhood residents to support such school integration measures at all costs encouraged activists to introduce and pursue an agenda based around specific Central Area needs. The Black Power movement introduced an element of separatism into the community that would later evolve under the banner of "community control." In advocating community control of Central Area institutions and resources to address Central Area problems, the Black Power movement and Black Panthers specifically recognized both the community's pride in the neighborhood and the need to unite the diverse Central Area around economic issues.

The Central Area identity resulting from this period was often perceived of as generally lower class and African American by both area residents and outsiders alike. In reality, the Central Area did celebrate a thriving African-oriented culture of its own and tremendous pride in Garfield High School, Mount Zion Church, and other neighborhood institutions. Yet the neighborhood was not so narrowly construed. While ethnicity provided a rallying point, the increasingly important economic issues that beset the Central Area prompted an inclusive agenda that brought in residents of all backgrounds. The Central Area's white, Asian, and middle-class populations of all ethnicities continued to play major roles in neighborhood affairs, including leadership of many agencies and organizations.

Unlike civil rights leaders who sought clear and quick integration into the larger city, leaders of the Black Power movement generally, and the Seattle Black Panthers specifically, introduced a sense of black pride and consciousness into the community. These differing ideologies caused enormous debate within the Central Area over the proper approach to the area's problems, but they did not cause turmoil and strife that would prevent forward motion or positive action. Indeed, the very ability to approach Central Area issues from a Central Area perspective indicated a neighborhood cohesiveness that was lacking in other parts of the city.

This Central Area identity—a mix of class, race, and geography—would reach its apex during this period, producing, arguably, the most cohesive neighborhood in the city.

The Party's Reputation

Some observers argue that the BPP's reputation for violence has been overstated. On the other hand, those who deny any truth to that image also go too far.[191] One reason for the disparate images of the Seattle BPP is the sheer volume of statements made by the Panthers. The young leadership spoke often to the media, and in some cases the sheer number of speaking requests required that a position be created to handle scheduling duties. These speeches often included fiery language that, at best, appeared calculated to draw the attention of mainstream America. At worst, the language could appear paranoid and bizarre—the UW Archives contains a transcript of an interview in which Aaron Dixon describes "a giant, huge gas chamber and concentration camp which has only one entrance in and one entrance out . . . the Medgar Evers swimming pool, which is heated by gas. This is nothing but a concentration camp. They have concentration camps in other parts of the state. And we're saying that the fascists are planning genocide upon Black people." In retrospect, Dixon recognizes how strange and conspiratorial his statement sounded, but, as he says laughingly, "at that time there were a lot of conspiracy theories going around and I bought into a few of them."[192]

There exist enough statements made by Seattle Black Panthers to support almost any view of the party. While some say the perceptions of the party as prone to violence is the result of media or police distortions, a few Panthers have admitted that they firebombed, shot at firefighters, and committed other acts of violence. Similarly, a large number of public speeches by Panthers in 1968 warned of tremendous violence and upheaval in an upcoming revolution. It is somewhat disingenuous to proclaim that the power one seeks "comes from the barrel of a gun" and wonder about the source of one's violent reputation.

Thus, while the public impression of the party as involved with violence may be overstated, it is not a fabrication. Eventually, the Seattle Panthers in particular recognized this and attempted to curtail inflammatory statements, but the imagery inevitably lingered in the minds of Seattleites.

Despite these complications, the more sensational aspects of the chapter's early years are not representative of the chapter's work, impact, and legacy. Indeed, the Dixons and others made a great number of thoughtful statements about working with groups of all races in a peaceful manner to serve the impoverished community within the Central Area and beyond. The Panthers enjoyed excellent relations with activists of all races and growing community support for their efforts to improve life in the Central Area. Very few who worked with the Dixons walked away unimpressed with their dedication or thoughtfulness. Even their occasional sparring partner city council member Sam Smith would comment positively on the party in his memoirs, adding with apparent pride that the Panthers had attempted to recruit him.[193]

More important than the group's bold statements were the vital services it offered at a time when such providers were not as consistent, expansive, or vigilant. "Years later I used to run into people all the time who ate at the breakfast program. It's amazing, these people are grown now, with families of their own," says Melvin Dickson.[194] Party members worked extremely hard at offering programs that were germane to local conditions. A typical workday for the Seattle Panthers was grueling. Gayle "Asali" Dickson put it in perspective: "Most people would consider what we did as hard work, but those days were the best days of my life. It was not work to me, I loved it."[195] In addition to providing sorely needed services, the Seattle chapter also provided a voice, encouraging Central Area residents to demand more from the city and from society at large. Such rhetoric would provide momentum that would help Central Area activists to demand an end to segregated schools, redlining, and discriminatory hiring throughout the following decade. When asked about the party's legacy, Aaron Dixon was quick to put it in context: "We brought a lot of pride and respect to the black community. We also set an example of service delivery that had not existed prior to the Black Panther Party. We became a model for superior service delivery. An example of this is the Carolyn Downs Medical Clinic that still functions today."[196] There is no doubt that the young activists who formed the Seattle chapter of the BPP made their mark on the city of Seattle, which history will be compelled to reflect.

Notes

1. *Seattle Post-Intelligencer*, November, 14, 1965.
2. Larry Richardson, "Civil Rights in Seattle: A Rhetorical Analysis of a Social Movement" (Ph.D. diss., Washington State University, 1975).

3. The most comprehensive book on Seattle's African American community is Quintard Taylor's *The Forging of a Black Community: Seattle's Central District from 1870 through the Civil Rights Era* (Seattle: University of Washington Press, 1994). The civil rights movement in Seattle has been aptly documented by Taylor and others, and will not be dealt with at length or in great depth here. However, a certain background to the local civil rights movement is vital to any understanding of the BPP in Seattle.

4. Robert C. Smith, *We Have No Leaders: African Americans in the Post-Civil Rights Era* (Albany: State University of New York Press, 1996), 11–16.

5. Richardson, "Civil Rights in Seattle," 21.

6. Ibid., 77.

7. John Guernsay, *Portland Oregonian*, June 6, 1963. Guernsay was writing on Portland's segregated schools.

8. On this scale, 79.7 is the percentage of African Americans who would have to move to completely integrate the city. With a rating of 100, 100 percent of the population would have to move. *Seattle Times*, May 30, 1966. The number is the percentage of people who would have to move to fully integrate a population. With a rating of 100, 100 percent of the population would have to move.

9. Although commonly referred to as *Jones v. O'Meara*, the suit was actually launched against a state bureau, *O'Meara v. Washington State Board Against Discrimination*, Case No. 535996 (Superior Ct. King Co. Wash., July 31, 1959), and *O'Meara v. Washington State Board Against Discrimination*, Case No. 35436, (Wash. State. Supreme Ct., September 29, 1961). In this case, the Washington State Board Against Discrimination issued a cease and desist order against O'Meara, who refused to sell his Federal Housing Authority–mortgaged home to Jones (an African American) for racial reasons. The King County Superior Court ruled against Jones, ruling that the statute clashed with O'Meara's freedom to choose with whom he would deal. The judge also used a narrow definition of "state action" to rule that the statute applied the equal-protection principles of the Fourteenth Amendment to a private action. This case was widely viewed very negatively. Contemporary writers dismissed it by stating, for example, "We have deliberately omitted any discussion of *O'Meara v. Washington State Board Against Discrimination* . . . because Judge Hodson's decision in that case, holding the Washington Housing law unconstitutional, is predicated upon an unsound theory and should be reversed on appeal." Milton Konvitz and Theodore Leskes, *A Century of Civil Rights: With a Study of State Law against Discrimination* (New York: Columbia University Press, 1961), 248. To the great surprise of many, it was upheld in a five-to-four decision by the state supreme court. Since the majority opinion did not address federal law, but upheld the decision on state statute grounds, the U.S. Supreme Court denied certiorari. The ruling was not widely cited as precedent, and the California Supreme Court dismissed it while supporting an open housing statute, writing, "We are aware that similar legislation was held invalid by the Supreme Court of Washington in a five-to-four decision . . . but we do not find that case persuasive authority." *Burks v. Poppy Const. Co.*, 20 Cal. Rptr. 609, 370 P.2d 313, 320 (Cal. 1962). *Jones v. O'Meara* is very well documented by Arval Morris and Donald Ritter in "Racial Minority Housing in Washington," *Washington State Law Review* 37 (Summer 1962): 139–151.

10. Harvard Sitkoff, *The Struggle for Black Equality, 1954-1992* (New York: Hill and Wang, 1993), 145.

11. The 1965 crash that took Wing from Seattle politics was a double blow to desegregation activists, in that the pilot was Sidney Gerber, an ardent foe of segregation. There were no survivors. Ellen Levine, *Housing and Race in Four Cities: A Report to the Foundation on Field Research in Denver, Seattle, Philadelphia, and Lexington* (New York: Ford Foundation Press, 1969), 81.

12. *Seattle Times*, March 11, 1964. Our discussion of open housing and the Seattle civil rights movement is merely a prologue to the Seattle Black Power movement and beyond. As such, we will not detail events already well documented by others. Those interested in greater detail should refer first to Rebecca Moore, "Anyplace but Here: The Seattle Campaign for Open Housing, 1950–1969" (master's thesis, Western Washington University, 1995). This is in addition to relevant parts of work on the subject by Taylor, *Forging of a Black Community* (especially chapter 6); and Richardson, "Civil Rights in Seattle."

13. Richardson, "Civil Rights in Seattle," 34, 85.

14. Ellen Levine describes various examples of real estate agents who found their jobs at risk after assisting black homebuyers. Levine, *Housing and Race*, 69–86.

15. Ibid.; *Seattle Times*, January 2, 1966, July 5, 1967, and August 3, 1969.

16. Taylor, *Forging of a Black Community*, 206.

17. Levine, *Housing and Race*, 104.

18. August Meier and Elliot Rudwick, *CORE: A Study in the Civil Rights Movement 1942–1968* (New York: Oxford University Press, 1973), 189; Congress of Racial Equality (CORE) Collection, University of Washington Archives and Special Collections [hereafter cited as CORE Collection]; Taylor, *Forging a Black Community*, chapter 7.

19. *Seattle Times*, March 22, April 3, 1964. Also described in Meier and Rudwick, *CORE*, 308.

20. Meier and Rudwick, *CORE*, 306–310.

21. Ibid., chapter 7; CORE Collection.

22. Meier and Rudwick, *CORE*, 384–385.

23. Planners had anticipated around 1,400 African American transfers. Dorothy Pieroth's dissertation is an excellent resource for those interested in Seattle public schools before 1968. Dorothy Hinson Pieroth, "Desegregating the Public Schools: Seattle, Washington, 1954–1968" (Ph.D. diss., University of Washington 1979).

24. *Seattle Times*, April 1, 3, 1966; Taylor, *Forging of a Black Community*, 213.

25. Taylor, *Forging of a Black Community*, 213. The figures for income in relation to whites not only reveals the depths of despair that Central Area black workers experienced but also hints at the relative wealth of those African Americans residing outside of the neighborhood.

26. Aaron Dixon, interview by Judson L. Jeffries, April 4, 2009.

27. Ibid.

28. Larry Gossett, interview by Jeff Zane, August 12, 1993; Elmer Dixon, interview by Jeff Zane, August 12, 1993; George Newsome, interview by Jeff Zane, October 4, 1994.

29. *Seattle Sun*, June 30, 1976; Taylor, *Forging a Black Community*, chapter 7; Gossett, interview; George Newsome interview by Jeff Zane, July 9, 1993; Newsome, interview, October 4, 1994.

30. Taylor, *Forging a Black Community*, chapter 7; Newsome, interview, July 9, 1993; Newsome, interview, October 4, 1994.

31. University of Washington Black Student Union (BSU) Papers, University of Washington Archives and Special Collections [hereafter cited as BSU Papers]; Gossett, interview; *Seattle Times*, December 8, 1970.

32. Diana Walker, "The University of Washington Establishment and the Black Student Union Sit-in of 1967" (master's thesis, University of Washington, 1980), 47; BSU Papers; *Seattle Times*, May 21, 22, 1967, and June 11, 1968.

33. *University of Washington Daily*, August 8, 1968.

34. BSU Papers.

35. CORE Collection; Meier and Rudwick, *CORE*, 384–385.

36. Meier and Rudwick, *CORE*, 385; Taylor, *Forging a Black Community*, chapter 7; CORE Collection.

37. CORE Collection.

38. Ibid.

39. *Seattle Times*, February 15, 1988.

40. Henry Hampton, *Voices of Freedom: An Oral History of the Civil Rights Movement from the 1950s through the 1980s* (New York: Bantam Books, 1990); Stokely Carmichael, *Black Power: The Politics of Liberation in America* (New York: Random House, 1967); Newsome, interview, October 4, 1994; Gossett, interview.

41. Dorothy Pieroth, interview by Jeff Zane, August 30, 1993.

42. *Seattle Times*, March 7, 1968.

43. Ibid.

44. Richard Gossett, Larry's younger brother, was a student at nearby Highline Community College.

45. Aaron Dixon, interview by Judson L. Jeffries, July 21, 2008.

46. BSU Papers; *Seattle Times*, April 2, 4, 1968.

47. Aaron Dixon, interview for the Seattle Black Panther Party History and Memory Project at the University of Washington [hereafter cited as the SBPP Project]. Oral interviews with former members of the Seattle Black Panther Party were conducted by Janet Jones and are maintained online by the project, under the oversight of James N. Gregory. This collection also contains an excellent three-part history of the Seattle BPP written by Kurt Schaefer entitled "The Black Panther Party in Seattle."

48. Ibid.

49. Aaron Dixon, interview, July 21, 2008.

50. Ibid.

51. Aaron Dixon, interviews by Judson L. Jeffries, April 5 and 6, 1968.

52. Aaron Dixon, interview by Judson L. Jeffries, July 24, 2008.

53. Ibid.

54. Ibid.

55. Aaron Dixon, interview, July 21, 2008.

56. Ibid.

57. *Seattle Sun*, June 30, 1976; BSU Papers; Gossett, interview.

58. Ron Johnson, interview for the SBPP Project.

59. *Seattle Times*; Gossett, interview; Newsome, interview, July 9, 1993; Newsome, interview, October 4, 1994.

60. Leon Valentine Hobbs, interview by Judson L. Jeffries, April 28, 2008.

61. Aaron Dixon, interview by Judson L. Jeffries, August 7, 2008.

62. Leon Valentine Hobbs, interview by Judson L. Jeffries, July 9, 2009.

63. Aaron Dixon, interview by Judson L. Jeffries, July 15, 2008.

64. Gossett, interview; Elmer Dixon, interview, August 12, 1993; Newsome, interview, October 4, 1994; CORE Collection.

65. Aaron Dixon, interview, July 15, 2008.

66. Bobby White, interview for the SBPP Project.

67. Gossett was acquitted. *Seattle Times*, July 2, 1968.

68. Ibid., July 2, 3, 5, 20, 30, 1968.

69. Bureau of the Census, *Characteristics of the Population 1970*, Pt. 21 Michigan, Table 27; Pt. 33n New Jersey, Table 27; Pt. 5, California, Table 27 (Washington, D.C.: Government Printing Office, 1971); Hampton, *Voices of Freedom*; Roger Sale, *Seattle: Past to Present* (Seattle: University of Washington Press, 1976), 218.

70. *Seattle Times*, March 7, 1968.

71. Gossett, interview; Elmer Dixon, interview, August 12, 1993; Newsome, interview, July 9, 1993.

72. They also chided the business owners for hiring practices and what many considered overpric-
    ing. Black Panther Party Papers, University of Washington Manuscripts, Special Collections,
    and University Archives; Taylor, *Forging a Black Community*, chapter 7.

73. *Seattle Times*, August 1, 31, 1968; Newsome, interview, July 9, 1993; Newsome, interview, October
    4, 1994; *New York Times*, July 30, 31, 1968.

74. *Seattle Times*, July 17, 1968.

75. It should be noted that there was no such official position. The convention also nominated
    Brisker, but he declined in order to devote more time to the BSU. Newsome, interview, October
    4, 1994.

76. *Seattle Times*, September 18, October 10, 1968; Aaron Dixon, interview, July 24, 2008.

77. Aaron Dixon, interview by Judson L. Jeffries, July 18, 2009.

78. *Seattle Times*, September 19, 20, 1968; BSU Papers.

79. Michael Newton, *Bitter Grain: Huey Newton and the Black Panther Party* (Los Angeles: Holloway
    House, 1991).

80. Aaron Dixon, interview by Judson L. Jeffries, April 22, 2009.

81. Aaron Dixon, interview by Judson L. Jeffries, October 6, 1968; *Afro-American*, October 10, 1968;
    Seattle Times, October 16, 1968.

82. *Seattle Times*, September 25, 1968.

83. *Seattle Post-Intelligencer*, February 28, March 4, 1969; Elmer and Aaron Dixon, Chris Mills of
    the UBF, Ron Carson of CORE, and activist Keve Bray arrived on Thursday to make an ap-
    pointment to speak, and encountered a very tense senate office. After Governor Evans returned
    from a trip that evening, he dispersed the police force that had gathered, and four of the leaders
    spoke the next day. Eight Black Panthers were permitted to march in formation on the grounds
    outside, but only after state police ensured their weapons were unloaded. It was generally por-
    trayed by *Seattle Post-Intelligencer* reporter Shelby Scates as a massive overreaction.

84. *Seattle Times*, October 24, 1986, and February 14, 1988; Gossett, interview.

85. Leon Valentine Hobbs, interview by Judson L. Jeffries, May 8, 2008.

86. Elmer Dixon, interview for SBPP Project.

87. Aaron Dixon memoirs, in SBPP Project.

88. Michael Dixon, interview for the SBPP Project.

89. To this day Aaron Dixon believes this incident to be no accident. A close examination of the
    weapon revealed that the casings were filled with a high explosive. His injuries required four
    separate surgeries over a twelve-month period. The pain that he experienced in his left arm
    persisted for at least five years. "I had to wear a cast up to my elbow for nearly a year."

90. Aaron Dixon, interview, July 21, 2008.

91. White, interview.

92. Aaron Dixon, interview, July 21, 2008.

93. Ibid.

94. Hobbs, interview.

95. Garry Owens, interview by Judson L. Jeffries, June 16, 2009.

96. Rashad Byrdsong, interview by Judson L. Jeffries, June 17, 2009.

97. Gayle "Asali" Dickson, interview by Judson L. Jeffries, June 6, 2009.

98. Anthony Ware, interview by Judson L. Jeffries, June 13, 2009.

99. Vernetta Molson, interview by Judson L. Jeffries, November 22, 2008.

100. Ware, interview.

101. Molson, interview, November 22, 2008.

102. Vernetta Molson, interview by Judson L. Jeffries, December 6, 2008.

103. Owens, interview, June 16, 2009.

104. Ron Johnson, interview by Judson L. Jeffries, June 6, 2009.

105. *Movement* interview by Bobby Seale, reprinted in the *Black Panther*, March 2, 1969.

106. "Youth Make the Revolution," *Black Panther*, August 2, 1969.

107. "Liberation School," *Black Panther*, February 7, 1970; "Vallejo Liberation School," *Black Panther*, August 9, 1969.

108. U.S. Congress, House of Representatives, Committee on Internal Security, *Black Panther Party, Part 4, National Office Operations and Investigation of Activities in Des Moines, Iowa, and Omaha, Nebr.*, 91st Cong., 2nd sess., 1970, Appendix A, 4979.

109. Melvin Dickson, interview by Judson L. Jeffries, June 19, 2009.

110. Ibid.

111. Ware, interview.

112. Ibid.

113. Garry Owens, interview by Judson L. Jeffries, June 17, 2009.

114. Melvin Dickson, interview, June 19, 2009.

115. Ware, interview.

116. Johnson, interview, June 6, 2009.

117. Vernetta Molson, interview by Judson L. Jeffries, November 11, 2008; Aaron Dixon, interview, July 24, 2008.

118. Gayle "Asali" Dickson, interview.

119. Hobbs, interview, April 28, 2008; Aaron Dixon, interview, July 21, 2008.

120. Johnson, interview, June 6, 2009.

121. Ibid.

122. Jake Fiddler, interview by Judson L. Jeffries, June 6, 2009.

123. Aaron Dixon, interview, July 21, 2008.

124. Jake Fiddler, interview by Judson L. Jeffries, June 9, 2009.

125. Hobbs, interview, May 8, 2008.

126. Ibid.

127. Hobbs, interview, April 28, 2008.

128. Leon Valentine Hobbs, interview by Judson L. Jeffries, June 22, 2009.

129. Ibid.

130. Mike Murray, interview for the SBPP Project.

131. Michael Dixon, interview.

132. Aaron Dixon, interview.

133. Leon Valentine Hobbs, interview for the SBPP Project.

134. Johnson, interview for the SBPP Project.

135. Aaron Dixon, interview by Judson L. Jeffries, April 22, 2008.

136. Gossett, interview; Elmer Dixon, interview; *Seattle Times*, August 23, 1968; *Afro-American*, May 30, 1968, 2.

137. Johnson, interview for the SBPP Project.

138. Ibid.

139. Wes Uhlman, interview for the SBPP Project.

140. Wes Uhlman, interview by Judson L. Jeffries, March 13, 2006.

141. Aaron Dixon, interview by Judson L. Jeffries, July 18, 2008.

142. Governor Evans had responded to a letter demanding a crackdown on the Seattle Panthers by writing that "if the Black Panthers, or anyone else, violates the law here in Olympia the state will take immediate action. However, there was no law violation by the Black Panthers and they, of course, have the same rights that any other citizen of the State of Washington has." Dan Evans to Mr. and Mrs. L. R. Picalolo, March 4, 1969, Evans Papers, Washington State Archives.

143. U.S. Congress, House of Representatives, Committee on Internal Security, *Black Panther Party*.

144. Leon Valentine Hobbs, interview by Judson L. Jeffries, June 18, 2009.

145. Ibid.

146. Aaron Dixon, interview by Judson L. Jeffries, June 17, 2009.

147. Aaron Dixon, interview, June 18, 2009.

148. Ibid.

149. Hobbs, interview, July 9, 2009.

150. Ibid.

151. Elmer Dixon, interview, August 12, 1993.

152. *Seattle Sun*, June 30, 1976.

153. Elmer Dixon, interview, August 12, 1993.

154. Ibid.; Newsome interview, July 9, 1993; Taylor, *Forging a Black Community*, chapter 7; *Seattle Sun*, June 30, 1976.

155. Michael Dixon, interview for the SBPP project.

156. *Seattle Sun*, June 30, 1976.

157. Elmer Dixon, interview for the SBPP Project.

158. White, interview for the SBPP Project.

159. Johnson, interview for the SBPP Project.

160. BSU Papers; *University of Washington Daily*, March 3, 1969; Newsome, interview, October 4, 1994; Gossett, interview.

161. *Seattle Times*, March 5, 6, 7, 8, 1970; *Seattle Post-Intelligencer*, March 10, 1970; BSU Papers.

162. *Seattle Times*, March 10, 24, 28, 1970; BSU Papers.

163. BSU Papers; *University of Washington Daily*, April 14, June 2, 1971, and February 1, May 8, 10, 1973; *Seattle Post-Intelligencer*, June 25, 1971.

164. Aaron Dixon, interview, June 18, 2009.

165. Ibid.

166. Kurt Schaefer, "The Black Panther Party in Seattle: Part 3—The Panthers and the Politicians" (citing Bobby Seale's talk at the BPP thirty-fifth reunion, Seattle, May 14, 2005, and Bobby Seale interview).

167. Ibid.

168. Michael Dixon, interview.

169. Elmer Dixon, interview by Judson L. Jeffries, April 24, 2009.

170. National leaders claim that the Seattle chapter was expelled. Elmer Dixon maintains that a group of Seattle Panthers made the conscious decision to break from the national group.

171. Aaron Dixon, interview, July 15, 2009.

172. Johnson, interview, June 6, 2009.

173. Elmer Dixon, interview by Judson L. Jeffries, May 5, 2009.

174. Ibid.

175. Elmer Dixon, interview by Judson L. Jeffries, April 23, 2009.

176. Ibid.

177. Ibid.

178. Ibid.

179. Ibid.

180. Elmer Dixon, interview by Judson L. Jeffries, May 16, 2009.

181. Today, Larry Gossett is the King County councilman for the Central Area.

182. *Seattle Times*, October 24, 1986; Newsome, interview, July 9, 1993; Michael Dixon, interview.

183. Michael Dixon, interview.

184. Aaron Dixon, interview, April 24, 2009.

185. Newsome, interview, July 9, 1993.

186. *Seattle Times*, July 25, 1968.

187. Ibid., March 7, 1968.

188. Ibid., September 3, 1968.

189. Herbert Haines, *Black Radicals and the Civil Rights Mainstream, 1954–1970* (Knoxville: University of Tennessee Press, 1988); Hampton, *Voices of Freedom*.

190. *Seattle Post-Intelligencer*, May 1, 1979.

191. Hobbs, interview for the SBPP Project.

192. Aaron Dixon, interview by Judson L. Jeffries, June 13, 2009.

193. *Sam Smith: An Oral History*. Interviewed by Dianne Bridgman. (Olympia: Washington State Oral History Program, 2000).

194. Melvin Dickson, interview, June 19, 2009.

195. Gayle "Asali" Dickson, interview.

196. Aaron Dixon, interview, April 22, 2009.

THE KANSAS CITY BLACK PANTHER PARTY AND THE REPRESSION OF THE BLACK REVOLUTION

Reynaldo Anderson

This chapter seeks to situate the local activities of the Kansas City, Missouri, branch of the Black Panther Party (BPP) in a context that connects them to the larger black freedom struggle in that city, the state, and the nation. The branch coordinated its specific activities, functioning as a subunit inside of the national BPP structure; in fact, the heartland chapters rotated members in order to carry out the BPP program effectively. These local events in the heartland help illuminate the rationale for a local formation of the BPP to address problems in the African American community that traditional civil rights organizations were unable to address. The study of these local activities have traditionally been either overlooked or subsumed under the rubric of an entire movement.

The study of these events helps to clarify the activities that occurred during the post–civil rights era. The BPP distinguished itself from the civil rights movement in two primary areas. First, the goal of the BPP was to gain control over institutions that impacted the lives of African Americans. Second, the BPP was willing to engage in armed self-defense tactics when confronted with violent oppression. The BPP was part of the African American tradition of armed resistance dating back to slave rebellions led by Nat Turner and Denmark Vesey.

The BPP has been frequently misunderstood by both scholars and the general public. The BPP emerged from a confluence of factors, including events in the world system, limitations of the civil rights movement, and white supremacy.[1]

The black revolution of 1968–1971 represented an antisystemic struggle against the world system in the United States—a society that was responsible for the enslavement and segregation of African peoples. The BPP was the modern manifestation of the black American freedom struggle against racial structures of power that created and sustained white skin privilege within the world system. The emergence of the BPP was in response to a convergence of elements that were destabilizing the world system circa 1968. These included the poor economy, the Vietnam War, the American culture of violence, and the limitations of the civil rights movement. The BPP was initially organized as a paramilitary self-defense black nationalist organization. However, with the advent of the black revolution, the Panthers evolved into a revolutionary nationalist organization attempting to seize power within the American polity. The Black Panthers attempted to harness the discontent of disaffected groups within the African American community (for example, prisoners, welfare mothers, students, and the black underclass) and organize them into a radical force to challenge the state and capitalist institutions in American society.

The theory that antisystemic movements behave differently in particular zones of the world system was substantiated by the ideological and rhetorical development of the BPP. Historically, social democratic parties represented the interests of working-class and underclass persons in core zones and organized around class distinctions and political ideas. However, the black revolution had the characteristics of antisystemic movements in peripheral and semiperipheral zones in the world system, utilizing both nationalist and socialist ideas to influence American political institutions.

The peripheral/semiperipheral character of the black revolution stemmed from black revolutionary theory that had coalesced into an antisystemic paradigm based upon four premises. First, because of its largely segregated and isolated residential relationship in relation to racist elements of the larger white community and its historical development in relation to the forces of production controlled by the white power elite, the black community was an internal colony within the United States existing in a neocolonial relationship with black compradors or petit bourgeoisie acting as agents for the white power elite. Second, the revolutionary cadre would include nationalistic black petit bourgeoisie, a radicalized black working class, and the black underclass, the vanguard element being the black lumpen proletariat composed of black prisoners, unemployed people, students, and poor black women. Third, the struggle would take place in an urban context, where most African Americans lived, unlike other third world revolutions, which were based in rural areas. Finally, this vanguard black element would lead other progressive elements in the United States in a revolutionary struggle to seize political power and fundamentally reorganize American society. Thus the ideological practice of the BPP was premised upon the demand for black equality and the attempt to gain power to determine the destiny of the African American community. However, the ideology of the BPP in its national content and form was sometimes contradicted by the manner in which local Black Panther cadres carried out or responded to the directives of the Central Committee.

This chapter focuses on the emergence and formation of the Kansas City BPP, the challenges and subsequent responses of cadre members, and the ultimate demise of the chapter. The rise and fall of the Kansas City BPP occurred roughly between July 1968 and March 1971. In order to put the Kansas City branch of the BPP in its proper context, a discussion of the sociopolitical environment in Kansas City is necessary.

Rising Militancy in the Heartland

After World War II, the Kansas City civil rights establishment focused on the areas of education, housing, employment, and political empowerment. The societal institution where African Americans first successfully directed serious political activity was in the area of education. The civil rights establishment experienced a great victory in the neighboring state of Kansas concerning segregated education. Nineteen fifty-four was an important year in the challenge to segregated education. The U.S. Supreme Court declared segregated education unconstitutional in *Brown v. Board of Education of Topeka, Kansas.* Segregated education was also challenged in the state of Missouri in *Arnold v. Kirkwood School District R-7.*[2] The effort to desegregate schools in the region was easier than in the South. Desegregation, however, was hampered by the concentration of the overwhelming majority of African American students in a few school districts in St. Louis and Kansas City.[3]

Housing and employment remained problems for African Americans in Kansas City into the 1960s. In Kansas City, 10 percent of the housing for African Americans was overcrowded and substandard. The overwhelming majority of African Americans were concentrated in low-wage jobs.[4] Under pressure from the civil rights movement, the government attempted to ameliorate African American social conditions with the passage of the Public Accommodations Act of 1964 and the Voting Rights Act of 1965. Although providing formal political enfranchisement, these laws did little to improve the economic status of the majority of African Americans.[5]

In 1962 African Americans in Kansas City finally tried to create an independent power base with the formation of Freedom Inc. Headed by Bruce Watkins and Leon Jordan, Freedom Inc. was created to rid local politics of organized crime.[6] Jordan became the first African American to become a lieutenant in the Kansas City Police Department and later served for several years in the West African country of Liberia training a local police force. Jordan launched his political and business career upon his return from West Africa, getting elected to public office in 1958.[7]

Bruce Watkins was chairman of the Jackson County Democratic Committee and actively served in the Republican Party.[8] Watkins and Jordan started Freedom Inc. to influence political/economic activities in the local African American community.[9] Specifically, it was developed to organize black voters more effectively and nurture the growth of future black leaders. In 1963 Freedom Inc. successfully got a public accommodations ordinance passed on a city ballot after organizing a huge voter registration campaign in the black community.[10] Freedom Inc. helped Jordan get elected to committeeman and Watkins to the city council. Freedom Inc. also successfully supported several candidates to elected positions in 1964.[11] Although organizations like Freedom Inc. and others successfully lobbied to end discrimination in public accommodations and voting rights, police brutality and economic conditions for many black residents changed little. However, Freedom Inc. suffered a serious setback when its president, Leon Jordan, was assassinated in July 1970.[12]

The growing dissatisfaction with discrimination and the perceived inability of the civil rights movement to deal with their problems caused many African Americans to criticize the nonviolent direct action tactics of Martin Luther King Jr. and the civil rights movement. Malcolm X, H. Rap Brown, and Stokely Carmichael appealed to a younger generation of African Americans who desired a more militant and nationalistic approach to the African American community's problems. The years of upheaval across the United States from 1965 to 1968 did not in any meaningful way impact the heartland region until King's assassination on April 4, 1968. Kansas City high school students protested because local officials refused to close school in King's honor and were hit with tear gas when they marched to city hall. That same night violence broke out in Kansas City; African Americans were seen throwing Molotov cocktails, and National Guardsman were brought in to restore order.[13] The black revolution, as it was viewed by some, had reached the heartland.

The Formation of the Kansas City BPP

The Kansas City chapter of the BPP was organized in early January 1969 under the leadership of Peter O'Neal. Originally known as the Black Vigilantes, the organization changed its name when it gained formal admission to the BPP in the summer of 1968. The Kansas City chapter promulgated the national organization's ideology, which had entered its revolutionary nationalist phase. The revolutionary nationalist position adopted by the party critiqued the role of capitalism and local capitalist exploitation of African Americans. The Kansas City chapter focused on the discontent of the African American working class and underclass, on the rage of black youth, on developing survival programs, and on building a functioning relationship with other community organizations. According to Andre (Weatherby) Rawls, the Kansas City BPP's membership was composed primarily of working-class, underclass, and a few middle-class African American men and women.[14] Many of the members had previous exposure to aspects of the civil rights movement, having been members of the youth branch of the National Association for the Advancement of Colored People (NAACP) or the Congress of Racial Equality (CORE). Pete O'Neal was the leader and deputy chairman of the Kansas City chapter of the BPP; Bill Whitfield was the deputy minister of defense; and Andre (Weatherby) Rawls was the communications secretary. Other key members were Charlotte Hill, the late Tommy Robinson and Billy Robinson, Phillip Crayton, Keith Hinch, and Henry Finley (who turned state's evidence and was branded a traitor and jackanape).[15]

As deputy chairman of the Kansas City chapter of the BPP, Pete O'Neil was responsible for carrying out the directives of the Central Committee specifically as they related to the party's Ten Point Program and Platform. However, Rawls points out that the Kansas City chapter, and the other Midwest chapters in Des Moines and Omaha, were under the regional supervision of the Illinois chapter of the BPP.

Andre (Weatherby) Rawls was the Kansas City chapter's communications secretary. This position made her responsible for the chapter's media correspondence and maintaining communication links with other heartland BPP chapters. According to Rawls, she joined the Kansas City Black Panther affiliate in 1969. Prior to her membership in the party, she was politically influenced by her exposure to the emerging black awareness movement on black college campuses and her initial involvement with CORE. However, she swiftly lost interest in CORE because of its perceived lack of direction. Rawls recalled: "Much later in life I realized that at the age of 12 on most Sunday afternoons while living with my Aunt in St. Louis we listened to a new minister on the radio who called himself Malcolm X. My exposure to revolutionary thinking had begun before I was aware."[16]

It was after Rawls attended a political education class hosted by the BPP that she became interested in seeking membership in the Kansas City chapter. The membership of the Kansas City BPP came primarily from what was considered the African American middle and lower classes. The majority of the Kansas City leadership came from two-parent homes and a middle- to working-class background, although a few came from single-parent homes. "Many parents were postal workers and factory workers. In the late 1960s very few African Americans drove public buses in Kansas City, therefore with a few exceptions there were limits as to how far African Americans could go."[17] The rank-and-file members of the chapter were from the African American lower class.

The party also functioned as an organizational means of teaching some members how to read in order to promulgate the party philosophy to the public. According to Rawls, many of the party's rank-and-file members were taught to read by studying the philosophy of dialectical materialism, Karl Marx, and Mao Zedong. Many evenings were spent teaching Marx's *Das Kapital* and Mao's *Red Book* in political education classes. Rawls noted: "We'd sit there in the wee hours of the morning teaching these brothers how to read word for word. Let's spell it, let's say it, let's spell it, let's understand what it means. . . . You got to know what you're talking about."[18] The rage of black youth was an important element in the formation of not only the national organization but the Kansas City chapter as well.

The Black Panthers were extremely effective in attracting the attention of the youth to the party's ideology and its radical stance toward society. African American children in the 1950s and 1960s had seen what their parents had to go through to make a living and had seen their spirits beaten down. They grew up during the television age and had witnessed African countries getting their freedom, the Emmett Till case, the Vietnamese people fighting for their freedom, and Bull Connor's dogs biting little black kids dressed for school, and this outraged many of them. Andrew Rollins noted: "When the four little Black girls were killed in the church in Birmingham I refused to march in a protest endorsed by the NAACP, my father asked me, 'Son don't you care about your people?' I replied, 'Yes I do, but before I participate in any more marches you all need to start talking like that man in New York City [referring to Malcolm X].'"[19]

The national party set up a variety of programs, which included a free breakfast program for children, free health clinics, free legal service, voter registration drives, black caucuses within unions, liberation schools, and a free clothing program. The Kansas City chapter successfully launched three major survival programs: the free breakfast program, black history classes, and free health screening for sickle cell and hypertension.[20] The free breakfast for schoolchildren was operated out of a local church. Initially, two sites were launched. Members of the Kansas City chapter visited local entrepreneurs and asked that they return a portion of what they had profited from the community by making a donation to the breakfast program. The ideas that influenced the program were that poor and oppressed children could not learn without proper nutrients, and breakfast was the most important meal.[21]

The health-care screening program was initiated with the assistance of African American physicians and other health-care professionals. The primary goal was to increase awareness of health issues in the African American community, and sickle cell and hypertension screening were among the services offered. Health care became an issue that encouraged many community residents who were afraid of the party's activities to embrace the activities of Black Panthers.[22] Rollins exclaimed: "We showed the people that we loved them by organizing the survival programs; that we cared for them more than the system. Also, we conducted political education classes when children came to breakfast or when members of the community attended the health clinics."[23]

The survival programs received different emphasis depending on the type of local support the heartland chapters were receiving. For example, while health-care screening and the free breakfast program were a focus in the Kansas City chapter, the Omaha and Des Moines chapters emphasized survival programs addressing a particular need that resonated in the community. However, because the members rotated between the three cities to operate the survival programs, authorities were unsure how many members were in a chapter. The Omaha BPP chapter started several survival programs, including a liberation school, political education classes, and a free breakfast program. Henry Poindexter recalled, "We published our own NCCF [National Committee to Combat Fascism] newsletter, held political education classes for the community, and sold BPP newspapers."[24] According to Murdock Platner, the liberation school operated at 2616 Parker Street in North Omaha.[25] The curriculum of the school was going to focus on various aspects of the Panthers' ideology. Platner recalls: "The announcement was made when this school stated that they were going to follow the teachings of Eldridge Cleaver, Huey P. Newton, and all the rest of the people who advocated revolution and the overthrow of the Government. In their public announcement to the press this is what they said they were going to have."[26]

The *Omaha World-Herald* also reported on the educational activities of the Omaha Black Panthers in an article, "Inside Labor: Black Panthers Tell Smirkers That They Mean Business": "Members must read two hours a day. Attendance is compulsory at two three-hour sessions weekly on revolutionary thought, theory and pragmatic action. . . . They have their own set of bibles. There are 12 to be exact: Among them are Mao's thoughts, Lin Piao's . . . , *The Communist Manifesto*, Lenin, and several Malcolm X books. . . . The rule is each member must 'own' and be proficient in the use of at least two guns."[27]

The BPP chapter in Omaha also coordinated the development of an organization that would both politically educate and instill cultural pride in young black students attending the local Omaha public schools.[28] The organization, called Black Association for Nationalism Through Unity (BANTU), was organized at Technical High School under the leadership of NCCF member Robert Griffin. The attempt to infiltrate the public schools did not go unnoticed. Platner noted: "During March of 1969 and June of 1969 the Black Panthers tried to organize . . . BANTU. The attempt to organize this was in Technical High School in Omaha. Robert Griffin is listed as a minister of student affairs in our records."[29]

The *World-Herald* reported that members of BANTU riding in a car were stopped and arrested by police officers during the Vivian Strong riots. In an article entitled "North Side Violence Continues a 3rd Night," the paper noted: "The occupants included Robert Cecil, 16, a leader of the Black Association for Nationalism Through Unity (BANTU) a wing of the Black Panthers. Police said it was a routine investigation. In the car were two shotguns, a rifle and two cameras. . . . The five were taken to Central Police station, questioned and released. . . . The weapons were returned to them."[30]

The members of the Kansas City chapter also collaborated with the Des Moines chapter in developing survival programs. Following the model designed by the national party, the Des Moines BPP chapter successfully started two survival programs, a drug and alcohol program and a free breakfast program. The drug and alcohol program emerged out of the need to insist cadres not consume alcohol while conducting Panther business. For example, it was discussed that a Panther could not be effective and function for the people because alcohol caused the body to deteriorate. According to Charles Knox:

What happened out of that was a series of lectures on alcoholism, this . . . need to talk about treating people who did have the problem and launched us into say Des Moines bringing people, taking people, to Kansas City to get treatment for drugs, for drug addition right; because Des Moines did not have a center. Or Kansas City when the person can't go there, go into Des Moines, if Des Moines had something or Omaha. So you see we moved into those areas because of necessity.[31]

The Des Moines BPP also successfully developed a free breakfast program that emerged out of the practical needs of the local African American population. Many African American leaders would not admit to the misery and did not like to discuss the level of hunger in the black community. The Des Moines chapter concentrated on issues related to malnutrition because traditional organizations were not addressing hunger in the community.[32] The financial independence of the party also made it a threat in the eyes of certain people because there was no reliance on government or state aid. Knox recalled:

So this is what we raised that other people were afraid to raise, that your organizations were afraid to raise because they would lose their money. But since we were not funded by anybody [laughter], we had no accountability to anybody but the people. This is why the masses of people had gravitated towards us. While the system saw a need to try to move to destroy us, try to infiltrate us, and destroy us, it would rise to a popular movement because of the kinds of problems that we were addressing.[33]

Therefore the creation of a free breakfast program was a practical response to the needs of the Des Moines community that ultimately allowed the BPP to connect with other communities of concern. With both the breakfast program and the drug and alcohol program, the Des Moines Panthers linked the concerns of African Americans with poor whites. Knox said:

Because they were going to school inadequately nourished and cold. . . . We were at the bottom of the system and we understood the problems better than anyone else. And how did we address them, we went ahead and established a breakfast program and didn't have any money. So look at how it works, if we can establish a breakfast program with no money—by donation—and the system has all of the money with taxes, why don't they have a national free breakfast program for children? which happened after the party established a free breakfast program for the children.[34]

Seventy-five to 100 elementary and junior high school children of different races and backgrounds were fed by the free breakfast program in Des Moines.[35] The free breakfast program was supported by other churches, including white denominations. Rev. Robert Kanagy, pastor of the predominantly white Forest Avenue Baptist Church, said, "We feel it's worthwhile or we wouldn't be involved in it. It serves a need that is real. I would hope that next year it might be done by the schools, where it ought to be."[36]

The conflicting ideologies between the BPP and local civil rights organizations apparently did not prohibit some local cooperation between the Kansas City BPP and the NAACP. The Kansas City Black Panther chapter earned a mandate of support from the NAACP. The Panthers were well integrated into the community, and party leaders were invited to sit on committees, speak as representatives of the community, and participate in community activities.[37] Party members were invited to sit on the United Fund disbursement committee. Party members met with groups of prison mothers and community celebrities to address specific issues. An example was a time when a new radio station was going to enter the market. The community invited the party to serve with them as spokespersons for the type of programming that would be acceptable. Petitions to deny licenses for television stations showing programs that were considered demeaning to the community were some of the actions taken by the party with the local community. In addition to the BPP, Kansas City had a group of young black entrepreneurs, calling themselves the Social Action

Committee of 20 (SAC 20). They worked in conjunction with the BPP on a number of occasions to open avenues of economic success for the community. Also, Kansas City BPP members had close alliances with organizations of welfare mothers, church community outreach workers, religious missionaries, and others.[38]

Challenges

The challenges that impacted the Kansas City BPP emerged out of Martin Luther King Jr.'s assassination, the segregated education and repression of angry black youth attempting to publicly mourn King, the BPP's national "Free Huey campaign," deteriorating economic conditions, residential segregation and white flight, and finally the repression by the state (represented by the local police). According to Rollins, black students were upset that school classes had not been called off following King's assassination; therefore, black teenagers from the segregated black high school organized a peaceful march to commemorate King. Rollins recalled:

My father told me not to go because the police would harm us. I was training to be a musician (I was a big fan of John Coltrane). However, following the Watts rebellion of 1965, I had a declining interest in studying music. After the King assassination, I put my instrument down and decided to become a revolutionary to fight for the liberation of Black people. The march by the students was ultimately stopped by police because of the use of violence and tear gas on the marchers.[39]

Increasingly, African American students were questioning the education they were receiving in schools and in many cases were openly fighting for a change in the curriculum. An article in the *Kansas City Star*, entitled "Youths Aim to Regain Black Identity," represented the views of a black youth who said:

We used to be ashamed of our African heritage because White people had conditioned us to see Africa as a backward jungle of naked cannibals. . . . We denied our ancestral identity in effect withdrawing from reality and thinking we were better or superior because we were American. . . . But now we see that our Black brothers in Africa are . . . ruling their own nation and managing their own affairs. . . . And we over here are still fighting to drink a cup of coffee in a public café. . . . We really are not better off at all. In fact we are not only hurting by American standards . . . we are hurting by international standards.[40]

The Kansas City BPP chapter had a good relationship with the national headquarters until differences arose over the distribution of funds related to the selling of the BPP newspaper. The Kansas City chapter followed the party line, which advocated the Ten Point Program and Platform, and the revolutionary philosophy, which included the history of African Americans interpreted through Marxism-Leninism. The party had emerged and had grown swiftly into an international organization between 1968 and 1969, and the Kansas City chapter was a part of that sudden growth, which also occurred during the "Free Huey campaign." However, the Central Committee located in Oakland was having some philosophical differences with its local branches. The party had started out as a local organization and was not organizationally prepared to grow into an international entity. Rawls recalled, "The local party was subsidiary to the National Office. However, on a day-to-day basis there was very little contact or control."[41] The leader of the Kansas City chapter, Pete O'Neal, traveled to Oakland to meet with Bobby Seale and Central Committee officers to discuss policy or strategy. Occasionally, Central Committee officers would travel to Kansas City to ensure that the party line and philosophy were being followed and that distribution of the paper continued, and sometimes issues of security were discussed. However, there was a constant tension that what was strategically feasible and beneficial to the African American masses on the East and West coasts may not be beneficial in the Midwest because of the Midwest's limited black population.[42]

The Midwest chapters were much different, in many ways. The relationship of the Kansas City BPP chapter with the Central Committee was a positive one. However, the Des Moines chapter was not in good standing with California, because of its members' refusal to sell the paper.[43] In the spring of 1970 there was an internal rupture among the leaders of the party that reflected the crisis of the national organization as a whole. Huey Newton, the driving force behind the creation of the BPP, was still incarcerated and publicly split with Eldridge Cleaver, and in the confusion and pressure of government repression, the party disintegrated.[44]

The Kansas City BPP chapter from its inception was attacked by the forces of the state in response to the chapter's activities, declared ideology of revolution, and attempt to overthrow the state. Rawls claims:

The K.C. Party was in consistent struggle with the local police, but more than that, the FBI kept the Party, as well as the families of Party members, under close surveillance. Cointelpro was in full operation from the inception of the organization of the party. Informants infiltrated the ranks of the party on a regular basis. The fight was external with Party members being arrested daily on charges that were considered "trumped up," or they were repeatedly being accused of possession of drugs and drug related paraphernalia. The internal fight was the continued destruction of Party property by infiltrators. For example, food for the breakfast program being rendered unusable, like a case of eggs inadvertently being dropped.[45]

The local enmity of the Kansas City Police Department was intense. Local news media worked in conjunction with the police to destroy the image of the party and limit its popularity with law-abiding citizens. Rawls asserted:

The local police *pigs* and their racist and oppressive treatment of both the African American community generally and the Party member specifically were the source of many articles and rallies in the community. One particular incident that warrants mention is an article that was written for the Black Panther paper with the headline that *The People of Kansas City were Ecstatic* because a police officer had been shot. That article was picked up by the *Kansas City Star* and touted as an example of the Party's anti-police rhetoric and the danger that the Party presented to the police.[46]

The Response

The response of the Kansas City BPP chapter revolved around several strategies that included a Marxist-Leninist vanguard orientation; the promulgation of the Central Committee's Ten Point Program and Platform; a strong antiracist message; the utilization of local African American slang and cultural concepts to communicate the party's message; and the strategy of using various forms of media to communicate to black residents. Andrew Rollins recalls:

The Party considered itself the Vanguard of the Revolution. We were organized according to the Leninist theory of the necessity of a vanguard element to bring about revolution. We considered ourselves soldiers of the people. We were committed to fight and die if necessary for the cause of liberation. Our structure was a disciplined military structure with a chain of command. We functioned on a need to know basis and we realized we were in a life and death struggle.[47]

However, because the party was a revolutionary nationalist organization, criteria relevant to African Americans were included in the rhetoric. The Ten Point Program and Platform, which was primarily targeted toward the mobilization of African Americans, was the foundation for all of the party's rhetoric.[48] The party's message was a revolutionary message, and the essence of the rhetoric was the government must be overthrown. Rollins claimed: "It was the government that maintained the political, legal, police and military system, which exploited African Americans. It was also the government which developed and maintained the educational system which crippled the minds of our people."[49]

Members of the BPP understood how racism had impacted the lives of African Americans. The Kansas City BPP used unique rhetorical methods of combating racism in the Kansas City community. Rawls recalls, "We used to have what we called 'Hang the Honkie' parties. This was where we could get a group of young white students who wanted to be exposed to The Party, and explain in fine detail the atrocities of slavery and degradation of oppression." Rawls describes the effectiveness of the gatherings: "If they, (whites) did not leave afraid and in tears we would not have considered the party successful. We would begin by discussing how Africans were stolen from Africa, packed like sardines in the slave ships, seasoned in the West Indies, and sold as slaves to build this country." Finally, Rawls remembered, "The detail would be graphic. Racism was combated by discussion of entitlement to determine our own destiny."[50]

Andrew Rollins remembered: "In our message we taught about the history of White racism in America. America was founded upon the genocide of one race, the Native Americans, and the enslavement of another, the African American. We also examined the various kinds of White racism namely: Institutional racism, individual racism, overt racism and covert racism."[51]

The Kansas City Panthers also maintained strict discipline. Rollins notes, "In keeping Party discipline, the Kansas City branch followed the *Party Line* developed by the Central Committee."[52] The basic difference between the rhetoric of the party and the rhetoric of the civil rights establishments was that the party's rhetoric was revolutionary, and the civil rights establishment's rhetoric was reformist.[53]

In Kansas City, Des Moines, and Omaha, political rallies were the primary form, outside of self-help programs, for the communication of ideas. In addition, the distribution of the *Black Panther*, flyers, pamphlets, and local newsletters that addressed specific topics were all modes of communication. Rawls also claimed that open political education classes and free summer school sessions for children and young adults were other methods of educating and communicating party ideas. Additionally, songs, poetry, and art were used to communicate the party line. For example, a song sung by the sisters included the lines:

No more brothers in jail
Pig's are gonna catch hell
Revolution has come
Time to pick up the gun.

Or there were these words from a revolutionary poem by Alprentice "Bunchy" Carter:

Black mother I must confess that I still breath
Though you are not yet freed
What could justify, my crying start
Forgive my coward heart
For I have just awakened from a deep deep sleep
And I be hazed and dazed and scared and vipers fester in my hair.

This poem ends with the line, "a slave who dies a natural death cannot balance out to two dead flies." This was a frequently quoted adage in the party.[54]

In conclusion, the political response of the Kansas City BPP was consistent with the Ten Point Program and Platform of the Central Committee. African American urban culture of the time, however, was unique in addressing racism with "Hang the Honkie" parties.

Demise of the Kansas City BPP

Four major causes led to the demise of the Kansas City BPP. First, the party lost the support of the local black civil rights establishment. Second, the Kansas City black elite was co-opted by support from the white power elite. Third, there was a marked increase in local state repression. Finally, internal BPP dissension hastened the demise of the Kansas Black Panthers. Initially, the relationship had been outwardly positive between the Kansas City BPP and the NAACP; however, the public relationship between the BPP and the NAACP changed after the shooting incident in which a white police officer was killed and the Kansas City BPP approved of the killing. Local NAACP leader Herman Johnson criticized the party for its stance in a newspaper article. The *Kansas City Star*, in an article entitled "Would Soften Panther View, Black Leaders Believe Most Decry Dacy Slaying," quoted Johnson as saying: "If Black people in Kansas City have any emotion about the recent slaying of John Edward Dacy, a White patrolman, that emotion is regret. . . . The Black Panthers are wrong in stating in their national publication that Black people here are ecstatic about the death of the officer."[55]

Although the members of the party did not back down from their statement concerning Officer Dacy, members of other civil rights organizations were equally critical of Chief Clarence Kelley and the local police force. Leon Jordan, leader of Freedom Inc., exclaimed that he was "not discouraged by the Panthers. . . . They see into some issues deeper than other people. . . . I am more disappointed in Kelley's statement. . . . Chief Kelley is a person with military and political power. He has an army, weapons, and the legal right to declare war. Pete O'Neal has none of that."[56]

The killing of Officer Dacy was a public relations disaster for the local party, for while the killing of Dacy may have been popular among the black underclass, the more conservative liberal black middle class was disturbed, and their organizations began to position themselves to quietly seize back the leadership of the African American community.

The *Kansas City Star* would be one of the primary vehicles for the local power elite to influence public opinion against the Black Panthers and point to the activities of responsible blacks working within the system. For example, in the months following a Panther incident at the municipal courthouse, the *Star* printed several articles about the future economic growth of the Kansas City area, future white flight, and the co-opting of the black petit bourgeoisie. The economic growth of the Kansas City metro area was tied to the development of the Crown Center redevelopment program. The *Star* reported in an article entitled "Progress 1969":

Most of these developments are in the first phase of four construction phases which are to make Crown Center by 1983, a unique central city concentration of homes (town houses and both high-rise and garden style apartments), upwards of 1 million square feet of offices in more than eight structures, the hotel and two motor inns, a cultural center, shops, restaurants and movie theatres and parking for upwards of 7,000 cars. . . . Fifty new buildings are programmed.[57]

The black bourgeoisie historically had been co-opted by the white power structure. However, following the King assassination in 1968, the black bourgeoisie or upper class was mute and in some ways was not antagonistic toward some of the activities of the black radicals. However, by mid-1969 this situation had changed. The BPP, locally in Kansas City and nationally, had been under heavy repression from the federal government since April 1969.[58] At the same time that the black revolution was being crushed locally and nationally, overtures were made to the black business class, which included local Kansas City citizens. Following the *Star*'s criticism of black revolutionaries apparently celebrating the death of a police officer and the urging of reprisals by police chief Kelley, the local power elite voted to deposit $100,000 into the black-owned Swope Parkway National Bank. The *Star*, in an August article entitled "School Funds to Negro Bank," reported: "The board action represents a shift from a stand in February when four of six school board members voted against putting $115,000 of Teacher Corps money in the bank. Henry Poindexter, board vice-president, voiced the majority view at that time when he said: 'We have created a lot of ill will in the banking community by practicing discrimination in reverse.'"[59]

The carrot-and-stick approach was used to offer some incentives for middle-class and upper-class blacks to support the American way of life (that is, affirmative action, educational opportunities, and minority set-aside programs). Those elements in the community that did not comply would be killed or incarcerated. This example of the practice of the carrot-and-stick approach to the African American community would be expanded nationally and locally to suppress radical activities in the African American community.[60] However, this action was also similar to what was going on in many former colonial nations; as the white residents were largely abandoning the inner city, the local power elite was ensuring that a certain class of the dominated ethnic group would remain to oversee the control and supervision of the colonized residents.

The framing of the Kansas City BPP's position in the aftermath of the death of Officer Dacy not only cost the party liberal black and some white support but also justified the repression of the party in the cause of law and order. In an August 1, 1969, article entitled "Panther View of Dacy Death," the *Star* wrote: "This week's issue of the Black Panther Party's national newspaper carries an article from Kansas City reporting 'ecstatic' reaction to the fatal shooting here last week of Patrolman John Edward Dacy. . . . Chief Kelley said last night the police officers shared a disgust over the article and added, 'I think that this type of thing indicates practically an open declaration of war.'"[61]

The article in question had been written by Andre (Weatherby) Rawls, then communications secretary in the Kansas City chapter, and appeared in the July 22, 1969, issue of the national BPP paper.[62] Entitled "Kansas City Fascist Pig Performing Final Duty," the article reported: "The people of Kansas City are in an ecstatic state today following the execution of a pig. Three unknown heroic brothers had the pleasure of offing a pig. . . . Dacy was a well known pig and well known exploiter of Black people. . . . Only on the Bones of the Oppressor can the People be founded. Only the Blood of the Oppressor can fertilize the soil for the People's self rule."[63]

In short, the demise of the Kansas City BPP can be attributed to some tactical errors related to the events surrounding the Dacy killing, which opened the door for more moderate black political formations to seize the impetus from the party. However, the reaction of the local party was due to the fact that government repression was intense. Party members had been brutalized, harassed, and imprisoned, and this reality probably caused them to strategically err in fighting for public opinion.

The Kansas City BPP emerged as a revolutionary vanguard party in January 1969 dedicated to opposing international capitalism and resisting the powers of the state. For example, in February, several weeks following the Kansas City chapter's public emergence, the BPP organized a local rally at the Gregg Community Center that drew several hundred people. The *Kansas City Star*, in its February 17 edition, reported in an article entitled "Large Turnout For Panthers:

The Black Panther Party served notice on White Kansas City yesterday afternoon that a revolution is coming if Black demands for justice and equality are not soon satisfied. . . . "We were forced to build this country." Pete O'Neal, deputy chairman of the party, said, "and if forced to we'll tear this . . . down!" "People are afraid of the word revolution," said Bill Whitfield, deputy minister of information. "They know the Black Panther Party are *Revolutionary* people. The system must be changed. We can't go on living the way we're living. . . . The revolution is coming."[64]

By the summer of 1969, when Officer Dacy was killed, the entire national organization had been under heavy repression by federal, state, and local authorities since earlier that spring. The local nationalistic bourgeoisie, Rollins remembers, "seemingly began to abandon support of the party following this incident and would eventually pursue electoral politics and affirmative action programs in the 1970s following the demise of the Kansas City Party."[65]

The repression by authorities intensified after Fred Hampton was killed in Chicago in December 1969. The Kansas City chapter was faced with a heavy police raid and would surely have been annihilated except for the arrival of some black preachers who surrounded the Panther headquarters.[66] The Kansas City BPP and the Central Committee vigorously opposed the power of the state to oppress and punish. Both entities attacked the brutality of the police and criticized the armed bodies of men who descended upon the black community as occupying armies. The Kansas City BPP and the Central Committee were also infiltrated by agents provocateur. Following the defeat of the Kansas City chapter, cadre members agreed not to communicate with each other for fear of observation and repression. "We would walk past each other on the street and nod at each other and not talk, for we were also not sure who were agents for the system or if we were under surveillance," said Rollins.[67] The Kansas City branch of the BPP was finally crushed and largely driven underground by January 1970. Peter O'Neal and his wife, Charlotte, were on the run at this time, fleeing to Africa.

Finally, it was revealed a couple of years later to a certain extent how long the federal authorities had been observing the activities and collecting intelligence on the Kansas City BPP. The U.S. House Committee on Internal Security, chaired by Congressman Richard H. Ichord of Missouri, convened hearings, for public consumption, to determine to what extent the Panthers were a threat to the internal security of the United States. The most interesting fact that emerged was the information that the Kansas City BPP had been under intense surveillance by the federal authorities since January 1969 following the changing of the name from Black Vigilantes, a local militant group, to the BPP, a revolutionary vanguard organization.

Following the Kansas City Panthers' public emergence, the local power elite began publishing editorials praising the benefits of working within the system. Although whites were abandoning urban centers all over the country, the need existed to establish a neocolonial relationship with the highly segregated urban population centers. The *Kansas City Star* opposed the ideological position of the BPP. Following the January 9 public emergence of the BPP in Kansas City, the *Kansas City Star* printed a series of articles that supported "Negro" capitalism. The paper reported: "Negro owned business enterprises in Kansas City are growing in number. Dozens of successes have been recorded in comparatively recent years. Many Negroes are forming an opinion that an improved climate now exists for their business success and are seeking the knowledge to participate."[68]

Finally, and perhaps most important, the party was undermined by the limited economic overture of the Philadelphia Plan—a government program later referred to as affirmative action—and antihunger programs similar to the free breakfast program. Affirmative action enabled qualified middle-class blacks to pursue careers in professions and jobs that had historically been denied to qualified African Americans and would impact the ability of the Panthers to recruit nationalist-oriented, middle-class blacks into their leadership cadre. Many scholarships were offered to black students to go to college. The government's introduction of the free breakfast program as a part of the federal budget, along with other federal programs targeting the black underclass lumpen, would also sap the ability to recruit rank-and-file soldiers from the black underclass for the black revolution.

However, Huey Newton's imprisonment and inability to influence daily operations, Eldridge Cleaver's erratic behavior, and Bobby Seale's limited ability contributed to the destruction of the organizational effectiveness of the party by the end of 1969. Seale's ability was especially limited due to his own incarceration and his inability to lead the various factions within the party. The destabilization of the Kansas City leadership involved the charges of transporting weapons across state line by Pete O'Neal and the repeated incarceration of the local leadership. As a result of the repression by authorities, by the beginning of 1970 the Kansas City chapter was no longer an effective functioning BPP affiliate.

The rhetoric of the Kansas City chapter members was effective in communicating the party's message because they would historicize from an African

American perspective. The utilization of Marxism and Leninism from an African American perspective allowed the Panthers to relate systematically to the black population the impact of the historic racist economic practices of capitalists on African Americans, as a distinct population, from slavery through segregation. Also, using words like "pig" to describe the police effectively demonstrated to blacks that the police were there to serve the community but instead were occupying armies in the community to protect the interests of the capitalist state.

Psychologically, the Kansas City Panthers, along with the rest of the national organization, would have a tremendous impact on the consciousness of African Americans, particularly on youth. The radical perspective the Panthers introduced into the black American population irreversibly influenced the community, particularly the black underclass, to violently oppose oppression. Following the dictum "repression breeds resistance," the Kansas City chapter and the national organization believed that the African American community would be psychologically transformed by the black revolution. The introduction of black studies programs in Kansas and Missouri was one outgrowth of this phenomenon. For example, the campus black student upheavals in conjunction with the Panther programs initiated the introduction of black history courses at Kansas State University.[69] In another instance, within a few short years between 1965 and 1968, almost an entire population shifted from a Negro referent to a black referent. However, a drawback of trying to revolutionize the black lumpen or underclass was the fact that many simply did not have the discipline to become good revolutionaries. For example, many of the more dedicated members of the Kansas City cadre were from working-class backgrounds or families or had been exposed to better elements of American society.

Consequences

A string of events contributed to dissension within the national and local leadership of the BPP and eventually caused its demise. Andre Rawls noted that during 1969 and 1970, events occurred that resulted in her exit from the party. Rawls asserts that after Fred Hampton and Mark Clark were killed in December 1969, police attacks against the party accelerated nationally.[70] The Kansas City chapter continued to function as an arm of the BPP while chapters in both Iowa and Nebraska were dissolving and becoming increasingly involved in court battles. These battles eventually resulted in their demise.

By the spring of 1970 the party was in disarray. Rawls began to drift from the party around March 1970 after leading a demonstration of high school students to address perceived ills at their school, which resulted in the entire group being shot with tear gas. Rawls left the city and went to live in St. Louis. In early 1970 the Kansas City chapter separated from the national organization and changed its name from the BPP to the Sons of Malcolm and later to the Heirs of Malcolm when someone pointed out that Malcolm X had only daughters. As the Heirs of Malcolm, the group continued to hold weekly political education classes that were open to the community but were usually attended by party members. They published their own newsletter for free distribution in the community. The free health clinic remained opened for about one year, but eventually closed because the services there were underutilized and resources were sparse. The breakfast program continued; however, donations in some areas were more difficult to obtain. Members of the group were still called upon to speak in a number of settings about the party's programs and political line.

In mid-1970 Pete O'Neal, the leader of the Kansas City chapter, fled the city to avoid a lengthy jail sentence, which would have resulted from him having been seen with weapons while on probation. Pete and his wife, Charlotte, left Kansas City by underground means and went to live in Algeria, in North Africa, with Eldridge Cleaver and other political exiles. The resources on the home front continued to dwindle, and eventually there was a very small band of predominantly brothers (diehards) who comprised the revolutionary cadre.[71] Rawls recalls: "One of my last activities with the party was in November of 1971 when Kathleen Cleaver visited Kansas City and spoke at Park College, in Parkville, Missouri. At that time she and her family were living in Algiers with Pete and the others. During her visit we were able to communicate by telephone with Pete. Kathleen was in the area for about two days, which was fully scheduled with appearances and speaking."[72]

In conclusion, the Kansas City Black Panthers were representative of the social exigencies that fueled the black revolution. The Kansas City BPP emerged during the Central Committee's revolutionary nationalist phase and the "Free Huey campaign." During its short history, the local party attempted to represent the interests of the African American masses in Kansas City with some successes and did strengthen the hand of the black bourgeoisie in their dealings with the white establishment. Finally, the Kansas City BPP represented the attempt by revolutionary movements to effect structural change at the local level in the world system and failed because of the repression of the state and the dissension within the national organization.

The stated purpose of this study was to analyze the political strategies of the heartland Kansas City BPP during the black revolution from 1968 to 1971. From a framework focusing on local perspectives, the study provides an analysis of the heartland Kansas City BPP's development from the late 1960s to September 1971. Second, the study provides insight into the context, choices, and effectiveness of the heartland Kansas City BPP cadres. Finally, through this study, theories have emerged about the role political activities played in local activities of the BPP.

The study reflects the importance and value of analyzing a movement from a local perspective to gain a perspective that may be different in some respect from that of national leaders. For example, the political strategies of the heartland BPP chapters were adapted to meet local exigencies. This was demonstrated in how local chapters would work with civil rights organizations or progressive white organizations. Additionally, the study demonstrates how local repression operated in concert with federal authorities. For example, the federal government observed all local chapters, and outright police repression and agents provocateur were used against the Kansas City chapter. Also, the study shows how it is difficult for a national message to be transmitted to the local level. The incarceration of Newton, Seale, and other Panther leaders from the Central Committee made it difficult to communicate effectively with the entire organization. This made it easier to create dissension within the party with agents provocateur, and made it harder for the leadership to maintain contact with the masses. Finally, the study examines how local conditions can impede the progress of a movement. For example, the cultural conservatism or regional focus of some heartland BPP members may have made them wary of certain social behaviors or strategies of cadres from the West Coast in regards to drug use and contradictory stances or attitudes toward women.

The heartland chapters, following the lead of the national BPP, attempted to establish survival programs to build support in their local communities to oppose the capitalist establishment in their communities. The anticapitalist dimension was connected to the survival programs. The heartland chapters initiated these efforts to persuade local African American communities that there were alternatives to capitalism that could ameliorate social conditions. Additionally, the heartland chapters developed survival programs unique to their locales based upon the recognition that alcohol and drugs were problems with which the black community needed to deal. However, these entities were limited in their effectiveness because of government initiatives related to the co-optation of local black elites or the local civil rights establishment. Although there was some initial cooperation with the black civil rights community, these initiatives were abandoned when the BPP made political miscalculations or criticized community organizations for being "poverty pimps."

These co-optation initiatives increased enrollment of black students in college and created affirmative action, free lunch and breakfast programs, and other federal programs that targeted the populations from which the Panthers drew their support. To oppose state power, the vanguard party dimension of the heartland chapters was characterized by the actions and politics of the local BPP cadres. For example, between the spring of 1968 and January 1969, all of the heartland chapters emerged in response to the King assassination, were recruited and trained during the "Free Huey campaign," adopted the revolutionary nationalist ideology of the national organization, and participated in behaviors designed to politically educate local African American communities and enlist their participation in the black revolution. Also, all three heartland chapters were attacked by forces of the state in the form of the police and other security forces of the United States.

The internal dynamics of the heartland chapters' political practice was crippled due to poor leadership and government repression. The heartland chapters were unable to effectively respond to government repression because of the Central Committee's poor leadership. The Central Committee was unable to establish any bases for cadres to train in urban guerrilla warfare or counterinsurgency that may have enabled the organization to survive longer. The leadership of the Central Committee during the period in question would have to be considered mediocre at best and atrocious at worst because of counterrevolutionary behavior at the Oakland headquarters that betrayed the hope and dreams of the local cadres who were incarcerated. Huey Newton, the inspirational founder of the organization, had the skills to start a local organization but was not prepared to promulgate a national revolution. Finally, the discipline of the party was in question because of its rapid growth, which permitted too many incompetent, overly romantic, unstable people to join the party's ranks.

However, there were different degrees of effectiveness between the three chapters. For example, the Omaha chapter was in operation as a BPP cadre for a shorter period of time than the Des Moines and Kansas City chapters. Also, the heartland chapters dissented from the policy of the national organization over the issue of selling newspapers and political education. The Omaha chapter was dissolved by the national organization within several months of its founding and was re-formed as an NCCF chapter under the supervision of the Kansas City chapter. Finally, by the spring of 1971 all of the heartland chapters ceased to be cadres of the national organization and began pursing local initiatives.

The antiracist dimension of the party was a consistent feature of the political practice of the heartland chapters, and there was some coalition building across racial lines, particularly with progressive local white religious denominations. However, the local cadres were never able to build any mass participation between whites and blacks to go beyond initiatives that had been gained as a result of the civil rights movement. Finally, the media effectively distorted the behavior of the party and terrified most whites and conservative blacks.

However, within the black community, the antiracist dimension of the heartland Panthers' rhetoric was effective because of its ability to mobilize the support of the African American community and positively impact the psychology of young African Americans. Heartland chapters were able to systematically relate to their communities the impact of racism and the impact of capitalism on the underdevelopment of the black community. Finally, the local cadres were able to utilize the historic mistreatment of blacks by the police to their rhetorical advantage by demonstrating that the police were not their community servants but were occupying armies that were there to protect the interests of capitalism. The psychological dimension of the heartland chapters' rhetoric was extremely effective in two areas: cultural identity and education. The rhetoric of the heartland chapters was effective in addressing and transforming the personality of the black community to adopt a more aggressive stance vis-à-vis the larger society and was able to gain some concessions as a result of these actions that, within a couple of years, transformed the Negro community to the black community. Finally, the political strategies of the heartland cadres influenced the inclusion of educational initiatives in secondary and university education that began to address the historical deficiencies in African American education.

In conclusion, the Kansas City BPP and other heartland cadres experienced defeats and victories, which impacted the future development of black politics in the United States. For example, the party at the local and national levels put power elites under pressure to reform the American polity. Second, valuable lessons were learned concerning the extent to which local political strategies could be used in attempting to reconstruct the American polity. Third, the political dimensions of the national and local BPP cadres demonstrated the possibilities and limitations of coalitions across racial lines. Also, the utilization of certain rhetorical strategies by party members galvanized a large section of the black community, forcing the African American population to reassess its relationship and its interests with respect to American society. Finally, when the BPP and its heartland cadres were defeated, this was consistent with the results of other revolutions in the world system circa 1968–1971; however, their *struggle* was in the tradition of previous African American rebellions and did ultimately have an impact on future trends such as multicultural education, affirmative action, food programs, and other services that are now taken for granted and are attributed to the civil rights movement and not the black revolution. Following the incarceration or death of several important members of the heartland chapters and the split with the national organization, Andre (Weatherby) Rawls, Charles Knox, Art Bronson, and other cadres formed the Black Revolutionary Party (BRP) in January 1971. The Kansas City chapter of the BPP and other heartland chapters left the national organization in the winter/spring of 1970. The BRP coordinated several political entities and engaged in international politics and programs before the fragmentation of the organization by the summer of 1972.[73]

The heartland BPP's transformation into the BRP guided or influenced several organizations to include local black student unions at colleges in the region to include Omaha, Des Moines, and Kansas City.[74] The BRP also worked with returning black Vietnam veterans, the Venceremos Brigade (an organization dedicated to supporting the Cuban Revolution), Operation Spearhead (a black tutorial program), the Free Angela Davis Committee, the Black Methodists for Church Renewal (BMCR), Rev. Phil Lawson, and the Cairo, Illinois, Black United Front with Rev. Charles Cohen.[75]

The Aftermath and Decline of Black Politics

African American politics was impacted by several factors. Black incorporation and institutionalization, presidential policy making, limitations on civil rights, symbolic politics, and racial symbolism impacted African American politics. The de-radicalization of the black freedom movement of the late 1960s and early 1970s was due to a dual strategy involving assassination and co-optation implemented by North American political economic elites. The incorporation and institutionalization of the black political/economic class operated in a top-to-bottom hierarchal fashion. The elite sectors in the United States include the corporate, government, and public interest arenas and involve over several thousand individuals not responsible to any democratic process. Of these several thousand elite positions, only twenty were occupied by African Americans by 1990, including Thurgood Marshall, Colin Powell, Andrew Brimmer, Patricia Harris, and others.[76]

As a result of affirmative action initiatives initiated during the Johnson administration, elections of urban officials, and larger representation in congress, the black middle class was successfully co-opted. However, the black middle class was symbolically and materially threatened by the efforts of the American conservative movement to sharply curtail civil rights and anoint their own conservative black leadership cadre.[77] Finally, at the same time the black middle class and upper class were incorporated and institutionalized, the black underclass was impacted by incarceration and drugs. The U.S. drug culture exploded in the late 1970s and early 1980s largely because of the influx of new criminal elements, joblessness, government reduction of public assistance, and the need for the U.S. government to raise money for covert operations.[78]

The impact of blacks in the presidential policy-making process steadily declined following the defeat of the black revolution in 1975. The Nixon administration had recruited African Americans with connections to the larger African American community such as Art Fletcher, who helped formulate set-asides for minorities in government contracts in the early 1970s.[79] However, under subsequent administrations, the African American community continued to lose influence in the policy arena for one main reason: Republicans realized they could govern without African American support.[80] This trend would continue until the election of Bill Clinton as president in 1992; however, many of the blacks who became members of his cabinet were not of the African American community civic society and had been members of the Democratic Leadership Committee (DLC), a more conservative elite political formation within the Democratic Party, following presidential electoral losses in the mid-1980s, to move the party away from liberal-leaning politics.

The influence of civil rights on the national conscience has steadily eroded since the late 1960s over two issues, busing and affirmative action. Although several black congressional leaders attempted to influence ideas that would restrict busing in exchange for increased financial support of predominantly African American school districts, the attempt was undermined by the NAACP and other civil rights leaders.[81] This important political miscalculation was the Vietnam of the civil rights establishment. The civil rights establishment strategically pursued busing as a tactic to get black children out of poor segregated schools instead of bargaining for increased resources for urban schools. Civil rights leaders argued for busing and integrated schools, which influenced white flight and abandonment of public education in many urban centers. This miscalculation impacted the national polity in three areas: rising racial conflict, a split in the black leadership organizations, and symbolic issues used by conservative administrations to appeal to voters.[82] Affirmative action politics have not been, in the twenty or so years following the implementation of affirmative action, commensurate with the political capital African Americans have spent on the programs. The symbolic politics following the black revolution were largely represented in the idea of a mythic rainbow coalition that was based on two ideas. First, because blacks represented approximately 20 percent of the vote for Democratic politicians, it was postulated the Democratic Party could be reformed. Second, nonblacks would ally with blacks to form a multiethnic coalition. A coalition was difficult because the majority of Asians, Latinos, and almost half of whites believed that blacks were prone to violence. Jesse Jackson, at the height of his success in 1988, never received substantial support from other minorities beyond the African American community.[83]

Finally, in regards to racial symbolism, by the late 1980s and early 1990s political pundits were blaming African Americans for a rightward shift in the American polity. The new racial symbolism contributed to a new orthodoxy in politics in which liberal political theorists supported the notion that blacks caused the political Left to collapse, although race had been a prominent feature in American politics since the country's inception.[84]

The decline of liberalism in the late 1960s led to a disturbing rise in what was referred to as the "new racist discourse," which characterizes new descriptions of cultural or family values, generates new topoi of racism, and shares similar forms across the ideological spectrum; those on the ideological Right celebrate the local, are monoculturalists, do not support the idea of a politically constructed multicultural community, are Judeo-Christian and English, and utilize argumentative rhetoric that separates Americans based on values.[85]

The subsequent decline in political and economic liberalism in the late 1960s and early 1970s was accompanied by the Black Power movement and the subsequent black revolution that attempted to articulate a new African American discourse. Harold Cruse, in his *The Crisis of the Negro Intellectual*, argues that with the passage of the civil rights bills of the 1960s, black liberal intellectuals had arrived at a crisis of leadership.[86] Cruse maintains that African American history was primarily a history of struggle between nationalist and integrationist politics. The philosophical decline of liberalism in the 1960s and 1970s also led to a decline in the liberal philosophy of integration. The decline of liberalism, the rise of reactionary conservatism, and the repression of black revolutionary intellectuals provided an opening for African American cultural nationalist intellectuals to address the ideological crisis within the African American community. One of the concepts that emerged in the mid-1970s was the philosophy of Afrocentrism. Afrocentric philosophy points out the historical fact that peoples or ethnic groups operate either out of their own worldview or someone else's, and Afrocentrism developed first in the African diasporic community because of the objective conditions confronting that community in the wake of the decline of the universalizing philosophy of liberalism. In conclusion, the defeat of the BPP represented, for some, the last serious attempt by African Americans to develop an independent African American political apparatus in the United States. The post–civil rights era required African Americans to reorganize internally to respond to new external challenges in a multiethnic, multiracial society in the twenty-first century.

Notes

1. Immanuel Wallenstein views the world system as a social system, one that has boundaries, structures, member groups, rules of legitimization, and coherence. Its life is made up of the conflicting forces that hold it together by tension and tear it apart as each group seeks eternally to remold it to its advantage. It has the characteristics of an organism, in that it has a life span over which its characteristics change in some respects and remain stable in others. One can define its structures as being at different times strong or weak in terms of the internal logic of its functioning.

2. L. Greene, G. Kremer, and A. Holland, *Missouri's Black Heritage* (St. Louis: Form Press, 1980), 135.

3. Ibid., 128–132.

4. Ibid., 145–146.

5. Ibid., 149.

6. A. Rollins, personal communication, July 8, 2001.

7. D. Conrads, *Biography of Leon Jordan, 1905–1970: Police Detective and Political Leader*, 1999, Kansas City Public Library, http://www.kclibrary.org/localhistory/, accessed April 1, 2004.

8. Ibid.

9. Greene, Kramer, and Holland, *Missouri's Black Heritage*, 165.

10. Conrads, *Biography of Leon Jordan*.

11. Greene, Kramer, and Holland, *Missouri's Black Heritage*, 166.

12. Ibid.; Conrads, *Biography of Leon Jordan*.

13. Greene, Kramer, and Holland, *Missouri's Black Heritage*, 153–154, 155.

14. A. Rawls, personal communication, September 3, 2000.

15. Ibid.

16. Ibid.

17. Ibid.

18. Ibid.

19. Ibid.

20. Ibid.

21. Ibid.

22. Ibid.

23. Rollins, personal communication.

24. E. Poindexter, personal communication, September 10, 2002.

25. U.S. Congress, House of Representatives, Committee on Internal Security, *Hearings Before the Committee on Internal Security, Black Panther Party, Part Four: National Office Operations and Investigation of Activities in Des Moines, Iowa, and Omaha, Nebraska*, 91st Cong., 2nd sess., October 6, 7, 8, 13, 14, 15 and November 17, 1970, 4887.

26. Ibid., 4893.

27. V. Riesel, "Inside Labor: Black Panthers Tell Smirkers That They Mean Business," *Omaha World-Herald*, June 25, 1969.

28. Poindexter, personal communication.

29. *Hearings Before the Committee on Internal Security*, 4887.

30. "North Side Violence Continues a 3rd Night," *Omaha World-Herald*, June 28, 1969.

31. C. Knox, personal communication, August 21, 2000.

32. Ibid.

33. Ibid.

34. Ibid.

35. S. Szumski, "Free Meal for Needy Youngsters," *Des Moines Register*, April 23, 1966.

36. R. Kanagy, quoted in ibid.

37. Rawls, personal communication.

38. Ibid.

39. Rollins, personal communication.

40. "Youths Aim to Regain Black Identity," *Kansas City Star*, January 23, 1969.

41. Rawls, personal communication.

42. Ibid.

43. Rollins, personal communication.

44. Ibid.

45. Rawls, personal communication.

46. Ibid.

47. Rollins, personal communication.

48. Rawls, personal communication.

49. Rollins, personal communication.

50. Rawls, personal communication.

51. Rollins, personal communication.

52. Ibid.

53. Ibid.

54. Rawls, personal communication.

55. C. Hammer, "Would Soften Panther View, Black Leaders Believe Most Decry Dacy Slaying," *Kansas City Star*, August 3, 1969.

56. "Panther View of Dacy Death," *Kansas City Star*, August 1, 1969.

57. "Progress 1969," *Kansas City Star*, January 12, 1969.

58. Rollins, personal communication.

59. "School Funds to Negro Bank," *Kansas City Star*, August 7, 1969.

60. Rollins, personal communication.

61. "Panther View of Dacy Death."

62. Rawls, personal communication.

63. "Kansas City Fascist Pig Performing Final Duty," *Black Panther Party News Service*, July 22, 1969.

64. "Large Turnout for Panthers," *Kansas City Star*, February 17, 1969.

65. Rollins, personal communication.

66. Ibid.

67. Ibid.

68. "K-State Astir over Student Protests," *Kansas City Star*, January 9, 1969.

69. Rollins, personal communication.

70. Rawls, personal communication.

71. Ibid.

72. Ibid.

73. A. Bronson, personal communication, July 11, 2003.

74. Ibid.

75. Ibid.

76. R. Smith, *We Have No Leaders: African Americans in the Post–Civil Rights Era* (New York: State University of New York Press, 1996), 140.

77. Ibid., 157.

78. G. Webb, *Dark Alliance: The CIA, the Contras, and the Crack Cocaine Explosion* (New York: Seven Stories Press, 1998).

79. Smith, *We Have No Leaders*, 137.

80. Ibid., 145.

81. Ibid., 153.

82. Ibid., 170.

83. Ibid., 241, 243.

84. Ibid., 245, 246.

85. R. Lee and K. Lee, "Myths of Blood, Property, and Maternity: Exploring the Public Argumentation

of Anti-Adoption Advocates," in *Argument in a Time of Change: Definitions, Frameworks, and Critiques*, ed. J. F. Klumpp (Annandale, Va.: National Communication Association, 1998), 256–261.

86. H. Cruse, *The Crisis of the Negro Intellectual* (New York: William Morrow, 1967).

MOTOR CITY PANTHERS

Joel P. Rhodes and Judson L. Jeffries

Detroit has a long history of contentious politics and left-wing activism that has impacted virtually every realm of the city's political, social, and civic life. These struggles sometimes paid off in observable gains, but never quite succeeded in bringing about full racial equality. Black people's struggles, in particular, at various times took separatist directions and, at other times, included coalitions with groups of other races and differing ideologies such as the Communist Party and the Socialist Workers Party. These political inclinations foreshadowed later developments involving the Black Panther Party (BPP). The earliest black struggles emerged in the form of the 1833 uprising when the black community rose up to prevent blacks from being carried back into slavery.[1] The next three decades were characterized by continual struggle to acquire the franchise and gain equal educational opportunities. During the Civil War, blacks fought in the Union army, in part to help destroy slavery just as they earlier had participated in the Underground Railroad and in the abolition movement.

Later, during Reconstruction, a small number of African Americans enjoyed a modicum of political and economic success. Unfortunately, with the close of Reconstruction effectively ending black people's access to resources that were once out of reach, violence against blacks increased drastically, as if to demonstrate to them the consequence for upward mobility. This form of terror continued at alarming levels well into the early 1940s. Undaunted, African Americans continued to wage battles against such matters as housing and job discrimination and were constantly pushing back residential boundaries.

The struggle took on an economic dimension during World War II when blacks engaged in strikes and work stoppages, first to pressure management into hiring African Americans at the Chrysler Tank Arsenal and then to force the improvement of working conditions for black workers at Packard.[2] It was also during World War II that the alliance forged in the 1930s between the Communist Party and many black United Auto Workers (UAW) members was strengthened. After World War II, the black struggle took many forms and iterations. Civil rights organizations like the National Association for the Advancement of Colored People (NAACP) and the Urban League sought to obliterate racial barriers via boycotts, the courts, and backroom deals with the city's establishment; yet blacks still lagged behind in virtually every conceivable socioeconomic aspect of human life—employment, education, housing, and the like. According to the Urban League, by the end of the 1950s more and more African American job seekers were demoralized, developing patterns of boredom and hopelessness with the city's state of affairs. The frustration and despair that prevailed among the young gave rise to a new movement, one that was more strident and brash than previous ones. When Martin Luther King Jr. led a march through downtown Detroit in 1963, the movement for racial equality was beginning to take on a different tenor. These younger blacks wanted action—they eschewed the slow wheels of the courts and the more palatable tactics (as viewed by many whites) of some of the more established organizations, and formed their own groups. In no time at all, the modern civil rights movement would give way to the Black Power movement that was sweeping across the nation, and Detroit would become a hotbed of black militancy.

It was against this backdrop that the Black Panthers sprouted up. Unlike in some other cities where the Panthers may have been the preeminent black militant group, in Detroit they were merely one in a long line of black radical groups jockeying for recruits, attention, and their place in the Black Power echelon. The history of the Detroit branch of the BPP is a complex and intricate one. The facts surrounding the founding of the branch, for example, are not as straightforward as with most other branches (more on that later). Moreover, the branch experienced a fair amount of attrition, making it somewhat difficult to identify former Detroit Panthers whose tenure cuts across the branch's entire life span. Finally, the Detroit branch consisted of an aboveground and underground cadre. Rumors of the underground activities are purportedly a screenwriter's dream, but since most underground comrades are understandably uneasy or unwilling to comment on such matters, some of which are highly delicate even after all these years, separating fact from fiction, for us, is a near impossibility. Hence, the bulk of this essay is, in the main, confined to those activities that occurred aboveground.

As part of a national organization, BPP members utilized their mutually exploitive relationship with the media, along with their own official newspaper, the *Black Panther*, to urge black people not only to stand up to but also move against those repressive forces, namely the police, whose purpose was—as far as many blacks were concerned—to keep blacks in their place, denigrating them in the process. The correct revolutionary meanings were narrated and interpreted in a way that created the perception of the Panthers—in the minds of many white radicals at least—as the vanguard of the New Left, carrying out an organized and efficient revolutionary assault against the state.[3]

The Detroit Panthers, who in 1970 became embroiled in at least three major confrontations with police, are an example of how urban guerrilla warfare was carried out and narrated by some Panther chapters across the country. Moreover, Detroit also highlights the often vast disparity between the carefully cultivated national image of a well-organized revolutionary army and local realities. Detroit demonstrates that because of the unique local situation, some young Panthers there did not interpret their violent actions as a theater of battle in a larger revolutionary struggle. Instead, for many of the rank and file in Detroit, their clashes with police officers were perceived as part of an ongoing war with an oppressive state whose sole purpose (as far as the Panthers and many other blacks were concerned) was to keep blacks powerless and mired in abject poverty. The difference was that, now empowered by the Black Panther phenomenon, for the first time they could ascribe meanings to their own actions that white society might actually be compelled to hear.[4] Most important though, the Detroit Panthers, like many other Panther branches across the country, gave the disaffected a sense of hope, pride, and efficacy. For some, the BPP was the only organization from which they received around-the-clock assistance—ranging from foodstuffs to clothes to financial assistance to emotional support. The Panthers worked long hours on behalf of the community. Gwen Robinson recalls that "the work was hard and tiresome. . . . We put in long hours 24/7. . . . You never got any rest."[5] Few organizations or agencies provided the kind of immediate, no-hassle relief as did the Detroit Panthers. Again, the Detroit Panthers were not atypical in this regard; rather, they were representative of the type of outreach efforts that the Panthers created in poor communities throughout the United States.

When the Panthers set up shop in Detroit, the African American population in that city faced many of the same conditions regarding education, economics, housing, health care, and police relations that bedeviled blacks in many major U.S. cities.[6] In the wake of the urban revolts of the 1960s, scholars commented on what urban historians such as Gilbert Osofsky referred to as the "tragic sameness" of urban ghettos in these key areas.[7] Although no scholarly consensus emerged regarding the meaning and measure of collective violence, one prominent school of thought theorized that the intensity of rebellions was often directly proportional to how intractable local racial conditions remained despite the efforts of some to ameliorate them. That being said, it is informative to begin by noting that in 1943 and again in the summer of 1967, Detroit was the site of two of the worst uprisings in the nation's history. The 1967 revolt is especially noteworthy as its instigators were, according to many scholars and laypersons alike, at the root of all that was fundamentally wrong in the sweltering repressive city of Detroit—that is, that the white power structure did not see blacks as equals but rather as some form of subhumans that needed to be cor-ralled or tamed.

The 1967 uprising was ignited by overzealous police officers who seemingly held little regard for Detroit's black residents. However, there were several events leading up to that muggy July night that created a climate for unrest. In 1959 William T. Patrick was elected as the city's first African American member of Detroit's nine-member Common Council. For reasons that are unclear, Patrick resigned in 1965, and a special election was held in which Thomas Poindexter, a white candidate, was elected in a campaign that centered on his petition-referendum drive to give homeowners a right to racial discrimination in the sale and rental of housing. During the general election of 1966, Poindexter was trounced, to the delight of many blacks, and Rev. Nicholas Hood, an African American minister, was elected to the council. Analysis of the votes showed that blacks had voted across racial lines, but whites only supported white can-didates. Furious, black ministers announced that they would, in the future, en-courage their congregations to vote for black candidates only. Liberal whites, in turn, became concerned over their electoral prospects; thus a coalition was formed that would prove valuable in later years.[8]

Although Hood was as concerned with police mistreatment of blacks as his constituents were, he was unable to effect any policy change regarding police-community relations. And since the council had no one other than Hood for whom police-community relations was a top priority, the police department had no incentive to protect African Americans from rogue officers and racist whites. Early in the summer of 1967, for example, a black man was killed by a group of whites when trying to protect his pregnant wife from their sexual advances. Adding to the tragedy was the loss of the baby. If anyone doubted that Detroit's law enforcement community viewed blacks differently, perhaps it was because they chose to ignore the evidence. For example, fifteen blacks had been shot by whites during the term of the incumbent prosecutor, and all had been ruled justifiable shootings despite a number of bizarre circumstances surrounding several of the deaths.[9] No surprise, then, that many Detroit blacks had little reason to believe that their welfare was given top billing by officials who had been entrusted with that very responsibility. Some within the black community warned of trouble if the police continued their menacing ways. At a Black Power rally in early July 1967, H. Rap Brown reportedly forecasted (some say instigated) trouble, saying that if "Motown" did not come around, "we are going to burn you down."

Within weeks, on July 22, 1967, violence broke out after police vice squad officers raided the United Community League located at Twelfth Street and Clairmont Avenue, which in the evening became an after-hours watering hole.

The police reportedly went there with the intent of rounding up a few patrons, but instead found more than eighty people inside holding a party for two returning Vietnam veterans, no less. Presented with the opportunity to make a big bust, the officers reportedly started roughhousing and arresting everyone there. While the officers awaited a "clean-up crew" to transport the arrestees to the station, a crowd assembled. After the last police cruiser left, a small group of men, angry over what happened, smashed the windows of an adjacent clothing store. Other acts of vandalism quickly followed. Looting and fires spread throughout the northwest side of Detroit, then crossed over to the east side. In less than forty-eight hours, the National Guard was mobilized, to be followed four days later by the army's famed Eighty-second Airborne. As police and military troops sought to regain control of the city, violence escalated.

The abysmal conditions faced by Detroit's inner-city blacks in the 1960s had been festering since the first great migration of southern blacks to Detroit during World War I. In the areas of education, economics, housing, and police relations, conditions in the late 1960s were in most cases continuations of decades-long trends. In a poll conducted in 1966 of Detroit's inner-city African American population, the overwhelming majority of residents indicated overall dissatisfaction with their environment. In the area of education, 36 percent were dissatisfied with the schools. According to the 1960 census, the nonwhite population of Detroit on average completed a little over nine years of schooling, compared to over ten years for whites, while almost half of nonwhites received less than eight years of education.[10] Inner-city schools were woefully overcrowded due in part to a black enrollment increase of almost 31,000 students between 1961 and 1965. Nearly 1,600 new teachers and 1,000 new classrooms were needed at the elementary school level alone, but with a deteriorating tax base and inadequate federal funds, schools were in no position to meet this increased enrollment or combat the over 50 percent dropout rate.[11]

Economic statistics and housing conditions were equally bleak. The median income for nonwhite inner-city residents was a little over $4,000, a good $1,600 below that of whites. The unemployment rate for inner-city black adults was 11 percent, more than triple the average for white workers in the Detroit metropolitan area. Detroit's War on Poverty program was one of the largest in the nation, but of the 360,000 residents living in poverty, only 70,000 were receiving direct aid. To make matters worse, Detroit, like many other major cities, was deindustrializing, and black workers, who had less seniority and lower job grades than white workers, were adversely impacted. Beginning in the 1950s, the big car manufacturers such as Ford, Chrysler, and General Motors (GM) began to automate their assembly lines and outsource parts production to subcontractors located in other cities as well as in foreign countries. Black males were especially hit hard by the combination of deindustrialization and entrenched job discrimination in the automotive industry. Young workers who had no postsecondary education found that entry-level jobs that had been open to their parents or older relatives in the 1940s and 1950s had dried up.

Henry Ford is credited with providing Detroit blacks with their first major employment opportunity.[12] The rest of the auto industry offered few job prospects for African Americans until forced by the labor shortages that accompanied World War I and World War II.[13] In fact, Herbert Northrup maintains that "perhaps if there had not been a shortage of labor during World War I, Negroes would never have found employment in the automobile industry."[14] Northrup's declaration is supported by the fact there were only 569 blacks among the 105,758 workers in the automobile industry in 1910, slightly more than 0.5 percent.[15] The migration of southern blacks and southern whites to Detroit was initially spurred by Henry Ford's announcement on January 5, 1914, that he would pay all workers a wage of $5 a day.[16] By 1919 there were approximately 10,000 blacks working in the automotive industry.[17] Of course, white workers received blacks with less than open arms, sometimes engaging in wildcat strikes against black employment or, in the rare instance, black advancement.

By 1960 conditions had not changed much. Data obtained from the three largest car manufacturers in 1960 shows that blacks were scarcely represented, comprising 15 percent of the metropolitan labor force at that time.[18] At GM, only 67 of 11,125 skilled tradesmen were African American; at Chrysler, just 24 of 7,425; and at Ford, approximately 250 of 7,000. Unions generally excluded blacks from membership if they had little potential utility and actively recruited them when they were essential to help unionize a factory or win a strike. The UAW national leadership gave lip service to racial equality, but did not impose their views upon local offices if they thought doing so would weaken or impede the union movement. Management often used blacks as strikebreakers and then abandoned them when the strike ended. Black workers became increasingly concerned about their lack of voice in local unions.

In an effort to gain leverage within the UAW, in 1957 a group of black unionists formed the Trade Union Leadership Conference (TULC). Walter Reuther had been successful in destroying the power of the Communist Party in the union, and with its demise, blacks supposedly lost their only real champion.[19] The TULC was able to establish a nominal level of influence after demonstrating its power by helping to defeat a union-backed candidate for mayor. The group endorsed Jerome P. Cavanaugh and worked to rally black voters on his behalf. Cavanaugh, a political novice, defeated incumbent Louis C. Miriani by 200,413 to 158,778.[20] This indicated to the UAW leadership that Detroit's black community had unified into a powerful political force; thus the union was forced to deal with the TULC in order to retain influence in the black community. In short, blacks achieved a meaningful voice in the UAW only after they realized and later demonstrated that they had too much power to be ignored. While some blacks in the auto industry were beginning to leverage their power to secure higher wages, advancement opportunities, and improved working conditions, many blacks barely squeaked by.

Overall, 32 percent of Detroit's blacks were below the national poverty line. Consequently, a great number of blacks were renting apartments rather than buying homes. The percentage of Detroit's nonwhite population who owned their own homes was almost half that of whites in the city overall. Part of the reason for the low numbers of black homeownership was the dearth of affordable housing available to blacks. Among that which was affordable were 38,000 low-income housing units that were substandard and/or overcrowded. In the Twelfth Street area alone, the population density reached more than 21,000 persons per square mile.[21] Apartments were subdivided, and six to eight families began to live in units that were designed for two families.

Discrimination in housing in Detroit dates back to the early twentieth century when black migrants first arrived and middle-class African Americans sought to integrate predominantly white communities. As early as the 1940s and 1950s, whites and their real estate agents worked to block blacks' entry into their neighborhoods by legal and extralegal means—for example, by erecting a six-foot-high concrete wall along Eight Mile Road to separate themselves from potential black neighbors. On the same front, white residents engaged in several bitter campaigns to prevent the integration of public housing located in predominantly white neighborhoods.[22] By the 1960s, despite the movement of some African Americans into formerly lily-white communities, segregation had become more pronounced. Not surprisingly, the quality and cost of housing differed substantially for blacks and whites, with blacks paying considerably higher mortgages and rents than whites for comparable accommodations.

Even though few blacks were able to penetrate the white housing market, Detroit experienced a tidal wave of white flight. During the 1950s, the white population declined by a mere 235 persons. Less than a decade later, that number increased exponentially. The fleeing of white residents, which began in earnest in the 1960s, approached a floodtide in the 1970s when both middle- and working-class whites began to move out. In 1970 Detroit's white population was 838,877, but by 1980 it had dwindled to less than 450,000.[23] On the other hand, the black population rose from 16 percent to nearly 30 percent, increasing from 300,000 to 480,000 in that decade alone. By 1967 blacks made up 30 percent of the city's total population. Despite the rather sizable increase in the number of black residents, African Americans, for the most part, were still unwilling or unable to exert their influence politically. In 1969 Richard Austin, a black politician who was purportedly popular among both blacks and whites, ran for mayor against Wayne County Sheriff Roman Gribbs. The election was a nail-biter; Austin lost by 1 percent of the vote.[24] Black turnout was 70 percent, down from the 80 percent that was recorded during the 1964 presidential election. To add insult to injury, Gribbs received 6 percent of the African American vote. Consequently, not only did blacks fail to leverage their numerical strength, but they failed to take advantage of the city's white flight. Needless to say, the loss was chalked up as a setback for the emerging black political elite.

Some communities experienced more white flight than others, especially the Twelfth Street area where nearly no blacks lived in 1940. By 1950 the area was nearly 40 percent nonwhite. By 1960 the proportion of blacks to whites had reversed: only 3.8 percent of its residents were white. Continual white flight left Detroit, in the words of prominent historian Godfrey Hodgson, "dying from the center outward."[25] In light of the fact that the first blacks did not move into the area until the late 1940s, the area underwent a complete racial transformation in little more than a decade. The first black migrants to the area were middle-class folks looking for a nice place to raise their families. By the mid-1960s some less desirable elements flowed in from the inner city. Some of the commercial establishments gave way to bars, pawnshops, and liquor stores.

The shortage of affordable and decent housing was further exacerbated by urban renewal. Entire neighborhoods were demolished to make room for freeways that linked the city to the suburbs. To build Interstate 75, Paradise Valley, or "Black Bottom," the neighborhood that black migrants and white ethnics had struggled over during the 1940s, was bulldozed. As the oldest established black enclave in Detroit, "Black Bottom" was not merely a point on the map, but was the commercial and cultural heart of Detroit's black community. There blacks socialized at the Flame Bar, the Chesterfield Lounge, and the Forest Club, each of which played host to some of the biggest names in entertainment, such as the irrepressible Josephine Baker, the inimitable Lionel Hampton, and the sultry and enchanting Sarah Vaughn.

The loss of this cultural mecca was, for many black residents, demoralizing, and their anger seethed for years thereafter. But aside from residential segregation, the situation most indicative of Detroit race relations by the 1960s was the long-standing dispute between the city's black population and the nearly all-white police force. Former Panther Elaine Brown maintained that "for black people, the police were all three prongs of the United States government, right on the streets—legislative, judicial, and mostly executive."[26] And as in many northern cities, the blatant racism of Detroit police officers and their contempt and disregard for African Americans were historically at the root of many of the city's racial problems. In his study of the Detroit African American community, historian Richard Thomas detailed the way in which the conduct of police reflected and reinforced the racial prejudices of Detroit's white citizens and city government as a whole, concluding simply that for many blacks in the postwar years, police brutality was "the symbol of everything that was wrong with Detroit."[27] It had certainly figured prominently in twentieth-century racial violence beginning with the 1942 Sojourner Truth housing project fracas[28] and the 1943 racial disorder,[29] where one observer noted "open warfare between the Detroit Negroes and the Detroit Police Department."[30] The 1950s and 1960s saw no significant improvement in police–black community relations. Part of the problem may have been the racial makeup of the department itself. Although the city of Detroit was becoming increasingly black, only 2.8 percent of its police force was African American.

According to a *Detroit Free Press* survey in 1967, blacks cited police brutality as the number one problem they faced in the months leading up to the July 1967 uprising. During the 1960s, the "Big Four," or "Tac Squad," roamed the streets, looking for bars to raid and people to rouse. These elite four-man units frequently stopped black males who were driving or walking through the Twelfth Street neighborhood, degrading them by calling them "boy" and "nigger."[31] By the late 1960s "abusive and discriminatory police actions" created a situation conducive to mass collective violence. Detroit blacks had every reason to believe that the Detroit Police Department was a racist agency. Complaint after complaint of police misconduct had been filed by blacks to no avail. Stories of blacks being roughed-up by police were in no short supply. Things had gotten so bad that many blacks stopped filing complaints, for they considered it a waste of time to do so.

A particularly egregious incident occurred on the morning of July 5, 1964. On that day, Cynthia Scott, aka Saint Scott, a black middle-aged prostitute who worked the Twelfth Street area, was shot and killed by police officers who claimed that she pulled a knife on one of them when he approached her. A boisterous and charismatic personality, Scott was widely known by both residents and law enforcement. According to witnesses, Officer Theodore Spicher and his partner began harassing and needling Scott unnecessarily in the early morning hours of July 5. Scott, despite being inebriated, went tit for tat with the officers, who, for reasons that are unclear, entered into a verbal sparring match with Scott. Upset over the verbal drumming they received from Scott, the officers became enraged. Fuming, Spicher leaped from the squad car and began menacing Scott. A scuffle ensued, and shots were fired. Scott was hit twice in the back and once in the stomach. Scott was no model citizen, but her death touched off a storm of protest. The outrage only increased when the officers were cleared of all wrongdoing. Hundreds of people picketed police headquarters on July 13. Blacks called for a retrial. Black attorneys assisted Scott's mother with a $5 million lawsuit against Spicher and the police department.[32]

With this lawsuit, the Detroit Police Department was officially put on notice; yet it still did not seem to deter police misconduct. For example, On September

12, 1965, four African American boys were playing football in the street when police officers approached them and began peppering them with questions. The officers demanded identification and told the youths to leave the area. When the boys protested, they were arrested and subsequently beaten, kicked, and stomped by several of the white officers at the precinct where they were being detained. That same year, when police officers placed Barbara Jackson (an alleged prostitute) under arrest, Jackson suffered injuries inconsistent with the police department's claim that she sustained them when "she fell attempting to escape." Jackson reported that "the officer picked her up and slammed her to the ground [and] then another officer pulled off her wig and kicked her with the comment 'now you're really going to the hospital.'" Even the liberal police commissioner, George Edwards, had to face facts, acknowledging that "90 percent of the 4,767–man Detroit Police Department are bigoted, and [a] dislike for Negroes is reflected constantly in their language and often in physical abuse."[33] Racial discrimination was also present within the department, so much so that black officers saw the need to form an organization called Concerned Officers for Equal Justice. Of course, there were many white officers who harbored no racial animus toward blacks, and as a result were presumably able to carry out their duties fairly and impartially.

In the months preceding the uprising, confrontations between police and blacks escalated dramatically, creating the volatile tinderbox situation that exploded into nearly six days of intense violence. Like many civil disorders of the era, police actions initially sparked the rebellion. Yet far more so than in other cities that experienced such upheaval, the strain between Detroit police and African Americans, which made authorities initially reluctant to even enter black neighborhoods during the extensive looting phase of the revolt, nearly guaranteed intense violence. Slow in their attempts to reestablish order through verbal dialogue or control of the looting with strategic action, because of their deteriorated relationship with blacks, when Detroit police finally responded to the disorder, they were clearly at a disadvantage. Faced with a situation nearly out of control, police unfortunately responded in kind, engaging in what some have referred to as a police riot.[34]

Consequently, in the wake of the violence, overall race relations may have worsened, as the white and black communities became even more divided and white hostility became even more pronounced. Convinced that blacks were ungrateful for the progress that had been made during President Johnson's administration, antiblack sentiment among whites hardened. One of the most violent clashes between police and blacks occurred on March 29, 1969, two years after the uprising. The Republic of New Africa (RNA), a black nationalist organization and one of the city's most visible militant groups, was commemorating its one-year anniversary at the Reverend C. L. Franklin's New Bethel Baptist

Church—ironically, near the flashpoint of the 1967 uprising—when at about midnight two patrol officers reportedly saw several armed members leaving the church. One officer stopped to question the men, but was reportedly shot to death before he could unholster his revolver; the second officer was also shot but somehow managed to call for backup. Police arrived on the scene and riddled the church with bullets, arresting 142 people in the process. However, the message had been sent—blacks would no longer serve as punching bags and target practice for the police. As luck would have it, George Crockett, the Recorders' Court judge, held an all-night marathon of bond hearings.[35] The speed with which he moved to allow the defendants to post bond did not win him any friends within the police department or within the larger white community. The New Bethel defendants were tried in two separate trials, but were acquitted in both cases. Not long after, a campaign was begun, supported by the Detroit Police Officers' Association, to have Crockett removed from office. The city's black militants declared the acquittals a major victory, but this episode, for all intents and purposes, sounded the death knell for the RNA in Detroit. After the dust settled, the RNA fully understood the dangers associated with remaining in a city where its police department may have been likely to seek revenge for the death of one of its own. Consequently, the RNA acquired land in the South and moved its headquarters to Mississippi. It is fair to say that the RNA had attracted a fair amount of support among young blacks in Detroit during the short time it was in existence.

The shooting death of a police officer signaled to some whites that Detroit had become a haven for black militants who were ready to kill whites with impunity, even white police officers if they stood in black people's way. Black militancy reached a fever pitch during the late 1960s. Numerous groups were formed in the wake of the 1967 uprising, and membership in some of those already established swelled. Attendance at Shrine of the Black Madonna meetings, for example, skyrocketed after the rebellion. Still, these black militant organizations did not carry the same sway among most blacks as did the organizations most commonly associated with the civil rights movement.

The New Detroit Committee (NDC), a multiracial organization of leaders from the worlds of business, government, education, unions, and neighborhood and community groups, was created that same year to coordinate community improvement efforts. And though grassroots efforts like this continued to mobilize people throughout the African American community, the NDC suffered a series of internal squabbles and other setbacks that led to the resignation of its radical black members and ultimately undermined its effectiveness.[36] The Detroit Urban League (DUL), long a pillar of activism within the black community, continued years of work in seeking equality of opportunity, as did the NAACP. More rambunctious blacks who deemed organizations like the

Urban League as either too moderate, too mainstream, or too slow in getting things done formed their own groups such as Group on Advanced Leadership (GOAL) and UHURU. Yet in the era of intensifying Black Power, with its demands for immediate equality and a penchant for radical forms of activism, other groups began organizing to the ideological left of these traditional civil rights organizations. Especially after the 1967 uprising, nascent radical groups such as local revolutionaries Glanton Dowdell's and the Reverend Albert Cleage's City-Wide Citizens Actions Committee (CCAC) were increasingly eclipsed in militancy by even more radical groups like the Sons of Malcolm, the Dodge Revolutionary Union Movement (DRUM, and its various RUM incarnations), Rev. Cleage's Shrine of the Black Madonna, the RNA, and the Black Panthers.[37] While never representing the views of the majority of blacks, these more militant organizations did garner considerable support among a sizable portion of the postrebellion African American community and for a time took the lead in community organizing. As for the older and more moderate organizations like the DUL, once viewed as being on the cutting edge, by the late 1960s they were steadily slipping in relevance to a new generation of younger, more eager blacks.[38] Said Rev. Cleage, a leading voice of Detroit's black theology and Black Power movement, "We are [the] new black establishment, the Toms are out."[39]

Activism, especially among the working class, has traditionally been a major avenue toward status in the Detroit African American community, due to the fact that social stratification in the black community has not been so rigidly defined by levels of income, education, and occupation as in the larger white society. Since racial discrimination has limited blacks' ability to achieve a maximum expression in any of these indexes, resulting in a "compression" on the social ladder, the urban African American community often measures a person's stature by his or her community activism in the struggle against forms of racial discrimination. In a city like Detroit, this also meant that union activism against labor exploitation and institutional racism in the auto industry was worn as a badge of honor. Because status within the Detroit black community was subjective in this way, and because community and industrial organizing were so closely linked, some young blacks without the means to move up the social ladder and without employment in the auto industry—which was also a prerequisite for joining the radical DRUM—may have perhaps thought that their participation in the Black Power movement would allow them to achieve a certain measure of status. After the uprising sent "a fresh surge of positive revolutionary energy" through Detroit's inner city, and finding few creative outlets for their passion within established community groups and local government, being a Panther afforded a young African American a certain status in the eyes of the nearly 40 percent of Detroit blacks who held a favorable impression of the Black Power movement.[40] It was among this group that the Black Panthers undoubtedly found many of their recruits.

The circumstances surrounding the founding of the Detroit branch of the BPP and the parties involved vary according to the source. Michael Newton, author of *Bitter Grain: Huey Newton and the Black Panther Party*, states that the Panthers "surfaced in Detroit in the summer of 1968."[41] In his work "Marching Blind: The Rise and Fall of the Black Panther Party in Detroit," Ahmad Rahman, a former Detroit Panther who relies heavily on interviews with Ron Scott, also writes that the branch was founded in May 1968 by Ron Scott, Eric Bell, Jackie Spicer, George Gillis, and Victor Stewart.[42] Phil Garner, an early member of the Detroit Panthers, and General Gordon Baker and Luke Tripp (both of DRUM) offer a less clear-cut and more colorful version of the Panther emergence in Detroit. According to Garner, there was a group of young activists that consisted of Ron Scott, Eric Bell, himself, and others who in the spring of 1968 were calling themselves Panthers, but were not Panthers because "we had not received authorization from national headquarters to start a branch." When asked why the group had not bothered to seek permission from national headquarters to start a branch, Garner replied that "when the Party and SNCC announced a merger in 1968 [the one that led to Stokely Carmichael being named prime minister, H. Rap Brown assuming the position of minister of justice, and James Forman accepting the role of minister of foreign affairs] that caused a great deal of confusion among many SNCC people, including me." "Members of SNCC like myself now assumed that we were Panthers," Garner recalls.

I believe at some point Panthers Sam Napier and Landon Williams came to Detroit and told us flat out that we could not be Panthers unless we received training and get certified or authorized. Somehow I, along with Omar, whose last name I don't remember, and Oliver Malik McClure were selected to go to San Francisco to get trained. We underwent a tremendous amount of training; a lot of testing to see if we were true believers. We were there for about three months. While there we received military training from Geronimo Pratt. We returned to Detroit in either late August or September, and the first thing we did was acquire an office on Indiandale. Once the office was in place we started recruiting.[43]

Garner quickly points out that when "we were finally given authorization to open an office in Detroit we were authorized as a National Committee to Combat Fascism (NCCF) not a branch of the BPP. We were later authorized as the Detroit branch of the Black Panther Party, but by that time I was long gone."[44]

Other sources claim that members of DRUM oversaw the founding of the Detroit branch of the BPP.[45] In an effort to influence the direction of the movement and preempt the potential allure that a Panther branch might have among black youth, some scholars submit that DRUM members supervised the local branch of the Black Panthers with the purpose of preempting its impact in Detroit. Their thinking was that in time, the national headquarters in Oakland would recognize DRUM as the established revolutionary group in Detroit and defer accordingly. Others claim that members of the League of Revolutionary Black Workers (a derivative of DRUM) actually started the first branch of the BPP in Detroit. The first scenario seems more likely than the second, especially since the League was founded in the fall of 1968 months after the so-called Panthers organized themselves. However, if the first is true, at worst this logic seems ill-conceived and at best naive. The idea that the national BPP would recognize DRUM as "the black radical" organization in Detroit given black people's long-standing and persistent problems—socially, politically, and economically—is unlikely. At most, the Panthers would have viewed DRUM as a strong advocate for black auto workers (a relatively small segment of Detroit's black poor), but because the issues on which the group focused did not address the concerns and problems of the wider black community, it is implausible that the Panthers would have deferred to DRUM or anyone else for that matter. Be that as it may, there appear to be elements of truth here.

Extensive interviews of General Gordon Baker and Luke Tripp reveal that in late 1967 or early 1968, Tripp, John Williams, and Marian Kramer got wind that some young community activists (a group that included Scott, Eric Bell, Victor Stewart, and others) wanted to start a Panther branch. Baker remembers that "these kids were especially intrigued after a visit by Kathleen Cleaver and Bill Brent at the Ghetto Coffee Shop in either late 1967 or early 1968."[46] Cleaver and Brent were apparently in town to drum up support for Huey Newton, who was in jail for allegedly killing a police officer; galvanize support around Eldridge Cleaver's presidential campaign; and gauge the community's interest in starting a local Panther branch. Tripp maintained that

because we were older and more experienced we felt some responsibility for these young upstarts. After all, most of them were inexperienced and naive. We knew that if left to do this thing on their own they would either end up in jail or be killed. We wanted to engage them in political education and put them to work building the Black Workers Movement. One of the things we did was get them involved in Eldridge Cleaver's presidential campaign. Our intent was to monitor the kids and eventually channel their energy around activities concerning Black workers. We were going to use the Panther branch as a feeder group for the League of Black Revolutionary Workers.[47]

Tripp admits that contact was made with Kathleen Cleaver during her visit, but no authorization was given to start a Panther branch by her or anyone else. Things began to unravel in the ensuing months when the self-anointed Panthers expressed interest in getting an office and adorning it with the typical Black Panther signage. "This created tension between them and us more experienced activists, because we didn't want the kind of attention that such an office would bring," Tripp recalled.[48] Little did Tripp know that his problems were just about to begin. According both Baker and Tripp, Tripp wrote a 1969 article provocatively titled "D.R.U.M.—Vanguard of the Black Revolution, Dodge Revolutionary Union Movement States History, Purpose and Aims" for the *South End* with the Panther symbol boldly blazoned across the top of the article. The article somehow landed in the hands of David Hilliard, who immediately dispatched a group of Chicago Panthers to investigate the matter. The Chicago Panthers, which included Fred Hampton, were ordered "to find out who was running around Detroit claiming to be Panthers." Tripp remembers that although Hampton was cordial and easygoing, he and the others arrived "strapped." "Hampton told us in no uncertain terms that in order to be Panthers we had to get certified and follow the rules and regulations of the national office. By that time I had grown weary of the whole thing so I decided to withdraw, I don't know what happened after that."[49]

The similarities in Garner's, Baker's, and Tripp's versions weaken the claim that the branch was founded in 1968. Not only do these versions run counter to the notion that the Detroit Panthers were an officially sanctioned entity in 1968, but they also undermine the often-told story that Detroit started as a branch, was expelled by the national headquarters, was later reinstated as an NCCF chapter, and then was granted BPP status thereafter.

Given that Garner, Omar, and Malik McClure were in California at the exact same time the Revolutionary Conference for a United Front Against Fascism was under way, out of which came the creation of the NCCF, it seems plausible that these comrades would have been granted an NCCF charter, not a branch of the BPP, especially since some of the party's national leaders expressed concern about getting the party's growth under control. A reported 3,000 delegates attended the three-day conference in the summer of 1969, which outlined the Panthers' new plan to link the efforts of "students, workers, farmer-peasants, and the lumpen-proletariat" in a united front against the state. Fifteen NCCFs were chartered to coordinate these ventures at the local level; according to Garner, he, Omar, and Malik McClure secured one. It appears, then, that Detroit was not given authorization for an official branch of the BPP until the early 1970s. Conversations with former Panthers, coupled with a close examination of the *Black Panther* newspaper, suggest that full-fledged Black Panther status was granted no earlier than 1971.[50]

Whatever the case, it is fair to say that the unauthorized Detroit cadre was by many accounts initially a constructive and low-key outpost, carrying out with varying degrees of success the numerous responsibilities and programs mandated by the national headquarters in Oakland.[51] Still, they were not an official branch of the BPP, and consequently had to be shut down. Upon returning from Oakland in late summer 1969, a meeting of "former" self-appointed Panthers was called to lay out the structure of the new NCCF while attempting to build the outpost from the remains of the unauthorized Panther branch. Working as an organizing arm of the Panthers, the official mission of the NCCF was twofold. In addition to everyday recruiting, teaching, selling newspapers, and various other duties, members were to concentrate primarily on circulating petitions requiring that the Panthers' longtime plan for decentralized, autonomous police forces be put on local ballots. Simultaneously, efforts to create "an army" with groups such as Students for a Democratic Society (SDS), RNA, and the Weather Underground were initiated, and in fact within months SDS, the Young Lords, and the Young Patriots in Chicago reached out to Detroit offering their assistance in obtaining weapons and ammunition. Of particular importance regarding the Detroit NCCF, members were also subject to the same expectations, rules, and directives as full-fledged Panthers, but in general the NCCFs were seen as the "proving ground" or probationary period before full Black Panther chapter status was conferred.

Rank-and-file membership fluctuated between thirty and fifty aspiring Panthers, and their backgrounds varied widely. Tracy Wilson, a descendant of Nat Turner, found her way into the Detroit Panthers via a most circuitous route. As a teen Wilson, along with her three siblings, were kicked out of the house by her abusive mother. One day while walking the streets of Wilmington, Delaware, a neighbor spotted Wilson crying and offered her solace. Later the neighbor and two other women decided to go to New York after a threatening encounter with Wilmington police. With no place to go, Wilson pleaded with them to take her. At first the women refused. Not one to take no for an answer, Wilson convinced the women to let her tag along.

Upon arriving in New York, Wilson spent the next eight months cleaning rich people's houses in Albany to make ends meet. From there she and the women went to Chicago, but according to Wilson, "Chicago was too much . . . the Blackstone Rangers were everywhere." Once again the women hopped on a Greyhound bus out of town—this time to Detroit. A few months later Wilson decided to go her separate way, as the women's treatment of her was reminiscent of the abusive environment in which she grew up. One day Wilson was so depressed she decided to go for a walk to clear her head. Walking aimlessly through the rubble and ruin left in the wake of the 1967 revolt, the sight of this destruction made Wilson even more depressed. After walking for what seemed like miles, Wilson stopped for a breather. As she was catching her breath, she looked up, and in front of her was the Westside office of the Detroit BPP. Said Wilson, who at the time was eighteen years old and pregnant, "I thought this was an omen, that this was where I was meant to be."[52]

Lorene Johnson's route into the BPP was less eventful than Wilson's, but noteworthy nonetheless. A twenty-six-year-old mother of four and student at Wayne State University, Johnson joined the party (actually the NCCF) in 1970, after a short stint in the RNA. Says Johnson: "I was a member of RNA from day one. I left the RNA when I got tired of the bickering—and the clash of egos between Richard and Milton Henry."[53] A native of Lake Charles, Louisiana, Bill Elder and his family moved to Fort Dix, New Jersey, when he was eleven years old. The son of an army drill instructor and career soldier, Elder also joined the Detroit branch in 1970 after serving nearly three years in the U.S. Navy, fifteen months of which (from October 1968 to January 1970) were in Vietnam. Elder admits that he stumbled into the party. After being discharged from the navy, Elder returned to New Jersey for a short while, before selling his car and boarding a plane to Detroit. He chose Detroit because several of the "brothers" he had met in Vietnam claimed that "Detroit was the place to be . . . they said Detroit had a lot to offer."[54]

When Elder arrived in Detroit, he found a much different city than the one he had envisioned. He could not find work, had barely enough money to pay rent, and had no telephone. "When I first arrived in Detroit I stayed at the YMCA before finding a room in a boarding house. My rent was $15 dollars a week, and I couldn't even afford to pay that. . . . It was hard securing employment because I had to ride the bus to get around town . . . and I had to use a pay phone to make calls. . . . It was tough."[55] One day while walking around downtown, Elder ran into two female Panthers who were selling the *Black Panther*. At some point during the conversation, the women invited him back to the Panthers' eastside office. Once there, the Panthers were showing the movie *The Battle of Algiers*. "There must have been about forty to fifty people there that night from the community," Elder remembered. After the movie, "the Panthers tried to give me the old sales pitch. . . . Simply put, they asked me to join the Party to which I replied, 'I'll think about it.'"[56] Elder weighed his options; he had no job, he could barely pay his rent and buy food, and he had no phone. Facing the stark reality of the situation, he joined the party a few months later in October 1970.

At twenty-one, Elder was the age of the typical Panther, the majority of whom were between eighteen and twenty-two years old—and in fairness a number of them were simply "Rally Panthers" who only appeared at public functions to don their black leather jackets and berets and shout slogans like "Off the Pig" and "Free Huey." When there was work to be done, "Rally

Panthers" were nowhere to be found. In 1969 the first of two purges were ordered, and between seven and eight of these "Rally Panthers" were kicked out for dereliction of duty, not keeping the books in order, coming up short on money from newspaper sales, and generally not taking their political work seriously. Even after the first purge, at any given time only a dozen or so Panthers could be counted on to do day-to-day grunt work, and these generally tended to be those who were attracted to the BPP because of its community survival programs.[57] According to Donald Berry—an army veteran who, early on, supposedly served as the Panthers' field secretary for the Twelfth Street area and later lieutenant of security for the state of Michigan in 1969—the officers in those early years were generally Panthers in their late twenties to early thirties like himself and future defense captain Michael Baynham, Officer of Finance Eric Bell, Lieutenant of Information Charlie Diggs Jr., and Anita Hartman, who coordinated the breakfast programs. How much credence one should attribute to Berry's testimony is unclear. First, a thorough examination of the Detroit branch of the BPP was conducted, and no such position as lieutenant of security was discovered. Second, Berry mentioned at a congressional hearing that he was a member of the 1960 Olympic boxing team. When asked if he went to Rome that year, he responded, "Yes, I went, but didn't fight because I received two broken hands in the trial."[58] Again, a rather meticulous investigation of the 1960 Olympic boxing team on which Cassius Clay (later Muhammad Ali) was a member did not uncover the name Donald Berry.

As Berry later testified, he and the others "joined the Panthers for the good the Panthers were doing." "I had studied the Panthers before I joined," he maintained, "and I had seen a lot of good things they were doing for the black community. This I wanted to be a part of, as long as they were helping our people working in the community, helping the children, working with the people, this was good. I wanted to be a part of this."[59] Indeed, early on the chapter's membership screening process probably reflected and reinforced this more exclusive sense of idealism and commitment to service among the core activists. When a potential applicant inquired about joining the Black Panthers, the officer of the day routinely collected vital information and a photograph so that a proper "investigation" could be conducted into the prospective comrade's background, sincerity, understanding of and commitment to the program, and potential association with the police department. During the investigation, which could last up to six weeks, probationary Panthers attended political education classes—routinely held every Saturday from five to seven o'clock in the evening—performed regular community work in the breakfast program, and sold their quota of newspapers. In chorus, members quizzed the recruits frequently to gauge their understanding of the Panther philosophy and platform and to determine whether the trainees harbored any uncertainty concerning what it meant to be a Black Panther. Much of the recruiting followed along these same lines as well. Following the investigation period, if found acceptable, individuals were deemed a "friend of the Panthers" and assigned a supplemental three-week training course.[60] Only after completing these last lessons was judgment finally passed as to membership.

In this way, the Detroit cadre deliberately kept a quality-over-quantity perspective in regard to its cadre. As Berry recalled, if the Detroit Panthers

felt when you were being interviewed that you had any doubt in your mind about the Panthers, at that time they would refuse you membership. A lot of people had a lot of doubts in their minds because they didn't understand and know what the Black Panther Party was really about. At the time they were so afraid, to them everyone that they didn't know anything about they considered them as being a policeman. They said they would rather have at the time a small membership of people that were dedicated rather than have a large membership of people they were not sure of.[61]

Those dedicated to the hard, often unglamorous grunt work of organizing utilized their membership in the Black Panthers to get out in the black communities of Detroit, soliciting the input of locals to help define their problems and ways in which the party might work to solve them. Much of this involved establishing dialogue between tenants and landlords, and businessmen and patrons, to, in some modest cases, just agree on the need to keep their neighborhoods clean.[62] The centerpiece of the Detroit Panthers' outreach became their breakfast programs, which commenced in May 1969 in several locations. As in other cities where Panther branches existed, the Detroit Panthers solicited food donations from chain stores as well as local businesses such as the Brothers Market. Lorene Johnson remembers that the Brothers Market was always very receptive to Panther requests.[63] These signature Panther programs did not begin until nearly a year after the unauthorized cadre first surfaced. However, once the programs began—one in the northeast section, one on the west side of town, and one on the east side of town in two church dining halls and a recreation center—the breakfast coordinator fed as many as fifty children a day at each site. Says Tracy Wilson, "I visited schools, and talked to principals who helped get the word out about the breakfast program."[64]

Over the years, the position of breakfast coordinator was held by different comrades. When Lorene Johnson joined the party in 1970, Chuck Holt was apparently the breakfast coordinator, and, according to government documents, Anita Hartman preceded him. Before Hartman, Phil Garner remembers Paulette Frye serving in that capacity for a brief time. Not long after Johnson joined the branch, she was put in charge of the breakfast program. "We were up at 6:30 in the morning from Monday through Friday serving breakfast. It didn't matter what your socioeconomic status was; anyone and everyone was welcomed to have breakfast," said Johnson.[65] "I loved the breakfast program. It was a very positive experience," said Gwen Robinson.[66]

The breakfast program that operated out of the 2228 Bewick Street office was very popular and always bustling with foot traffic, partly because it was located across the street from Scripps Elementary School. As part of the party's efforts to heighten young people's consciousness, the Panthers took the opportunity to expose the children to the party's Ten Point Program and Platform as well as lead them in a chorus of "Power to the People" and the Panthers' own rendition of "Everywhere We Go," two of the group's most popular melodies.[67] After the children ate a hearty breakfast, which consisted of eggs, sausage, and sometimes grits and pancakes—but always orange juice and milk—Panthers would walk the children to school. Gwen Robinson maintains that "the breakfast program was very important to the community, because for some of the kids it may have been one of the few meals they would eat in a given day."[68]

Community residents played a vital role in the day-to-day operations of the free breakfast program; they helped solicit donations, they served food, they washed dishes, and they also cleaned up. Many of them were between the ages of fifteen and seventeen, many of them young men. According to Tracy Wilson, "If one stopped by the Bewick Street office one might find more young men serving food than young women." When asked to explain this phenomenon, Wilson maintained that "a number of the young men in the neighborhood were being raised by single mothers, hence some of them were hungry for male mentors and father figures. . . . They admired the Panther men and thus wanted to emulate them." When asked how the gender dynamics played out in the kitchen, Wilson laughed and shot back, "Hey the men were the best cooks. . . . They could cook better than any of the women. Edgar Robinson was the best cook in the chapter. If Edgar was cooking everyone showed up."[69] Gwen Robinson recalls that Robinson was famous for his barbecue chicken.[70] Alvin Brown, who cooked for the free breakfast program, was also a great cook. He was a southern-style cook.[71]

The Panthers augmented their free breakfast program with a short-lived lunch program and various free food giveaways. Gwen Robinson was the brain-child behind the lunch program. Robinson approached Pastor Harold Wasner at the Lutheran Church of the Cross, where she herself worshipped, with the idea of partnering with the church to offer a lunch program for youth during the summer of 1972. Pastor Wasner agreed, and the lunch program went off without a hitch. By summer's end, however, Robinson learned that while the pastor supported the idea of a lunch program, members of the church's board did not share the pastor's sentiments. Board members were uneasy about having any association with the Panthers, and as a result the program was discontinued. That same year the Panthers initiated their free food giveaway. Johnson remembers that "we used to give away full bags of groceries once or twice a year."[72] In the June 10, 1972, issue of the *Black Panther* newspaper, the free food giveaway is featured prominently. An article entitled "Free Food All Over Motown!" says that "the Detroit Branch of the BPP implemented a Survival Day, initiating the Free Food Giveaway Program into the Jeffries housing projects."[73] Although the actual event, which occurred on May 20, 1972, was set up in the park area on Gibson and Selden streets, the residents of the Jeffries projects were the target audience. The Jeffries complex consisted of thirteen separate high-rise towers, five smaller towers, and 415 low-rise town homes, housing nearly 8,000 people. Once a clean, safe, and sought-after place to live, the Jeffries projects, built after World War II, fell into disrepair in the late 1960s during the heroin epidemic.

Tracy Wilson recalls handing out tons of leaflets about Survival Day and advertising the event on radio to help spread the word.[74] The event was well received; 1,500 people reportedly came out for the Panthers' first Survival Day, where 1,000 bags of groceries were given away. The Survival Day took on the aura of a festival. The event started at 11:00 a.m.; at that time the Panthers conducted free sickle cell anemia testing and registered people to vote. Attendees were treated to, among other things, an array of musical groups such as the Sins of Satan, the Skies Unlimited, and Sharon Hicks the Psychedelic Sister Plus One.[75] In addition to the musical guests, attendees enjoyed the work of local artists, who were invited to showcase their wares. There were speakers throughout the day representing various groups, including the effervescent Mother Waddles (from Mother Waddles Charity Mission), a well-known community activist in Detroit. In addition to food, entertainment, and health screenings, the Panthers also took the opportunity to set up voter registration booths. Hundreds of residents registered to vote that day. This effort was especially timely as the 1973 mayoral election was fast approaching. The election featured the unheralded Coleman A. Young, on whose behalf the Panthers worked fervently.

Many in Detroit's black and progressive and white communities considered Coleman a godsend. In Coleman, a former state senator, they saw someone who could be trusted to keep the struggle for racial equality on the "front burner," who was firmly within the Democratic liberal and radical tradition, who was committed to housing reform, education reform, and, perhaps most important, reforming the city's police department. And unlike Richard Austin (the African American candidate who had run for mayor in 1969), Coleman displayed a fire and passion that many found inspiring. The Panthers threw their support behind Coleman as early as 1972 when many, including some blacks, viewed Coleman as an afterthought. Initially, few gave Coleman little chance of defeating John Nichols, the city's former police commissioner and creator of Stop Robberies, Enjoy Safe Streets (STRESS). Formed in early 1971, with the blessing of the mayor, STRESS wreaked havoc on the city's leftist groups specifically and the black community in general.

The BPP was one of several groups who were critical of STRESS's methods. In 1972 the Panthers called for the dissolution of STRESS. On March 26, 1972, the Panthers, along with the Southeastern Black Caucus and Malcolm X Black Hand Society, organized a "mass rally" at the University of Detroit in response to an incident involving five black youths and a member of the STRESS unit. The officer maintained that the youths were committing a robbery when he fired on them, wounding three, one of whom was killed. A flyer entitled "A Message to Our Community on STRESS" states, "We cannot allow this incident to become history—written off and forgotten. It may be your son or brother the next time. We must stand together to end this menace to Black life. STRESS must be discontinued at once! We must not settle for less than complete abolishment."

During the latter stages of the campaign, it was reported that Coleman was running a distant third among the candidates. Even though Nichols had never held elected office, and despite the widespread unpopularity of STRESS within the black community and certain sectors of the white community, Nichols was viewed as the front-runner. Less than one month before the election, the *Detroit News* predicted an easy victory for Nichols, stating that "if white voters follow their usual pattern of higher turnout than Black voters . . . Nichols will be the next tenant in the Manoogian Mansion."[76] While in retrospect one wonders how the *Detroit News*'s prediction could have been so off, the paper was only reporting what many of Detroit's residents thought, either publicly or privately. The gloomy forecast, however, did not deter the Panthers from their organizing efforts. While the Detroit branch of the BPP did not officially work for the Coleman campaign, its members canvassed neighborhoods—going door to door speaking to residents about the importance of the election, not to mention its historical significance. Panthers also registered thousands of voters and drove people to the polls on election day. As strong critics of the city's police department, the Panthers found in Coleman exactly the kind of radical reformer that many black communities across the country wished they had. That Coleman was African American gave the Panthers even greater incentive to work toward his election.

Coleman promised to transform the police department from a lily-white agency to one that more was reflective of the racial makeup of the city. He blasted white police officers who lived in the suburbs, saying they were like an "army of occupation" and charging, "They don't give a damn about the city. They come in and kick some ass and go back" to their suburban homes. Once in office, Young suspended police officers who lived outside the city, demoted others, promoted a large number of African American officers, recruited women and other minorities, and, to the delight of many, disbanded STRESS.

The Panthers understood that there was a time and place to work within the system. At no other time during their existence did the Panthers combine masterfully their own machinery, which included their community survival endeavors and consciousness-raising efforts, with the city's political apparatus than during the years 1971 to 1973. The Panthers' work appeared to have caught the attention of the national headquarters, as it was during this time that the NCCF was apparently granted full-fledged BPP status. Articles began to appear in the *Black Panther* newspaper referring to the Detroit cadre as the Detroit branch of the BPP.

The Panthers unique way of politicizing and educating Detroit's black and white communities by way of human sustenance enabled them to access certain areas of Detroit that perhaps may have been unreceptive to the message of other groups, let alone certain politicians. The free breakfast programs and free food giveaways were financed through donations from local merchants, chain grocery stores, mom-and-pop establishments, and private citizens located within the service area. In keeping with the early leadership's organizing style, solicitations were done with respect and not inappropriate coercion and/ or illegal intimidation tactics as was perhaps the case in other parts of the country. Regarding the donations, Donald Berry claimed to have personally kept a careful tally of all donations as early as 1969 in a notebook and gave receipts, although he admitted that in the early years some of the foodstuffs never made it to the breakfast programs but were confiscated by the Panthers themselves.[77]

Historian Heather Ann Thompson's take on the breakfast program is refreshing. Thompson opines that the Panthers' breakfast programs and food giveaways were offered under the aegis of economic justice, something to which most blacks could relate.[78] According to a reporter with the *Michigan Chronicle*, the city's black newspaper, "The Panthers get food donations from all merchants in the community . . . [and] if they refuse, they tell them that they are not going to be allowed to stay in the community if they don't put something back into it."[79] Even if they sometimes accomplished their goals through threat and intimidation, the Panthers won a degree of respect in Detroit's black community because they operated programs to feed poor people and educate citizens under the law.[80] The Panthers were held in such high regard in certain communities that food would be donated without them having to solicit it. Rita Smith, the Panthers' communications secretary in the early 1970s, remembers suggesting to the teachers at Post Middle School—where she was a student—that "we should donate the food left over from the graduation party to the Black Panther Party."[81] The following day a group of students, including Smith, accompanied by one of the teachers, went to the Panthers' office on Indiandale and dropped off the food. Melvin Peters, the teacher to whom Smith referred, remembers that day: "The black students at Post were politically motivated. They had an enthusiasm for activism that I had not seen at other schools where I had taught."[82]

Perhaps the Panthers most laudable effort was their free busing to prison program. Organized out of the Collingwood Avenue office, the program was initiated in 1972. A flyer titled "Motor City Buses Rolling: Free Busing to Prison Program" included the scheduled runs as well as the items and information needed to visit inmates. Buses left from the Collingwood Avenue office at 9:00 a.m. and returned at 6:00 p.m. Although buses departed at 9:00 a.m., the Panthers were sticklers for keeping to the schedule; thus riders were encouraged to arrive at the office by 8:00 a.m.

Says Panther Tracy Wilson, who joined the party in 1971, "We ran two buses every other week to Joliet Prison [in Joliet, Illinois] and Jackson State Prison.... The program was so popular that the buses were always filled to capacity, sometimes we had to turn people away. Initially, there were bus trips every week, but that became too expensive, so we settled on every other week."[83] Although Wilson remembers that buses ran every other week, the flyer mentioned above suggests that, on occasion, bus trips to prisons were made weekly. JoNina Abron, who joined the Detroit branch in 1972, recounts her involvement with the free busing to prison program in *The Black Panther Party (Reconsidered)*: "I drove one of the vans that transported families to visit their incarcerated relatives at Jackson State Prison. Having grown up as the sheltered daughter of a minister and a music teacher, I was overwhelmed by my experiences at Jackson State Prison, which was my first visit to a penitentiary."[84]

In addition to ensuring that inmates maintained contact with their friends, relatives, and loved ones, the Panthers also sent care packages to inmates that included personal hygiene items and nonperishable goods. Members of the branch also took it upon themselves to provide attorney referrals to inmates, an effort that did not go unappreciated given the limited contact that many inmates had with the outside world.

While the free busing to prison program may have been the branch's most commendable offering, the local branch also felt compelled to couple its food programs with free clothing giveaways. For example, in 1972 the Panthers initiated a free shoe giveaway to go with the free clothes that the Panthers provided members of the community. Said Gwen Robinson, "We would go to the dry cleaners and ask for clothing donations, then people would come by the office and get what they needed." When asked if the branch ever had trouble giving away items, because of low demand, Robinson replied, "No, demand was always high. . . . There were always people who were glad to get what we gave away."[85]

From the inception of the Detroit group, one of the primary duties for the rank and file revolved around the sale of the *Black Panther* newspaper. On the one hand, for the various chapters, the *Black Panther*, as the "official organ" of the party, remained the primary vehicle for promoting the Panthers' programs. And given the paper's expressed goal of "Circulate to Educate," it became for those in Detroit specifically a means of disseminating the party's evolving revolutionary ideology. Besides the paper's usual stories on "the plight of Black America" solicited from branches and chapters across the country, the *Black Panther*—with a nationwide weekly circulation of 140,000 by decade's end—covered a wide array of issues from health care to international politics to foreign policy. The newspaper undoubtedly helped nurture the image of the paramilitary Panthers as romantic vanguard figures carrying out an organized and efficient revolutionary assault against the state.[86] With the revolutionary art of Emory Douglas and other Panther artists, along with proclamations from the national cadre, the newspaper introduced terms such as "pig" and "offing the pig" into the wider lexicon of radicalism, while, in the words of the national headquarters, shouldering the chief responsibility of educating potential Panthers in "the correct handling of the revolution."[87] This type of in-house journalism facilitated the relative sea change in the course of the Detroit branch. For better and worse, on a much larger scale the *Black Panther*—coupled with the party's mutually exploitive relationship with the national media—eventually positioned the Panthers as the most celebrated American revolutionaries in the Vietnam War era.[88]

In a more immediate sense, hawking the *Black Panther* on the street was a moneymaking staple for the Panthers. Based on quotas and a fee schedule set by the national office, each Detroit Panther was responsible for selling a given number, and for every paper sold, the individual kept five cents, the chapter received a dime, and a nickel went to Oakland. Here again, local leadership insisted on sales being carried out in a respectful and orderly manner and worked out arrangements whereby local stores agreed to carry the paper as well. In early 1969 Detroit Panthers were reportedly selling somewhere between 1,500 and 1,600 issues a week.[89] As the officer of the day at the eastside office on Pennsylvania Avenue during the early 1970s, Bill Elder's job was to make sure that the office ran smoothly, that everyone was accounted for and had their assignments. He remembers that "Panthers were given 100 papers, assigned a certain part of the city and told to get out there and sell those papers. Each Panther had an entire week to sell 100 papers a day."[90] Other party members recall being given 200 papers a day to sell. Whatever the case, everyone had to shoulder his or her own load. Gwen Robinson remembers standing outside in perhaps below-freezing temperatures hawking the paper. Says Robinson: "It was either in the winter of 1970 or 1971, and I had just had surgery on my left hand. . . . I had a cast all the way up to my elbow, my fingertips were exposed, and it was freezing outside, and here I was selling the paper."[91]

Party members had an extra incentive to sell their allotment of papers because "it didn't look good if you returned to the office not having sold all of your papers. Returning with unsold papers was frowned upon. Those who did so were called out by other members."[92] Therefore, to avoid being singled out or embarrassed, most members hawked the newspaper with a greater sense of urgency than was perhaps the case in some other branches. Elder recalls that one of his best spots to sell the paper was in front of a corner store located on Mack Avenue and Bewick Street: "I would move a whole lot of papers right there."[93] Gwen Robinson, who started out as a community worker in October 1969 at the age of sixteen, remembers being able to unload a lot papers in front of Hudson's Department Store in downtown Detroit. Unfortunately, hawking the paper in front of Hudson's also had its disadvantages, as one was likely to receive a citation for the curious charge of impeding the flow traffic.[94]

Despite the lack of a sophisticated distribution apparatus such as vending machines and the like, local Panthers did relatively well at selling the newspaper. According to Elder, one of the reasons for their relative success is that once a week they would rent a car and hit fifty to sixty stores in a day. "We would drive out to places like Inkster, Dearborn, and other suburban areas that had a decent-size black population, and we would collect the money from the papers sold, retrieve the remaining papers of which there always very few, and drop off that week's shipment."[95] By 1971 the national headquarters was sending the Detroit branch more than 7,000 papers a week.

Three other modest revenue-generating enterprises were created via relationships with entertainers and alliances with various local groups. Like the Panthers in Oakland and Los Angeles, the Detroit Panthers developed relationships with people in the entertainment industry. In the early 1970s the Panthers held a Free Huey rally in Kennedy Square in downtown Detroit. The acts included the Dramatics, Bill Withers and the local band General Assistance and the ADC Band.[96] In 1972 two other fund-raising efforts were undertaken by the Panthers—one that featured the Ohio Players, who agreed to do a concert at a local club, and another that starred the Staple Singers, who performed at a venue at the University of Detroit.[97] Other monies came from relationships established with other militant groups. One of these, the Black Berets, was formed by African Americans in Ann Arbor, Michigan, after they were unable to secure a Panther charter. In consultation with the Detroit Panthers, the Ann Arbor group organized anyway, and after taking its name from that distinctive element of the Panther uniform, the Black Berets operated as almost an auxiliary of sorts to their Michigan brothers and sisters, setting up a breakfast program and contributing money whenever they could.[98]

By far the most colorful and notorious, at least from the perspective of law enforcement, of the allied groups was the White Panther Party (WPP). Founded in November 1968, the WPP was the offspring of the radical countercultural fascination with the mantra "Revolution in Our Time," which for a period, according to writer Tom Wolfe, made the Black Panthers "radical chic" among white socialites and left-wing activists.[99] Its paternity could more narrowly be traced to a union of John Sinclair, once described as the "High Priest of the Detroit hippies," and the Detroit Black Panthers.[100] Sinclair, who now lives in Amsterdam, recalls that "the creation of the WPP was in response to the Panthers' call for whites to support them by going into white communities and organizing among themselves."[101]

Sinclair and his wife, Leni, along with artist Gary Grimshaw, were the founding members of "The Trans-Love Energies Unlimited," a psychedelic Detroit commune populated with hip activists who, like Sinclair, viewed rock and roll as a weapon of cultural revolution. In promoting local concerts and lightshows, and printing posters and an underground newspaper, Sinclair became acquainted with the Detroit Panthers and began doing some of the chapter's printing. In time, the two groups explored more substantive avenues of collaboration, with plans to use each other's access into poor white and black neighborhoods of the city, respectively, to thus maximize their collective organizing in these communities. For example, Sinclair says, "When we were in Detroit, whenever the Panthers called for a demonstration we joined them. We were especially active in those demonstrations that were held in front of the Federal Building in support of Huey Newton."[102]

Sinclair and members of the commune, many of whom were Wayne State University hippies, ultimately moved their operations to Ann Arbor, and in the spirit of that Detroit alliance reformed as the WPP. Despite their moderate successes in community organizing, the White Panthers' proclivity to merge music and politics resulted in a number of benefit concerts—often featuring MC5 (the Motor City Five), a rock band and revenue generator for the WPP—whose proceeds helped support the Detroit Black Panthers.[103] The concerts were performed under the aegis of Rainbow Media, a subsidiary of the WPP. The purpose of Rainbow Media was to put on blues and jazz festivals. Ray Charles and Sippy Wallace were among the acts secured.[104] Most of the concerts were held in various sites around Ann Arbor, such as West Park and Gallup Park. On occasion, the MC5 performed in Tartar Park near the campus of Wayne State University. In addition to concert benefits, Pun Plamondon, a cofounder of the WPP, says that "we also helped get food donations for the Panthers Free Food programs." He continued:

We secured brown rice, whole grain noodles, day old bread, that sort of thing. You see, we had connections with the entire "hippie" community, organic food stores; we also had contacts with organic growers, so getting foodstuffs was no big deal. I remember one time in the summer of 1969, some pot dealers in Ann Arbor had a load of weed delivered from Mexico in a refrigerated truck with the herb buried under 75 cases of lettuce. After the pot was unloaded the dealers contacted me to see if anyone needed the lettuce. I contacted the Panthers in Detroit and delivered the produce to them.[105]

Helping the Panthers circulate their newspaper was also something in which Plamondon was involved. "I served as a Midwest newspaper distributor for the Party's national headquarters. I worked mainly with Sam Napier. He would send a couple hundred papers either weekly or bi-weekly; and I would pick them up at Air freight and deliver them to head shops,[106] record stores— anyplace that would sell the underground press. Using the WPP's Rainbow Trucking Company I set up a whole distribution network throughout southern Michigan, even Toledo."[107]

Often underappreciated and/or unacknowledged by scholars was the support provided the Panthers by black student unions around the country. True, black student union members participated in and attended Panther rallies, but their contributions were often much more substantial. Detroit was no exception. Students from Wayne State University and the University of Michigan attended Panther political education classes and helped facilitate discussions. They also played an integral part in the Panthers' liberation school, which was held during the summer months at the Collingwood Avenue office. Approximately twenty to twenty-five children, ranging from eight to thirteen years of age, arrived in the morning prepared to take on the day's lesson. The curriculum focused on black history. Thomas Amar Casey, a member of the Black Student Union (BSU) at the University of Michigan, served as a volunteer instructor for the liberation school for at least two summers, 1969 and 1970. "We utilized black history to educate the children while improving their reading skills. Black Freedom Fighters were often the focus of the lessons; people like Kwame Nkrumah, Julius Nyerere, Nat Turner, and Malcolm X. Children received a heavy dose of Malcolm X."[108] Like the free breakfast program, kids were served breakfast when they arrived, but were also treated to lunch before the day concluded. The Panthers recognized that children were not being exposed to black history in school, but instead of lamenting the fact that curricula omitted black people's contribution to America, the Panthers took it upon themselves to fill a very important void. In addition to learning black history, children were instilled with a sense of pride and an appreciation for black people's accomplishments, not to mention a burning desire to aspire to heights that they perhaps once thought unattainable. Children began to look at themselves differently.[109]

The Panthers also cultivated relationships with groups closer to home. Gwen Robinson distinctly remembers that in the summer of 1973, several churches and other groups, including the Panthers, collaborated to do a Radiothon at Callahan Hall at the University of Detroit with the expressed purpose of raising funds for sickle cell anemia. Gladys Knight was the main attraction. Tracy Wilson recalls that day well because "it was Gladys Knight's birthday and we presented Gladys with a surprise birthday cake."[110] The Radiothon was a rousing success, raising close to $10,000. Other fund-raising efforts that occurred in 1973 included a dance for teens on January 20 at St. Margaret Mary Church on Lemay Avenue. "Let's Crazy Leg for Survival" was the theme for the evening; all proceeds went to help finance the community survival programs.

When the Panthers were not overwhelmed with the necessary day-to-day grunt work to keep the branch afloat, they were training for the impending revolution. As proponents of self-defense, the Detroit Panthers obeyed national directives to conduct classes on the use of firearms, physical education, and political education. Under orders from national headquarters that all members become qualified with weapons in order to be "prepared for the revolution," early on firearms classes were held weekly. Panthers were instructed on the maintenance, carrying, loading, aiming, and firing of 12-gauge shotguns, .33 Winchesters, and .22 revolvers. These classes sometimes drew as many as fifteen to twenty people, with several members voluntarily shooting at local rifle ranges on Saturdays. Although never stockpiling weapons at the Panther house—in fact, Panther leaders apparently forbade the storage of guns and ammunition in the Panther office—there was no questioning of the national directive that each member own at least two weapons and 2,000 rounds of ammunition—not surprising considering that maybe as many as one-third of Detroit's inner-city residents owned guns.[111] In addition to the weapons training, Donald Berry claims to have conducted weekly physical fitness and nutrition classes, attended mainly by female Panthers.

Besides the *Black Panther*, Detroit Panthers also disseminated the prevailing Panther ideology through weekly political education classes. Taught on a rotating basis, these evening classes were well attended and generally well received by the public, sometimes drawing as many as fifty people. Sometimes discussions revolved around or centered on Mao Zedong's *Little Red Book*; other times they centered on articles in the *Black Panther*, the party's Ten Point Platform and Program, or important local issues. The purpose of these discussions was to raise issues that were relevant to the community and to find solutions to whatever problems were considered pressing at the time. Thomas Amar Casey maintains that the political education classes literally transformed people's lives. "There were brothers who, when they initially started participating in the P.E. [political education] classes, were functional illiterates, but over time learned to read; not just your basic stuff, but advanced material. Brothers who literally couldn't read when I first met them were reading and understanding sophisticated Marxist-Leninist principles several months later. . . . The growth in literacy was astounding."[112] Suffice to say the eclectic demographic of the participants made for a fair amount of spirited intellectual discourse. Says Tracy Wilson, "Sometimes P.E. classes got a little heated, because people may have disagreed with someone, but that was encouraged."[113]

More often than not, the classes attracted curious non-Panthers and therefore usually focused on discussions of the party's Ten Point Program and Platform while routinely clarifying the "meanings and definitions of certain words that were used by the Panthers."[114] This in particular required a great deal of rigor on the part of the instructors, as Panther ideology was often obscured by Huey Newton's penchant for complex theoretical principles, frequent redefinition, and constantly evolving paradigms. Always experimenting with variations of classical Marxist-Leninist doctrine and incorporating different historical revolutionary experiences whether or not they actually applied to black people's predicament, over time Panther philosophies evolved into a complex and, for some members, confusing amalgamation. Like other revolutionary nationalists of the late 1960s, founders Newton and Seale would eventually see the struggle for Black Power as a worldwide battle for black liberation against American-led capitalist imperialism. Believing that no blacks could be free until all were free, they viewed localized community control and blacks' ability to create their own institutions in the much larger context of worldwide revolution.

Subscribing to the nationalist belief that black ghettos constituted an "internal colony of the United States," the Panthers made the connection that, in conjunction with the proliferation of nationalist revolutions then under way in colonial Africa and other parts of the world, African Americans had to join the battle, thereby creating a simultaneous international and national assault on white American domination. Seeing the second consecutive "long, hot summer" of urban upheaval in 1966 as the opening salvo for the American phase of this revolution, Newton and Seale became convinced that the energies and passions of young urban blacks could, if harnessed properly, be redirected to more productive avenues of activism. Newton, in particular, believed that while riots were frivolous acts of violence that lacked a political purpose, they were, nevertheless, a prelude to the revolution.

In this regard, Frantz Fanon's *The Wretched of the Earth*, the psychiatrist's account of the Algerian revolution and his interpretations of anticolonial revolutionaries in Africa, emerged as one of the most profound and enduring influences in the formulation of Panther tenets on the nature and origins of struggle.[115] Newton and Seale saw not only themselves and their small coterie of followers but also a large segment of the inner-city youth culture of which they were products in Fanon's concept of a "lumpen proletariat." According to Fanon, with the proper education, this fringe element—composed of the millions of black domestics, janitors, cooks, maintenance workers, thieves, welfare mothers, gang members, pimps, prostitutes, hustlers, and thugs—constituted the revolutionary force in the colony's urban centers.[116] Thus, in accordance with Fanon's advice, the Panthers' mission in these years revolved around organizing and mobilizing America's outcasts by raising their level of consciousness and molding them into revolutionaries capable of engaging in sustained urban guerrilla warfare.[117] In the eyes of some early Panthers, they were just such a group and therefore had the power and considered it their obligation to educate the "lumpen" with radical principles necessary for them to assume their roles as "troops" in the revolution. Through Fanon's interpretations of the meanings and uses of violence, the Panthers found a raison d' etre applicable to their colonial status, as they perceived it, as well as to the more ambiguous cultural aspects of Black Power. Some thought the Panthers interpreted Fanon too literally and that his blueprint for revolution was not applicable to the United States. Specifically, those in the League of Revolutionary Black Workers believed that the Panthers were undermining the revolution by focusing on the politicization of the lumpen rather the workers. As far as members of the League were concerned, the lumpen could not be counted on in times of war—they were too easy to corrupt and too undisciplined, and possessed no leverage, an argument first postulated by Karl Marx.

Many of these finer details of the Panthers' plan for revolution—which created pronounced rifts and factions at both the national and local levels—were undoubtedly discussed and argued in Detroit. Yet it is certainly worth noting that based on later testimony by Donald Berry, the political lessons of this particular cadre stressed the desirability of living in the spirit of the "Self-Defense" portion of the party's official name (the Black Panther Party for Self-Defense, the group's original name, was shortened to the Black Panther Party in 1967), which cast violence and confrontations with the police as decidedly counterproductive to community organizing. The Detroit Panthers did apparently take up the gun on at least three separate occasions prior to 1969 when small cadres of Panthers, including Berry, raided the residences of known drug dealers. Some of the Panther offices around the country were located in some of the city's roughest and most depressed areas. On this point Bill Elder (who again joined the party in 1970) exclaims, "Our Eastside office on Pennsylvania Avenue was in a drug infested and crime ridden area."[118]

Raiding drug houses served two purposes: doing so enabled the Panthers to supplement the chapter's revenue: "We took their money . . . we knew the drug dealers couldn't call the police, so they had no legal recourse";[119] and some Panthers thought that if they raided drug dealers often enough, the dealers would simply move their operations elsewhere. Elder remembers that on at least one occasion in the early 1970s, a Panther cadre was given inadequate intelligence, which made for a very hairy experience. When the team arrived to kick in the door of one house, they encountered a solid oak door. "Kicking the door did absolutely no good nor did shooting at it. . . . The bullets barely even chipped the wood. . . . Bullets bounced off that door as if it was made of iron."[120] Quickly assessing the situation. The men decided to abort the mission; the team fled down the snowy and icy streets of Detroit, barely escaping with their lives. The Panthers' effort to rid the community of drugs was commendable, not to mention noble, even if their motives were not entirely altruistic. These operations continued off and on for some time before they were eventually shut down. Some say that these vigilante drug busts created friction with elements of organized crime, on the one hand, and the police department, on the other, and were summarily discontinued. However, there is little evidence to support this theory. Truth be told, there does not seem to be any evidence of confrontations or shootouts between police and Detroit Panthers before 1969.[121] That, however, would change.

Late 1969 was a turning point for the Detroit cadre. Reportedly, in the wake of criticism from various unnamed sources within the ranks as well as from the national office, the NCCF was put on notice. Supposedly the office was being shabbily run; some members were running amuck and not taking their responsibilities seriously, while others were using the party's name to gain stature within the community. Several members had virtually abandoned their earlier community involvement, directing their attention toward the police, which incidentally coincided with Eldridge Cleaver's exhortation to "take it to the streets."[122] According to Berry, he and other older activists were reportedly struck by the profound commitment to violence on the part of this new cadre. "All they would talk about is violence, destruction, kill the pig," Berry recalled.[123] For this reason, Berry and other older activists shied away from their more adventuristic comrades. Only four members of the original wannabe Detroit Black Panthers reportedly embraced the new direction, and essentially they made up the cadre of its leadership. Malik McClure became chairman, Chuck Holt took over as the breakfast and lunch coordinator, Larry Powell assumed the position of lieutenant of information, and Norman McKee reportedly oversaw the development of the liberation school for young people.

Moreover, in response to a critical letter sent in 1969 allegedly from a Detroit Panther and forwarded through Chicago, Landon B. Williams and Rory Hithe were dispatched to Detroit from the Oakland office to investigate a laundry list of allegations involving money and food coming up short, papers not being sold, money not being sent to the West Coast, and the disintegration of the NCCF into a dysfunctional and cliquish club of petty jealousies and dissension. Inspection tours from Oakland were not unheard of; in fact, Raymond "Masai" Hewitt and Donald Cox were reported to have visited numerous branches across the country as part of a regular inspection of each branch's books and operations. Nonetheless, the arrival of Williams and Hithe was understood to be different, as the letter itself seems to have broken the protocol and chain of command whereby communication with Oakland was routinely done by phone and then only by two authorized officers—the communications secretary and defense captain. Moreover, Charlie Diggs Jr., for one, recognized the inspectors as what he referred to as "the goon squad from California" who were not there to examine the branch's checkbook but to take the locals out into the alley and break their legs. "These guys you have to be scared of," Berry remembered Diggs saying, "because that is why they sent them, if anything goes wrong in the chapter. . . . These guys come from out of town and wax you; they take care of you."[124]

To put Detroit's office in order, over the course of two days the Oakland Panthers gathered most members of the branch together and announced that they had compiled a list of ten names designated to be purged. As each name was read—including Diggs's—the ex-Panthers were to immediately leave the premises or face consequences. At the conclusion, all new officers were installed save for Berry, who, according to him, alone remained in his capacity as lieutenant of security. This shake-up of leadership included the supposed elevation of Michael Baynham as defense captain.[125] According to government documents, not long after, under very mysterious circumstances, Michael Baynham was shot in the head while standing in the hallway of a Panther house. Though numerous Panthers were present—several from Detroit and a few from Chicago—inexplicably no one could come up with a motive or identify the killer. Since neither the police nor the Detroit Panthers themselves pursued an investigation with any zeal, no one was ever charged with the crime. As Berry later testified in regards to who might have murdered Baynham: "Well, truthfully we don't know. . . . Now with 14 Panthers in the house and the defense captain shot, nobody claims they knew what happened. The police didn't investigate it, the Panthers didn't bother to investigate it, so the national office asked for a report on what had happened. They didn't get one. The central office [Chicago] asked for a report, they didn't get one. Everybody went into hiding."[126]

One Panther who was in the house at the time remembers being "shocked that no one saw anything or seemed to have any clue as to what happened that day; it was strange."[127] According to him, there were Panthers on the first and second floors as well as on the front porch, yet there were no witnesses. Years later, Pun Plamondon said that in the summer of 1969, a Panther woman approached him and asked if he could help her find a safe place to hide. The woman had confided in him that her boyfriend was killed and that she believed the murderers to be other Panthers. "She was absolutely terrified. I took her and a friend to one of the Victorian houses the WPP owned on fraternity row in Ann Arbor and before I left I gave her a gun."[128] The boyfriend she was referring to was Baynham. She left the party shortly after that.

Already under fire to pull their weight, Chief of Staff David Hilliard, who Huey Newton officially left in charge while incarcerated, now ordered the NCCF closed for its members' apparent lack of interest in solving the murder of one of their own. All activities were to cease until, if and when, Oakland judged them worthy of reopening. According to Berry, he and a handful of older Panthers kept working in the community out of a sense of obligation and fear that if their programs lapsed, trust and respect between the people they served and those who donated to their cause would suffer in the long term. Even after the Chicago Panthers made the national headquarters aware of their activism—and David Hilliard made it explicit that they were not to impersonate Black Panthers—their work continued, although they no longer called themselves Panthers.[129] The group was eventually reinstated, but only after convincing the brass in Oakland that they were fully committed to serving the people.

While eventually growing in size to nearly forty members by 1970, the Detroit NCCF attracted a whole new rank and file of younger activists, both male and female, mostly in their mid to late teens. A profile of the new NCCF conforms very closely to Charles E. Jones and Judson L. Jeffries's observation that, at the local level, the Panthers made up a cross section of young African Americans with "individual adherence to the party's centralized structure . . . as varied as the members."[130] Most remained committed to community service, and, as a matter of fact, the NCCF carried on a breakfast and a lunch program while also exploring the idea of starting a free medical clinic.[131]

A small group of Panthers were far less interested in these tedious types of programs and activities, and by the spring of 1970 the NCCF had let the breakfast program dwindle to just one center. Due to a dedicated cadre of workers, the breakfast programs were later rejuvenated under new leadership. Unfortunately, though, newspaper sales continued to decline as certain members became more abrasive in their technique. Most important, some of these young activists, regardless of their individual agendas, were now operating within a system in which they were indoctrinated with the expectation that the only way to be a "true Panther" was to follow the new violent directives.[132] From our discussions with former Panthers, Chuck Holt seemed to be the strongest advocate of this doctrine. Unlike Newton and Seale, who believed that the party needed to highlight and expand its community survival programs, Holt fell squarely within the Cleaver camp, who believed it was time to escalate the revolution by stepping up the attack against anyone who stood between the Panthers and black people's liberation. For Cleaver, a real Panther had a gun in one hand and a copy of Carlos Marighella's *A Minimanual of the Urban Guerilla* in the other. To one unnamed Panther, it was somewhat ironic, if not amusing, that Holt adopted such a position, because, according to him, Holt was not physically capable of leading such an assault, even if he were so inclined, which, says the unnamed source, he was not. "Holt was about five feet eight inches and 250 pounds"—not exactly the prototypical revolutionary. Ahmad Rahman remembers a very different Holt than the one Elder paints, stating, "Yes, Holt was stocky, but he was actually very skilled in hand-to-hand combat.... He was a martial arts expert.... Holt was dangerous."[133]

Chronological age is an important variable when studying participation in violence, and it is no coincidence that a younger rank and file in Detroit would more likely be attracted to this new emphasis toward confronting the police. Having grown up in the mounting "conflict climate" of the Detroit inner city, several had reportedly participated in the 1967 rebellion and, like many Detroit blacks, blamed the police for starting that violence and inflicting the vast majority of bodily harm and death.[134] Unlike many older African Americans who were still committed to established civil rights goals, organizations, and tactics, they were in the first place generally more receptive to unconventional modes of political participation and community activism. They were often also more receptive to the call for Black Power and possessed a stronger belief in their own ability to control events in their lives and shape their own future. The civil disturbances of the 1960s, whether experienced on television or firsthand, exposed them to the use of violence as a legitimate form of social protest and political communication.[135]

For these particular kids who found their way to the NCCF, the glamorous swagger of the Panthers—a black leather jacket, a beret, and dark glasses—was indeed attractive despite the fact that Panthers in Detroit rarely donned the Panther uniform, choosing to wear street clothes instead. Moreover, according to some who lived in Detroit at the time, the young Panthers were reportedly alienated from some of the most prominent radical groups, which were oriented toward autoworkers, students, and professionals. These other organizations preferred to keep a comparatively low profile, abstaining from shouting "Off the Pig" and generally pursuing a less aggressive and more reformist agenda.[136] For the Panthers, this worker orientation and strategy did not align with the mandates from Oakland, nor did it appeal to those who were just along for the ride, imitating the Panther style rather than being in it to help blacks actualize their potential. "It was about being cool on the street," instructed former Detroit Panther Charles White. "We didn't give a shit about good grades, that stuff didn't mean a thing."[137] At the time of the 1967 upheaval, approximately 30 percent of blacks age eighteen to twenty-four were unemployed in Detroit. For some misguided youth, the Detroit Panthers were "the leaders of the community." They were the right group to join. After all, they were on television.[138]

Without question, some of the young Detroit NCCF members embraced violence for diverse reasons and engaged in it to varying degrees. It cannot be assumed that these rank-and-file Panthers lacked the political sophistication to synthesize and evaluate the often convoluted revolutionary doctrine disseminated from Oakland regarding self-defense against violence. The words of Eldridge Cleaver, who became the national figure who most embodied the Panthers' increasingly violent nature during Newton's incarceration for most of the late 1960s, were certainly clear enough. Cleaver's autobiographical book, *Soul on Ice*, oddly established his credentials among white radicals and liberals, and a number of young urban African Americans, as a man of the people who spoke with authority regarding the struggle. The photogenic, charismatic, and articulate Cleaver repeatedly admonished blacks to pick up the gun and arm themselves to the teeth, pruning bad "pig apples off the tree of life." In the spring of 1968, he openly proclaimed that "the violent phase of the black liberation struggle is here, and it will spread. From that shot, from that blood, America will be painted red." In no uncertain terms, Cleaver called on "stone-cold revolutionaries" and "cold, calculating killing machines" to "face down the pigs at their level."[139] Tragically and irresponsibly, Cleaver's ill-fated position got Bobby Hutton killed.

For Cleaver, it was now time for all Panthers to confront the police, building up to a "total war" against the oppressor in the very near future. Cleaver maintained at the time that victories could no longer be won "in the courtrooms and at press conferences, but in the streets of Babylon, doing it in the road, but doing it. As long as we kill pigs."[140] It is true that relatively few in Detroit read all their Marx, Mao, and Che as required, and some failed to study past revolutions, but one did not need to have read Fanon or necessarily been fully versed in the Panthers' political philosophy to understand Cleaver's powerful battle cry that "in order to stop the slaughter of the people we must accelerate the slaughter of the pigs. Those who can't stand the sight of blood, especially your own, should stay at home and pray for those who come outside to move, to do it, and pray for victory and not for an end to the slaughter."[141]

When the first author asked Charles White if Detroit Panthers used violence to liberate the black community, carry out a guerrilla war, or be the vanguard in a popular struggle against American capitalism, White laughed. "OK," White qualified, the rank and file were "not stupid," and "maybe a few had that fantasy in their head," but "this shit [violence] was nothin' new, the Panthers weren't tellin' us to do nothin' out of the ordinary."[142]

Studies conducted in the late 1960s, such as the one by the Center for the Study of Metropolitan Problems in Education, found that among black teenagers, the Black Panthers generally attracted those already predisposed to violence. Indeed, for some of the "street kids," as White called them, in the NCCF, organized tactics to confront police may have differed in the degree of extremity, but not in kind from what might be considered ordinary behavior.[143] Some had engaged the police in violence for years before joining the NCCF, and several would have continued to have done so even without the Black Panthers. Many were street savvy, and some had prior associations with several Detroit gangs.[144]

Apparently, only a hardcore group of the Detroit Panthers were actually "warriors," fully embracing Cleaver's philosophy and taking to heart the late Fred Hampton's conviction that Panthers "might kill a few and get a little satisfaction. Kill some more and you get some more satisfaction. Kill 'em all and you get complete satisfaction." A few were status seekers, and some simply went along with what they were told, afraid to question the established leadership's indoctrination. According to White, "Most of these kids were followers, you tell them what to do . . . they do it."[145] Already convinced of the party's basic philosophy and possessing limited life experience and little familiarity with abstract thinking, these very impressionable young Panthers were significantly influenced by the exhortations of charismatic local advocates of violence and by the powerful imagery, slogans, graphic language, and revolutionary art in the *Black Panther*.[146] By design, the paper's stark accounts of the "fascists pigs of Detroit [constantly roaming] black communities in search of victims, unleashing their sadistic desires and violence, harassing and brutalizing in the name of 'law and order'" educated many for whom the subtle ambiguities in the Black Panthers' ideology may have been lost.[147] Perhaps most important, the constant barrage of Emory Douglas's graphic depictions of policemen being liquidated by various methods proved to be worth a thousand words, encouraging a few to imagine themselves doing that to a policeman and instilling the conviction, according to Donald Berry, "I can do this; I can do that."[148]

Gender can also be accounted for here as well. There were always young women in the Detroit Black Panthers, and like female Panthers across the nation, they, too, sought to negotiate the proper role of a comrade in arms within the masculine and sexist world of the Black Power movement. For Newton and the early years of the party, the prerequisite for the recapturing of black masculinity—an integral aspect of the Panthers' revolutionary strategy for black liberation—was the necessity of the black man to, in his words, "recapture his mind" and, at the same time, "recapture his balls."[149] In the chauvinistic world of the Black Power movement, where, for some, "aggression and bravado defined manhood," some women were initially given very limited roles. Like most areas of Panther doctrine, the official role of women in the BPP was rather ambiguous, with many contradictions between rhetoric and performance and from chapter to chapter. But according to historian Tracye Ann Matthews, while the national office in Oakland set about crafting its imagery of black masculinity and patriarchy, "presumably, Black women's role in this revolutionizing process was to respond favorably to the new entity, created at least in part with the intention of attracting their awe, admiration, and participation in lionizing the new Black man." This was certainly the case in Detroit, where women were ostensibly viewed as warriors on equal footing with men; at the same time, the sexism question still remained, but nowhere near to the degree that it existed in Oakland.[150]

As the Panthers became a national phenomenon, the role of women in the party slowly expanded in the late 1960s, as women became more outspoken about the grave prognosis for a revolution divided by sex and relying solely on the efforts of men. Between 1969 and 1971, events conspired to raise the consciousness of Panther women and eventually alter the perceptions of what a woman's role in the revolution should be. For one, the emergence of strong Panther women such as Audrea Jones (Boston), Elaine Brown (Oakland), Assata Shakur (New York), Connie Felder (Baltimore), and Barbara Easley-Cox (Philadelphia) and the revolutionary example of third world women inspired many male and female Panthers to question male chauvinism and separate gender-specific offices within the national hierarchy.[151] Likewise, women's success in the Panthers' community programs emboldened many women to voice their opinions and assert themselves in other areas of party procedure. Still, more than anything, it was when women began to more fully share in the armed defense facets of the Panther program that a discernable renegotiation of their role in the organization was possible. The increased frequency of Panther women being arrested, imprisoned, and brutalized by police, and the value placed on this by men, afforded women the impetus needed to begin synthesizing their struggle against the chauvinism of Panther men within the context of the overall revolution. Though this renegotiation was uneven, halting, and full of contradictions, "the new Black woman," contends Matthews, "was expected to be a mother, sexual partner, *and* full time revolutionary."[152] Nevertheless, in a movement inherently linked to masculinity in the eyes of some, sexism proved especially intractable.

Although Rita Smith maintains that some of the brothers in Detroit were chauvinistic, she conceded that sexism was not as prominent in Detroit as it was rumored to be in Oakland and other places.[153] Said Gwen Robinson: "We did not have to put up with the type of foolishness that reportedly went on in Oakland. Women in Detroit were not subjugated in any way. The men did not try to take liberties with us. There were no domestic abuse issues or anything like that. If we sensed any overt sexism on the part of the men, the women as a collective would deal with it. . . . If push came to shove we might go on strike or something."[154]

Conversations with several Detroit Panther women make clear that both the men and women were encouraged to take on the duties and responsibilities of a revolutionary, regardless of gender. Sisters pulled their own weight, says Lorene Johnson. Panther women were admonished to take up the gun "just like the brothers."[155] Besides involvement in the most significant instance of urban guerrilla warfare in the history of the Detroit branch—the "Detroit 15" showdown in which several rifle shells of the same caliber that killed Officer Glen Smith were found in the knee socks of one of the eight women arrested—police reported several other instances where women such as Delphine McCray joined with male Panthers in skirmishes with the police. In addition to investing considerable effort into the Detroit branch, whether by contributing clerical skills in the office, propagandizing on the street, or implementing the group's survival programs, female Panthers repeatedly proved themselves in the most powerful and highly regarded manner in a time of war—that is, under fire.[156]

Judging from the prominent role women were given in the narration of Panther activities in Detroit, it seems likely that certain women were seen by the rank and file as integral and vital to the NCCF's conceptions of urban guerrilla warfare. Be that as it may, Rita Smith remembers that a number of sisters were disappointed that not enough of them were involved in the guerrilla warfare operations for which the underground cadre was known. In other words, some saw their exclusion as a form of male chauvinism.[157] However, as former Detroit Panther Charles White said, simply, "they were with us." Although some were considered "revolutionary warriors," some female Detroit Panthers still did not always receive the full respect of their male counterparts. This is undoubtedly because, as other scholars have pointed out, young rank-and-file men brought considerable preconceptions and habits regarding women with them into the party.[158] It may also reflect the conscious decision of anxious young men to subordinate female Panthers in an effort to augment their own assertions of masculinity. As Kathleen Cleaver maintained, when "black men move to assert themselves, to regain a sense of dignity, to regain a sense of manhood, to regain a sense of humanity . . . they many times take out resentment of their position against their own black women." Charles White did not recall a great deal of emphasis put on analyzing gender exploitation or equality in Detroit. But quite tellingly, he concluded, "They knew what was required," and when the time came, "they fought too."[159]

In 1970 both male and female Panthers—undoubtedly under the influence of Eldridge Cleaver—began to follow "specific orders to get down" with the Detroit police. Culminating in the October shooting death of police officer

Glen Smith, most instances were actually relatively minor, and more than a few were instigated by police. Although other radical groups such as the Weather Underground, the RNA, and the Black Liberation Army—groups rumored to be in concert with the Panthers under the United Front Against Fascism—engaged in their own acts of urban guerrilla warfare in Detroit, there is little evidence to suggest that the groups coordinated their efforts. It should be noted, however, that collaborations of this kind are often clandestine in nature, which might explain why there is no evidence to support the coordinated effort theory. In February, at a downtown rally for the Chicago 7 organized by SDS, NCCF members Larry Powell, Norman McKee, and James Pita responded to overzealous police officers brusquely dispersing the nearly 159 demonstrators by hurling bottles at the officers and wrestling another to the ground when the officer became too abrasive.

Publicly retaliating in this way served two purposes—to effect a defensive posture and to educate the onlookers. With such a large audience on hand to witness their symbolic refusal to accept police heavy-handedness, this approach had the potential to disabuse some of their image of the police as omnipotent and therefore give some a sense of efficacy, whereas before they may have felt helpless to defend themselves against the police. After the three were arrested, the police interpreted the men's actions as part of the overall sharp increase in the disregard for authority. But under the headline "Pigs Run Amuck," an NCCF bulletin highlighted the lesson with rhetorical flair. Praising the stand taken by the three and referring to them as the "best humanity possesses," the Detroit NCCF spelled out future assignments with the ominous warning that the "racist butchers [police] must cease their wanton murder and brutality of black people or face the wrath of the black community."[160] Promising to do what "it takes to have the fascists remove his funky feet from off our necks," throughout the spring and early summer clashes between the Panthers and the police ensued.[161] In a reportedly unprovoked attack in July 1970, Larry Powell struck an officer, knocking him nearly unconscious, and then pummeled him while he lay on the ground. Later that month the media reported that Ahmad Rahman supposedly attacked police officers after a routine traffic stop. Police officers reported a story that Rahman followed the rhetorical example of Eldridge Cleaver by striking a police officer and extolling the crowd to "Kill the pigs" and "Help me free our brothers." In a recent conversation with Rahman, he says that the police fabricated this entire story. What happened, says Rahman, is the following:

Me and a few other brothers were on Woodward Avenue directly across the street from J. L. Hudsons, which was in the center of downtown Detroit. Two "brothers" were flat on their stomachs, handcuffed behind their backs, and cops had their boots on their faces. One was Oliver Shows, who would be shot dead by Detroit Police three years later. The other was Mark Bethune, who would be shot dead two years later by members of STRESS. Shows and Bethune were community workers. I crossed the street from where I was selling the papers. I told people nearby that this was the kind of police brutality that our party opposed, and they would learn more by buying the latest edition of the *Black Panther* newspaper that I held up for them to see. The police grabbed me and said I was under arrest. I asked, "For what?" They said for attempting to incite a riot. Then they stuffed me into their squad car and proceeded to beat me all the way to the police station. Later the officers testified during my trial that we had attacked one of them. The people in the courtroom protested so loudly that instead of the ninety days that he could have sentenced me to, the judge sentenced me to ten days instead.[162]

These were but a few of such confrontations, involving no fewer than nineteen NCCF members.[163] Since the mid-1960s, violence against police officers increased markedly in inner-city Detroit, and publicly the Panthers articulated their belief that their actions would serve to "educate and politicize the masses," creating a text from which the increasingly besieged black community could supplement the Panthers' narration with appropriate actions of their own in the future.[164] Toward this end, certain Detroit Panthers continued to issue sensational revolutionary interpretations and caveats to accompany their acts of urban guerrilla warfare, consistently imparting a colorful variation of the common ultimatum that authorities must immediately end "the brutality and murder of black people or the racist dog policemen will face the wrath of an armed people."[165]

According to anthropologist Allen Feldman in his groundbreaking work on the performative violence of the Irish Republican Army, paramilitary groups create conditions wherein the body-as-object becomes a symbolic political text to be read and interpreted apart from the real consequences of the violence itself. The act of performative violence invests the body with the power to become a political statement, situated in the larger political discourse in which the group is engaged and the history of that movement in general.[166] This concept of the body as political text has particular significance for black Americans, whose bodies have historically been objectified through assorted displays of slavery, whipping, hunting, lynching, burning, and other forms of brutality. For black women, this was amplified through sexual objectification, exploitation, and abuse.[167] Traditionally, whites possessed the power to both inscribe the dominant society's message on the black body and then also explicate the black body to the dominant society, creating a succession of stereotypes and myths designed to perpetuate the inequality of American race relations.

For years, southern institutions brought violence to bear on the bodies of activists, thus investing their bodies with political value in which the nation as a whole could interpret to the advantage of the movement. Yet the rank-and-file Panther's body was invested with power of its own creation, thus reversing this trend. In the spirit of revolution, some Panthers welcomed skirmishes with the police, and although (for the most part) not the instigators of these confrontations, they at times dictated the sites and stagings of graphic urban guerrilla warfare themselves, as was the case in three separate snipings during 1970. Under these conditions, their bodies became not just the medium but also the origin of power, making it possible to retain the ability to narrate their actions even when they were the victims of police repression. When acting as individuals, they may have known what their clashes with police meant, but they did not have a voice that the dominant white society was apt to acknowledge.

Acting "in the name" of the BPP gave them a voice, allowing blacks to narrate and edit their own bodies, explaining to society what their own actions meant.[168] Certain members of the national office manipulated this message, but because of the BPP's national image, and both the fear and fascination it evoked in white society, Panthers in places like Detroit, or again Oakland and Los Angeles, could use violence on the party's behalf to communicate with the dominant society in much the same way that the rebellions of the mid to late 1960s had.[169] When doing so, they were not engaged in actions that white society could cursorily dismiss as random examples of black pathology. Historically, when African Americans engaged in random, usually black-on-black violence, the dominant society found it distasteful but tolerable and largely expected. But when deliberately presented against white institutions cumulatively by the national party and then further framed by both underground and mainstream media, print and television, the combined local efforts of the Black Panthers created the perception of a well-organized, efficient revolutionary force moving forward on a variety of fronts.[170] In this way, the Panthers were part of a larger revolution, and their retaliatory and other times preemptive strikes against police gave their actions new meaning and purpose—not criminal activity but more noble efforts to "create machinery for [the] defense of our black communities right here in Detroit."[171] Through acts of guerrilla warfare, they were empowered to deliver a message to society, in passionate oratory and graphic imagery, that chronicled the realities of America's ghettos. If only for that moment, Panthers were invested with a power virtually unknown in daily inner-city life.

In the spring of 1970 several Detroit police officers were reportedly the victims of snipings when they entered certain black neighborhoods. Unable to come up with a motive or any legitimate grievance, the police attributed the shootings to members of the party. Regardless of how the police interpreted these acts, if true, these actions were perhaps about "space-claiming." According to historian Thomas Sugrue, racially motivated space-claiming was actually a nearly constant feature of postwar Detroit as the black population surge in the ghetto strained the city's commitment to residential segregation. Between the 1940s and 1960s, reaching a peak in the late 1950s, "small disturbances, near-riots, and riots" broke out in the city's neighborhoods undergoing racial turnover. These widespread violent attempts to mark one's territory symbolically set the price for transgressing Detroit's invisible racial boundaries and also reflected high degrees of organized planning. Yet unlike the sniping mentioned above, historically it was whites who harassed, demonstrated and picketed against, vandalized, assaulted, and generally terrorized blacks moving into formerly all-white neighborhoods.[172]

However, the Panthers were not like some of their "black elders" who rarely resisted white-initiated violence on the neighborhood battlegrounds. By meeting violence with violence, the Panthers' gunshots were instead a preemptive strike to claim the area of the city already broadly defined as the black community against the presence of a menacing white "other." In keeping with the Panthers' contention that Detroit police were seeking to ambush and destroy the party, the NCCF utilized the sniping incident to further its efforts to mobilize the masses, glowingly depicting the shooters as "people's warriors [standing] between the fascist pigs and the black community with [the] honorable dignity of warriors standing as one with the people." In an open letter to the black community, the NCCF again clued authorities in on the motive, maintaining that "these brothers said and did what the Black Community has always wanted to say and do for themselves for so long. That is to move and destroy the power structure and all its parts and components in our community."[173]

Nearly three months later, two more Detroit NCCF activists took up the gun in another instance of carefully staged urban guerrilla warfare. Accounts of the shooting are contradictory, but it appears that on the evening of June 28, 1970, two police cars on the predominantly black east side of Detroit were fired upon by Lawrence White and Michael Anderson. What also appears clear is the ambush was at least partially planned beforehand by White, Anderson, and three others. According to the police, they supposedly received information from an ex-NCCF or Panther that there was a "plot to assassinate Detroit police officers."[174] Acting on this tip, they were already trailing the car containing the five men from the NCCF office in the northwest section of Detroit to the area of the ambush around the Edsel Ford Expressway. At this point, White and Anderson got out and continued on foot, carrying unidentified objects and briefly eluding the police. Near midnight, White and Anderson reportedly opened fire on a police car stopped at a red light, slightly wounding two officers. When a second unmarked squad car arrived, the two Panthers, armed with a Belgian Mauser rifle and an M-1 carbine, fired at least ten more rounds into it, again wounding an officer, before fleeing to White's house on nearby Rohns.[175]

Testifying before a congressional committee, Donald Berry recalled White's obsession "with always wanting to kill a policeman," giving weight to the police department's conviction that the shooting involved a degree of planning as part of a larger plot.[176] If indeed the shooting was a planned ambush, it is interesting that the NCCF chose not to glorify White and Anderson, as had been done after the sniping incident. Instead of ascribing to them what Frantz Fanon referred to as the "positive and creative" qualities that go along with revolutionary forces carrying out urban guerrilla operations, local Panthers constructed a much different political statement around their role as the victims of frequent police efforts to provoke an attack.

Building the case that Detroit police sought to "herd them off to prison camps," the NCCF chose not to evoke images of an organized and efficient act of violence, but the party pronounced the two had simply done "as any human being would have done had their family and/or community become the target of racist pig oppression, stood up and defended their human right of life by any means necessary, in this case the gun."[177]

This choice of framing by the Panthers may have been in response to the ways in which the police aggressively publicized their narration of the ambush. Unlike the earlier sniping where police professed they knew of no motive, in the *Detroit News*, the city's evening paper, police sought to divide the Panthers from any potential constituency, clearly portraying them and their actions as wholly counter to the city's much-publicized bids for improved race relations in the wake of the rebellion. "The purpose of these activities was clearly to provoke an incident that could be exploited by a few to wreck our community," Police Commissioner Patrick Murphy was quoted as saying. Outside of that, the commissioner maintained, "I am unable to equate the violence, the viciousness that occurred that night with any kind of legitimate grievance." Murphy's view of the Panthers was that of marginal characters, riffraff, whose deviance disqualified them from a legitimate position within current community dialogues, explaining: "The department has worked long and hard to establish and improve good relationships with every segment of this community. The individuals who would commit this type of violence, in my humble opinion, will not be influenced by any efforts by this department to improve community relations."[178]

Perhaps feeling the image of "victim" would carry more weight with the black community at that particular time, the Panthers countered by downplaying the initial shooting and instead drawing attention to the use of tear gas and the abusive conduct of the "over one hundred and fifty bloodthirsty pigs" toward the two Panthers and their family members inside the house on Rohns during the resultant early morning showdown.[179] In their reading of events, the roles were reversed, and the episode was politically significant as an example of the police department using a "ridiculous excuse" to "invade the Black Community, indiscriminately shooting and gassing members of the community with intent to murder."[180] On a personal level, it may be impossible to determine exactly which way White and Anderson interpreted the shooting. Yet given White's alleged reputation for wanting to kill a police officer, it seems likely that Eldridge Cleaver's larger vision of things like a North American Liberation Front against the police resonated with these two men's own perceived role in "a war with the cops." "The hard core [probably speaking of White and Anderson, among others]," Charles White remarked, tellingly cutting to the central issue, "they understood Cleaver, but this was all about our war, and the Black Panthers didn't start that."[181]

Violence between Panthers and members of the Detroit Police Department reached a crescendo in October with an encounter that led to the shooting death of officer Glen Smith and the incarceration of the Detroit 15. As would be expected, several accounts of the incident exist, but apparently around dusk on October 24, 1970, Detroit police officers confronted two Panthers distributing party literature on a street corner near the NCCF's new headquarters on the city's west side and attempted to cite them for harassing passersby. Perceiving another instance of police brutality in the making, a small crowd formed as the two Panthers resisted, eventually breaking free from the police and running to the nearby NCCF house on Sixteenth and Myrtle with handcuffs still dangling from one man's wrist. By this time, a jeering crowd had gathered in the street and began pelting the police with rocks and bottles, prompting the officers to call for backup.[182]

One of the police officers responding to the call was Marshall Emerson, a black plainclothes officer. Upon arriving on the scene, Emerson swept through a vacant lot in his unmarked patrol car, drawing high-powered rifle fire from somewhere in the vicinity. In reaction to the gunfire, which wounded Emerson in the hand, another black plainclothes officer, Glen Smith, drew his service revolver and crouched behind his unmarked car across the street from where Emerson was shot. While peering over his car toward the direction of the NCCF residence about fifty feet away, Smith was shot and killed.

As the police presence increased, more and more Panthers sought refuge in the NCCF office, reinforced with sandbags and well stocked with assorted weaponry, dynamite, and pipe bombs, according to police accounts. For nearly six hours police laid siege to the house, firing several canisters of tear gas, but by most accounts abstaining from a bloody head-on assault of the residence. Newly appointed Police Commissioner John F. Nichols went to the scene and took charge of the operation.

Only after numerous attempts by local black community leaders such as Rev. Willis Tabor, Frank Ditto (director of the Eastside Voice of Independent Detroit), William Penn of the NAACP, and several members of the city council to mediate, along with a call from the Panther brass, did the fifteen Panthers—eight women and seven men—surrender to police.[183] Nadine Brown, a columnist for the *Michigan Chronicle*, was called a heroine for her role as emissary between the authorities and the occupants of the house. She made several trips into the house, which resulted in the activists' surrender.[184]

Aside from the revulsion and hostility of many Detroit whites, for whom the death of a policeman led to several condemnations of certain "gutless" and "spineless" city officials for not allowing the police to destroy those in the NCCF house, the event also confirmed their worst fears about Black Power as a means of blacks "taking over." The shooting was generally synthesized as an extreme example of that alarming 68 percent increase in assaults on Detroit police between 1969 and 1970. Anxiety over this trend manifested itself fully in the widely held belief that, in the words of a Detroit officer, the events in Detroit were just local instances of a much larger "national conspiracy across this nation to attack and harass and, if possible, kill police officers."[185]

Like many police officers around the nation, Detroit police feared that the 1967 insurrection, these "cop killings," and other attacks on police were indeed part of an organized and coordinated assault on them. Testifying in October 1970 before a Senate subcommittee investigating assaults on law enforcement officers, Detroit Detective Lieutenant William R. McCoy answered in the affirmative that not only could this offensive be traced back to black self-defense pioneer Robert F. Williams and his emphasis on urban guerrilla warfare, but "in fact," McCoy incorrectly stated, "I believe it dates back further than that, when our New Left started and the SDS originated."[186] McCoy was referring most immediately to two bombs (each consisting of up to thirty-four sticks of dynamite) that Detroit police discovered at their own Thirteenth Precinct Station and Police Officers Association building on the same day in March 1970. In connection with these bombings, a federal grand jury in Detroit that summer indicted thirteen members of the Weather Underground for transporting explosives in interstate commerce with the intent to engage in a bombing campaign of police stations and banks in Michigan.[187]

Detective McCoy continued that this conspiracy "does not involve any one single organization, I believe it involves several different organizations" and is definitely "countrywide, nationwide."[188] When questioned about the role of the BPP in this "nationwide conspiracy," McCoy referred to literature with titles like "Long Live the Revolution," "America's House on Fire: Freedom Now or Let It Burn," and "Praise the Lord and Pass the Ammunition" distributed by the Detroit Panthers and the League of Revolutionary Black Workers. "Words don't kill cops," another police official was quoted in the *Detroit News* regarding the proliferation of "rhetorical violence" from the Panthers in the last year. But, he pointed out, "any policeman who has ever read the *Black Panther* might be more than a little uptight in his dealings with Panther members."[189]

In the estimation of the Detroit Police Department, the Panthers' literature and actions "capture the minds of [these] young students" and indoctrinate them with the conviction that, in the words of the Panthers, "All self-defense groups must strike blows against the slave master until we have secured our survival as a people, and if this takes shooting every pig and blowing up every pigsty, then let's get on up."[190] Detective McCoy concluded his testimony with the theory that, ultimately, the objective of this conspiracy to harm the police, which "I am sure . . . is not confined to the Detroit area," "is a means to another end." "I think they would like to overthrow the Government of the United States," he gauged, "and the police are our first line of defense." As far as some others were concerned, by interfering with the "effectiveness and efficiency of the police and the firefighter" in the major and minor cities, militants could achieve their final objective, "a state of anarchy."[191]

Incredible as this theory may sound, nothing could be farther from the truth. In the minds of some Panthers, by singling out the police, they were merely putting the police on the defensive or, as some might say, giving the police "a dose of their own medicine." Blacks had been harassed, manhandled, and made to feel like second-class citizens on a daily basis since the founding of the first American police department in the 1800s. The Panthers believed that blacks had suffered long enough. They would no longer be horded around like chattel. Blacks would deal with the police on an equal footing, and no one felt more strongly about this than Eldridge Cleaver, who in a warning to the "pigs" wrote: "The next time you [the police] come into the Black community and take another Black life you gonna have to bring ass to get ass."

On this matter, the Cleaver-influenced factions at both the national and local levels were in accord. In Detroit, Cleaver's followers interpreted the shooting of Emerson and Smith as justifiable retaliation for systematic repression on the part of Detroit police, maintaining the killing was only the "black community [beginning] to respond to the continuous pig brutality and the murder of black people with shots of gun fire and dead pigs."[192] As revolutionary internationalists seeking allies in a united front against American capitalist oppression, the Panthers often subordinated questions of race. In the Panther ideology, "pigs" meant all agents of repression—white or black—acting in an unrevolutionary manner. This may explain why the Panthers showed just as much contempt for black police officers who mistreated blacks as they did for white officers who mistreated blacks, and why the Detroit Panthers never made any recorded mention of the fact that both Emerson and Smith were black.

Charles White refused to comment directly on the Smith killing but distinctly said it had been building for quite some time and that anybody could have seen that this showdown was coming.[193] Throughout 1970 some members of the Detroit NCCF decried what they called "police efforts to get the Panthers" through constant surveillance, harassing those selling the party's newspaper, defacing party posters on the streets, and sabotaging Panther property.[194]

As expected, some members of the Detroit NCCF attributed the shooting to certain members at the national level who crafted the image of the Panthers as leaders in a wider revolution, proclaiming in the pages of the *Black Panther*, "With every pig attack on the vanguard party the people's willingness and ability to deal with the pigs grow."[195] Partially to satisfy this undertaking, the Detroit 15 were portrayed on the pages of the *Black Panther* as heroic figures standing up for an appreciative black community who in turn aided the Panthers' resistance to police brutality.[196] This type of framing began with the events that led to the shooting. While the *Detroit Free Press* reported the initial scuffle resulted from two Panthers' recalcitrance upon being cited by police for distributing Panther literature, according to the Panthers' narration, the two Panthers simply came to the aid of a nine-year-old boy being beaten by police. From there, according to the Panthers, police instigated the entire episode by attacking the two with "clubs and blackjacks" before arresting them.[197]

By first considering the size of the boisterous crowds that gathered during the standoff and the fact that, in addition to stoning police, non-Panthers also set three patrol cars ablaze, there is probably some basis for the Panthers' contention they received a measure of community support that evening. The *Michigan Chronicle* buttressed this claim with its analysis that the Detroit 15 were unafraid during the standoff only because they believed they had the black community behind them.[198] The newspaper responded sympathetically to the Panthers in the wake of the shootout. While lamenting the violence and shooting death of Officer Smith, Nadine Brown expressed her frustration at the city of Detroit for not opening a dialogue with young blacks sooner. "My anger never subsided," she wrote of her role in helping the Panthers surrender to police without additional bloodshed, "but it was joined by a profound concern for those young people inside who were fighting for a cause, and the people in the community."[199] Judging from these reactions, the Panthers' clashes with the police over the preceding months had apparently reached at least some in the audience.

Additionally, several eyewitnesses also told authorities that the "trigger-happy cops" should be blamed for the violence, not the Panthers, pointing out that their undue show of force was a "common occurrence" in the neighborhood. Regardless of how much actual support they enjoyed, the Panthers undoubtedly exaggerated it in constructing official accounts of hundreds of people in the streets throwing "a nigga wrench into the man's machinery" to be used by the national party. For their purposes, the bottom line was that the support, whatever its level, was proof, as the *Black Panther* announced, that "with every pig attack on the vanguard party the people's willingness and ability to deal with the pigs grow."[200]

Only three of the Detroit 15—Erone Desaussure, Benjamin Fondrun, and David Johnson—were ever convicted of felonious assault, but while some remained incarcerated for nearly eight months awaiting trial, the Panthers also carefully cultivated their martyrdom.[201] In a local variation of a much overused 1960s slogan, the city was repeatedly called to "Free the Detroit 15." To inspire support for the cause, numerous "pig attacks" against jailed Panthers were relayed to the public, including accounts of police deliberately burning Jerome Lee in his cell and assaulting Diane Brown. Nevertheless, despite long hours of the police's "inhumane schemes" to break their backs and spirit, the Panthers assured the black community that police could not "stifle the love for the people's struggle felt and generated by our revolutionary comrades."[202]

Ultimately, however, the most salient interpretations of the Detroit 15 were not those of the Panthers, but instead those formulated within the dominant society. Certain members of the Detroit Panthers enthusiastically played their part in Cleaver's plan to escalate the revolution "by taking it the pigs," but it was precisely these localized instances of urban guerrilla warfare in cities like Detroit that, when perceived cumulatively by the nation as a whole, truly gave the appearance of a rather well coordinated guerrilla campaign against American institutions. More so than any other militant group of the Vietnam War era, as white America and its media increasingly bought into Panther propaganda or embellished it, the localized political texts created by acts of urban guerrilla warfare were read as a carefully orchestrated revolutionary strategy. The image of organized, disciplined, and empowered—armed—blacks carrying out what was perceived to be such a sustained and efficient national campaign of urban guerrilla violence against America's police stretched society beyond its endurance. It was as if the age-old fear of the slave rebellion was given new and terrifying expression by thousands of Panthers across the nation appearing to move in unison. That the Panthers were so successful in creating this image was evident not only in the testimony of Detroit police but more profoundly in the swift and ruthless campaign of repression carried out by the Federal Bureau of Investigation (FBI), which by the early 1970s facilitated the Panthers' demise.

And again, maybe more so than in any other U.S. city, violence and the perceptions of violence in the isolated and decaying inner city of Detroit had a profound and immediate impact on race relations, affecting both whites and blacks. Although the Panthers never had a massive following in Detroit, their rhetoric and actions still impacted how more established and perhaps influential black groups operated. For whites, who already felt on the defensive in the face of "the economic and racial transformation of the city"—and who often blamed blacks for their own status—the proliferation of violent resistance by frustrated blacks reinforced already strong prejudices about the "colored problem" while solidifying the city's considerable racial polarization.[203]

Despite this well-documented polarization and conflict in Detroit, specifically examining the interpretations and reactions to the political violence of the Black Panthers by the city's white citizens proves problematic because acts of urban guerrilla warfare by the Panthers in Detroit were not the only show in town, not by a long shot. The late 1960s and early 1970s brought a frightening increase in assaults on police, a "minirebellion" on the Lower East Side in 1966, spiraling homicide rates in the central city, and the activities of several Black Power and New Left groups, including the Panthers. By the early 1970s Detroit led the nation in crimes of violence and murder. Incredibly, in 1973 homicides in Detroit were triple the number killed on all sides during "the troubles" in Northern Ireland the same year.[204] All of these figures, however, pale in comparison to the revolt in historical memory and scholarly research. Variously referred to as the Great Rebellion, the six days of intense violence in the summer of 1967 eclipsed all other forms of American political violence, save the 1965 Watts uprising. The upheaval left forty-three people dead (nine whites, thirty-four blacks), 347 injured, thousands arrested, 5,000 homeless, some 2,700 buildings either looted or burned, and $163 million of insured property damage—apart from the countless millions in incalculable uninsured property and personal economic hardships.[205]

Thus, in the dense forest that was political violence in Detroit, it may well be impossible to isolate and measure a single tree like the Black Panthers. Still, the acts of urban guerrilla warfare on the part of the Panthers in 1970 were perceived as another of the menacing manifestations of violent resistance by frustrated blacks, which along with the uprising, "hardened white racial prejudices" and "gave urgency to white resistance" in Detroit. The discernable white backlash in Detroit during the 1970s and 1980s over affirmative action, busing, attempts to alter the residential racial status quo, and the "'excesses' of Black Power" were all influenced directly or indirectly by white judgments and opinions drawn in part from all the violence.[206]

Fear of violence and apprehension over its continuation accelerated Detroit's postwar trend of white flight. Whites historically had been extremely reluctant and in many cases violently opposed to black encroachment into previously racially unmixed neighborhoods on the edges of the city's invisible, yet very real, racial boundaries. In hundreds of instances, on a grassroots and block-by-block basis, whites attempted to hold back the open housing movement of the 1950s and 1960s, choosing to "hold 'til the dam bursts, then run like hell." No doubt directly reflecting continued consternation over black violence, whites bolted in record numbers in the late 1960s. In 1967, 47,000 whites had retreated from the battleground of the city to Detroit's growing suburbs; in 1968, 80,000 joined the exodus as did 46,000 more in 1969, and nearly as many in 1970.[207]

Like many working- and lower-middle-class whites in the United States, thousands of whites in Detroit reacted to the violence with support for racially conservative candidates. Again as was the case in many cities and states that experienced rebellions, in the 1968 and 1972 presidential elections, Richard Nixon, a Republican, overwhelmingly captured Detroit's white precincts. Maybe more astonishing, in those same years third-party candidate Governor George Wallace, the renowned defender of segregation at the University of Alabama in the early 1960s, cultivated an impressive political base in the city, and to a lesser degree the state, winning 10 percent of the votes cast in Michigan in 1968 despite the massive anti-Wallace campaign launched by the UAW, the state AFL-CIO, and the Michigan Teamsters. Warmly received when he campaigned there again, in 1972 Wallace exhibited a strong showing by sweeping every predominately white ward in Detroit on his way to a stunning victory in the Michigan Democratic Party primary.[208]

Perhaps the city's most consequential interpretations of the violence resulted in the police department's tangible attempts to keep the have-nots (mainly blacks) subjugated and physically cordoned off from the rest of the city. Once again adhering to the adage that the best defense is a good offense, it was from this general thinking that the STRESS unit was born. This "secret, elite section of Detroit undercover assault squads" operating in the inner city was viewed by white Detroit as a neo-vigilante posse cleaning up the ghetto.[209] STRESS meted out its justice on the streets with highly questionable extralegal tactics and disturbing lethal force. In addition to an estimated 500 raids without search warrants during the thirty-month lifespan of STRESS, the Detroit Police Department posted the highest number of civilian killings by police per capita in the nation, twenty deaths within the same two-and-a-half-year period. Ten people were killed—ten of the first eleven were black—and nine others wounded in just the first six months of STRESS.

Statistically, in 1971 Detroit police killed civilians at a rate of 7.17 per 1,000 officers, more than one-third of which was done by STRESS, itself comprising probably no more than 2 percent of the department.[210] Its very existence and strong support by white Detroit speaks directly to the anxiety of the city's population regarding black violence and the siege mentality that settled over the predominantly white Detroit police force. On the other hand, largely campaigning on the conduct of the Detroit police, and in particular STRESS, Coleman Young's victory over white police commissioner John Nichols, the creator of STRESS, in 1973, to become the city's first black mayor, was seen by many African Americans as a final vindication of their resentment and opposition to the abuses and excesses of STRESS.[211]

It was also in this atmosphere that such unscrupulous programs as the FBI's Counter Intelligence Program (COINTELPRO) flourished. Instigated by the FBI and sanctioned by the Justice Department, COINTELPRO involved FBI agents working in conjunction with local police departments to disrupt, misdirect, discredit, and generally neutralize the activities of leftist groups like the Black Panthers. Between 1968 and 1969 COINTELPRO raids on thirty-one Panther offices nationwide, including Detroit, were responsible for the incarceration of hundreds of Panthers. Simultaneously, disinformation efforts preoccupied and divided leadership, while exorbitant bail drained party funds. In all, COINTELPRO was instrumental in hastening the Panthers' demise.[212]

By 1974 the Detroit branch of the BPP had withered away. Lorene Johnson "was one of the last members of the branch to leave, leaving Detroit for Oakland in the winter of 1973."[213] In the end, though, the Detroit branch of the BPP "exemplified to many urban Blacks qualities of bravery and compassion."[214] Melvin Peters calls the Detroit Panthers "some of the bravest people I have ever known."[215] The Panthers attempted to organize and mold an eclectic group of mostly young people into a revolutionary movement for social change. At the same time, they used their community survival programs to help sustain members of the community who might otherwise have fallen by the wayside, all the while instilling in them a sense of consciousness that might compel them to act in a revolutionary manner against the forces of oppression. For some residents, the Panthers were the only organization from which they could receive around-the-clock assistance. The assistance that the Panthers provided went beyond their established mandated community survival programs. It was not uncommon for the members of the Detroit branch to check on their neighbors, especially the elderly; provide shelter for runaways; or transport sick people to the hospital. Residents could request services without feeling embarrassed, be treated like human beings rather than being degraded by the bureaucrats who ran the city's social service agencies, not be burdened with mounds of paperwork typical of most service agencies, and be free from intrusive questions that infringed on one's privacy.

Contrary to the widely held belief that the Panthers were the products of broken homes, poor environs, and troubled backgrounds, many members were raised in two-parent households that may have been considered middle class at the time. Among this eclectic group, at least in the early years, was also an element that could be considered "lumpen." In some ways, the Detroit Panthers were representative of many other Panther branches and chapters throughout the country. Yet in the area of urban guerrilla warfare, on the streets of Motown there were some Panthers who viewed their clashes with police not as a coordinated alliance with the National Liberation Front, Fidelistas, or even the Weathermen, but rather as a battle in an ongoing war of disrespect, retaliation, and revenge. Again, the difference was that, in the Panther uniform, they might now assign meanings to their own actions. That being said, the problem still remained that if much of white America was inexplicably perplexed by the Panthers' overall message, dealing with a hostile nonwhite enemy was something white America knew all about.

Notes

1. On July 3, 1833, as his wife, Lucie, was about to be sold down the river, Thornton Blackburn planned a daring escape from their Louisville masters. Followed to Michigan, the couple was captured and sentenced to return to Kentucky. Upon hearing this, Detroit's black community rallied to their cause in the Blackburn uprisings of 1833, the first racial uprising in the city's history. Thornton and Lucie were ushered across the river to Canada, but their safety proved tenuous when Michigan's governor demanded their extradition. Canada's defense of the Blackburns set the tone for all future Canada-U.S. relations over the issue of fugitive slaves and confirmed the British colony as the main terminus of the Underground Railroad.

2. James Geschwender, *Class, Race and Worker Insurgency* (New York: Cambridge University Press, 1977).

3. See, for example, "Guerilla Attacks in USA," *Black Panther*, February 27, 1971; "Revolutionary Self-Defense: The Correct Method for Dealing with the Mercenary Pig," *Black Panther*, March 20, 1971; and "Pigs Executed in Dallas, Texas," *Black Panther*, February 20, 1971.

4. Charles White, interview by Joel P. Rhodes, November 17, 1997. After months of searching in vain for a former Detroit Black Panther willing to talk about the violence of 1970, the first author placed a classified ad in the *Michigan Chronicle*, the Detroit-area African American newspaper, requesting that former Panthers contact me by phone. As part of the agreement to be interviewed, this respondent stipulated that he would not use specific names and he himself must remain anonymous, even to the interviewer. Despite this, the caller exhibited a quick grasp of the people, places, and events I questioned the caller about, which quickly made me confident that the caller was a reliable source. Hereafter, I refer to this source by the pseudonym Charles White. It should be made clear, however, that although White exhibited a strong grasp of Detroit Black Panther history, I cannot say with 100 percent certainty that he was indeed a member of the Detroit branch of the BPP. His statements should be read bearing that in mind. Kathleen Rout, *Eldridge Cleaver* (Boston: Twayne, 1991), 101.

5. Gwen Robinson, interview by Judson L. Jeffries, May 26, 2009.

6. For an excellent study of postwar Detroit, see Thomas J. Sugrue, *The Origins of the Urban Crisis: Race and Inequality in Postwar Detroit* (Princeton, N.J.: Princeton University Press, 1996); and Richard W. Thomas, *Life for Us Is What We Make It: Building Black Community in Detroit, 1915–1945* (Bloomington: Indiana University Press, 1992).

7. Gilbert Osofsky, *Harlem: The Making of a Ghetto; Negro New York, 1890–1930* (New York: Harper and Row, 1968).

8. James Geschwender, *Class, Race and Worker Insurgency* (New York: Cambridge University Press, 1977).

9. Ibid.

10. *Report of the National Advisory Commission on Civil Disorders* (Washington, D.C.: Government Printing Office, 1968), 90, 132, 152, 429, 430.

11. Ibid., 49–50, 80, 240, 351; Joel A. Lieske, "The Conditions of Racial Violence in American Cities: A Developmental Synthesis," *American Political Science Review* 72, no. 4 (December 1978): 1324–1340.

12. Lloyd H. Bailer, "The Negro Automobile Worker," *Journal of Political Economy* 51 (October 1943): 416; Herbert R. Northrup, *Organized Labor and the Negro* (New York: Harper, 1944), 189–194; Herbert R. Northrup, "The Negro in the Automobile Industry," in *Negro Employment in Basic Industry* (New York: Harper and Brothers, 1970), 1:56.

13. Lloyd H. Bailer, "The Automobile Unions and Negro Labor," *Political Science Quarterly* 59 (December 1944): 566.

14. Northrup, *Organized Labor and the Negro*, 186.

15. Bailer, "Negro Automobile Worker," 415.

16. B. J. Widick, *Detroit: City of Race and Class Violence* (Chicago: Quadrangle, 1972), 26.

17. Ibid.; Bailer, "Negro Automobile Worker," 415.

18. Reynolds Farley, Sheldon Danziger, and Harry J. Holzer, *Detroit Divided* (New York: Russell Sage Foundation, 2000), 42.

19. Geschwender, *Class, Race and Worker Insurgency*.

20. Ibid.

21. Ibid.

22. Farley, Danziger, and Holzer, *Detroit Divided*.

23. U.S. Census 1940–1980.

24. Wilber C. Rich, "Coleman Young and Detroit Politics: 1973–1986," in *The New Black Politics: The Search for Political Power*, ed. Michael B. Preston, Lenneal J. Henderson Jr., and Paul Puryear (New York: Longman, 1987), 220–221.

25. Godfrey Hodgson, *America In Our Time: From World War II to Nixon, What Happened and Why* (New York: Vintage Books, 1976), 439.

26. Elaine Brown, *A Taste of Power: A Black Woman's Story* (New York: Pantheon, 1992), 247.

27. Thomas, *Life for Us Is What We Make It*, 316–318. For perceptions of the police as an occupying army, see also Dan Georgakas and Marvin Surkin, *Detroit: I Do Mind Dying, A Study in Urban Revolution* (New York: St. Martin's Press, 1975).

28. Thousands of southerners, mainly blacks, migrated to the city of Detroit in search of defense industry jobs in the early 1940s. The Sojourner Truth homes were built in order to accommodate the workers and their families. On January 20, 1942, federal housing officials in Washington announced that the Sojourner Truth homes would be designated for whites instead. Mayor Edward Jeffries, Detroit housing officials, certain union leaders, and Detroit civil rights activists protested. Fights broke out between black and white protesters. Whites were adamant about maintaining the racial purity of their neighborhood. In April of that year, the mayor prevailed. Under the protection of the state police and the Michigan National Guard, blacks were allowed to move into the Sojourner Truth homes.

29. Altercations between black and white youth began on June 20, 1943, at Belle Isle Park. Things soon escalated to the point where black and white mobs were assaulting one another, beating innocent motorists and passersby, burning cars, destroying storefronts, and looting businesses. Both sides were said to have been equally responsible for the violence, as both blacks and whites reportedly encouraged others to join in with false accusations that one of "their own" had been unjustly attacked. The violence lasted three days, resulting in thirty-four people dead, twenty-

five of whom were African American. Out of the nearly 600 injured, blacks accounted for more than 75 percent, and of the roughly 1,800 people who were arrested, blacks accounted for approximately 85 percent. The violence finally ended when Mayor Edward Jeffries and Governor Harry Kelly asked President Roosevelt to intervene.

30. *Report of the National Advisory Commission*, 48.
31. Sidney Fine, *Violence in the Model City: The Cavanaugh Administration, Race Relations and the Detroit Riot of 1967* (Ann Arbor: University of Michigan Press, 1989), 98.
32. Angela D. Dillard, *Faith in the City: Preaching Radical Social Change in Detroit* (Ann Arbor: University of Michigan Press, 2007).
33. As quoted in William Serrin, "God Help Our City," *Atlantic Monthly*, March 1969, 115.
34. Hodgson, *America In Our Time*, 434–437.
35. George Crockett, a lawyer and jurist, would later win a congressional seat, serving from 1980 to 1991.
36. See Helen Mataya Graves, "New Detroit Committee/New Detroit, Incorporated: A Case Study of an Urban Coalition" (Ph.D. diss., Wayne State University, 1975).
37. For an analysis of arguably the most prominent revolutionary nationalist group in Detroit, the Dodge Revolutionary Action Movement (DRUM), and the working-class African Americans who organized around its founding ideals in various shops throughout the city's auto industry, see Geschwender, *Class, Race and Worker Insurgency*.
38. Herbert Haines, *Black Radicals and the Civil Rights Mainstream, 1954–1970* (Knoxville: University of Tennessee Press, 1988), 70–71.
39. Fine, *Violence in the Model City*, 373.
40. Thomas, *Life for Us Is What We Make It*, 86–87; Georgakas and Surkin, *Detroit*, 1.
41. Michael Newton, *Bitter Grain: Huey Newton and the Black Panther Party* (Los Angeles: Holloway House, 1991), 138.
42. Ahmad A. Rahman, "Marching Blind: The Rise and Fall of the Black Panther Party in Detroit," in *Liberated Territory: Untold Local Perspectives on the Black Panther Party*, ed. Yohuru Williams and Jama Lazerow (Durham, N.C.: Duke University Press, 2008), 181–231.
43. Phil Garner, interview by Judson L. Jeffries, June 22, 2009.
44. Ibid.
45. Geschwender, *Class, Race and Worker Insurgency*; Heather Ann Thompson, *Whose Detroit? Politics, Labor, and Race in a Modern American City* (Ithaca, N.Y.: Cornell University Press, 2001); Dillard, *Faith in the City*.
46. General Gordon Baker, interview by Judson L. Jeffries, June 15, 2009.
47. Luke Tripp, interview by Judson L. Jeffries, June 26, 2009.
48. Ibid.
49. Ibid.
50. A close read of the *Black Panther* reveals that articles about the Detroit cadre did not begin referring to them as the Detroit branch of the BPP until 1972. Before that time they were cited in the *Black Panther* newspaper as an NCFF. However, several members of the branch maintain that by 1971 they were a full-fledged branch of the BPP.
51. In theory, the paramilitary BPP was structured with a definite chain of command. Outside of the national headquarters in Oakland, there were regional headquarters that supervised nearby Panther branches. For example, the New York chapter served as the regional headquarters for the entire East Coast; Chicago for the Midwest; Winston-Salem, North Carolina, for the South; and Seattle, Washington, for the Pacific Northwest.
52. Tracy Wilson, interview by Judson L. Jeffries, October 28, 2009.

53. Lorene Johnson, interview by Judson L. Jeffries, December 7, 2008.

54. Bill Elder, interview by Judson L. Jeffries, May 8, 2009.

55. Ibid.

56. Ibid.

57. U.S. Congress, House of Representatives, Committee on Internal Security, *Black Panther Party Part 3 Investigations of Detroit, Philadelphia, and Indianapolis Chapters*, 91st Cong., 2nd sess., July 21–24, 1970, 4440–4441, 4431–4443 [hereafter cited as *Investigations of Detroit*].

58. Ibid., 4431.

59. Ibid.

60. Ibid, 4474.

61. Ibid., 4467, 4473, 4474.

62. It should be noted that Berry's altruist account, while certainly in the spirit of the Panthers' mission of serving the people, was given while testifying before the House of Representatives Committee on Internal Security and may reflect his efforts at self-promotion. Ibid., 4432.

63. Johnson, interview.

64. Tracy Wilson, interview by Judson L. Jeffries, May 15, 2009.

65. Johnson, interview.

66. Gwen Robinson, interview by Judson L. Jeffries, May 20, 2009.

67. Robinson, interview, May 26, 2009.

68. Ibid.

69. Wilson, interview, May 15, 2009.

70. Robinson, interview, May 20, 2009.

71. Tracy Wilson, interview by Judson L. Jeffries, March 31, 2009.

72. Robinson, interview, May 20, 2009.

73. *Black Panther*, June 10, 1972, 7.

74. Wilson, interview, May 15, 2009.

75. *Black Panther*, June 10, 1972, 7.

76. *Detroit News*, October 8, 1973.

77. *Investigations of Detroit*, 4447

78. Thompson, *Whose Detroit?*

79. *Detroit News*, November 16, 1970.

80. Thompson, *Whose Detroit?*

81. Rita Smith, interview by Judson L. Jeffries, July 24, 2009.

82. Melvin Peters, interview by Judson L. Jeffries, October 12, 2009.

83. Wilson, interview, May 15, 2009.

84. JoNina Abron, "Serving the People: The Survival Programs of the Black Panther Party," in *The Black Panther Party (Reconsidered)*, ed. Charles E. Jones (Baltimore: Black Classic Press, 1998), 187.

85. Robinson, interview, May 26, 2009.

86. Brown, *Taste of Power*, 292.

87. The pig became a powerful symbol for the Black Panthers around 1968 and entered wider usage immediately thereafter. "Off the Pig" actually had dual meanings, the first being any act of violence against the police but also the demand to remove the police from the black community. U.S. Congress, House of Representatives, Committee on Internal Security, *Gun-Barrel Politics: Black Panther Party, 1966–1971*, 92nd Cong., 1st sess., August 18, 1971, 42–43 [hereafter cited as *Gun-Barrel Politics*]; Brown, *Taste of Power*, 292.

88. Rout, *Eldridge Cleaver*, 101; Philip S. Foner, ed., *The Black Panthers Speak* (Philadelphia: J. B. Lippincott, 1970), 16–18.

89. *Investigations of Detroit*, 4455.

90. Bill Elder, interview by Judson L. Jeffries, March 17, 2009.

91. Robinson, interview, May 26, 2009.

92. Bill Elder, interview by Judson L. Jeffries, May 16, 2009.

93. Bill Elder, interview by Judson L. Jeffries, May 17, 2009.

94. Robinson, interview, May 20, 2009.

95. Elder, interview, May 16, 2009.

96. Robinson, interview, May 20, 2009.

97. Johnson, interview.

98. The Detroit Black Panthers also swore an allegiance to the Black Student Union of Detroit, but this effectively meant little more than attending each other's rallies and events. *Investigations of Detroit*, 4458.

99. Tom Wolfe, *Radical Chic & Mau-Mauing the Flak Catchers* (New York: Farrar, Straus, and Giroux, 1970).

100. *Detroit News*, May 2, 1967.

101. John Sinclair, interview by Judson L. Jeffries, June 23, 2009.

102. Ibid.

103. *Investigations of Detroit*, 4454–4455.

104. Pun Plamondon, interview by Judson L. Jeffries, July 27, 2009.

105. Ibid.

106. "Head shop" was the term used to describe boutiques that sold drug items and counterculture artifacts: bongs, rolling papers, underground press, roach clips, poetry books, hippie clothing, jewelry, hard-to-find records, incense, astrology books, posters, black lights, political books—stuff you would never find in J. C. Penny's or Sears.

107. Pun Plamondon, e-mail correspondence with Judson L. Jeffries, July 6, 2009.

108. Thomas Amar Casey, interview by Judson L. Jeffries, July 23, 2009.

109. Ibid.

110. Wilson, interview, May 15, 2009.

111. David Courtwright, *Violent Land: Single Men and Social Disorder from the Frontier to the Inner City* (Cambridge, Mass.: Harvard University Press, 1996), 30–32. See also Bertram Wyatt Brown, *Honor and Violence in the Old South* (New York: Oxford University Press, 1986).

112. Amar Casey, interview.

113. Tracy Wilson, interview by Judson L. Jeffries, May 18, 2009.

114. *Investigations of Detroit*, 4431–4437.

115. G. Louis Heath, ed., *Off the Pigs! The History and Literature of the Black Panther Party* (Metuchen, N.J.: Scarecrow, 1976), 50–58.

116. Frantz Fanon, *The Wretched of the Earth* (New York: Grove Press, 1963), 94; Brown, *Taste of Power*, 136.

117. Brown, *Taste of Power*, 67.

118. Elder, interview, May 16, 2009.

119. Ibid.

120. Ibid.

121. *Investigations of Detroit*, 4476.

122. Eldridge Cleaver, "Requiem for Nonviolence (The Death of Martin Luther King, Jr.)," *Ramparts* 7, no. 9 (December 1968); Rout, *Eldridge Cleaver*, 133–136, 139, 148–149.

123. *Investigations of Detroit*, 4438, 4440.

124. Ibid., 4441–4442

125. Ibid., 4441–4442, 4457, 4473.

126. Ibid., 4435.

127. Garner, interview.

128. Plamondon, interview.

129. *Investigations of Detroit*, 4437.

130. Jones and Jeffries, *Black Panther Party Reconsidered.*

131. Unfortunately, the medical clinic never materialized for two reasons: the long days of hard work prevented the Panthers from giving that project the attention needed to jump start a medical clinic, and over the course of the next few years, when the groundwork for the clinic had finally been laid, the Detroit cadre were ordered to go to Oakland to work on the political campaigns of Bobby Seale and Elaine Brown.

132. *Investigations of Detroit*, 4438.

133. Ahmad Rahman, conversation with Judson L. Jeffries, October 24, 2009.

134. White, interview; Fine, *Violence in the Model City*, 423.

135. White, interview; John Forward and Jay R. Williams, "Internal-External Control and Black Militancy," *Journal of Social Issues* 26, no. 1 (1970): 88; Donald Warren, *Black Neighborhoods: An Assessment of Community Power* (Ann Arbor: University of Michigan Press, 1975), 38–43; Joel Aberbach and Jack Walker, "The Meanings of Black Power: A Comparison of White and Black Interpretations of a Political Slogan," *American Political Science Review* 64 (June 1970): 384.

136. Georgakas and Surkin, *Detroit*, 74.

137. White, interview; Sugrue, *Origins of the Urban Crisis*, 261.

138. White, interview.

139. *Gun-Barrel Politics*, 38; Rout, *Eldridge Cleaver*, 121, 133–136, 139, 148–149; William L. Van DeBurg, *New Day in Babylon* (Chicago: University of Chicago Press, 1992), 160.

140. *Gun-Barrel Politics*, 38; Rout, *Eldridge Cleaver*, 121, 133–136, 139, 148–149; Van DeBurg, *New Day in Babylon*, 160.

141. *Gun-Barrel Politics*, 38; Rout, *Eldridge Cleaver*, 121, 133–136, 139, 148–149; Van DeBurg, *New Day in Babylon*, 160.

142. White, interview.

143. Daniel Levine et al., *The Attitudes of Students at Black High Schools in Five Cities, Spring 1970* (Kansas City: Center for the Study of Metropolitan Problems in Education, 1971), 32; White, interview.

144. White, interview; *Investigations of Detroit*, 4443.

145. White, interview.

146. Ibid.; Aberbach and Walker, "Meanings of Black Power," 384; *Investigations of Detroit*, 4444; Gail Sheehy, "Black Against Black: The Agony of Panthermania," *New York*, November 16, 1970, 38; Carolyn Calloway, "Group Cohesiveness in the Black Panther Party," *Journal of Black Studies* 8 (September 1977): 63; Brown, *Taste of Power*, 139.

147. *Black Panther*, September 26, 1970, 8.

148. *Investigations of Detroit*, 4445, 4447, 4450, 4461.

149. Huey P. Newton, quoted in *Black Protest Thought in the Twentieth Century*, ed. August Meier, Elliott Rudwick, and Francis I. Broderick, 2nd ed. (New York: Bobbs-Merrill, 1971), 8, 506.

150. Tracye Ann Matthews, "'No One Ever Asks What a Man's Place in the Revolution Is': Gender and Sexual Politics in the Black Panther Party, 1966–1971" (Ph.D. diss., University of Michigan, 1998), 90; *Investigations of Detroit*, 4456–4457.

151. Not all reactions to these women were favorable. Brown and Huggins formed the core of what became known in the party as "the clique," a group of Panther women in Oakland who dedi-

cated themselves to the hard work of the party's community organizing without subordinating themselves. Many Black Panther men around the country became resentful of the "smart bitches" with bad attitudes in the "clique," variously accusing them of identifying with the "white" women's liberation movement or conspiring to keep black men emasculated. Brown, *Taste of Power*, 191–192.

152. Matthews, "'No One Ever Asks,'" 317, 331, 357 (emphasis added); Heath, *Off the Pigs!*, 339–342.

153. Smith, interview.

154. Robinson, interview, May 20, 2009.

155. Johnson, interview.

156. *Detroit Free Press*, October 26, 1970; *Investigations of Detroit*, 4457. Unfortunately for the historian, the Wayne County recorder's court transcripts of the Detroit 15 trial were routinely destroyed after twenty-five years, just two years before the first author began this research.

157. Smith, interview.

158. *Investigations of Detroit*, 4457; White, interview. Several Detroit Panthers came from street gangs and maintained connections to this subculture. This may have been key regarding their conceptions of violence and women in general. David Courtwright argues that gangs brought together "young, undersocialized, armed, intoxicated men" and put them in a position to constantly test and prove their manhood. Certainly these are the ingredients of a feminist nightmare. Courtwright, *Violent Land*, 239.

159. Heath, *Off the Pigs!* 434; Rout, *Eldridge Cleaver*, 162; White, interview.

160. *Gun-Barrel Politics*, 307–309; NCCF Bulletin, in ibid.

161. *Black Panther*, August 8, 1970, 4.

162. Ahmad Rahman, interview by Judson L. Jeffries, October 28, 2009.

163. *Investigations of Detroit*, 4446. Those Panthers who returned from the Revolutionary Conference for a United Front Against Fascism in Oakland apparently had specific instructions from the national office to avenge Fred Hampton's and Mark Clark's deaths by acts of sniping and other violence directed at police. Donald Berry believed this directive was sent out to many Panther chapters nationwide.

164. "Assaults on Law Enforcement Officers," in *Gun-Barrel Politics*, 309; *Investigations of Detroit*, 4446.

165. *Black Panther*, July 25, 1970, 9.

166. Allen Feldman, *Formations of Violence: The Narrative of the Body and Political Terror in Northern Ireland* (Chicago: University of Chicago Press, 1991), 7, 30.

167. Patricia H. Collins, *Black Feminist Thought: Knowledge, Consciousness, and the Politics of Empowerment* (New York: Routledge, 1991), 172.

168. White, interview.

169. "Revolutionary Self-Defense: The Correct Method for Dealing with the Mercenary Pig," *Black Panther*, March 20, 1971; "Pigs Executed in Dallas, Texas," *Black Panther*, February 20, 1971.

170. Between the fall of 1967 and the end of 1968, nine police were killed and fifty-six wounded in clashes with the Panthers nationwide. Although there is some controversy concerning the actual number of Panthers killed by police during the same time, at least ten were reported killed and countless others wounded. Edward J. Epstein, "The Panthers and the Police: A Pattern of Genocide?" *New Yorker*, February 13, 1971.

171. "Assaults on Law Enforcement Officers," 315.

172. Sugrue, *Origins of the Urban Crisis*, 231–240.

173. "Assaults on Law Enforcement Officers," 290; *Detroit Free Press*, March 9, 1970; *Investigations of Detroit*, 4453; *Black Panther*, September 26, 1970, 8.

174. *Detroit News*, June 30, 1970; "Assaults on Law Enforcement Officers," 290.

175. *Michigan Chronicle*, July 4, 1970; *Detroit Free Press*, June 29, 1970; *Detroit News*, July 5, 1970.

176. *Investigations of Detroit*, 4444.

177. NCCF press release, in "Assaults on Law Enforcement Officers," 300; *Black Panther*, July 24, 1970, 8; *Detroit Free Press*, June 30, 1970; *Detroit News*, July 5, 1970.

178. *Detroit News*, July 5, 1970.

179. White, interview; *Black Panther*, September 8, 1970, 4.

180. NCCF press release, in "Assaults on Law Enforcement Officers," 300.

181. White, interview.

182. *Detroit Free Press*, October 26, 1970; *Detroit News*, October 25, 1970.

183. *Detroit Free Press*, October 27, 1970; *Detroit News*, October 26, 1970. Besides the Detroit 15, Jimmie Hall, Benjamin Baker, Donald Armes, Paul Allen, Roger DuBois Armstrong, and Minnie Johnson faced lesser charges stemming from the shooting.

184. *Detroit News*, October 26, 1970.

185. "Assaults on Law Enforcement Officers," 317.

186. Robert F. Williams's neo-vigilante commitment to African American armed self-defense in the rural South is seen as a vital link between the traditional civil rights movement and the Black Power movement. See Timothy B. Tyson, "Robert F. Williams, 'Black Power,' and the Roots of the African American Freedom Struggle," *Journal of American History* 85, no. 2 (September 1998): 540–570; "Assaults on Law Enforcement Officers," 317.

187. "Assaults on Law Enforcement Officers," 268, 276, 279, 317. The thirteen named in the indictment were a "who's who" consisting of Mark Rudd, Bernadine Dohrn, William Ayers, Kathy Boudin, Linda Evans, Cathy Wilkerson, Diane Donghi, Russell Neufeld, Jane Spielman, Ronald Fliegelman, Larry Grathwohl, Naomi Jaffe, and Robert Burlingham.

188. Ibid., 315, 325.

189. *Detroit News*, October 27, 1970.

190. "Assaults on Law Enforcement Officers," 315, 325.

191. Ibid., 268–325.

192. *Black Panther*, November 14, 1970, 5.

193. White, interview.

194. *Michigan Chronicle*, October 24, 1970.

195. *Black Panther*, October 31, 1970.

196. *Black Panther*, July 24, 1971; *Detroit News*, October 26, 1970. The Detroit 15 included June Williams and Beverly Fleming, both juveniles; seventeen-year-olds Jerome Lee and Diane Brown; eighteen-year-olds Erone Desaussure, Cassandra Parker, and William Cunningham; nineteen-year-olds Benjamin Fondrun, David Johnson, and Carole Smith; twenty-year-olds Shanti Jones, Linda Wormsley, and Patricia Duncan; and twenty-one-year-olds Victor Grayson and Sylvia Robinson.

197. *Black Panther*, July 24, 1971.

198. *Michigan Chronicle*, October 31, 1970.

199. Ibid.

200. *Black Panther*, October 31, 1970, 12. For one thing, instead of three police cars being burned in all other versions, the Panthers claimed there were four, and in what may be an outright fabrication, the NCCF gave credit to the masses for the shooting death of a fireman and at least five other policemen.

201. In actuality, Patricia Duncan had been released on bond prior to the trial because she was pregnant, and charges were dropped against June Williams because she was a juvenile.

202. *Black Panther*, April 3, 1971, 7.

203. Sugrue, *Origins of the Urban Crisis*, 265.

204. Georgakas and Surkin, *Detroit*, 4–5. "The troubles" are the generation-long series of violent clashes in Northern Ireland during the last third of the twentieth century between elements of the Catholic and Protestant communities.

205. *Report of the National Advisory Commission.*

206. Sugrue, *Origins of the Urban Crisis*, 4, 265–266.

207. Ibid., 256–257; Fine, *Violence in the Model City*, 384.

208. Sugrue, *Origins of the Urban Crisis*, 265.

209. Although estimated to be made up of around 100 officers, the Detroit Police Department never released specific information regarding membership, numerical strength, or the specific duties of STRESS.

210. Georgakas and Surkin, *Detroit*, 202–203.

211. Fine, *Violence in the Model City*, 456–457.

212. David Farber, *Chicago: '68* (Chicago: University of Chicago Press, 1988), 128–129, 130.

213. Johnson, interview.

214. Steven Malik Shelton, "The Panther Walk," *Michigan Citizen*, http://www.michigancitizen .com.

215. Peters, interview.

THE DES MOINES, IOWA, AFRICAN AMERICAN COMMUNITY AND THE EMERGENCE AND IMPACT OF THE BLACK PANTHER PARTY, 1948-1973

Bruce Fehn and Robert Jefferson

On one fateful evening during the mid-1960s, Black Power politics and civil rights activism in Des Moines, Iowa, shared equal billing in America's heartland. On July 4, 1966, young African Americans assembled at Good Park, located in Des Moines' largest black neighborhood, and participated in a violent disturbance lasting several hours. According to *Des Moines Register* reporters Dick Spry and Stephen Seploy, "the clash between youths and police apparently [had] been brewing for several nights. Negro youths, on several occasions [had] refused to leave the park swimming pool at closing time." The night before the rebellion, young African Americans were upset at what they perceived as two policemen's rough handling of two youngsters in the park after the 10 p.m. curfew. The Independence Day festivities with fireworks, which were illegal in Iowa, disturbed a neighbor, who called police. When police soon arrived on the scene, the mood of the people there grew restive. After being accosted physically and verbally, young people jumped on the police cars and rocked them back and forth. They barricaded the park entry at Seventeenth and University with benches and a trash barrel. As police removed the barricade, insurrectionists hurled rocks and bottles at them.[1]

To quell the Good Park rebellion, Wendell Nichols, the white acting police chief, called upon three prominent black community members: John Estes, Perry Hooks, and James B. "Brad" Morris. Estes, a funeral home director, had for years been active in the black community. In 1968 he became president of the Des Moines branch of the National Association for the Advancement of Colored People (NAACP). Joining Estes at Good Park was Perry Hooks, director of the Des Moines Human Relations Commission, and attorney Brad Morris, head of the local NAACP chapter at this time. Well known among youth in the African American community, they succeeded in convincing the young people to disperse. The July 4 rioting, however, had not exhausted their discontent. The next evening, at 9:30 p.m., another disturbance shook the neighborhood. Again, police enlisted Estes's and Morris's assistance. This time someone threw a brick and hit Morris in the ribs. After a sweep through the park and neighborhood, police arrested five men and two women, ages eighteen and nineteen.[2]

The July 1966 Good Park rebellions were prelude to the emergence in Des Moines of more radical politics, channeled two years later into new programs by members of the Des Moines chapter of the Black Panther Party (BPP). In 1968, the same year the BPP came into national prominence, urban sociologist Herbert L. Gans used the term "spontaneous rebellions" to conceptualize uprisings such as those that took place at Good Park. A "spontaneous rebellion," Gans argued, must be understood as part of a larger and longer social, economic, and political process. "This process begins," Gans explained, "with mounting anger that is expressed at an inciting incident, expands to a community-wide uprising, and often ends with revengeful oppression by the forces of law and order."[3] This pattern of development unfolded in Des Moines' near northside black neighborhood in the quarter century between 1948 and 1973. Without question, the Good Park rebellions were expressions of "mounting anger" with roots in Des Moines' racist history and African American mobilizations to fight back.

Although historian Reynaldo Anderson correctly observed that mounting black frustration created conditions for the Des Moines Panthers' emergence, he neither specified the specific sources of discontent nor connected the Panthers' politics to African Americans' previous and ongoing struggles against discrimination and segregation. While the Black Panthers, with their militant rhetoric, confrontational behavior, and independent survival programs, gave a radical shove to black politics, they built programs upon extant political and economic resources. In Des Moines, moreover, Black Panthers found traditional African American leaders, and even members of the white community, sympathetic to their survival programs, cultivation of black pride, and forceful challenges to a racist society that segregated and oppressed black people. While Anderson provided valuable analysis on the Des Moines Panthers' ideological differences with Oakland headquarters and leadership's approaches to educating recruits, he did not connect the party's development to African Americans' long history of struggle and protest against racist institutions, segregation, and discrimination.[4]

The signature event energizing African Americans' post–World War II efforts to fight back against white racist oppression in Des Moines was the 1948 desegregation of Katz Drug Store. For eighteen years, leaders of the NAACP's Des Moines branch attempted unsuccessfully to prosecute the Katz Drug

Company for refusing to serve African Americans at the store's cafeteria and soda fountain. On July 7, 1948, Edna Griffin, however, initiated direct action protests against Katz to supplement the NAACP's approach of filing criminal or civil suits for blacks who had reported discrimination. With expectations they would not be served, Griffin and another black activist, John Bibbs, went to the Katz soda fountain and ordered ice cream. After a waitress told Griffin and Bibbs she could not serve them because of their race, Griffin complained to the store owner and manager, Maurice Katz. As he had done for the previous eighteen years, Katz again refused to serve African Americans.[5]

This time, however, Katz met his match. Griffin used this instance of Katz's refusal to serve blacks as an incident around which to organize both public protests and legal actions. For weeks she marched in integrated picket lines in front of Katz Drug's central downtown store. Pedestrians at Seventh and Locust could hardly avoid picket signs that read, for example, "The Bullets Weren't Meant for Whites Only"—a reference, of course, to African Americans' equal sacrifices in the World War II fight to defeat racist, totalitarian fascism. While pickets marched, Griffin set in motion lawsuits that eventually required Katz to quit discriminating against black people. On December 2, 1949, Katz Drug Store began to serve all patrons regardless of their skin color.[6]

Activists such as Griffin, who had been a member of the Progressive Party and Communist Party and also founded in Des Moines a chapter of the Congress of Racial Equality (CORE), infused a militant brand of politics into the Des Moines civil rights movement. Other leaders of the Des Moines black community, some radical and others more mainstream, also worked to defeat housing segregation, challenged police harassment, or fought to end employment discrimination. In the 1940s and 1950s black attorneys, including Charles P. Howard Sr. and Robert Wright Sr., defended African Americans who believed they had been unfairly treated by police, businesses, or the judicial system. Community organizers in the 1950s and 1960s fought white landlords' and realtors' segregated housing practices, as well as the discrimination blacks experienced at hotels, restaurants, and other public accommodations. In early May 1964, for example, over 100 black civil rights activists demonstrated around city hall and the state capitol building to demand a fair housing measure for city residents.[7]

A particularly important development in the city's civil rights history was establishment of the Des Moines Human Rights Commission. Starting in 1951, a coalition with members from the League of Women Voters, United Packinghouse Workers of America, NAACP, National Conference of Christians and Jews, American Friends Service Committee, and Council of Churches persuaded the Des Moines City Council to establish a permanent commission to pursue cases involving potential violations of civil rights in the city. From its formal establishment in 1954 as part of the mayor's office, the commission was a highly visible presence in Des Moines, fighting against segregated housing and other forms of racial discrimination.[8]

Other black women and men, who may or may not have been leaders of black organizations, performed the important community work of providing adults and young people with places to go and things to do. Historian Lynda C. Walker-Webster identified nearly 100 social and civic clubs that served Des Moines' African Americans. Among them was the Negro Community Center, later called Willkie House, which was founded in 1917. Besides serving adults as a space for meetings and rendering community services, Willkie House provided children with opportunities to participate in dance, arts, crafts, music-making, sports, dramatics, and other activities.[9]

Good Park, the site of the July 1966 youth rebellions, was another place where black children and teenagers went to play, socialize, and recreate. The park was roughly a square block of green space with a wading pool, shelter house, and basketball courts. Located near the west end of Des Moines' black neighborhood, the Des Moines freeway bordered the park on the south. On the north, the park sloped down to University Avenue, a busy east-west city thoroughfare. To the park's immediate west, near and along Seventeenth Street, was an integrated working-class neighborhood, which was increasingly black in composition. To the east, a steep incline dropped down to Keosauqua Avenue, a busy street that cut northwest-southeast through the black community. Keosauqua bisected the Center Street neighborhood and business district, which, until urban renewal and freeway construction, "embodied the spirit of the city's black residents" and was a "focal point" of black life in Des Moines.[10]

What some African American leaders at the time saw in the July 1966 Good Park rebellions as "defiance of law and order" perpetrated by a "few misguided youngsters" was in fact a watershed moment in the city's racial politics and civil rights history. Simmering frustrations associated with racial discrimination in housing, education, and employment and the de facto segregation of swimming pools and other public facilities boiled over into demonstrations for recreational space wherein blacks could comfortably assemble and socialize.[11] With the 1966 Good Park rebellions, young African Americans began a process of bold and public agitation to effect changes in their neighborhoods, including defense of the park and the near northside black neighborhood from what they regarded as police intrusions. Over the next five years, young black people's many subsequent confrontations with police and city officials reshaped a much longer African American movement of social change and justice in the capital city.

The energetic responses of young people to police brutality like those witnessed by *Des Moines Register* reporters at Good Park in the mid-1960s prefigured policies and programs later undertaken by the members of the Des

Moines chapter of the BPP. They harnessed and organized the post–World War II energy of black discontent and gave it a militant charge. Although the Des Moines BPP chapter lasted as a formal organization only two years, from January or February 1968 to January 1970, the organization had a permanent and significant impact on Des Moines' economic, political, and social landscape, an impact that can only be understood within the longer context of African American history in Des Moines.

The Des Moines Panthers mined African Americans' discontent that had been festering in the city for a century. It was in the wake of World War II, however, that African Americans sharply intensified demands for equal opportunity and an end to de jure and de facto segregation. After fighting fascism in the European and Pacific theaters as well as wartime discrimination on the home front, black women and men, and their white allies, were ready to mobilize against white-dominated institutions keeping them down. The desegregation of Katz Drug Store became a historical touchstone inspiring African Americans to sustain the fight. And between 1948 and 1968, under the leadership of Robert Wright Sr., John Estes, Edna Griffin, Brad Morris, and many others, the civil rights movement attained increasing momentum, power, and influence.[12] This power and influence, however, was never sufficient to overcome white residents' determination to keep blacks out of their neighborhoods or overturn white employers' and trades unions' tendencies to discriminate against blacks in hiring and job placement.

The frustrations with white intransigence set the stage for the Black Panthers' emergence in Des Moines with their more militant brand of local politics. As historian Yohuru Williams observed, an objective assessment the national BPP and its individual branches or chapters requires appraisal of their "relationship not just to the civil rights movement but also to Black Power and its influence in the late 1950s and 1960s."[13] Fully realized histories of local chapters also require fine-grained assessments of local historical conditions and actions that set the stage for each branch's particular development. In recent years, scholars have taken us beyond the widely held view of the party as antiwhite and wedded to a politics of armed self-defense of the black community. Scholars recognized the national party and its individual chapters never "espoused blanket antiwhite racism as its critics alleged. Instead, they formed alliances with white radicals even as they touted an armed revolution and promoted community service, i.e., 'survival,' programs."[14]

In Des Moines, the chapter's leaders and rank and file forged practical programs built in view of circumstances faced by the city's black residents. Local BPP leaders, virtually all of them reared in Des Moines, understood local circumstances and accordingly forged their political and community programs. Such problems as poor housing and the black community's general deterioration ("urban blight") stemmed directly from urban renewal and freeway construction in the late 1950s and early 1960s, which seriously disrupted black life and created conditions for the Des Moines Panthers' emergence.[15] Although the Black Panthers, with their militant rhetoric, confrontational behavior, and survival programs, gave a radical shove to black politics, they built programs upon already available political and economic resources, as well as widespread black frustration with municipal projects, policies, and whites' refusal to allow them to move into most sections of the city.

According to 1966 Department of Commerce data, which the *Des Moines Tribune* published in its July 8, 1968, issue, African Americans constituted 10,875 of Des Moines' total population of 206,739, or just 5.3 percent. Although representing only a little over 5 percent of Des Moines' total population, most blacks lived in just four of the forty-seven "tracts" into which the U.S. Commerce Department divided the city. Perry Hooks, director of the Des Moines Human Rights Commission, described the tracts as "ghettos." "Most Des Moines Negroes," he told a *Des Moines Tribune* reporter, "live in areas set apart by imaginary borders beyond which they are not supposed to move. . . . That makes these areas ghettoes." Hooks expressed frustration with whites' successful resistance to desegregation even into the "'lily-white' tracts surrounding the Negro districts."[16]

All of the predominantly African American tracts were along or near University Avenue, a major east-west thoroughfare. Two of them, on the west side of the Des Moines River, were in an area known as the "near northside." In these tracts lived just over 3,000 African Americans, who represented 63 percent of a total population of 4,829 living in the area. A significant number of blacks, over 1,000 in each case, also lived in two other tracts to the immediate north and west of the black-majority tracts on the near northside. Another substantial population of African Americans lived in two other census tracts. Located in the "Logan area" of the city, these tracts were just two miles east of the near northside, on the opposite side of the Des Moines River. African Americans in the Logan area constituted 73 percent of the total population of 2,183 in one tract and 62 percent of 1,865 residents in the other.[17]

The "concentration" and "strict segregation" of African Americans in these tracts, as well as the Des Moines Independent School District policies, required African American youngsters, for the most part, to attend elementary and secondary schools nearest their homes. Young African Americans living in the eastside census tracts went to Amos Hiatt Junior High and then East High School. Young people living in the near northside went to Washington Irving Junior High and then to either North High or Des Moines Technical High School. Although never more than 10 to 15 percent of the large high schools they attended, black students' altercations with their white counterparts helped, as we shall see, to fuel and focus black discontent upon the high schools. Black students' expressions of discontent with curricula, including the failure to teach black history, helped generate grassroots political energy among both students and their parents—energy mined and channeled in 1968 and 1969 by the newly formed Des Moines BPP.[18]

In face of white racism, discrimination, and segregation, the previous generation of African Americans had built in the first half of the twentieth century their own institutions, organizations, and lifestyles in the Des Moines' segregated urban landscape. In the 1930s, 1940s, and 1950s the focal point of black economic, social, and cultural life was on or near Center Street, which bordered the near northside to the south. In the Center Street neighborhood, black-owned businesses served mostly black customers, with a few whites occasionally going there for the good music to be found in bars and clubs. Urban renewal and the Des Moines freeway construction in the early 1960s, however, led to Center Street's disintegration as the hub of black business and culture. Until its demise, Center Street was the place for African Americans to get their hair cut or styled, dine at a good restaurant, visit the pharmacy, or socialize. Black citizens submitted orders for flyers, directories, business cards, and menus at Hobart DePatten Sr.'s print shop. Women trained as beauticians at Pauline Brown Humphrey's Crescent School of Beauty.[19] The Center Street neighborhood provided many opportunities to enjoy music at the Billiken, 1113, and Sepia nightclubs, among several others. During Center Street's heyday in the 1930s and 1940s, the neighborhood "brimmed with activity," wrote journalist and historian Raymond Kelso Weikal. "And its music flowed like flood waters."[20]

For white residents of Des Moines, "Center Street" was synonymous with the black part of town. While "a lot of whites" went to Center Street to hear good music at its nightclubs, few entered the neighborhood for other purposes. As the neighborhood freeway construction and urban renewal displaced mainstream black businesses, however, some whites went to Center Street and pursued illegal activities. Underage whites found places or individuals who would sell them liquor. Prostitution began to take hold, and the Des Moines Police Department's vice squad became a regular presence in the area. According to Hobart DePatten Sr., who lived just a few blocks from Center Street, police would no longer "cut you a break," but would arrest people for the most minor offenses.[21]

The Des Moines' white establishment's decisions in the late 1950s to begin urban development projects, including freeway construction, drove daggers into the Center Street neighborhood and seriously disorganized the black community. DePatten, whose father, Robert Patten, for many years ran the only printing business on Center Street, expressed the magnitude of the disaster for many of Des Moines' black residents: "Urban renewal was our 9/11."[22] Urban renewal projects and the new freeway wiped out affordable housing for black families. White realtors worked with white residents to keep displaced African Americans from moving into white neighborhoods. So blacks found themselves ever more tightly confined within the deteriorating near northside neighborhood.[23] Like his father, Hobart DePatten Sr. was a businessman and landlord who became very active in Des Moines politics after freeway and urban renewal destroyed his home. In the early 1960s he founded the Concerned Citizens Committee to represent African Americans who thought they were unfairly treated by city authorities.[24] As we shall see, Hobart DePatten's son Clive would a few years later join, and become very active in, the Des Moines chapter of the BPP.

White citizens, moreover, enforced segregation by means of verbal and sometimes physical intimidation. There was at least one case of a front yard cross burning when an African American moved into a white neighborhood.[25] In the mid-1960s even well-off, professional African Americans encountered "institutional racism designed to keep blacks both literally and figuratively 'in their place.'"[26] And, of course, whites of all ages reinforced their own sense of superiority through racist jokes and taunts directed at Des Moines' black citizens.

Small wonder, then, that young African Americans cherished Good Park as a social and recreational space more or less isolated from the racism and discrimination that permeated the city. Historian Ralph Crowder, who grew up near Good Park, remembered it as a "wonderful Black institution in Des Moines." Crowder observed that in the 1950s and early 1960s, both blacks and whites "accepted what now would be called segregated spaces without any problems." He remembered Good Park in those years

as a wonderful setting where Black athletic traditions were passed on to younger generations. Shared historical information usually was passed on to younger Black men from as far back as the 1940s. . . . Basketball and swimming were the major formal activities. . . . In the mid and late 1950s, the Good Park Pool was the center of our young social circle. This is where young Black boys learned how to swim, dive, court women, and developed strong bonds of friendship. . . . As we grew older, Good became an all purpose social center that embraced so much of my preteen and teen years. . . . There were certainly problems and some folks had clashes with racist white cops. But my generation and close friends who went to North [High School] all longed for some athletic accomplishments rather than anything that had to with gang culture.[27]

For Crowder, Good Park, like black churches, was a treasured social space that "filled Black male youth with some solid options."[28]

The "solid options" of Good Park and other black institutions proved insufficient to stem the tide of growing black discontent. When *Des Moines Register* reporters Jerry Szumski and Stephen Seploy investigated the sources of the July 4 and 5, 1966, Good Park disturbances, African American teenagers and young adults told them there was not enough for them to do at night. Some complained of the inability to find jobs and expressed concern about rough police treatment. Others pointed to policemen's disrespectful language and demeanor expressed toward young blacks. The latter told community leader John Estes "that when ... police officers approach [young African Americans], they should approach as a gentleman and not with 'Boy' or 'Hey, you.'" One nineteen-year-old told reporters that the Good Park incidents began when young people in the park were having a party after the 10 p.m. curfew and "[a] couple of police came in with nightsticks. One grabbed a kid, called him names and pushed him."[29]

The 1966 Good Park rebellions occurred at a time when blacks in many cities expressed violent discontent often sparked by instances of what they perceived as police brutality directed at African Americans. African Americans, many stuck in northern urban ghettos with few economic opportunities, grew impatient with the progress of the mainstream civil rights movement. In 1964 blacks rebelled in Rochester and Harlem, New York; Jacksonville, Florida; Newark, Patterson, and Keansburg, New Jersey; Chicago; and Philadelphia. In 1965 even larger spontaneous rebellions occurred in the Watts area of Los Angeles and again in Chicago.[30] In 1966, the year of the Good Park rebellions, additional racial insurrections took place in American cities, including one just 150 miles west of Des Moines in Omaha, Nebraska. In Omaha, a revolt also broke out on July 4 and lasted three days.[31] Two years later, on July 7, 1968, a huge race skirmish erupted just 100 miles northeast of Des Moines in Waterloo, Iowa.[32]

As in other cities, a police confrontation with disaffected young people triggered the July 1966 Good Park uprising, as increasingly the presence of law enforcement became a focal point of African American outrage.[33] Blacks in Des Moines distrusted the city's predominantly white police force.[34] African Americans often complained that police pulled them over for no apparent reason as they drove through the city. In wide circulation among blacks at the time was the mistreatment police applied to prisoners in "the elevator" carrying those arrested from the parking lot behind the Polk County courthouse up to the "drunk tank" and jail cells.[35]

Blacks' resentment toward police deepened when police made arrests in the black community or even killed an African American. For example, several weeks after the Good Park rebellions, on August 15, 1966, patrolman Charles Park shot dead Dwight Green, who allegedly refused Park's order to "halt" when Green was leaving through the window of a laundry. This incident sparked, on

August 19, 1966, an integrated march of young people on Des Moines police headquarters, with marchers demanding that police form a "grievance board" and the establishment of stringent rules on the use of highly lethal "riot guns" (12-gauge shotguns with shells loaded with pellets the size of .22-caliber bullets), the kind that killed Green. Once assembled, the crowd taunted police. Soon African Americans formed the Citizens Committee to End Police Brutality. Organized at Good Park, the Citizens Committee signaled African Americans' deepening disdain with police force members' application of force exercised toward black citizens. The African American newspaper, the *Iowa Bystander*, reported that the committee's ambitious and primary goals were "the removal of shotguns from patrolman's cars and a review board to investigate such police violations as shotgunnings, mis-arrests and 'trips up the elevator.'"[36]

These 1966 Good Park rebellions and the police killing of Dwight Green took place at the same time Black Power rhetoric began to infuse black neighborhoods, rhetoric that deeply aggravated the city's white population. Just a few weeks before Green's death and the subsequent demonstration at police headquarters, the *Des Moines Register*, the city's most widely circulated newspaper, editorialized that the employment of the term "Black Power" by the Student Nonviolent Coordinating Committee (SNCC) and CORE aroused "angry belligerence . . . among those who accept it and anger and misunderstanding among those (white and black) who oppose it." The editorial sympathized with African Americans who suffered at the hands of "Kluxers and cruising shotgunners" in the Deep South, "but making it sound like revolutionary violence doesn't help a bit."[37]

Many of Des Moines' mainstream black leaders, in contrast, came to understand the appeal of a more confrontational brand of rhetoric and politics. They recognized the disaffection of young blacks who were "denied voices and . . . aligned themselves . . . with so-called militant groups."[38] In Des Moines, racism, segregation, and discrimination remained intractable. White police officers in the mid-1960s seemed, at least to some African Americans, to have become increasingly aggressive in arresting black citizens.[39] For blacks, residential segregation was intensified by variations of de facto segregation in schools, public accommodations, and neighborhoods where African Americans were not welcome.

African American discontent reached a boiling point in the two years following the first Good Park rebellions. In 1967 those displaced by Interstate 235 construction and the accompanying urban renewal projects grew upset with the Des Moines City Council for failing to make provisions for good housing and smooth relocation procedures. Brad Morris and W. Lawrence Oliver, attorneys for displaced residents, accused the council of designing a "planned program of segregated housing." Displaced persons also were angry about low appraisals for homes and businesses, especially those businesses including the Crescent Beauty Shop, Wells Billiard Parlor, and Hardaway's Tonsorial Parlor. On March 27, 1967, home and business owners complained before a Des Moines City Council meeting that the city offered residents prices too low to buy comparable homes elsewhere. They complained that the "secretive" appraisal process aroused suspicions among displaced persons. One of the African Americans at the city council meeting "wanted to know about a person who had struggled to buy a house and lived there 40 years, only to, in Urban Renewal, have to pull up his roots and accept a price that would not let him buy another such dwelling comparable to the first." J. Taylor worried specifically about displaced elderly residents who had to relocate. Taylor gave sharp expression to elderly residents' anxieties when he told the council, "It would be a lot more human if you took them out and shot them."[40]

The black community also had grown increasingly frustrated with employment discrimination in Des Moines, as poverty and unemployment disproportionately affected the near northside neighborhood. As measured by the *Bystander*'s coverage of hiring discrimination, this was a major and long-festering issue within the African American community. In 1967, for example, blacks were angry over the fire department's refusal to hire qualified black applicants. In April the fire department's rejection of Milford Fonza's and Walter William's applications prompted the *Bystander* to refer to Des Moines city officials as "jack asses by managing to block the appointment of any Negroes to the fire department."[41] Finally, "after over a year's hassle between the Civil Service Commission, the Des Moines Human Rights Commission, [and], the Civil Rights Commission," reported the *Bystander*, "Milford Fonza, 22, was accepted and certified as a fireman." Williams also joined the fire department in 1967. Besides the fire department, labor unions, such as the local plumbers' and bricklayers' unions, blocked African Americans from entering apprenticeship programs. This discriminatory practice also deeply angered members of the black community.[42]

One year later, African American community leaders were again thwarted as entrenched white city officials blocked legitimate avenues for rectifying employment discrimination. Although Perry Hooks was able to apply pressure to various Des Moines agencies to address employment discrimination, the Des Moines Civil Service Commission refused to include any African Americans among its membership. When in April 1967 the commission appointed a new member, it chose a white applicant, overlooking three distinguished leaders of the Des Moines black community: John Estes, president of the Des Moines branch of the NAACP; Robert A. Wright Sr., the Iowa state NAACP president; and attorney Brad Morris.[43]

By the summer of 1967, mainstream black leaders began to issue grave warnings about the Des Moines white establishment's failures to adequately meet black demands for enforcement of fair housing laws and antidiscrimination statutes. John Estes, for example, told members of the Iowa Cities Task Force on Community Relations they should expect an "insurrection." In July 1966 Estes, along with Perry Hooks and Brad Morris, had helped police defuse the Good Park rebellions. Now Estes was far from sanguine about their ability to do so. "Don't ask us to help stop an insurrection if it comes," he told members of the task force, "we won't be able to. We told you for years about the problems and you wouldn't listen. Then comes Newark and Detroit and you ask us [again] what we've telling you all along."[44] Less than one year later, in the wake of Martin Luther King Jr.'s assassination, young African Americans in Des Moines participated in insurrections that Estes and other African Americans warned about.

On Thursday, April 4, 1968, James Earl Ray's assassination of King heightened African Americans' indignation, which Estes had so often tried to explain to the Des Moines white establishment.[45] The murder sparked rebellions in 125 cities throughout the nation.[46] In Des Moines, too, some African Americans violently expressed their futility and despair. Such expressions first took place on the Sunday following King's death. On that day, April 7, African Americans and white allies had marched to a demonstration at the state capitol building. Starting in the heart of black Des Moines, at Good Park, an estimated 3,000 to 5,000 marchers linked arms and walked four abreast down Keosauqua Avenue. They walked underneath the Des Moines freeway through what had been the Center Street neighborhood and into the city's downtown. The marchers proceeded to Ninth Street, turned south, and then east up Locust Street toward Capitol Hill and the statehouse. Once there, the marchers joined other mourners to listen as speakers memorialized the life and work of King.[47]

One of the speakers was Representative June Franklin, a black woman who represented the predominantly African American near northside neighborhood in the Iowa legislature. She delivered to the crowd a powerful message infused with the rhetoric of Black Power. Franklin proclaimed:

It is time for the few black citizens of Iowa who sit on policy-making boards and commissions, or hold jobs where they can help their black brothers to stop compromising, stop scratching, stop shuffling, stop grinning, stop being handkerchief heads and Uncle Toms . . . to stand up and step forward and be counted. Let us all be black together, march together, work together. Let us be black together. Dr. King never accepted half a loaf. He was never an Uncle Tom. He walked in peace and fought for dignity and equality of people. It is time for the black ministers of this city to stand up and step forward and show leadership—start leading our people to the promised land.[48]

Representative Franklin delivered just one of several fiery speeches that preached black solidarity and demanded equality. One speaker warned, "The poor giveth, the poor taketh away."[49]

As a harbinger of increased African American militancy, and the even more deeply fractured police-black relations, the memorial service had barely ended when, at 5 p.m., an angry confrontation occurred between police and a group of African American young people. A report of the incident in the *Des Moines Tribune* stated that Police Chief Vear V. Douglas, who had recently returned from sick leave, led "40 helmeted police officers . . . who ran at the group with clubs and ordered them to remain on the sidewalk." The policemen confronted the young people, who apparently were returning from the memorial service back to the near northside on the Locust Street bridge that spanned the Des Moines River and led into downtown. "Several officers jabbed at youths [with their nightsticks]," the *Tribune* reported, and "the youths shoved back." Police authorities also jabbed newsmen at the scene. Police officers subsequently arrested eleven young African Americans for breaking seven downtown store windows. Later that evening arsonists ignited six fires that caused $25,000 in damages.[50]

The police assault upon young black people on the Locust Street bridge unleashed a firestorm of grassroots political turbulence as news of the arrests quickly spread through the black community. The night after the incident, 200 people showed up at the Des Moines City Council's regular Monday night meeting to complain about police conduct at the Locust Street bridge, in particular, and police behavior, in general, toward black people. Another seventy-five protestors showed up to complain about the police at a separate meeting of the council's special Police–Community Relations Committee, which met the same evening at a different location.[51]

The discontent stirred by police actions at the Locust Street bridge aroused the ire of African Americans of all economic classes and political persuasions. John Estes, for example, criticized police. In particular, he placed blame on Chief Douglas for pulling his gun, which Estes claimed provoked the young people's violent responses. Estes believed, moreover, that the confrontations' "real destruction" would derive from young people's deepened distrust of authority, especially the police. Black leaders, including Representative Franklin, called upon the Des Moines City Council to fire Chief Douglas. Police officers, in turn, publicly supported Douglas and expressed frustration at the public criticism the police force received. They pointed toward constant harassment they experienced while working twelve-hour shifts in the days following King's murder.[52] In spite of African Americans' call for Chief Douglas's ouster, the council voted to retain him as head of the police force.[53]

Meanwhile, young African Americans organized to confront what they perceived as racially motivated policing of the black community. On Wednesday, April 10, 1968, three days after the Locust Street bridge incident, fifty young people attended a special session of the Des Moines City Council held to discuss relationships between the police and the black community. The group's leaders presented the council with a list of thirteen demands, and then walked out of the meeting. Nine of their demands insisted upon reforms of police procedures and practices within black neighborhoods. They included the following: only one police car should be dispatched to a scene instead of three or four; riot guns and nightsticks should not be so routinely "displayed or brandished"; and police must end "watchdog" surveillance in the black community.[54]

Unsurprisingly, given the long history of racist policing in Des Moines, the city council's and police department's efforts to smooth relations between police and young blacks were probably bound to fail. In early June 1968 the Des Moines Police Department resumed a program it inaugurated the previous summer and hired eight young African Americans as part of a "Des Moines Police Youth Patrol." According to Acting Police Chief Wendell Nichols, who had replaced Chief Douglas, who was on disability leave, black members of the Youth Patrol would walk the streets of the near northside to help smooth relations between African American young people and Des Moines police officers.[55] After the Locust Street bridge incident, however, such a move could not interrupt the continued downward spiral of police–black youth interactions. The downward spiral was marked by numerous small insurrections directed at police officers who patrolled the near northside neighborhood. The police responded with beefed-up patrols in the area. Increased police patrols further enraged young people and helped establish conditions for additional confrontations. In early June 1968, for example, police shot a fleeing African American whom they suspected of breaking and entering. Subsequently, African American youths went on a rampage of firebomb and rock throwing.[56]

Besides launching spontaneous insurrections, black youth also organized demonstrations in front of city hall to protest police actions in their neighborhood. On June 5, 1968, for example, African Americans marched in front of city hall to support Stanley Lee Williams, whom police arrested following a disturbance at Ninth and University. The demonstrators carried signs reading "Get the Police Off University Avenue," "Stop Police Brutality and Oppression," "Our Human Rights Have Been Violated We Demand Freedom Now," "Get Those Racist Cops Out of University [Avenue]," "Racist Cops and Government Are Guilty of Black Genocide," and "Black Control of the Black Community."[57]

With demonstrators expressing anger at Des Moines police by using expressions such as "black genocide," "racist police," and "black control," *Des Moines Register* reporters wanted the police department's views on what appeared to be a rapidly deteriorating relationship between near northside blacks and members of the police force. A policeman interviewed at the scene of the June 5 demonstration reported that a number of University Avenue–area residents had called to support police patrols of the area. He said the police wanted to recruit more black officers, and the department's "mobile recruiting unit had been in the area to try and enlist blacks into the police force." This statement, which could be interpreted as another police effort to reach out to the black community, contrasted sharply with Acting Police Chief Nichols's statement to the *Register's* reporters. In response to black demands that police stay out of the black community, Nichols said ominously: "I can tell you one thing. We're not moving out of University Avenue."[58]

In addition to young people's protests against police behavior, welfare rights activists also prepared the way in Des Moines for the emergence of the Black Panthers' confrontational politics, as well as the organization's survival programs. In the summer of 1968 black women waged a number of highly public and well-publicized protests against the Des Moines and Polk County welfare systems. The unquestioned leader of this group of women was Joeanna Cheatom, who later worked hand-in-glove with BPP members to build survival programs in the near northside. Cheatom, a forty-three-year-old mother of four, organized the Welfare Rights Organization in Des Moines and served as its president.[59]

Starting in June 1968, Cheatom led welfare recipients in a series of confrontations with the Polk County Welfare Office and the Polk County Welfare Board. On Tuesday, June 10, 1968, Cheatom and ten other mothers who received support from the federal Aid to Dependent Children (ADC) program went to Polk County Welfare Director Leland Ahern's office. There the women demanded what a *Des Moines Tribune* reporter identified as "sweeping reforms of the welfare system," which included "a greater voice in the administration of programs." Operating in the direct action tradition of Edna Griffin and other civil rights pioneers in Des Moines, Cheatom threatened to "sit in" with her fellow protestors unless the group's demands, previously presented to the Polk County Welfare Board five days earlier, were met. With some protestors wearing signs stating, for example, "We Want a Fair Hearing," the women's demands included: ADC recipients would not be cut off from funds without a hearing; applications for ADC would be immediately acted upon; and food stamps would be distributed by a "mobile unit" rather than exclusively at the Welfare Department Office.[60]

Three weeks later Cheatom led the group on a march from the Des Moines city hall to Capitol Hill, where they conducted an all-night "vigil" on the steps of the Iowa statehouse. The next morning, July 1, 1968, Cheatom and her fellow protestors presented further demands, this time to Iowa Social Services Commissioner Maurice Harmon.[61] In mid-July welfare officials accused Cheatom of mishandling funds associated with the welfare organization she founded, as well as misuse of ADC money she had received to support her children. Cheatom fought back, accusing the Welfare Board of "Gestapo" tactics in its efforts to regulate her behavior.[62] While never becoming an official BPP member, Cheatom had, by mid-July 1968, allied herself with members of the Des Moines chapter of the BPP to develop community-based programs for the poor.

With young African Americans and single black women paving the way, conditions were ripe for organization in Des Moines of a BPP chapter. Young African Americans demonstrated readiness for a more confrontational brand of politics through their confrontations with police and city officials. Black women were fed up with the treatment administered them by public welfare organizations. Mainstream black leaders, moreover, became more sympathetic with the rhetoric of black pride and Black Power.[63] Into this situation stepped Mary Rhem and Charles Knox, who had prepared themselves to organize and channel African Americans' discontent into a new politics and establishment of new community-based programs.

Rhem and Knox had joined a revolutionary organization established in October 1966 in Oakland, California: the BPP. By early 1968 Panther organizations had already emerged in Harlem, Chicago, Indianapolis, and Detroit. However, the Oakland BPP became the recognized center of party ideology, politics, and image. While working to organize programs in Oakland's black communities, the headquarters published the *Black Panther Intercommunal News Service*, edited by David Hilliard, which the Oakland chapter distributed to other branches throughout the nation. Although individual chapters focused on local concerns, the paper gave Black Panthers in other cities a shared identity and helped the party's nationwide image as a group determined to exert economic and social control over their own communities. The Oakland party's highly successful distillation of the Panthers' intentions into the famous Ten Point Program and Platform also helped the Oakland chapter emerge as the ideological hub for chapters nationwide.[64] With the national media's attention riveted on the Oakland chapter members' May 2, 1967, disruption of the California legislature, as well as Huey P. Newton's arrest and trial for murder and the subsequent "Free Huey campaign," the Oakland party attained sufficient political cachet to officially sanction formation of BPP chapters throughout the United States. Among these was the new chapter formed in the small midwestern city of Des Moines.

In Des Moines, Mary Rhem and Charles Knox by 1968 had already concluded that in the North's segregated cities a new breed of African American leader had to organize community members into programs for economic survival. Born in Arkansas, Rhem moved with her mother to Des Moines at age nine. They settled in Des Moines' near northside. Inevitably, she soon felt the sting of racism and prejudice. A graduate of Des Moines North High School, Rhem, at age nineteen, went in early 1968 to Los Angeles to visit her brother. Together, they went to a BPP rally, which inspired Rhem to attend political education sessions. By July of that year Rhem was back in Des Moines, mobilizing blacks into a political organization, the Des Moines chapter of the BPP.[65]

As she walked the streets of her northside neighborhood, near the corner of Thirteenth and University, Rhem ran into Charles Knox. She knew virtually everyone in her neighborhood. So she was immediately curious about this stranger. Rhem soon learned that she and Knox had a lot in common. Knox had come from Chicago, by way of Kansas City, Missouri, to Des Moines as part of the antipoverty program, Volunteers in Service to America (VISTA). VISTA workers had a demonstrated record of organizing poor black communities, especially in the area of welfare rights.[66]

From his year serving in the VISTA program, Knox deepened his commitment to addressing the needs of the urban poor. In early 1967 he had reported to VISTA's regional office in Kansas City, Missouri, where he received orders to report to Des Moines. Upon his arrival, the Office of Economic Opportunity (OEO) in Des Moines placed Knox, along with nineteen other volunteers, with neighborhood opportunity centers. Under the VISTA program, volunteers worked for one year, providing assistance to the community's working poor. In exchange, volunteers received housing and food allowances, as well as a modest stipend for personal expenses. While a VISTA volunteer, Knox quickly became involved in near northside neighborhood issues. He attended meetings of Forest Avenue residents, who lived on one of the main thoroughfares cutting east-west through the near northside black community. Knox listened while they voiced displeasure over the deteriorating conditions in the near northside community. After completing his year with VISTA, Knox decided to stay in Des Moines to develop neighborhood programs to address the needs of the black community. He landed a job with the Polk County Board of Education as a special school social worker. Knox's employment, however, came to an abrupt end. The Board of Education fired Knox for failing to show up for work for two weeks. During this time, Knox had traveled to Kansas City to register his discontent over the firing of six Des Moines VISTA workers.[67] It was while walking the streets in hope of finding employment elsewhere in the city that Knox met Mary Rhem.

Soon after their first encounter, Rhem and Knox joined forces to establish in Des Moines a chapter of the BPP. They quickly recruited new members. In the course its brief existence, the Des Moines Panther chapter had roughly 100 members, with about fourteen "hard line workers" who strove to build programs intended to enable African Americans' self-reliance within their own communities. Group leaders emphasized community action over rhetoric. "Our thing," Knox recalled in a 1976 interview with a *Des Moines Tribune* staff writer, "was to work, go to school, or head some project full time. You didn't sit on the street corner and philosophize."[68] Lesser-known individuals who were vital to the Des Moines chapter included nineteen-year-old Charles Smith, who worked as the deputy minister of defense; Beverly Williams, the deputy minister of finance; and Stephen Green, the party's lieutenant for distribution, offering goods and services to individual African Americans in particularly dire straits.[69]

The Des Moines Panthers quietly made their public presence known for the first time as the Des Moines City Council sought ways to address growing anger among black citizens. At a meeting in late June 1968, council members discussed ways to "beef-up" ordinances to prohibit "racial discrimination in housing, subpoena powers in investigating charges of racial discrimination and improved cooperation from city departments."[70] Silas Ewing, chairman of the Des Moines Human Rights Commission, attended the meeting to report on his organization's recent meeting with young black people who complained of heavy policing of the near northside, especially Thirteenth and University, as well as police mistreatment of them. Ewing complained that his organization was powerless to investigate such charges.[71] After Ewing's appearance, Richard Brooks, a Young Men's Christian Association (YMCA) youth worker whom the organization had assigned, interestingly, as a liaison to the newly formed Des Moines BPP, read a letter from BPP members to the city council. After first stating the Panthers' goal was "self-security for the black community," Brooks read from the letter. The letter stated that black members of boards and commissions should "take a chance on losing your good jobs" and go into the black community to assist their less fortunate brothers and sisters. "The eyes of the world," Brooks read, "are on white America." John Estes, Des Moines branch NAACP president, subsequently told the city council that without additional enforcement powers, the Human Rights Commission was not "relevant to the black community."[72]

On July 18, 1968, eighteen days after the city council meeting at which the Panthers made known their chapter's existence in Des Moines, they submitted to the Iowa Secretary of State's office articles of incorporation for the establishment of a permanent organization to "promote, implement and develop the well being of the entire black community in Iowa." In its application, the "Black Panther Organization, Inc." included the names of twelve "initial directors," three women and nine men. Executing the articles before a notary public were Rhem, Knox, and Michael Harris, who also became a central figure in the Des

Moines Panthers. In the articles, the authors expressed their intention to "promote and develop black power in the community which means the economic, political and cultural control of the black community by black people." Except for Harris, who lived on Twentieth Street, other "directors" lived very close to one another, between Eleventh and Nineteenth streets, in the heart of Des Moines' near northside black community. They also resided near the chapter's registered office near the corner of Eleventh Street and University Avenue.[73]

During July and August 1968, the BPP openly solicited funds from mainstream public and private organizations. At the Greater Opportunities, Inc. (GO), Des Moines' antipoverty agency, they applied for $1,500 to bring an African American festival and other cultural projects to their neighborhoods. The GO board of directors denied the Panthers' application for the apparent failure to explain how they would account for the money. In addition, the board stated the application failed to provide sufficient information concerning the Des Moines' chapter's leadership and membership.[74]

After weeks of not hearing about the results of their application, approximately twenty party members gathered outside the Forest Hills Opportunity Center to confront the GO board and register their displeasure with the delay. "You shot us through the grease and put us through the mill," Rhem complained. "Now you close us out and tell us to wait while you make a decision affecting us. We don't want it." Meanwhile, the Panthers applied for contributions from the Retail Merchants Bureau of the Des Moines Chamber of Commerce to sponsor an "Afro-American festival." The bureau's committee established to review such solicitations denied the Panthers' request, stating the "Party did not merit the financial support of the business community."[75]

The BPP's GO application had in fact spurred heated discussion among the GO's integrated eight-member executive committee, which eventually approved the party's funding request. During the closed-door meeting, several African American leaders, such as municipal judge Luther T. Glanton Jr., and some white members of the agency's governing body favored the project without reservation. A local clergyman, however, agreed to support funding only if the BPP accepted guidance from a "responsible group" of volunteers. In addition, funding would occur on the basis of reimbursement, BPP projects would be subject to the agency's accounting office, and only "qualified teachers" could provide instruction in African history and culture courses offered by the party. Other executive committee members categorically rejected the proposal, arguing that the Des Moines group was connected with the national BPP headquarters and was therefore ineligible for funding. Still others suggested postponement of a decision, claiming that they did not have enough information about the project to render an informed judgment of the application's merits.[76]

One of those who supported the proposal complained that "it is ridiculous to turn down something like this for only $1,500." Another expressed "skepticism about the project but I would like to see this board approve the plan to see what this Black Panther group will do. We hear a lot about the destructiveness of [the Black Panthers], let's see what a group can do when it asks to do something constructive." Shortly afterward, members of the agency unanimously approved the request, granting the party $1,500 to sponsor cultural projects along University Avenue.[77]

Although BPP members had difficulty obtaining sufficient funds for survival programs, they found many African American leaders, and even some whites, sympathetic to the need for the Panthers and their survival programs. In June 1969 members of the white-dominated Catholic Charities of Des Moines provided the Black Panthers with a house, rent free, in which to set up chapter headquarters. The house was located at 1207 Eleventh Street in the heart of the near northside black community.[78] Mainstream black leaders such as John Estes appreciated the party's cultivation of black pride and its forceful challenges to a racist society that segregated and oppressed black people. BPP members also learned that with secretive approaches, they could garner funding from white-dominated organizations in the city, such as the Des Moines branch of the American Friends Service Committee (AFSC). Mary Rhem remembered the predominantly white AFSC as providing "drive-by donations" at Panther headquarters in order to keep its donations to the organization out of the public eye.[79]

While Rhem was the undoubted founder of the BPP in Des Moines, and demonstrated her willingness to lead public demonstrations, Charles Knox soon became the public face of the organization. The BPP in Des Moines, as elsewhere, was a male-dominated organization, wherein talented women exerted leadership behind the scenes forging relationships with neighborhood leaders and developing programs to benefit black community members. So Rhem, while head of the Des Moines BPP, also set about doing the practical, hard work of organizing breakfast programs for children and health programs for adults.[80] She made connections, for example, with Joeanna Cheatom and worked with the latter in efforts to help black women exercise their rights to welfare support.[81]

Knox, too, worked hard at organizing party programs and making connections with community groups, but he also caught the ears and eyes of public officials, including the Des Moines Police Department, with his militant voice and highly visible political theater. He was frequently the subject of local newspaper stories. In one issue, the *Des Moines Register* published a lengthy article on Knox's work with a breakfast program.[82] In another issue, the *Register* reported how the public variously regarded Knox, with some viewing him as an honorable individual committed to the black community and others seeing him a phony who played upon "white guilt" to squeeze dollars from "liberals."[83]

Above all, the *Register's* articles reported on crimes and court cases involving Knox, which brought him notoriety as an outspoken leader of the Des Moines Black Panthers. The *Register* first brought Knox to prominence when, on October 10, 1968, a spectacular fire destroyed the Jewett Lumber Company on the city's east side. Shortly after eleven o'clock on the night of October 9, the main offices and yard at the Jewett Lumber Company were engulfed in flames. A half an hour later, a second fire erupted at an A & P supermarket located nearby, but inflicted very little damage. By one o'clock the next morning, the Jewett blaze had destroyed the lumber company's two-story building, collapsing a brick wall on a building behind it. Police arrested five African Americans, including Knox, Joeanna Cheatom, and the latter's sixteen-year-old son, Marvin. The other two charged with arson were Calvin Jones Jr. and Terry McDonald, both nineteen years old. The Des Moines police and Polk County Attorney indicted the five for setting the fires after unidentified witnesses claimed that they saw a station wagon carrying Knox and the Cheatoms in front of the lumberyard and the A & P near the time of the blazes.[84]

Knox's and the Cheatoms' trial got under way five months later, in April 1969, with Calvin Jones Jr. as one of the state's key witnesses. As a result, Jones's and McDonald's trials were to be held two weeks after those of Knox and Joeanna and Marvin Cheatom. In Oakland, Panther headquarters covered the trial in their national newspaper. The *Black Panther* identified Knox and the Cheatoms the "Des Moines 3."[85] Roughly thirty, mostly white supporters from Grinnell College and the University of Iowa took the cue. They prepared signs saying "Support the Des Moines 3," which they carried in front of the courthouse as the trial got under way. Presiding Judge J. P. Denato asserted he would not tolerate any attempts to disrupt the trial after a demonstrator tried to hand a juror a piece of "left-wing literature." At the start of the trial's second day, Judge Denato threw out the case because McDonald refused to corroborate Jones's testimony, which Iowa law required to convict a defendant in an arson case.[86]

Although the case against Knox, the Cheatoms, and the others was thrown out of court, the Jewett Lumber Company fire set in motion a constant, bitter entanglement between Black Panther leaders—especially Knox—the police, and the judiciary. While Knox and his codefendants apparently remained quiet during their arson trial, this was not to be the case in Knox's other encounters with Des Moines police and the judiciary system.[87] In the coming days and weeks, police arrested Knox many times, and the party's efforts to demonstrate support for Knox during his trials drained energy and attention from survival programs. Knox said as much in an interview nine years after the Jewett fire. "Police began to focus in on us for these silly things," he told a *Des Moines*

Tribune staff writer. "And we were then too busy defending ourselves to concentrate on the problems of the community."[88] Moreover, the Jewett fire was the first in a series of literally incendiary incidents, including the bombing of the Des Moines police station; the bombing of Des Moines Panther headquarters; the bombing of Soul Village, the black recreation center; and the bombing of the Story County courthouse in Ames, Iowa, thirty miles north of Des Moines.

In spite of constant distractions from police surveillance, arrests, and trials, the Des Moines BPP chapter leaders developed survival programs designed for near northside citizens to exert control over their own community's wellbeing. The BPP survival programs were central to both the national party's and its local affiliates' commitment to self-determination for the black community. Former Black Panther JoNina Abron identified four areas within which the Panther chapters sought to enable community self-determination: human sustenance, health, education, and criminal justice.[89] The Oakland Panthers had enshrined these areas of necessary community development in the famous Ten Point Program and Platform, which they widely disseminated to serve as principles guiding programs for community survival.

While Des Moines Panthers took seriously the party's Ten Point Program and Platform, they adhered in practice to those points most significant for the conditions of African Americans living in Des Moines. The Des Moines chapter, for example, paid a lot of attention to Point Five, which demanded high-quality education for young black people. Point Five stated:

We want education for our people that exposes the true nature of this decadent American society. We want education that teaches us our true history and our role in present-day society. We believe in an educational system that will give to our people a knowledge of the self. If you do not have knowledge of yourself and your position in the society and in the world, then you will have little chance to know anything else.[90]

To implement education that "expose[d] the true nature of the decadent American society," Des Moines Party leaders required new members to attend six weeks of "political education." In his October 8, 1970, testimony before the House Internal Security Committee, Clive DePatten, who had quit the Panthers before its dissolution in early 1970, told committee members that Deputy Minister of Education Charles Knox usually led new recruits in analyses of Mao Zedong's *Little Red Book* and other Marxist-Leninist texts.[91]

Many of the Des Moines chapter's recruits were recent high school dropouts, and they first needed to learn how to read before they could begin to understand the revolutionary analyses contained in Mao's *Little Red Book*, Marxist tracts, or articles published in the *Black Panther*. In correspondence with historian Reynaldo Anderson, Charles Knox indicated literacy instruction for recruits was a foundational, revolutionary activity. "You have to remember," Knox wrote Anderson, "that the folks who came to the party, many of them couldn't even read. This is very important. They couldn't read. They couldn't distinguish letters. The political classes taught them to read. We would take the *Red Book* and ask brothers to read a paragraph out of the book. Dictionary and Thesaurus next to us, and we read and we read and we read and we learned to read. And we learned analysis."[92] In Knox's view, new, illiterate BPP members learned to read because for the first time they *wanted* to read. They wanted to read in order to understand problems in their neighborhoods. They wanted, moreover, to apply political lessons learned at the chapter's political education classes to solve, and not just understand, problems of poor housing, health, inadequate public services, and the poverty that beset their community.[93]

In addition to literacy and political instruction for new Des Moines chapter recruits, the Panthers held each week an "open political education" class. Every Tuesday night, up to the April 29, 1969, bombing of Panther headquarters, blacks and some whites assembled in the headquarters' basement to discuss local, national, and international politics. During the political education classes, which were well attended, Panther leaders discussed how distribution of economic and political power maintained grotesque social inequities in terms of health care, education, and nutrition. The Panthers showed films, including *Off the Pig*, wherein Huey Newton, from inside the Alameda (California) County Jail, explained how police colonized African Americans in a manner not unlike the American government's military effort to colonize the Vietnamese. In the film, Newton's and other Panthers' explanations of class struggle overlay images of black women serving at the free breakfast programs and Panthers marching under the BPP flag singing, at one point, "Revolution has come, time to pick up the gun."[94]

With such a large number of dropouts among its membership, the chapter articulated its own sixteen–point program focused entirely on improving education for blacks in the Des Moines public schools. The party organized high school students into the Black Committee for Student Power, which presented the party's "sixteen wide-ranging demands to the school board." Included were demands for more black teachers who would teach African American history. In addition, committee members also demanded an end to academic tracking, which tended to channel most black students into "basic" or the newly emerged "special education" classes rather than those for college-bound white students. They also demanded dismissal of racist teachers.[95] Black Panthers' efforts to politicize high school students paid dividends as students in fall 1968 became openly militant in their demands for improved education. This was just the kind of grassroots political turbulence Des Moines BPP members sought to cultivate and channel into improved life chances for African American citizens.

In coherence with Panther national leadership's emphasis on "sustenance," Des Moines chapter members, in March 1968, followed the Oakland headquarters' lead and launched a free breakfast for children program. In the September 7, 1968, issue of the *Black Panther*, the party announced that, in Oakland, members would offer free breakfasts to children attending grade school and junior high. They located the free breakfast for children program in community centers and churches in the city. The party also asked for both black and white volunteers and for businesses, especially those operating in black neighborhoods, to donate to the breakfast program. Party leaders regarded the breakfast program as a highly significant signal to the black community that the BPP existed to serve them. They also saw the program as exposing and challenging the capitalist system, which allowed children to attend school even though their morning nutrition was insufficient for them to stay alert and learn. The free breakfast programs rapidly spread, and, according to a historian of the program, Miriam Eve White, Des Moines was among twenty-three BPP chapters conducting free breakfast for children programs by the end of 1969.[96]

In ways similar to Panthers at the Oakland headquarters, the Des Moines Panthers served free breakfasts in the basement of the predominantly white Forest Avenue Baptist Church, which was just a couple of blocks from the Des Moines chapter's office at Twelfth Street and University Avenue. Leo Pidgeon, who owned a grocery store at Ninth and University, was among those who donated food to the program. He recognized the program was vitally needed in the neighborhood. With contributions of food and money from various sources, men and women in the party served breakfast to children on Monday, Wednesday, and Friday. Available for the children were eggs, bacon, cereal, and biscuits, as well as milk and fruit juice.[97] Charles Knox, who was among those serving breakfast to the children, told a *Register* reporter that the program provided food to 75 to 100 youngsters of elementary and junior high school age in two shifts. In line with the Panthers' goal of fostering self-determination in the black community, Knox stated that he hoped neighborhood parents would take over the program. He also advocated breakfast programs in the schools, but, in the meantime, the Panthers intended to start breakfast programs in the Logan Street and Southeast Bottoms areas, where many poor and black people resided.[98]

In addition to serving breakfast, Des Moines Panther members educated the children who attended the free breakfast for children program. Using instructional practices and props tailored to educate the children, Panthers helped them comprehend the meaning of capitalism, imperialism, and socialism. The teacher, for example, showed children five pieces of candy. If just one child had most or all of the candy and kept the pieces to himself or herself, then this was a capitalist system. If, on the other hand, the five pieces of candy were distributed to all of the children, then there was a socialist system in operation. Many people, the Panthers instructed the children, worked to make the candy. So the candy needed to be fairly distributed among those who worked to produce it. In the basement of the Forest Avenue Baptist Church, moreover, the Panthers taught children that an unjust system of distribution should and would be overthrown.[99]

While sharing facilities with other activists at Forest Avenue Baptist Church, Panther leaders often gathered to discuss conditions that affected the lives of individuals and families, and developed programs, often ad hoc, to help them.[100] In line with the party's efforts to foster community sustenance, for example, BPP members and twenty neighborhood residents boycotted and demonstrated outside of Griger's Food Market, demanding that the store lower prices charged to African Americans and others who shopped there.[101] To address community health needs, they provided direct and immediate help to community members struggling with drug addiction. Since in the late 1960s there were not any drug treatment centers in Des Moines, Panther members drove people who were addicted to a treatment center in Kansas City, Missouri. Panthers also conducted "individual policing" of the illegal drug trade in the black community and applied unsuccessfully for federal funds to start a treatment center.[102]

As they worked to address Des Moines' unique problems and conditions, Des Moines BPP members sold the Oakland national headquarters' newspaper, the *Black Panther Intercommunal News Service*, to raise funds and inform community residents about the issues of the day. Party members hawked the publication on street corners along University Avenue, which ran east-west through the entire length of the eastside and near northside black communities. BPP members also sold the newspaper statewide, mostly in university and college towns, including Ames, Iowa City, Cedar Falls—Waterloo, and Des Moines. The paper was also sold in Des Moines junior high and high schools. The *Black Panther*'s hostile expressions and revolutionary rhetoric deeply troubled white leadership and ordinary citizens of Des Moines and the state of Iowa. Many shared the views of U.S. House Representative William R. Scherle, who served on the House Committee on Internal Security and collected Panther publications to use as evidence in congressional hearings on BPP activities and programs.[103] The images of the police as pigs and the paper's violent representations of African Americans shooting police and even other black people, whom the paper called "Uncle Toms," appalled Scherle, many other whites, as well as some African Americans.

While working on program development and fund-raising, party leaders, whenever opportunities arose, encouraged African Americans to participate in visible, militant actions on the streets, in schools, and in the halls of the city's municipal buildings. In the fall of 1968, around the time that the Jewett Lumber Company fire called attention to the Des Moines Panthers' existence, many African American youngsters in the Des Moines public schools began to appear more militant. This behavior, in turn, antagonized some of their white schoolmates. On November 1, 1968, tensions between white and black students at East High boiled over into a confrontation, which included the knifing of the white student council president. When policemen arrived at the scene of the altercation, they arrested thirteen students, and East High administrators suspended five others.[104]

The interracial violence among the high school students increased hostility among black and white communities on Des Moines' north and east sides. At a meeting called by concerned parents and teachers, held at East High, located at East Fourteenth and Walker streets, near University Avenue, some black parents encouraged others to keep their children home from school. The meeting, which Des Moines School District Superintendent Dwight Davis hoped would "improve race relations" and "bring about better understanding and unity between all white and black students," drew skepticism from both white and black parents. Instead of unifying, each group formed its own organization to advocate for their children.[105] Meanwhile school officials worked to punish and undercut students who wanted to keep the school's racial problems in the public eye. Soon after the interracial fight at East High, the school board expelled four students, three from East and one from Des Moines Technical High School (Tech). School officials at Tech suspended between fifteen and twenty-five students after they left school before classes ended for the day in a show of support for black students at East High.[106]

At this point, the white school board president, George Caudill, attributed turmoil in Des Moines schools to the agitation and militant rhetoric of the Black Panthers in Des Moines and other cities. He linked the Panthers and black high school students' demands to the radical college campus organization Students for a Democratic Society (SDS), which "paraphrase[ed] the Communist Manifesto with 'students of the world unite.'" In anticipation of possible "walk outs, sit-ins, and open conflict," the school board adopted "strict disciplinary policies to cope with such events."[107]

On December 3, three days after the student walkouts, 450 (presumably white) citizens met at the Bellizzi-MacRae American Legion Post Hall and organized the Concerned Parents Association. According to the *Des Moines Register*, Dwight Hummell, the new organization's spokesperson, stated that the Concerned Parents Association "[is] not a white backlash group and not racist." Through his comments to the *Register*, Hummell "invited Negroes to join the association," an association those at the Legion Post Hall had organized to claim, among their other "concerns," that "school officials have discriminated against good students by inviting preferential treatment to the habitual trouble makers." The organization went before the school board to express support of the board president's determination to exert discipline in the schools and expel, not just suspend, students guilty of serious violations of the board's newly strengthened discipline policy.[108]

During this period, in fall 1968 and spring 1969, as interracial tensions intensified in the Des Moines schools and elsewhere, BPP members organized and attended a rally on April 13, 1969, at Good Park to promote the free breakfast for children program. The rally proceeded smoothly and nearly came to a close when about twelve police officers moved in to arrest participants on charges of unlawful assembly and resisting arrest. Des Moines police sergeant Ed Harlan told reporters that when policemen arrived at Good Park, Knox "turned his attention to the officers and advised the crowd to 'rise up and strike out' and to turn on the Des Moines pigs (police).'" As police moved to arrest Knox, BPP member Charles Edward Smith came to Knox's aid by trying to pull him from the clutches of arresting officers. At the same time, boisterous groups moved down University Avenue, hurling rocks and bricks at squad cars and passing vehicles, smashing windshields in the process.[109]

By nightfall, the April 19 "spontaneous rebellion" turned the area between University Avenue and Forest Avenue into a veritable war zone, with both streets closed to traffic and patrolmen stationed at virtually every corner in the area. When the fracas ended, a young black woman was taken to a hospital after sustaining gunshot wounds in the shoulder. Several of those returning home from the Good Park rally were beaten and arrested. Besides Knox, police arrested Mary Rhem and Stephen Green, two other key chapter leaders. Evelyn, Clive, and Hobart DePatten Jr. were among the battered and bruised. As Hobart DePatten Sr. recalled, "They arrested my son Clive, and then my other son, Hobart Jr., when he protested the arrest of Clive. When my wife, Evelyn, asked police what was happening, they arrested her too. If I hadn't been inside my house, they would have arrested me."[110] This experience with police had a profound impact upon Hobart Sr.'s youngest son, Clive. After being treated at a nearby hospital, Clive DePatten was returned to police headquarters, where he was charged and booked. While confined in the Polk County jail, he joined the BPP, immersing himself in party organizing and getting involved in the United Black Federation–sponsored Soul Village (a black meeting hall and recreation center) as a program training counselor.[111]

Mayor Thomas Urban tried to allay black community unrest by holding a special meeting on April 15, 1969, to discuss problems contributing to the most recent Good Park conflagration. Among those who attended the gathering were members of the Des Moines Police Department, BPP leaders, and approximately thirty residents from the near northside neighborhood. During the meeting, citizens demanded to know why police were on hand at the rally since there was no threat of violence. Police Chief Nichols and Detective Ed Rand claimed that police moved in only after receiving calls from nearby residents who complained that Knox and other BPP leaders used obscene language during the gathering. After several heated exchanges between city officials and Panther leaders, the meeting ended when Urban refused Knox's request that an officer actually present at the scene appear before the group to explain police actions.[112]

While Urban tried to foster communication between the Des Moines police force and the African American community, the Black Panthers garnered increasing support from black students and white allies in Iowa's colleges and universities, including Grinnell College and the University of Iowa. Black Panther leaders accepted invitations to appear on campuses, sometimes visiting classrooms to discuss their purposes and programs.[113] Two days after the April 13, 1969, Good Park rally and ensuing insurrection, nearly 100 people—mostly students from Iowa State University and the University of Iowa—assembled in Iowa City at the east steps of Old Capitol, the University of Iowa's signature building. Many voiced support for the BPP members. Speakers at the rally claimed the police arrests of party members in Des Moines were intended to turn the public against the BPP. Over the next few days, University of Iowa students led a wave of demonstrations at the Des Moines courthouse, registering their displeasure with the actions taken by the city's police department.[114]

Against this backdrop, the situation in Des Moines suddenly turned even more violent. The day following the Good Park rally, on April 14, 1969, someone set off an explosion on the near northside, apparently intended to topple a telephone pole into an electrical substation. Then, around midnight on April 26, a terrific explosion leveled the entire back end of the BPP headquarters, shattering windows in at least fifty homes in the neighborhood. As Panthers Edward King and Johnson Hughes proceeded to leave the demolished eight-room facility, they fought with police officers after the police attempted to spray them with mace. Police arrested both men and charged them with interfering with the duties of a police officer and resisting arrest. Bedlam ensued as groups of angry black residents stormed into the streets heaving gasoline-filled Molotov cocktails and rocks at police and parked cars. The next morning the sun rose on scores of anxious police officers, who sealed off access to the Panther house and the police station downtown in hopes of guarding against the possibility of further bombings.[115]

In the following days and weeks, mutual suspicions further intensified between local blacks and the police. Many African Americans were convinced the police knew the dynamiters' identities and that some officers at least conspired in the bombings. Panther member Charles Smith reported that on the night the headquarters was destroyed, police arrived at the scene moments after the explosions. "They were at our door thirty seconds after the explosion," he recalled. "I've never seen them get anywhere that fast in my life."[116] Police and city officials, for their part, accused Panther members of bombing their own headquarters. Albert Gladson, a Des Moines police intelligence officer, alleged that "approximately two weeks after the bombing of the Panther headquarters, Clive DePatten, Michael Smith, and one other party member spoke before a group in Minneapolis, Minnesota, and openly admitted that they had exploded a device to blow up their own headquarters to gain national recognition for the Black Panther Party."[117]

After the bombing, the Panthers sustained their survival programs, while preparing to defend themselves against the police. They quickly built a fence around their heavily damaged headquarters, and armed party members "sat on the front porch and patrolled the immediate area in front of their home."[118] The Black Mobile Street Workers, a local welfare rights organization founded by Joeanna Cheatom, moved into the bombed-out headquarters. In June 1968, however, the Panthers decided to move their operations into a small office nearby, at 1210 University Avenue, sharing the building with a mattress factory. While some Panthers armed for personal, as well as chapter, survival, others continued the party's survival programs.[119] On July 31, 1969, as part of the National Welfare Rights Organization's call for a "politics of disruption," BPP member Katherine Bryson led a march of eleven adults and seven children to the Polk County Welfare Department, where they applied for "increased ACD grants 'to a level that will provide an adequate standard of living.'" Understanding welfare rights agitation as integral to community survival programs, Bryson then led her group to a "camp-in" on the statehouse grounds. The camp-in was intended to help draw attention to the needs of welfare recipients in Iowa and nationwide.[120]

Although the Des Moines Panthers continued to try and implement survival programs, the bombing of their headquarters severely damaged the organization. Historically, in the United States and elsewhere, government's violent repression (legal or extralegal) has successfully disrupted formal organizations wanting fundamental political and economic change. Violence, combined with mainstream political leaders' desire to punish Black Panthers, administered the coup de grâce to the Des Moines chapter of the BPP. In February 1970, furthermore, the BPP national office expelled the Des Moines chapter from the national organization. Clive DePatten believed the Des Moines chapter was kicked out because of ideological differences concerning whether local chapter members should present themselves as Communists devoted to Marxism-Leninism-Maoism or as indigenous community workers fighting to better the lives of black people.[121] The national party was also angry at Des Moines chapter members because they failed to sell enough issues of the *Black Panther* in Des Moines. The national party, according to Knox, had increasingly relied on sales revenues from the *Black Panther* to keep the national organization afloat financially. According to Knox, the Des Moines BPP preferred to study and apply analyses in the *Black Panther* to local problems rather than spend time trying to reach the national headquarter's sales "quota."[122]

As Des Moines chapter leaders worked to keep serving the near northside community, the chapter suffered from continued police disruptions of their lives and activities. Quickly after Oakland leaders expelled the Des Moines chapter, Knox and others organized in Des Moines the Black Revolutionary Communist Youth, which met in the former Panther headquarters as well as Knox's apartment, which was located in a building wherein other former Panthers, now Revolutionary Community Youth leaders, also resided: Mary Rhem, Charles Smith, and Peter Williams. The Black Revolutionary Communist Youth continued to enlist volunteer support for the free breakfast program, now operated in Des Moines by the United Methodist Church.[123] On October 2, 1970, however, the police raided the apartment building where Panther leaders resided in search of explosives. Later the same day, Mary Rhem was on the streets of the near northside distributing a leaflet that read in part: "Again the fascist authorities of Des Moines unjustifiably harassed the Black Revolutionary Communist Youth by ransacking our apartment while we were not at home (the brothers and sisters were serving the people by assisting with the free breakfast program)."[124]

Soon after police raided the Panther apartments, the Des Moines City Council, mayor, and others lodged loud and vociferous protests when, in October 1970, Larry Scales, director of the Iowa Children's and Family Services, hired Knox, at a salary of $7,000 per year, to counsel juvenile delinquents. Scales hired Knox because the former was "impressed" with the latter's "confidence, concern and ability in working with black youth." From his position on the Internal Security Committee of the U.S. House of Representatives, Iowa's Seventh District representative William Scherle insisted that a federal investigation be launched to determine how a person with Knox's background and political views could possibly be qualified and hired for a position working with young people.[125]

For several days in October and November 1970, members of the Internal Security Committee conducted hearings on the threat Black Panthers represented to the security of the United States and its citizens. Consisting primarily of congressmen from southern and midwestern districts, the committee was cochaired by Richard Ichord of Missouri and Richardson Preyer of North Carolina. Its membership included Claude Pepper from Florida, Edwin

Edwards from Louisiana, Louis Stokes and John Ashbrook from Ohio, Richard Roudebush from Indiana, Albert Watson from South Carolina, and William Scherle from Iowa. The committee was charged with "investigating the activities and objectives of the national office of the Black Panther Party."[126] The members also worked to determine whether the pronouncements voiced by party officials and the material printed in the *Black Panther* were merely rhetorical or if they actually advocated strategies to overthrow the U.S. government.

In many instances, the testimony that Internal Security Committee members heard about the Des Moines BPP activities contained rumor, innuendo, and speculation intended to reinforce the members' preconceived notions of the party as a violent organization.[127] In an overt effort to create an image of the party as a militant organization that advocated armed violence, committee witnesses tended to associate violent incidents in Des Moines with the fiery, outspoken Charles Knox. According to Scherle, Knox "had a long and shady history of involvement with the wrong side of the law, and an equally long and open career with revolutionary groups including the Black Panther and Communist Parties." In light of Knox's background and activities, Scherle argued, "The people of Iowa will not let this issue lapse into oblivion. They have the right to expect their representatives in government to use their influence to root out extremists from Iowa antipoverty programs."[128]

In fall 1970, while Scherle and his colleagues conducted hearings on the Black Panthers, Knox converted his arrests into opportunities to denounce the judicial system and promote revolution. Often the charges stemmed from open displays of contempt for Iowa law enforcement officials. For example, on November 5 police arrested Knox on a charge of operating a motor vehicle with a suspended license. When he appeared in court later that afternoon, however, Knox faced far more serious legal action after failing to acknowledge Judge Ray Harrison in the Municipal Court of Des Moines. Upon hearing the charges preferred against him, Knox refused legal counsel, but not before calling the judge "a pig fascist" and John King, the Polk County assistant district attorney, a "degenerate punk."

As a result of Knox's contempt, the judge sentenced him to five days in the Polk County jail. At a subsequent contempt trial, the judge asked Knox if he wanted to testify on his own behalf. Knox replied, "For what? I tell you, man, if I'm guilty of anything I'm guilty of serving the people and that's all I need to say and nothing more." "You can jail a revolutionary, but you can't jail a revolution," he was overheard muttering to the judge as he was being led from the courtroom. During the trial, Clive DePatten, Stephen Green, and Mary Rhem were also charged with contempt after staging demonstrations while the court was in session and shouting epithets such as "fascist court" and referring to the officers as "pigs." On April 9 of the following year, each stood trial for contempt, where they received sentences ranging from ninety days to six months in the county jail.[129]

In August 1971 the House Internal Security Committee convened for the last time its investigation into the motives and methods of the BPP. After concluding that the days of the BPP's grassroots politics and community influence were over, Richardson Preyer exclaimed, "Panthers, put down your guns and find your voices."[130] Congressman Preyer and his colleagues, however, could not realize at the time that former Des Moines Panthers had never lost their voices in the first place. Rather, they had merely moved behind the platforms of legitimate urban politics or the desks of conventional jobs to voice the needs of the black community and continue working for its residents.

In fact, in subsequent years the Des Moines Black Panther chapter and individual members were celebrated as having had a significant and valuable impact upon the black community and the city as a whole. In a 1991 interview, Representative June Franklin, who delivered the stirring speech at the memorial for Martin Luther King Jr., asserted that it was the BPP that finally moved Des Moines' white elites to attack housing discrimination in the city. "It scared the pants off those people," Franklin claimed. "Business people, I guess they had visions of Des Moines burning down and all that kind of thing, that they'd never had before. . . . I think they got together and decided, hey, we don't want this for Des Moines, and I think they [the Panthers] helped bring it about, the change in attitude."[131]

Looking back forty years later, historian Ralph Crowder, who grew up on the near northside, expressed surprise to recognize names of African Americans who emerged after 1968 as leaders in Des Moines in the near northside black community. With the emergence of the BPP, Crowder wrote, "many . . . working-class blacks in D[es] [M]oines [attained] a voice that was usually never heard." These new voices challenged "traditional middle class Black leadership that dominated not only D[es] M[oines] but other communities where the Panther Party thrived." "The transformation of some local people I knew," Crowder remembered, "[was] truly amazing."[132]

Black youth, whom the party had transformed into political or social activists, would continue to have a positive impact on the black community for years to come. In 1980, for example, the collective voice of the Des Moines black community was the radio station KUBC, founded the previous year by Charles Knox and his close friend Joeanna Cheatom. Former Panther Stephen Green, now Imam Ako Abul-Samad, served on the station's board of directors as well as the station's general manager. Mary Rhem, now Sister Haadasha, was a member of the station's board of directors. KUBC listeners heard, and continue to hear at 89.3 FM, music, dramas, and messages relating to African American history broadcast over 50,000 watts twenty-four hours, seven days a week. Program developers also offered news affecting African and Asian peoples throughout the world. In April 1982 a talk show directed to Des Moines' rapidly increasing Hispanic population was set to go on the air. Most important, recalled Mary Rhem, the station enabled BPP members to broadcast information of particular concern to the black community and provided direct access to their neighbors in ways that the newspapers did not. "When a child was lost in the community," she recalled, "or something was up in the neighborhood, a brother or sister disc jockey would announce that 'all programming must stop because we have a crisis in our community.'" "Regular radio broadcasting," she remarked, "would return to normal only after the situation was resolved."[133]

These new voices and transformed individuals included Clive DePatten, who had testified before William Scherle and other members of the House Committee on Internal Security. Later, as Kalonji Saadiq, he served the black community as station manager of KUBC. Until his death of heart failure on November 16, 1996, at age forty-six, Saadiq was famous in the black community for serving the community and monitoring the police. "We would patrol the police," Saadiq told a *Des Moines Tribune* reporter. "Anytime they'd arrest someone, we'd make sure nothing funky went down." Saadiq frequently appeared before the Des Moines City Council to represent African Americans. He was especially vocal "in his bitter relentless criticism of the Des Moines police department."[134]

Mary Rhem (Sister Haadasha), founder of the Des Moines BPP, worked for many years at Oakridge Neighborhood Services serving poor people, most of them African Americans, on Des Moines' near northside. Stephen Green, who took the name Ako Abdul-Samad, organized or worked with a number of organizations serving poor and black people. As representative to the Iowa legislature from Des Moines' near northside neighborhood, Abdul-Samad has for several years worked on issues of particular concern to African Americans, such as Iowa's terribly disproportionate incarceration rates of blacks.[135]

The political, cultural, and social legacy of the Des Moines chapter of the BPP remained evident in the collective memory of its city's residents. The legacy was recognized by African Americans and some whites who acknowledged that Des Moines previously had not responded to mainstream African American leaders' repeated calls for program funding and services in the black community. While uncomfortable with Black Power rhetoric and the Black Panthers' confrontational politics, they knew the party's programs, demonstrations, and posturing spurred the city toward more equitable employment of black citizens. As early as 1969 Des Moines high school students could take courses in black history, and those with special learning needs could attend the Frederick Douglass School, established in 1972. Police officers never again could abuse a prisoner without risking the wrath of black community members such as

Kalongi Saadiq. And Joeanna Cheatom, who had been arrested for setting fire to the Jewett Lumber Company, gained immortality when members of the Des Moines City Council designated a recreational area as Joeanna Cheatom Park after her death on May 2, 1984. The park commemorated her long-standing service to Des Moines, which included her founding of the Pre-Trial Support Program, giving those who awaited trial what Cheatom herself called a "second chance."[136] Cheatom Park is located in the near northside community, just a few blocks away from Good Park, where so much of Black Panther history in Des Moines rushed forward.

Notes

This chapter is an expanded version of an article prepared for the *Annals of Iowa*, forthcoming. Thanks to Marilyn Upchurch for helpful research assistance at the Des Moines (Central) Public Library. Thanks also to Hal Chase for his help with, and enthusiasm for, this project's contribution to African American history in Iowa.

1. *Des Moines Register*, July 5, 1966.
2. *Iowa Bystander*, July 7, 1966 [hereafter cited as *Bystander*].
3. Herbert J. Gans, "The Ghetto Rebellions and Urban Class Conflict," *Proceedings of the Academy of Political Science* 29 (1968): 42–51. For Gans's analysis of community disruption stemming from urban renewal, see Herbert J. Gans, *The Urban Villagers: Group and Class in the Life of Italian Americans* (New York, 1965).
4. Reynaldo Anderson, "Practical Internationalists: The Story of the Des Moines, Iowa, Black Panther Party," in *Groundwork: Local Black Freedom Movements in America*, ed. Jeanne Theoharis and Komozi Woodard (New York: New York University Press, 2005), 283–299.
5. Noah Lawrence, "'Since It Is My Right, I Would Like to Have It': Edna Griffin and the Katz Desegregation Movement," *Annals of Iowa* 67 (2008): 298–330; Noah Lawrence, "Griffin, Edna Mae Williams," in *The Biographical Dictionary of Iowa*, ed. David Hudson, Loren N. Horton, and Marvin Bergman (Iowa City: University of Iowa Press, 2008), 196–197.
6. Lawrence, "'Since It Is My Right,'" 298–330; Lawrence, "Griffin," 196–197.
7. Jeremy Brigham and Robert Wright Sr., "Civil Rights Organizations in Iowa," in *Outside In: African American History in Iowa, 1838–2000*, ed. Bill Silag et al. (Des Moines: State Historical Society of Iowa, 2001), 304–331; Bruce Fehn, "Howard, Charles P.," in Hudson, Horton, and Bergman, *Iowa Biographical Dictionary*, 253–254; Hal S. Chase, "Glanton, Luther T.," in Hudson, Horton, and Bergman, *Iowa Biographical Dictionary*, 191–192.
8. Brigham and Wright, "Civil Rights Organizations in Iowa," 310.
9. John Estes, interview, August 8, 2008, Des Moines, Iowa; Lynda C. Walker-Webster, "Social, Cultural and Civic Organizations," in Silag et al., *Outside In*, 402–462, passim.
10. Jack Lufkin, "'Higher Expectations for Ourselves': African Americans in Iowa's Business World," in Silag et al., *Outside In*, 205; Raymond Kelso Weikal, "The Song of the River: African American Music and Entertainment in Iowa," in Silag et al., *Outside In*, 529.
11. Edward S. Allen, *Freedom in Iowa: The Role of the Iowa Civil Liberties Union* (Ames: Iowa State University Press, 1977), 99–104.

12. Brigham and Wright, "Civil Rights Organizations in Iowa," 304–310; Richard, Lord Acton and Patricia Nassif Acton, "A Legal History of African-Americans from the Iowa Territory to the State Sesquicentennial, 1838–1996," in Silag et al., *Outside In*, 77–82.

13. Yohuru Williams, "Some Abstract Thing Called Freedom: Civil Rights, Black Power, and the Legacy of the Black Panther Party," *Organization of American Historians Magazine of History* 22 (2008): 18.

14. Ibid.

15. Anderson, "Practical Internationalists," 284, 289.

16. *Des Moines Tribune*, July 8, 10, 1968.

17. James Fleming, *A Racial-Sexual Study of Employment in Des Moines* (Des Moines, Iowa: Des Moines Human Rights Commission, 1971), 1; *Des Moines Tribune*, July 8, 10, 1968.

18. Fleming, *Racial-Sexual Study*, 1; *Des Moines Tribune*, July 8, 10, 1968.

19. Lufkin, "'Higher Expectations for Ourselves,'" 205–209.

20. Weikal, "Song of the River," 530–534; Tom Gary, "A Place Called Center Street," *Straight Ahead* (Winter 2007): 1, 3. Besides local artists such as Speck Redd and Irene Myles, national or international stars including Josephine Baker, Duke Ellington, and Nat "King" Cole all appeared at Center Street's entertainment venues. See http://www.livingblues.com/product_information. php?product, accessed October 9, 2008; Jack Lufkin, "Patten's Neighborhood: The Center Street Community and the African-American Printer Who Preserved It," *Iowa Heritage Illustrated* 77 (1996): 122–144, passim.

21. Hobart DePatten Sr., interview, August 8, 2008, Des Moines, Iowa; Gaynelle Narcisse, *They Took Our Piece of the Pie: Center Street Revisited* (Des Moines, Iowa: Iowa Bystander, 1996), 11.

22. DePatten, interview. Hobart DePatten Sr. added the "De" to his father's name ("Patten") because "Patten" was a name white slaveholders had given to his ancestors. He wanted to exert control over his family name. DePatten Collection, Introduction, African-American Historical and Cultural Museum, Cedar Rapids, Iowa.

23. U.S. Commission on Civil Rights, Iowa Advisory Committee, *Urban Renewal Programs and Their Effects on Racial Minority Group Housing in Three Iowa Cites* (Washington, D.C., June 1964), 3–12.

24. DePatten Collection, Introduction.

25. *Bystander*, September 7, 1967.

26. Steven Berry and Erin Herndon, "Healing Hands and Questing Hearts: African-American Physicians in Iowa," in Silag et al., *Outside In*, 243–244.

27. Ralph Crowder to Bruce Fehn, e-mail correspondence, August 19, 2008.

28. Ibid.

29. *Des Moines Register*, July 7, 1966.

30. Peter M. Bergman, *The Chronological History of the Negro in America* (New York: Harper and Row, 1969), 584–599, passim. For more on the urban disturbances of the period and their underlying causes, see *Report of the National Advisory Commission on Civil Disorders* (Washington, D.C.: Government Printing Office, 1969), 19–131.

31. Bergman, *Chronological History*, 598; *Des Moines Register*, July 5, 1968.

32. *Bystander*, July 13, 1968.

33. Between 1963 and 1969, tensions between black youths and police in other areas such as Wyandanch and Nyack, New York; Massillon and Sandusky, Ohio; and Planfield, Rahway, Livingston, Elizabeth, East Orange, Paterson, Irvington, Jersey City, and Montclair, New Jersey, often resulted in looting and arson, and millions of dollars worth of damage. For more on this, see Thomas J. Sugrue, *Sweet Land of Liberty: The Forgotten Struggle for Civil Rights in the North* (New York: Random House, 2008), 325–326.

34. In 1968 six African Americans worked in the Des Moines Police Department out of a total 270 employees. This was 2.952 percent of the department. "Nonwhites" in Des Moines composed 5.5. percent of Des Moines' total population. *Des Moines Register*, December 5, 1968.

35. *Bystander*, August 25, 1966.

36. Ibid., August 18, 25, 1966.

37. *Des Moines Register*, July 7, 1966.

38. Robert A. Wright Sr. to Gloster B. Current, September 25, 1970, NAACP papers, Part 29, Series A, Reel 14.

39. DePatten, interview.

40. *Bystander*, March 30, 1967.

41. *Bystander*, April 13, 1966, and May 18, 1967. See also the report of the League of Women Voters of Des Moines, which documented high levels of concentrated unemployment and poverty in those areas of Des Moines where most African Americans resided. "The League of Women Voters of Des Moines" (February 1967) clipping file, "African Americans," Des Moines Public (Central) Library, Des Moines, Iowa.

42. *Bystander*, April 20, 1966; *Des Moines Register*, September 10, 2009.

43. *Bystander*, April 20, 1967.

44. Clipping file, "African Americans," Des Moines Public (Central) Library; Estes, interview.

45. Clipping file, "African Americans," Des Moines Public (Central) Library; Estes, interview.

46. Bergman, *Chronological History*, 609–610.

47. *Des Moines Tribune*, April 8, 1968.

48. Quoted in Suzanne O'Dea Schenken, *Legislators and Politicians: Iowa's Women Lawmakers* (Ames: Iowa State University Press, 1995), 118. See also *Des Moines Register*, April 8, 1968.

49. *Des Moines Tribune*, April 10, 1968.

50. Ibid., April 8, 1968.

51. Ibid., April 10, 1968.

52. Ibid., April 8, 1968.

53. Ibid., April 10, 1968.

54. Ibid.

55. Ibid., June 8, July 1, 2, 1968.

56. Ibid., June 7, 1968.

57. *Des Moines Register*, June 6, 1968. On black youth demonstrations against police actions, see also *Des Moines Tribune*, June 17, 1968. In this article, black minister William Heath told Mayor Thomas Urban that the city should get tougher with young people's law breaking. At the same time Heath made his remarks, a group outside again protested police activity in the near northside.

58. *Des Moines Register*, June 6, 1968; *Des Moines Tribune*, June 6, 1968.

59. *Des Moines Register*, March 8, 1984. This article contained a tribute to Cheatom, who died of cancer in 1984.

60. *Des Moines Tribune*, June 11, 1968.

61. Ibid., July 1, 1968.

62. Ibid., July 11, 1968.

63. Phil Parks, interview, August 8, 2008, Des Moines, Iowa; Estes, interview.

64. Deidre Mullane, ed., *Crossing the Danger Water: Three Hundred Years of African-American Writing* (New York: Doubleday, 1993), 683–685. The Ten Point Program and Platform was widely circulated and published. The Black Panthers in Oakland first published the Ten Point Program and Platform in the May 4, 1969, issue of the party's newspaper, the *Black Panther*. See David Hilliard, ed., *The Black Panther: Intercommunal News Service, 1967–1980* (New York: Atria Books, 2007), 24.

65. Sister Haadasha and Charles Knox, interview, October 10, 2006, Des Moines, Iowa.

66. Ibid.; Frances Fox Piven and Richard A. Cloward, *Poor People's Movements: Why They Succeed, How They Fail* (New York: Vintage, 1979), 292, 293.

67. *Des Moines Tribune*, February 7, 8, March 8, 1968.

68. Ibid., October 19, 1976. This action approach coheres with remarks made in the interview with Sister Haadasha and Charles Knox.

69. U.S. Congress, House of Representatives, Committee on Internal Security, *Hearings Before the Committee on Internal Security, Black Panther Party, Part Four: National Office Operations and Investigation of Activities in Des Moines, Iowa, and Omaha, Nebraska,* 91st Cong., 2nd sess., October 8, 1970, 4792.

70. *Des Moines Tribune*, July 1, 1968.

71. Ibid.

72. Ibid.

73. *Hearings Before the Committee on Internal Security*, 5009–5011.

74. *Des Moines Register*, August 10, 1968.

75. Ibid., August 6, 27, 1968.

76. Ibid., August 27, 1968.

77. Ibid., August 29, 1968.

78. *Hearings Before the Committee on Internal Security Committee*, 4832

79. Sister Haadasha and Knox, interview.

80. For broader discussions of gender politics within the BPP during the period, see Tracye Matthews, "'No One Ever Asks What a Man's Place in the Revolution Is': Gender and the Politics of the Black Panther Party, 1966–1971," in *The Black Panther Party (Reconsidered),* ed. Charles E. Jones (Baltimore: Black Classic Press, 1998), 267–304; Angela D. LeBlanc-Ernest, "'The Most Qualified Person to Handle the Job': Black Panther Party Women, 1966–1982," in Jones, *Black Panther Party (Reconsidered)*, 305–334.

81. *Hearings Before the Committee on Internal Security*, 4834.

82. *Des Moines Register*, April 23, 1969.

83. Ibid., April 22, 1969.

84. Ibid., October 10, December 1 and 28, 1968; *Bystander*, January 2, 1969.

85. Alex Michael Carr, "The Struggle and Repression of the Des Moines Black Panther Party for Self-Defence" (master's thesis, University of Iowa, 2006).

86. *Des Moines Register*, April 19, 22, 1969.

87. *State of Iowa v. Charles Knox*, 185 N.W.2d (2nd Cir. 1971).

88. *Des Moines Tribune*, October 19, 1976.

89. JoNina M. Abron, "'Serving the People': The Survival Programs of the Black Panther Party," in Jones, *Black Panther Party (Reconsidered)*, 179–187.

90. Hilliard, *Black Panther*, 24.

91. *Hearings Before the Committee on Internal Security*, 4796–4797.

92. Anderson, "Practical Internationalists," 288.

93. Ibid., 289; *Hearings Before the Committee on Internal Security*, 4792–4793

94. *Hearings Before the Committee on Internal Security*, 4811, 4820; *Off the Pig*, http://www.youtube.com/watch?v=HSlpRp4wLCw, accessed June 15, 2009.

95. Anderson, "Practical Internationalists," 286–287.

96. Miriam Eve White, "The Black Panthers' Free Breakfast for Children Program" (master's thesis, University of Wisconsin–Madison, 1988), 29–32.

97. *Des Moines Register*, April 23, 1969.

98. Ibid.

99. *Hearings Before the Committee on Internal Security*, 4812–4815.

100. *Des Moines Register*, December 28, 1966, and May 10, 1969.

101. *Hearings Before the Committee on Internal Security*, 4845–4846.

102. *Des Moines Tribune*, October 19, 1976; Sister Haadasha and Knox, interview; Anderson, "Practical Internationalists," 289.

103. William L. Scherle Papers, State Historical Society of Iowa, Des Moines.

104. *Des Moines Register*, December 4, 1968.

105. Ibid., November, 22, 1968.

106. Ibid., November 22, December 4, 12, 1968. The December 12 *Register* article noted black and white parent groups formed with different visions of school problems and solutions.

107. Ibid., December 4, 1968.

108. Ibid.

109. DePatten, interview.

110. *Des Moines Register*, April 30, 1969.

111. Ibid., April 14, 1969, and October 15, 1970; *Hearings Before the Committee on Internal Security*, 4812; *Black Panther*, April 27, 1969, 3.

112. *Des Moines Register*, April 14, 1969.

113. *Hearings Before the Committee on Internal Security*, 4810.

114. *Des Moines Register*, April 22, 1969.

115. Ibid., April 27, 28, 1969.

116. Ibid., April 28, 1969.

117. *Hearings Before the Committee on Internal Security*, 4833.

118. Ibid.

119. Ibid., 4834.

120. *Des Moines Register*, June 23, July 1, 3, 1969.

121. *Hearings Before the Committee on Internal Security*, 4834, 4837.

122. Anderson, "Practical Internationalists," 291–292.

123. *Hearings Before the Committee on Internal Security*, 4837.

124. Ibid., 5031.

125. *Des Moines Register*, October 14, 1970.

126. *Hearings Before the Committee on Internal Security*, iv–v.

127. Ibid.

128. Ibid., 4833, 4862–4863.

129. *Clive DePatten v. Ray Harrison, Steven Green v. Ray Harrison, Mary Rhem v. Ray Harrison*, 185 N.W.2d (2nd Cir. 1971).

130. U.S. Congress, House of Representatives, Committee on Internal Security, *Gun-Barrel Politics: Black Panther Party, 1966–1971*, 92nd Cong., 1st sess., August 18, 1971, 77, 145.

131. A. June Franklin, interview by Suzanne O'Dea Schenkin, Iowa Women's Archive, A Political Dialogue, Box 2, Transcript, University of Iowa Libraries, Iowa City, 1991.

132. Crowder to Fehn.

133. Sister Haadasha and Knox, interview; *Des Moines Register*, April 8, 1982, and January 12, 1991.

134. *Des Moines Tribune*, February 7, 1979; *Des Moines Register*, December 27, November 15, 1996.

135. *Iowa Independent*, October 24, 2007, http://iowaindependent.com, accessed August 23, 2008.

136. *Des Moines Register*, March 8, 1984.

THE BIG EASY WAS ANYTHING BUT FOR THE PANTHERS

Orissa Arend and Judson L. Jeffries

The Big Easy, as a site for the National Committee to Combat Fascism (NCCF), presented the aspiring Black Panthers with a unique set of circumstances. New Orleans differed from other major southern cities both in its storied intraracial history and in its civil rights movement activity. To start with, New Orleans had a significant African American population from its earliest years, and prior to the Civil War this population included sizable numbers of free black men and women who, with their descendants, called themselves Creoles. Creoles (light-hued free black Catholics of mixed-race French ancestry) tended to fare better than other blacks in most areas of public and private life. Some non-Creole blacks resented the advantages that were afforded light-skinned blacks, making it somewhat difficult to forge the kind of close-knit African American community that may have existed in other southern cities.

Activists attempting to organize the black community around issues of race may have found their work challenging. Moreover the long tradition of well-educated Creoles, coupled with the city's Roman Catholic and Latin heritage that encouraged tolerance and cooperation, made the civil rights struggle in the city different in some ways from that in other major southern locales. The New Orleans civil rights movement was not intense and forceful, as was the case in other southern cities. The movement mirrored the easy-going, relaxed nature of the masses. In an interview with historian Adam Fairclough, Harvey Britton, Louisiana's National Association for the Advancement of Colored People (NAACP) field secretary, noted, "We had worked at our own pace, and things were going to generally get better, but it was not on a national time schedule, it was on Louisiana's time schedule."[1] Well, there was a generation of younger New Orleanians, both black and white, who believed that progress was moving at a much slower rate than warranted. In their minds, the timetable for black progress needed to be moved up. Consequently, a group of young aspiring Black Panthers (mostly in their late teens and early twenties) set up an NCCF office with the expressed purpose of accelerating the struggle for black equality. Before long they would catch the attention of the city leaders and find themselves in the crosshairs of the New Orleans Police Department (NOPD). Concerned with what the NCCF might be planning, the NOPD was prepared to thwart any armed insurrection or mass violence in the city, which had gone through the turbulent 1960s without a hint of a rebellion, something in which the city leaders took pride.

Donald Guyton, now known as Malik Rahim, was one of those on whom the police set their sights. When Rahim (who was in charge of security for the up-start NCCF office in 1970) crawled on his belly through the Piety Street house that had been teargassed and riddled with bullets in the fall of 1970, it was impossible for him to foresee the mild evening thirty-three years later when he would again come face to face with the powers responsible for that onslaught. The NCCF charter, established in December 1969, was not even a year old when the group became embroiled in a highly publicized standoff with members of the NOPD in mid-September 1970. Rahim remembers, "The shooting had stopped, and Charles Scott had instructed me to go from room to room and assess the carnage."[2] Rahim, a Vietnam veteran, was no stranger to death and mayhem, but he dreaded what he might find as he made his way through the house. To his and everyone else's amazement, there were no casualties.

The shootout on Piety Street between the aspiring Panthers and the NOPD lasted approximately thirty minutes. But the tensions leading up to the shoot-out had been building for months. During the previous summer, Rahim and his wife, Barbara, went to their friend Puchimo's house every day for Panther meetings. Those were the early days of the Black Panther Party (BPP) in New Orleans, and Puchimo's house was one of several gathering places. The oldest of the prospective Panthers, Rahim was only twenty-two. Even though he was well traveled, his encounter with the Panthers in his hometown awakened him to new ideas and new possibilities. Thirty-three years later he would reflect, "It was the first time I ever talked to a brother who had no fear."[3] The person to whom Rahim referred was nineteen-year-old Steve Green, the reported founder of the local office of the NCCF and a native Louisianan who had come to New Orleans in May 1969 by way of California. Initially, when Rahim and Barbara tried to join the NCCF, Green urged them not to. They had two children, and Panthers had to be ready on a daily basis to put their lives on the line for their principles. "Too dangerous," Green told them. Rahim and Barbara, however, would not take no for an answer, and by the fall of 1970 they were members of the NCCF. According to the July 25, 1970, issue of the *Black Panther*, the NCCF acted as "organizing bureaus of the Black Panther Party ONLY." The NCCF was sanctioned as a Black Panther chapter only after it proved its worthiness via various community initiatives.⁴ This approval, interestingly, came after the much-ballyhooed confrontation with members of the NOPD.

Headquartered on Piety Street, the prospective Panthers were just outside of the largest, poorest housing development in New Orleans. The $23 million project opened to tenants on May 21, 1956, with 388 four-bedroom apartments and 968 three-bedroom apartments. The project, located within the Ninth Ward in a cypress swamp and dumping ground, was named, among all things, Desire. The *New Orleans Times-Picayune* would later call it a "disaster from its inception . . . a mind-numbing series of careless decisions that amounted to a blueprint for disaster." "It wasn't designed for people to live in; it was designed, rather, as warehousing for the city's poorest residents," according to Ed Arceneaux, a former Desire manager and housing management specialist with the federal Department of Housing and Urban Development (HUD). Larry Jones, the executive director of the Housing Authority of New Orleans (HANO) in 1989, blamed racism. Said Jones in the *Times-Picayune*: the aim was quantity not quality, and so housing officials built an unwieldy giant. "This was for poor black people. I just think that the commitment was not there. . . . They just felt like poor people don't deserve a whole lot."⁵

In the early 1960s, when some previously all-white projects opened their doors to blacks, some residents, who were initially confined to Desire, began moving out in search of better housing. However, by the mid-1960s Desire became increasingly overcrowded as the city was hit hard by Hurricane Betsy in 1965, putting parts of the city, including Desire, under six feet of water. Eighty-one lives were claimed. Levees along the Mississippi River Gulf Coast Outlet along Florida Avenue in the Lower Ninth Ward, as well as on both sides of the Industrial Canal, were breached. Sections of the Lower Ninth Ward were destroyed, and many buildings and businesses were not rebuilt due to a lack of city loans and grants. Moreover, thousands of jobs and millions of dollars in tax revenue were lost, making grim conditions worse. Hurricane Betsy tested the city's levee system and forced massive black displacement and relocation, resulting in tremendous human suffering and death. These adverse conditions forced some black families to, as a last resort, move into Desire, where they remained. By 1970, 10,594 residents, 8,312 (75 percent) of them under the age of twenty-one, were crowded into an area twelve blocks long and three blocks wide.⁶

On a typical summer day, women sat on their porches fanning the tepid air and exchanging news and banter while children jumped rope and played ball in the dirt. Broken glass, old shoes, cigarette butts, and drug paraphernalia littered trampled weeds between apartments. Holes in walls and broken pipes accommodated a sizable population of rodents. Yet the city's administration did not publicly acknowledge the squalor of Desire until the NCCF, demanding attention and advocating revolutionary action, established a headquarters on Piety

Street half a block from the project. At the same time, the NCCF was setting up services to provide some relief and to point out that simple and humane remedies could be provided, if not by the city, then by young black revolutionaries who believed that blacks were being treated more like chattel than citizens.

In August 1970 the city finally took notice. Mayor Maurice "Moon" Landrieu sent Robert H. (Bob) Tucker, his idealistic young black special assistant, to Desire to investigate. Tucker spent seventy-two hours "living" in the home of Henry Faggen. Describing Desire as "one of the most explosive areas of the city," Tucker wrote: "Life in any multi-family structure for the low income family is a very difficult proposition, to say the least. The Desire housing project is a classic study of the worst."[7]

He reported that children waded in clogged sewers for lack of recreation facilities; families were afraid to leave their homes at night for fear of being robbed, mugged, or raped; piles of garbage went uncollected for days, even weeks. Desire was isolated, Tucker found, culturally and geographically from the rest of the city. Located in the Ninth Ward, downriver from the city, it was bordered by railroad tracks, the Mississippi River, the Industrial Canal, and a corridor of industrial plants.[8] But it had nonetheless spawned community leaders, entrepreneurs, and social activists.

Desire Community Center leaders told the *States-Item*, New Orleans's second-largest daily newspaper at the time:

We are fighting against the top . . . to acquire operational funds, against ignorant powers . . . against public leaders who are all too often ignorant of the misery and frustration that cause addicts to revert to drug-dependence behavior. . . . We are fighting against the bottom—the crummy building we live in, reeking with the smell of urine, the dirty floors and broken windows, the backyard that's littered with garbage; the millions of cockroaches crawling over us when we are asleep, sharing our coffee when we are awake; the huge flies and tiny mosquitoes that come through our window, left open in summer heat so that we can breathe "fresh pollution."[9]

Tucker reported that 61 percent of the families in Desire lived on less than $3,000 a year. Food stamp recipients were held up in broad daylight by junkies and vagrants. In 1970 the median family income for blacks in New Orleans generally was $4,745 as compared to $7,445 for whites. This means that white median family income was just over one and a half times that of black median family income. In other words, for every dollar earned by a white family, a black family earned 64 cents.[10] By 1980 little had changed, as black median income increased by less than $3,000 while white median income nearly doubled ($14,898).[11] At any rate, Tucker told reporters at the *Times-Picayune* that a major source of irritation in the community was a local grocery store that failed to meet health standards and, to make matters worse, inflated prices on days when welfare checks arrived in residents' mailboxes. This store, owned by Clarence Broussard, an African American, would become an even larger source of contention.

Just days before the shootout that put Rahim on his belly, Tucker had proposed an eleven–point program to Mayor Landrieu to help alleviate some of the conditions. Included in the program were suggestions that the New Orleans Public Service return regular bus service to the area after midnight; the Board of Health rigidly inspect the grocery store in question; the HANO and the City Sanitation Department provide more jobs for neighborhood residents, particularly ex-addicts; and the sewers in the community be unclogged and kept cleaned.[12]

The reality of the housing development stood in stark contrast to its evocative street names. Piety intersects Pleasure, Humanity, and Desire streets, each of which was named by an eighteenth-century Frenchman who first developed that part of town. In this Catholic city, the names of the daughters of landowners, Desiree and Piete, morphed into a primary human emotion and its superego counterpart, desire and piety. "Piety" means fidelity to natural obligations, faithfulness to that which one is bound by a pledge, a duty, or a sense of what is right or appropriate. In many ways, Piety was the right street for the Panthers. That duty, pledge, and sense of what is right was the Panthers' commitment to self-determination for black people. And Piety intersected Desire. Desire was a fitting name also because, in this housing development, there was a pervasive feeling, angrier than hopelessness, born of a longing that could never be fulfilled.

Birth of the New Orleans Branch

Geronimo ji Jaga (formerly Elmer Pratt) was not directly involved in the founding of the NCCF, although he helped set it in motion. Though the Central Committee in Oakland questioned the viability of a proposed New Orleans branch, ji Jaga pushed for the establishment of one, citing the militant history in Louisiana of groups like the Deacons for Defense and Justice in Bogalusa and Jonesboro, who had armed themselves to combat the activities of the Ku Klux Klan. Ji Jaga, who had been well schooled by members of the Deacons while growing up in Louisiana, knew the benefit of having the NCCF in New Orleans. In 1970 the Central Committee agreed to let ji Jaga send Steve Green, Harold Joseph Holmes, and George Lloyd to help launch the New Orleans branch of the BPP. After the Piety Street shootout, ji Jaga reportedly asked Jane

Fonda to come to New Orleans to publicize the Panthers' cause and to transport the Panthers to the Revolutionary People's Constitutional Convention in Washington, D.C.[13]

The Panthers' first brief home was adjacent to the St. Thomas Housing Development. St. Thomas was like Desire in its large concentration of poor African Americans. Located between downtown and the posh Garden District, it was, however, much more a part of the city than the isolated Desire. Until the 1960s St. Thomas had been all white. The building that housed the Panthers' headquarters at 2353 St. Thomas Street was owned by the wife of Criminal District Court Judge Bernard J. Bagert. The Panthers' political education classes held there attracted crowds of young people—a development that reportedly gave Police Chief Joseph Giarrusso some cause for concern.

In the summer of 1970 Chief Giarrusso sent several memos to newly elected Mayor Landrieu to present "intelligence information on certain activists in the New Orleans area." He stated, "The organization of greatest concern and considered most dangerous was the BLACK PANTHER PARTY." He quoted Federal Bureau of Investigation (FBI) director J. Edgar Hoover as saying, "Extremist all-negro, hate-type organizations such as the Black Panther Party, continue to fan the flames of riot and revolution. . . . Many of these groups, whose leaders preach violence and hatred of the white race, have been involved in shootouts with local police. Many attacks on police by black extremists are unprovoked and nothing more than planned ambushes."[14]

In June 1970 Judge Bagert started eviction proceedings against the NCCF. According to the alternative newspaper *NOLA Express*, Judge Bagert was a slum landlord who evicted the Panthers from their first headquarters because he abhorred what they stood for. He told the *Times-Picayune*: "I'm only glad I don't live in the project. . . . We ought to take a bulldozer [to the buildings] and start over."[15] Reports out of the HANO revealed some startling facts: from 1967 to 1970 Desire consistently ranked near the top of the city's housing developments with the most grievances registered by its tenants. After the June eviction of the prospective Panthers from the St. Thomas property, NCCF members met to chart their next course of action. They decided to move into a house near Desire on Piety Street in mid-July. Frequent acts of police brutality in the area and deplorable living conditions fomented an atmosphere that was receptive to the Panthers' message of self-defense, self-reliance, and self-determination. After settling into their new digs—in the same building as Johnny Jackson's group, Sons of Desire—the Panthers resumed recruiting and organizing.

On July 30 Chief Giarrusso sent another memo, informing the mayor of the Panthers' move. Underscoring his point, he wrote, "As I have stated in previous memos to you concerning this organization, it is considered the most dangerous of black militant organizations and its activities are of great concern to this department."[16] High on Giarrusso's list of concerns was the Panthers' free breakfast program for children. Barbara Guyton was the breakfast coordinator. She wrote and distributed a flyer that became part of Mayor Landrieu's personal papers, now housed in the New Orleans Public Library:

All children in grammar schools, and growing young adults in junior high schools, can receive a full hot breakfast, free of charge. The fact that the Black Panther Party, in implementing this program, has fed over 100,000 children over the past year, is reason enough for the continuance of the free breakfast program.

Because we realize that our children cannot receive an effective education on empty stomachs, we're asking for your full support in seeing to it that the children begin their school day on full stomachs.[17]

The free breakfast program demonstrated to both blacks and whites that black people could in fact be self-reliant and did not need to rely on the government for assistance. The free breakfast program may have been an organizationally mandated program, but this was not the impetus for putting one in place. In response to impoverished conditions, members of the NCCF canvassed the community to find out what its residents were in need of most. They learned that many families could not afford to give their children breakfast in the morning before heading off to school. Consequently, a breakfast program was created; children were served bacon and eggs, toast, juice, and other items. The free breakfast program was a huge hit, as scores of children were served daily. At breakfast, children were exposed to the Panthers' Ten Point Program and Platform and treated to lessons in black history, something which they undoubtedly received little of in school.

Chief Giarrusso, however, was leery of this "effective education" and concerned about what the children were being fed. In an August 20 memo to Mayor Landrieu, he wrote: "The breakfast program is used, primarily, to reach young children with their hate philosophy. This tactic may be more dangerous than the attacks on law enforcement. It is easy to see the far-reaching effects of continually propagandizing children with a hate philosophy that poisons the mind against all established authority, and especially the white race."[18]

Preparations on Piety Street

Less than three weeks after the NCCF's move to Piety Street, the police received a report about a disturbance in the neighborhood. When the police arrived, they were jeered by a gathering crowd. Believing that the incident was deliberately staged by the NCCF, the NOPD quit patrolling Desire. They operated on the periphery, except for two black patrolmen, Raymond Reed and Joseph Orticke. Reed, who had grown up in Desire, was accused of being overly aggressive in his handling of black suspects. Suffice to say, both officers were labeled "Uncle Toms."[19]

On November 14, 1970, the *Black Panther* reported some additional police presence:

The pigs moved into the house directly behind us. They also occupied a two story house a block away behind our house and placed informers in a house across the street. On Piety Street itself, the pigs moved into a house one block away and made many raids on the community from that position. The black bootlicking pig capitalist [Clarence] Broussard, who owns most of the rat infested houses (including the house the NCCF rented) [and the grocery store mentioned in Tucker's report] on the block, filed a criminal trespassing complaint against the members of the NCCF and the pigs gave until Friday to move.[20]

Chief Giarrusso continued to monitor the Panthers' activities. He reported to Landrieu that Harold Joseph Holmes was sent to New Orleans from Des Moines, Iowa, to organize a Panther chapter. His report continued:

Information has just been received from a very reliable source which indicates that Holmes' superiors are not satisfied with his lack of militancy and he is being recalled and will be replaced by one George Lloyd. This could indicate a stepped-up program which would parallel [P]anther activities in other parts of the nation. My Intelligence Division has information indicating that these people now have in their possession at least three hand guns, two of which are 357 Magnums, a very powerful weapon, four shotguns, and several boxes of shotgun cartridges. These shotgun cartridges are of the oo buckshot "slug variety." This type of ammunition is seldom used for sporting purposes and is considered offensive in nature. In addition to these weapons, they have a 22 caliber rifle that is equipped with a scope.

One room of the new headquarters building located at 3544 Piety Street has been sandbagged up to window level, partially barricading the building. This situation should be of a great deal of concern to the entire community. The Police Department is attempting to maintain sources of information in an effort to determine the path to be followed by this group. You will be advised of all future developments immediately.[21]

At the time of Giarrusso's report, Steve Green left town, reportedly to take care of business elsewhere. The reasons for his departure one month prior to the shootout still remain a subject of debate. Meanwhile, the NCCF was busy building its community survival programs. Barbara Guyton's breakfast program was drawing more and more children every day. Landrieu and Tucker were planning their site visit to Desire, scheduled for September 15, to take a closer look at its problems. Tucker would be making a site visit that day without Landrieu; but it was not the scheduled one. Giarrusso was redoubling efforts at gathering intelligence about the supposed danger of the group and sending memos to Landrieu. He wanted the city administration to give its full attention to his assertion of the need for a high alert primarily because he would be leaving his post in a few weeks, handing it over to his brother Clarence.

The battle lines were being drawn.

Two Young Black Men Take Different Paths

In 1965, when he was seventeen years old, Malik Rahim enlisted in the U.S. Navy as it seemed the only way he could get out of Algiers, a community where he lived all his life, located across the Mississippi River from New Orleans. In the mid-1960s Algiers was fairly isolated, and Rahim did not watch the news; he did not even know that the United States was ensnared in the Vietnam War. At boot camp, when he heard that Malcolm X had been killed, he acknowledges that he was oblivious as to who Malcolm was. After boot camp, he was shipped off to Vietnam. When he arrived, he refused to fight. "In order to kill people, you had to think of the Vietcong as 'gooks.' The soldiers who called Vietcong gooks also called Black people 'niggers.'"[22] He discovered in Vietnam that the racism he had experienced in New Orleans was indeed a worldwide problem.

After Rahim was discharged from the service, he moved to California, where he held numerous odd jobs. To his disappointment, he was unable to land a job at the Post Office like many ex-servicemen he knew; therefore he decided to return to New Orleans to do pipeline construction and apply for his seaman's papers. Shortly after returning to New Orleans, he met Alton Edwards, who was selling the Panther newspaper on Canal Street. Rahim's interest was piqued, and he started going to Panther meetings. He imbibed most of the Panthers' principles. Said Rahim, "They held out respect for everyone—black and white and all colors; but I had come back from Vietnam with a hatred for white people. The Panthers had to re-educate me on that."[23]

Most of the Panthers whom Rahim encountered were raised in public housing. "Mayor Moon Landrieu complained about outside agitators. But I looked around and couldn't find them. The New Orleans Panthers could have used some outside help."[24] Even Steve Green—or "Steve from the West Coast," as the media referred to him—had grown up in New Orleans. The erroneous notion that members of the NCCF were transplants was one to which many subscribed. Said Leontine Luke, an NAACP leader and longtime activist in New Orleans: "I felt . . . that the youth of our city was letting an organization like the Black Panthers come in and direct their movements. And I don't think that was right. Because I don't think that anyone can come in and tell you more about how to go about business in your home than you yourself—or your city."[25] Further evidence that runs counter to Giarrusso's claim that the prospective Panthers were outside agitators can be found in the arrests of Panthers over an eighteen-month period beginning in 1970. Of the fewer than fifty people arrested in all local Panther incidents, most were from New Orleans.[26]

Rahim recalls that it was the Panthers' community work that drew him and many others to the party. And because the Desire complex was in dire need of so many services, the NCCF not only established several mandated programs but a few ad hoc programs as well. With little outside help, the New Orleans cadre set up a breakfast program that reportedly served over 300 children weekly, established free sickle cell screenings, conducted classes on self-determination, and organized and carried out clean-up projects.

The NCCF also set up patrols in the Desire complex to help rid the area of drugs. They "made it clear to drug dealers on the corner that they had to move on."[27] Early on, members of the NCCF occasionally ran into the hard-headed or self-proclaimed tough guy; in those instances, the person was, more often than not, moved by force. Eventually everyone got the message and moved on, allowing the aspiring Panthers to refrain from the rough stuff. These patrols helped the group deal effectively with crime in general. In 1970 the murder rate in New Orleans reached an all-time high.[28] Upon learning this, the prospective Panthers sprung into action by patrolling the sprawling housing complex around the clock, checking on the elderly, generally ensuring the safety of its residents like New York City's Guardian Angels some ten years later. Panthers did chores for the elderly, escorted them to the grocery store and to the bank so that they could cash their checks, and guarded people's houses when they were away. Some Panthers were even asked to house-sit while the occupants were out of town. Astonishingly, during an interview years later, Rahim claimed that they had "reduced crime [in Desire] to just about 0 percent."[29]

Of the NCCF's offerings, many people found the political education classes to be intriguing. At these classes, participants were introduced to Mao Zedong's *Little Red Book, The Autobiography of Malcolm X,* and the teachings of Huey P. Newton. Initially, classes started with approximately ten to fifteen children. However, as the parents became increasingly interested in what the NCCF was doing with their children, they, too, felt compelled to get involved. As more and more adults were drawn to the NCCF's political education classes, a bigger venue had to be secured in order to accommodate the large crowds. Both adults and the youth soaked up the lively and engaging discussions about issues that pertained to black people in general and black New Orleanians in particular. Law enforcement officials maintained that these classes were not meant to enlighten but instead were used to indoctrinate both children and adults in an effort to get them to stir up trouble.

The NCCF's community survival programs were always in high demand given the state of black affairs. By 1970 New Orleans's economy was failing. Its major industries—including tourism, oil and gas, wholesale and retail trade, and shipping—were in decline. Manufacturing, once a strong element of the city's economy, had dipped substantially since 1960. Among the city's leading sources of employment were wholesale and retail trade, services, and government.[30] Unfortunately, blacks made up a disproportionate number of these employees. As the recession hit, unemployment soared.[31] By 1970 one out of every three black persons was out of work. According to James R. Bobo, New Orleans's failing economy was directly related to inadequate economic development:

The local economy has experienced economic stagnation tendencies since the mid to late 1950s, with chronic and severe stagnation since 1966, not because there was an absence of economic growth, but because economic development did not provide adequate employment opportunities for an expanding labor force. . . . Employment opportunities have been inadequate since 1966. . . . Consequently, unemployment has increased both absolutely and as a percentage of the labor force since 1966, reaching 9.0 percent in 1975.[32]

Rahim's theory is that the authorities wanted the deplorable conditions in Desire to continue because federal funds were awarded in the early 1970s based on poverty and high crime rates. But the Panthers had decided that "it was time we stopped destroying ourselves."[33] As the first author interviewed Rahim on a fall day in 2002, the setting sun began to come through the living room window at an angle that produced a halo backlight to his below-the-shoulder dreads. "New Orleans is a city based on tribalism," he stated. "But, for a time, under Panther leadership in the Desire, rivalries between residents of different housing developments were set aside. People came together for the good of the most oppressed."[34]

Larry Preston Williams Sr., an African American, joined the police force at the age of nineteen. The NOPD was only about 15 percent black in the late 1960s; but Williams's draft number was ten, and he had no desire to go to Vietnam. He wanted to finish college instead, and he saw the NOPD as a means to an end. In 1970, when he was twenty-two, Williams was assigned to NOPD's Intelligence Unit. Among his responsibilities was to find people willing to infiltrate the BPP, the Republic of New Africa, the Ku Klux Klan, and the American Nazi Party. He loved the assignment, which was a welcome change from the routine police work in "the District."[35]

Williams described the police academy as "difficult racially." The training instructor used the "n" word. All six of the black recruits in Williams's class threatened to leave, but their superiors convinced them to stay. He was assigned to street duty in March 1969. Williams recalled:

I worked with some good, decent white officers. But I noticed that white police officers were overall *terrible* at dealing with black males. Black males had hostility against police officers.... I mean sometimes you'd get on a scene of a crime and for no reason you'd find black males being hostile to police officers because it was fashionable and politically correct at the time. If they were hostile to a white officer, they were more hostile to me.[36]

When asked if he had any inner conflict about managing the infiltration of the BPP, Williams responded: "The only conflict I had was my views of radicals, because I always considered myself to be as far to the left as I could get. So my conflict was managing the infiltration of groups that I wouldn't say I identified with—but groups that I had admiration for. Having that assignment was very, very interesting."[37]

Instructions and guidelines regarding whom to infiltrate were provided by the U.S. Attorney's office. That office kept a list of activists and subversives who were considered dangerous. As Williams noted, "If they were on the list, we watched them." Williams said he was, and is, a nonviolent person: "If the Panthers hadn't threatened violence," he says, "I wouldn't have taken the job to infiltrate." Williams saw the potential for violence in a community, and Desire, he thought, did not

deserve to be in the cross-fire. If something had happened between the Panthers and the police department, a lot of innocent people would have been killed. That bothered me. But an organization that was sensitive to police brutality, wanted to feed kids, wanted to get drug dealers out of the neighborhood—had I not been a cop—was an organization that I would have supported. I don't think I would have joined, but I could have supported it, because in theory those were good ideas.... So of course there was no conflict there. It was a matter of violence.[38]

Williams looked somewhat embarrassed when he was reminded that although the Panthers frequently spewed inflammatory rhetoric, they did not actually perpetrate any acts of violence in New Orleans. Said Williams:

The police department probably became convinced that these people posed a danger to the police department, and of course the police department would try to convince people that they posed a direct threat to the community, especially the white community. But there was nothing that I saw or heard from infiltrators to convince me that these people disliked white people because they were white. There were particular white people that they thought were oppressive. There were cops, black and white, that they thought were the arms of an oppressive society that they would resist. But just hating people because of the color of their skin—I never got that from the Panthers.[39]

Regarding their program, Williams noted: "As a group I thought this chapter was pretty devoted to doing things for the Desire area. I thought generally their stated goals were good. I thought they went about them fairly efficiently given the resources they had. I thought they were sincere. I thought they were good people." He added: "The only problem I had with them was that they seemed to have an intense dislike for most police officers. It wasn't individual. They just didn't like police officers."[40]

Williams loved being in the Intelligence Unit; it was everything he expected and more:

The challenge was to get information from the groups. I found that I could get more information from the groups if I infiltrated them with women rather than men. Men did not suspect women of being undercover agents. Women could form confidential relationships. Women always know things that the guys didn't know, saw things that the guys didn't know. They could go places where the guys would be suspicious. They could ask questions that wouldn't arouse suspicion; whereas if a guy asked the same question, there would have been suspicions.[41]

Williams says he had a female in the Panthers and one in the Klan, both of whom worked out well. "All you need is one female. And she doesn't need to be intimate with anybody. What's important is the role that she plays. She's always in there. She's supposed to take care of the house, and so she sees everybody who comes in. She feeds people. She has all the telephone numbers. She makes all the telephone calls. She has a list of people to call if something happens. I mean it's just great. *One woman!*"[42]

A New Moon in the Crescent City

Prior to 1970 blacks had been, for the most part, effectively kept out of the city's political affairs, and this was done by the city leaders without violence or the threat of violence. In New Orleans, there was no need for a "Bull" Connor or Sheriff Jim Clark type, as there seemed to be an unusually high degree of cooperation (relatively speaking) between certain sectors of blacks and whites. Unlike in some racially hostile cities such as Birmingham, Montgomery, or Selma, Alabama, it was not uncommon for large numbers of local whites to join the struggle for equality. A good example occurred in September 1963, when more than 300 whites participated in a march of 10,000 blacks to city hall to present to the mayor and city council a list of grievances. The following year the Citizens' Committee (a group of black lawyers) threatened a selective buying campaign against Canal Street merchants. After several merchants respond-ed with "commitments" to hire blacks, the leaders postponed their boycott. Blacks and whites via the Urban League, the NAACP, the Interdominational Ministerial Alliance, and other groups engaged in a variety of tactics to change racial policy, including negotiations, litigation, and the occasional sit-ins. Activism among both blacks and whites in New Orleans could be characterized as "genteel protest."

New Orleans's rigid social structure also helped keep blacks at bay politi-cally. The pinnacle of the city's social and political sphere was dominated by a small number of wealthy white families whose New Orleans lineage could be traced back several generations. The elitism propagated by the city's influentials is, ironically, best illustrated during Mardi Gras. While the masses make an art form out of participating in an open, freewheeling epicurean revelry, the elites attend elegant balls that "are closed not only to the general public but also to everyone except those whose families have been . . . [in New Orleans] since the turn of the century."[43] Suffice to say, this rigid social structure undercut any ef-fort at a more diversified civic and political leadership in New Orleans.

By 1970 Rahim's consciousness, as well as that of many other black New Orleanians, was evolving; so, too, was the city administration. Newly elected Mayor Landrieu shocked many by appointing African Americans to top lead-ership positions in city hall. During Mayor Victor Schiro's tenure, city hall had been virtually lily-white, with no African Americans holding a position higher than clerk.

Under Landrieu, blacks were able to make significant inroads into city gov-ernment. Terry Duvernay was named the city's chief administrative officer; Cecil Carter was named deputy director of the Human Relations office; and Don Hubbard became director of the Total Community Action neighborhood center in the Desire Housing Development and, later, director of the Division of Youth Services for the city. He succeeded Charles Elloie, who would later become a judge. Five of the twelve department head slots were filled with blacks, including finance, recreation, welfare, property management, and model cities. It is ironic that an African American headed the city's finance department, given that municipal finances had been especially difficult for blacks to penetrate. More important, the chief administrative officer provides overall executive supervision and coordination of the day-to-day functions of city government as well as appoints, subject to the mayor's approval, eleven of the thirteen executive department heads. In addition to the department head appointments, Landrieu also appointed a number of blacks to important administrative positions below the department head level, including the director of policy planning, the manpower director, and the mayor's executive assistant. During Landrieu's eight years as mayor, the number of blacks working in municipal government increased from 10 percent to 40 percent.

Carter, Tucker, and Hubbard, well grounded in civil rights history and active players on the local scene, were "on the ground" in Desire as tensions escalated. Each helped in important ways to avert what appeared to be inevitable, massive bloodshed.

One could argue that Landrieu's appointment of blacks to important positions was not entirely motivated by a fair sense of equality and justice. Landrieu understood that the political and racial landscape in New Orleans was changing and, equally as important, that they were inextricably linked. Blacks constituted 45 percent of the city's population, and that number was growing. However, their voter registration numbers were not commensurate with their potential, politically. No black had ever held the mayoralty or occupied a seat on the city council. It was not until 1967 that the city sent its first African American (Ernest Morial) to the Louisiana state legislature. Landrieu recognized that a massive voter registration effort over the next several years could ensure Democratic rule (including his reelection) ad infinitum.

The move toward African American inclusion signaled a radical transition in a city where the voting majority was still 55 percent white. But the Voting Rights Act of 1965 had altered the political landscape. In 1964, 63 percent of the city's eligible white population was registered to vote, but less than 25 percent of eligible blacks were registered. Ten years later the latter number had swelled to nearly 42 percent.[44] With strong support from black political organizations such as the Southern Organization for Unified Leadership (SOUL) and Community Organization for Urban Politics (COUP), Moon Landrieu was New Orleans' last white mayor. As he took office in 1970, selecting a police chief was among his highest priorities. Landrieu had two requirements for his new police chief: that the top cop be absolutely, impeccably honest, and that he had a "good, solid, rational attitude on race." Frankly, Landrieu said in a 2003 interview, "that was extremely difficult to find."[45] His choice was Clarence Giarrusso, brother of police chief Joe Giarrusso. Landrieu's comments regarding the difficulty finding a person of high character is interesting, if not odd, given that he apparently needed to look no farther than the brother of the then current police chief. The selection of Clarence Giarrusso seemingly took the guesswork out of this very important hire.

In a 2003 interview, Clarence Giarrusso boasts that in 1970, he had many dependable informants in the community. He considers Israel Fields and Melvin Howard, the undercover police who had infiltrated the BPP soon after its inception, real heroes and some of his greatest assets at that time. "I knew what was coming, anticipated some things," he said, "and we could smooth things out. Information is very important for police work, and there were many pieces of string that I could pull at that time."[46]

Giarrusso downplayed the drama of the 1970 confrontation. Fear is not part of his personality, he notes: "It didn't bother me that they called us pigs. I knew where they were coming from. . . . I talked with the Panthers. They were dissatisfied people. The things they didn't like made sense. They were treated as second-class citizens. . . . American society was in a revolutionary mood, a . . . changing mood." Giarrusso remembers going into Desire before the confrontation with Mayor Landrieu and Ben Levy, the chief administrative officer. He had second thoughts about trying to talk to the Panthers, but "there's always some people with whom you can talk. . . . America was engaged in social maturing."[47]

When Clarence Giarrusso assumed the position of chief, he appointed Louis J. Sirgo, a white seventeen–year veteran of the NOPD, as his deputy chief.[48] Deputy Chief Sirgo was a visionary. In a speech to civic leaders shortly before he died, Sirgo warned that "a thin blue line of police officers, working against the odds is able to partially contain the violence and prevent criminal anarchy." But that containment, he said, could not last for long. "Police forces were not designed for, nor are they capable of coping with the kind of [social ills] which exists in most of our urban areas, conditions which are becoming worse by the day." He deplored what he called the "vindictive system" of crime and punishment. And he deplored "the greatest sin of American society—the status of the American Negro."[49]

"If there were no 'Desires,'" he said, "there would be no Panthers. What I am saying is that we have to get our heads out of the sand, for, after all, it is an unsafe position. An ostrich buries his brains, and that part of his anatomy [that] remains visible makes a very good target for a sniper."[50]

Sirgo's comments about the plight of American cities are hard to argue with; even his remarks about the police departments' inability to cope with the type of social ills that exist in America's urban areas have some merit. Missing from

Sirgo's analysis was his assessment of the officers that made up the NOPD. An examination of the attitudes of New Orleans's police officers about themselves and their work may help to explain why the NOPD was unable to or unwilling to tackle the kinds of problems that a police department is especially equipped to handle. A survey of New Orleans police officers in the 1960s revealed, for example, that two-thirds or more of the officers considered such acts as taking graft, accepting bribes so a suspect could avoid being issued a ticket, and cheating on an examination for promotion to be highly immoral; but 46 percent saw nothing seriously wrong with discriminating against minority groups. More disconcerting, most officers seemed to accept a relatively low assessment of their qualifications and their ability to make significant social inroads. The survey reported that while most officers considered themselves moderately dependable and extroverted, many ranked themselves low on other characteristics. Only 9 percent regarded themselves as highly ambitious, 4 percent ranked themselves as highly intelligent, and none rated themselves as highly sophisticated.[51] It is possible that a lack of self-esteem may have had an impact on the performance of their work.

In 1970 there was an amazing convergence of political events and personalities in the Crescent City. At the same time a band of black revolutionaries formed in town, New Orleans had a new mayor who was not consciously racist, a new police chief who was humane, and an assistant police chief who had a unique understanding of both the past and future. Talented young black men served in the city's administration for the first time, and there was at least one black undercover cop who considered himself as far to the left as one could get. Thus the defining racial event in New Orleans of the post–civil rights era did not become the bloodbath that many people feared.

Just Before the Shootout

On September 14 it was getting dark outside of Robert Glass's Central City New Orleans Legal Assistance Corporation (NOLAC) office. He was working late to ensure that his files and records were in order because he suspected that he would not be working for NOLAC much longer. His current clients were too controversial. The previous June, when Judge Bagert had started eviction proceedings against the revolutionaries on St. Thomas Street, the Panthers asked Glass and fellow attorney Ernest Jones to represent them. Even though the Panthers had very little money, neither Glass nor Jones thought twice about taking the case—they considered the cause to be righteous.

Thirty-three years later, Glass is working late again, this time in an elegant but comfortable downtown office with brick walls, wide plank floors, and plenty of New Orleans charm. Glass is a busy man, in demand as a defense lawyer, with the reputation of having an acerbic personality. But he was willing to give a lengthy interview that evening. He ended it with this story, almost as an afterthought:

I got a call that some trouble had occurred down in the Desire Housing proj- ects. I called Ernest [Jones] at home and we agreed to meet down there. I got down there. And on the edge of the project was a liquor store called Champs. I walked into the store. I was a little young and prideful. After law school I had bought a Mont Blanc fountain pen and that's what I used in my office late at night to write. They cost $35 at the time. And I had the pen with me when I drove down to the Desire project. I walked into Champs liquor store and there was a young Black man with a bandolier and a gun. He said, "My kid sister could use that pen at her school." And he took it. It took me five years . . . be- fore I could afford another one![52]

According to most reports, the immediate precipitating cause of the September 15 shootout on Piety Street between the police and the Panthers was the outing of two undercover police officers. Local and national newspapers featured headlines about the mock trial and beatings of infiltrators Melvin Howard and Israel Fields at the hands of the Panthers. But thirty-five years later, Fields says that "there was no mock trial, but rather a little scuffle" with people shouting accusations. Fields says he remembers three other NOPD un- dercover officers being there that night as well as at least one person from the FBI. "We never admitted to being undercover."[53]

"Tyrone Edwards hit both of us in the head with a pot. When he hit me a second time, that started a fight," Fields recalled. Fields and Edwards fell to the floor—neither would let the other go—and both of them took some licks. But others intervened to stop the fight, and the Panthers ended up putting Fields and Howard out on the street. Once out of the Piety house, Fields says he was stabbed in the back and hit by a two-by-four with nails in it. He did not know who his assailants were. When he noticed the blood coming out of his head, he nearly fainted. "If I had, I probably would have been dead." But instead, he picked up a metal garbage can to shield himself against blows from a metal pipe and started running. "I was out on my feet."[54] Fields managed to reach Foreman's grocery store, which was next to Broussard's. From there, he called police headquarters, and they sent someone to escort him to Charity Hospital, where twenty-seven stitches were required to reattach his nearly severed ear.

Fields had joined the force in 1969 at age twenty. He joined the narcotics squad under its head, Clarence Giarrusso. "I had a narcotics buy on one of the guys." Fields had bought marijuana from Ron Ailsworth on St. Thomas Street, after which he was encouraged by both Giarrussos to hang around Panther headquarters. He officially went undercover in August 1969. Young and still "green" in 1970, he muses, "Maybe I was trying to stay out of the war, and I wound up in another war." Contrary to popular belief, he and Melvin Howard worked independently; it took him some time before he discovered that Howard was undercover also. Fields says that his escape from Piety Street was quite frightening. Comparing his stint with the narcotics squad to his undercover work, he reflects, "I would rather buy drugs."[55]

Rahim recounts the events this way: He says two little boys selling the *Louisiana Weekly* on the corner of Tulane and Broad—right outside of police headquarters—had tipped off the Panthers weeks before the shootout that Howard and Fields were cops. In late July they said to a party member, "Hey, them two is police, pigs," setting in motion a hair-raising chain of events. Apparently, the two boys had spotted Fields and Howard going in and out of the local police precinct and, on occasion, riding in the front seat rather than the backseat of a police cruiser. According to Rahim, the Panthers knew how to handle undercover police officers. "We'd call them Uncle Toms and we'd run 'em off. But the two young ones with big, gigantic bushes [Afros], Melvin Howard and Israel Fields—there was a lot of debate about what to do with *them*. First we said we were going to expose them. But then Charles Scott said, 'No, we won't expose them 'cause then they [the police] gonna send some more and it might take us too long to find out who they are. Let's just keep them here. We're gonna feed them with a long-handled spoon." At that same meeting, a Panther imposter who had not yet been discovered, a federal agent who had infiltrated the unit, yelled, "Kill them." "But Charles [Scott] objected. We'll either educate them or use them until they realize they are Uncle Toms. Maybe they'll see the light."[56]

As the weeks passed, it became more and more obvious that the police would find an excuse for a raid on the Piety Street headquarters. Meanwhile, the Panthers continued to feign ignorance. Rahim remembers that the night before the shootout, the police cordoned off the project, restricted access, and continually hovered over it in a helicopter. There was sniping all night long, probably from Broussard's store, Rahim believes. The Panthers evacuated all the children from the headquarters.[57]

Given all the commotion, Althea Francois was surprised at the number of people who had come for the public education class conducted by Charles Scott that evening. She noticed that Scott was rushing through the class. Then Scott announced, "There are two pigs in the office." Francois felt a chill go through her body. Scott instructed Francois to take the children to the safe house (a house less than a block away from the headquarters) and wait for instructions; and so she did. She gathered up the five or six children, all under the age of five, and headed out. "It was a very strange night," Francois recalls. "I didn't sleep at all; but the children slept through the night, because they were too young to know what was going on." "If things get really hairy, throw a mattress over the children and lie on top," Scott told her.[58]

On the day of the shootout, according to the *States-Item*: "During the early morning hours, many Panther sympathizers in Desire pleaded with Panther leaders to 'lose themselves' in the project's labyrinthine complex of buildings to avoid arrest." But the Panthers had their own way of doing things. "They stayed to face the riot squads," the paper reported.[59] Indeed, Rahim had an escape plan. There were bunkers all through Desire. "Get as close to the Gulf as you can," he thought, "take a boat, and go to Cuba." Again Scott saw it differently. He said, "No, man. This is political. And we gonna make a political stand." He was not moving the group into the projects either because "they gonna destroy a lot of people's houses. These people are poor. They can't afford to lose nothin'. We gonna stay right here in our office."[60] Rahim remembers that even with the sniping, people from Desire were coming over to see if they needed something and to help with the children. One woman came over and put a prayer cloth, a plain black cloth, on the wall and said, "Ain't nothin' gonna happen to y'all."[61]

As tensions rose, it became harder to deal with the so-called Panthers who were cops. A month and a half of pretending not to know had created a strain. According to Rahim, the night before the shootout, he lost patience with Fields and punched him in the mouth when Fields denied being a cop. But Charles Scott, the principled strategist, said, "No man, don't hit him. Don't beat him. Don't do anything to him."[62]

Meanwhile a crowd had gathered outside the Piety headquarters as word on the street circulated that something was about to happen. "Charles reasoned that Fields and Howard, if they were all right, if what they were standing for was right, if they were there to protect their people, they would not have any problem going out of the Panther office and walking in front of the people. So [the Panthers] tossed them out there," recalls Rahim. "Howard and Fields tried to run through the crowd; several Panthers created a path to allow them to escape. Charles figured, if they get jumped, that's just the excuse the police want to come in here and raid. When the Panthers cleared the way, one of the men ran straight for Broussard's store."[63]

According to the *New York Times*, "Mr. Fields said he took refuge in a grocery store and waited to be rescued. Mr. Howard said he jumped a seven-foot fence and outran his pursuers."[64]

Rahim claims that "as soon as they got to the store, the police opened fire. That's where they killed a young brother [the next day] who just happened to be there. He didn't even have a rock."[65] The first shots of the thirty-minute volley came from Broussard's store. The *States-Item* reported that patrolmen Reed and Orticke had driven by the Piety headquarters shortly before midnight on Monday and had seen two men who looked like they had been beaten running toward Broussard's grocery store. Reed and Orticke had gone there to investigate a car burning.[66] According to the *NOLA Express*, the car reportedly belonged to Fields and Howard.[67] How this could have been is unclear given that Fields and Howard claimed not to have known one another's true identity.

The *States-Item* report goes on to say that "gunfire then sent bullets ripping through the patrol car, injuring Reed and Orticke."[68] Sporadic shooting occurred throughout the night, keeping Althea Francois from getting any sleep. Around 7:00 a.m. on Tuesday morning, the children awoke, and "they wanted their breakfast, their bottles, their mamas and daddies." Francois could see the Piety Street house from where she stood in the doorway, but she did not know whose parents were still there; and she had no way, at that moment, of finding out. She recalls twenty-five minutes of nonstop shooting. "I didn't know which of the parents were in the building. Hearing the gunfire and the way it happened I knew nobody was alive. I had to just wait."[69] Francois proceeded to do the only thing she knew to do: she gathered up the children, fed them a hearty breakfast, and pretended it was a normal morning.[70]

The Shootout

After Fields and Howard fled, several Desire residents were wounded by snipers during the night. Attorneys Jones and Glass left Desire that evening during a lull in the shooting. But in the morning the police department's plan took shape. "The scene of the Central Lockup as police geared up for the raid was grim," reported the *Times-Picayune* on September 15, 1970. "It's a job," a black policeman, was quoted as saying. "It has to be done by somebody." The article continued: "The first bus pulled out at 8:04 a.m. A convoy of police buses, police cruisers and newsmen in private cars wended its way through the downtown morning rush-hour traffic and onto Interstate 10. By 8:45 a.m., the battle was on. 'My god, it sounds like a war,' one policeman exclaimed as automatic rifle and machine gun fire punctuated the early morning stillness."[71]

Rahim tells the story of the shootout on Piety Street in this way:

There were twelve of us in the party office at the time, and almost a hundred police with everything from a .50-caliber machine gun and armored cars to their revolvers. We had about nine shotguns, and a couple of .357 revolvers. But everything we had was legally purchased, and it was registered to our office. Our position was that African Americans should no longer be lynched or beaten or attacked and have their rights taken away without any form of resistance. We believed that you had a right to defend yourself. You had a right to defend your community. You had a right to defend your family. And you had the right to defend your honor as a human being.[72]

Roy Reed offered this report on September 15, 1970, in the *New York Times*: "The police came shortly after 8:30 a.m. just as the winds from nearby tropical storm Felice churned up a black cover of clouds that dumped a downpour of rain on the Desire neighborhood. Several hundred New Orleans policemen and twenty or thirty state policemen descended on the organization's headquarters—a large old frame building decorated with posters of Panther heroes."[73]

Rahim remembers:

The police came in busloads. They got in their positions and just started shooting. They shot up the office maybe twenty minutes straight. It seemed like it was all day. I said, "Boy, they gonna kill us." The firing was coming in so fast we literally had to pour water on the walls because you could see the sheet rock expanding from the heat till you could touch it and it would just pop. The tear gas canisters came in as fast as we could toss them out. We put bread in wet towels. The yeast in the bread helped with the tear gas. The front door weighed about 300 pounds. It was constructed from drain covers scavenged from the nonfunctional Desire sewer system.[74]

Among the revolutionaries and defenders of the people was a fourteen–year-old boy who was in the Piety house when the shootout occurred. The Panthers did not have enough time to evacuate him. In the midst of the shooting, the boy rose up and uttered a plea that probably voiced the fears of the slightly older people as well: "I want my Mama!" Someone yelled, "Get down, fool!" and tackled him. Seconds later, the area in which he stood was riddled with bullets.[75]

Time magazine described it this way: "Shots of unknown origin were heard, and police opened fire with automatic rifles and shotguns. Some of the ammunition was powerful enough to rip through three rooms and emerge from the building's opposite wall.... The besieged were presumably saved from death or injury by sandbags they had piled against their walls."[76]

"All of a sudden the shooting stopped," Rahim continues.

After about three or four minutes Charles asked me to crawl to the different rooms and find out how many were injured and how many were dead. I went to the first room. I asked, "How many people in there are shot? How many are dead?" Ron [Ailsworth] responded, "Ain"t nobody in here shot or dead."

I crawled to the next room. Nobody shot or dead. The back room—nobody. I went back to Charles, and he asked, "Who they done killed?" I said, "Nobody." He said, "What!? All that shootin' and they ain't shot nobody!?" I said "no," and we all burst out laughing. He said, "Well, we done did all we can do in here. Now we gonna take it to court. Tell everybody to come down." I said, "No. I ain't gonna let them take me out and hang me, beat me to death. Whatever they gonna do to me, they gonna do to me right here."

Charles proclaimed, "That's not what we here for. We gonna come out of here *as men and women* and we gonna take it to court. Whatever happens from there happens. If they take us out of here and kill us, everybody in this community gonna know what happened because we gonna walk out of here *as men and women.*"

We all assembled in the second room, and that's when Charles gave one of the greatest inspirational speeches I ever heard. He said, "We're the Black Panther Party and we ain't gonna bow down and we ain't gonna allow anybody to degrade us or what we stand for. We gonna let everybody know that we stand for our rights as human beings, and we gonna take it to court. If they convict us, we gonna let everybody know that in this country there's two kinds of justice. There's justice for the rich and powerful, and there's injustice for the poor and the disenfranchised. When you walk out of that door, everybody raise their hand and holler POWER TO THE PEOPLE."[77]

The prayer cloth had worked—or perhaps it was the sandbags, the 300-pound fortified door, or Scott's inspirational speech. Rahim prepared for the surrender.

Charles told me to tie a white flag on my shotgun and stick it out the window. As we started walking out, I said, "Hey, Charles, they might not honor that white flag." Charles replied, "Well, hey, if that's what they gonna do, let me be the first one to die." As Charles walked out he raised up his hand at the door and called out "POWER TO THE PEOPLE." I was the last one to leave the office. The first policeman that had me put a gun in my ear and tried to trip me to make it look like I was gonna run so he could shoot me. A sister named Charlene Duckworth who was looking out her window yelled, "Don't you shoot that Brother!"

When Charlene started hollering, another police officer, a lieutenant [Rahim thinks it was Sirgo], jumped that officer who was trying to shoot me and made him leave. He put another police officer with me and brought us through the house. They took Ron and me back in and kept asking us, "How many up there dead? How many left in there?" Ed (one of the brothers) hollered "FIVE. Get two of them big ones!"[78]

The Panthers were perhaps foolishly taunting the police even at that very tense time. Rahim laughs as he remembers that at the time of the shootout, he was the biggest, at a whopping 147 pounds. He continues:

That's when I was able to get a look, a real look, at how everywhere you looked there were bullet holes. I looked and I said, "Boy, how in the world did we survive this? Lord have mercy." They had Ron [Ailsworth] and I sit on the porch and it started raining. One white police officer commended us, "Hey, I respect that's what y'all stand for, that's what y'all believe in. But this is what I believe in." I said, "Well, I respect that, too." Then we talked about the Saints, about the season they were having. Then they took us to jail.[79]

At a press conference on the afternoon of September 15, Giarrusso and Landrieu commended all of the law enforcement personnel involved in the fracas, including the Jefferson Parish Sheriff's Department, the Louisiana State Police, and various members of the U.S. Attorney's office. "Today was an excellent example of teamwork, harmony, cooperation and coordination," the police superintendent said.[80] "We are very grateful to the people in the Desire Project, many of whom were not aware of what was going on who found themselves in a battle area," said the mayor.[81]

On September 16 the *States-Item* reported: "The arrested Panthers marched out of the headquarters with arms raised and were ordered to walk across a narrow bridge over the Higgins Canal. They were told to lay on the ground, spread-eagled, while they were searched. The Panthers were then taken to Central Lockup for booking."[82] Larry Preston Williams and Rahim saw the shootout differently. Like Rahim, Williams was twenty-two years old, was African American, and had grown up in New Orleans. But instead of going to Vietnam, as Rahim had, he joined the NOPD. This is Williams's account:

I arrived there in the afternoon, if I remember correctly. There were large numbers of police officers standing outside. We were there because we understood that the Black Panther Party was prepared to confront two men that were thought to be undercover agents. The assumption was that that would cause some kind of conflict. The FBI informed us that the chapter was well infiltrated with police officers and undercover agents. I think at any time there were probably at least five—at the high point maybe eight or nine—police officers and/or paid or leveraged informants. And we didn't know if the people they were going to accuse were really *our* police officers. But in the event that they did accuse our officers and in the event they were in danger, there was a contingent of officers prepared to go in and rescue them. So our presence there was really not to move the Panthers out of the premises, but to be there to rescue our officers in the event they needed to be gotten out, extracted.[83]

When Williams joined into the Intelligence Unit, Fields and Howard were already undercover. "I would hear people say that there were two undercover cops; eventually, I figured it out because they just kind of stood out. They didn't have the rhetoric. They didn't have the background. They were not from the same kind of home life. They just stood out. I just kind of suspected; but I wasn't certain."[84]

The Piety Street office was bugged, but whether the transmitter was planted or whether undercover officers had body transmitters, Williams did not know. In any case, from police headquarters he was able to hear the discussion in the Panther office.

Somebody said, "There's a pig in here!" And Mr. Fields said, "Off the pigs!" And my memory is that shortly after that Mr. Fields and the other undercover officer, Melvin Howard, left Panther headquarters and took refuge at a grocery store across the street. Later on, there was some firing back and forth. I'm not clear as to who fired the first shot. I didn't get any specific instructions. When I arrived officers were standing around pretty angry, but at the same time under control. You didn't have officers—angry as they were—totally out of control, running around, storming the place, trying to kill people. I attribute that to Clarence Giarrusso's leadership. His brother [Joseph Giarrusso] was entirely different. He was old school—reactionary, rule by force. I think if it had been up to Joseph Giarrusso the cops would have stormed the place. There would have been a bloodbath. That's the way you did it in those days. You didn't let people like the Panthers dictate what you did. You didn't give them a break. Not that you order people to kill suspects, but you understand that in that kind of frenzy—with setting that kind of example and tone—that someone was going to get killed.[85]

"Well, Clarence's tone was just the opposite," Williams continues.

He had always had the reputation for being an easy-going, sensible, compassionate person. He would avoid violence if possible. Miraculously, no one was injured. I probably arrived just as the shooting was winding down. I had a carbine, and I do remember firing two or three shots. Our information was that somebody had switched out live ammunition for blanks. The reason I believe that was the case is that as we stood and fired at the Panthers, it would have been impossible for them to shoot into this large gathering of police officers and not hit anyone. Of course our ammunition was live. I was there when they surrendered. They came out with their hands up. We cuffed them and took them to Orleans Parish Prison. . . . The Panthers *did* give up—to their credit—because that was not a confrontation that they could have won. . . . With all the grenades they had it still would have been a bloodbath, and the people who would have shed the most blood would have been the Panthers. . . . When it came down to it, they put their hands up and walked out of their headquarters like any bank robber. They weren't ready to pay the ultimate price. Not ready at all. . . . I mean, what kind of serious Panther just gives up? . . . Now to me that was a miracle. I am *glad* that they surrendered. But serious Panthers would have fought to the end. These guys were different. It's *good*.[86]

Williams, of course, had not been privy to Charles Scott's inspirational speech. After the Panthers surrendered and were taken to the Orleans Parish Prison, Giarrusso called a press conference at 1:30 p.m. at city hall. A reporter asked the chief, "What does an incident like this do to the man-power situation, working around the clock?" Giarrusso answered, "I think that this community should recognize that we are terribly, terribly short of men. What it does to us . . . some of us have been up thirty consecutive hours." "How long can you keep up at such a pace?" the reporter wanted to know. "I don't know but we will if we have to. These people will not get a foothold in this community," the chief vowed.[87]

The *New York Times* reported that "with the shooting stopped, neighbors drifted out to the front yards of their small houses across the street to watch. About 400 other Negroes gathered behind the committee headquarters and shouted anti-police slogans."[88] By 2:30 p.m. order had been restored to the Desire area. City buses crossed the creaky bridge and headed into the project. "A young Negro and two companions sauntered by the firehouse, while blowing on a clarinet. Another . . . frolicked past while holding his umbrella high to ward off the September sun."[89]

On September 21 the *States-Item* reported: "Thirteen persons [including three women] were arrested when police stormed the Black Panther headquarters. . . . They were charged this afternoon with five counts each of attempted murder." Bond was set at $100,000 per person.[90]

Reactions and Reflections

After the shootout, the Panthers seemed even more ominous to some whites. Still, they, and particularly their breakfast program, garnered support among a fairly broad spectrum of New Orleans's citizens. Five days after the Piety Street havoc, the Reverend Joseph Putnam, a white pastor of St. Francis De Sales Catholic Church, had this to say from the pulpit on Sunday, September 20:

Black Panthers, your platform and your program embraces what every self-respecting man wants for himself and his people: Freedom, power to the people, full employment, decent housing, and education. To achieve these basic goals you demand an end to capitalist exploitation and robbery of black people, an end to compulsory military service for black people, an end to police brutality and murder, an end to unfair and unjust trials of black people and freedom and amnesty for all blacks who have been convicted unjustly. You want land, bread, housing, education, clothing, justice, peace and self-determination for the black community. In all of these things that I too believe. For all of these things I too work daily. It is for these things that I live and struggle and suffer. And yes, like you, it is for these things that I will gladly die.

This is why I welcomed a free breakfast program at the Church I serve with full knowledge that some members of the sponsoring group were Panther sympathizers.[91]

After describing the church politics that brought the program into being, Putnam continued:

During the months that have followed, these young people demonstrated their ability to feed about one hundred to one hundred twenty hungry children every weekday and to deal with the problems and details that accompany such a program. Perhaps their greatest trial came from the internal turmoil caused when one of their helpers tried to cause conflict between the black children and the five to ten little white children who were hungry and were also being fed. The group had sufficient character to make the decision to feed the hungry no matter what the color of their skin, and sufficient self-discipline to deal with the dissident brother. I must confess, my experience has not always been the same in some white church groups when black children have come to participate.[92]

Putnam concluded on a cautionary note:

But, Black Panthers, in spite of your magnificent platform, your great goals and objectives, if what I read, hear and see in news reports and in reports from the community is true, I cannot agree that your attempt to arm yourselves with guns and bombs will bring better conditions. I cannot agree that strong-arm, fascist-like tactics will effectively combat fascism. I cannot agree that police-like methods will eliminate police brutality. I cannot agree that exploitation of black brothers will eliminate exploitation of black brothers. I cannot agree that freeing your will on the minds and hearts and bodies of black people is the way to freedom for blacks. Many blacks who are working in breakfast programs and in other fine programs and who love your goals but do not agree with your strategy and tactics are now suffering considerably because of your actions. Somehow your actions are not liberating but enslaving to those who associate with you.

Nevertheless, in spite of our differences of opinion, I hope we can continue to work together on things where we agree. Thank you.[93]

In 1970 a wide range of people could empathize with black people's plight and the Panthers' efforts to ameliorate the conditions that afflicted the city's poorest residents.

How did the mayor assess the upheaval? In 2003 Moon Landrieu reflected:

The Panthers apparently had won a good bit of support down there by giving out meals and breakfasts and becoming part of the community in [Desire]. And they developed a good bit of sympathy, both from the standpoint of "charity" work they were doing as well as this whole question of race, which was and still is today (not as much today) a boiling question. Minority rights, the repression of blacks, police brutality, poverty—these played a huge part in it. When I ran for office I got a minority of the white vote, a vast majority of the black vote. There was no reason for me to be frightened of black people.[94]

Landrieu, the last white mayor of New Orleans, from 1970 to 1978 did indeed enjoy substantial black voter support over the years. In both his 1969 and 1973 mayoral campaigns, Landrieu garnered more than 90 percent of the black vote.[95] "I felt comfortable with black people. Still do, always will. But I was going to enforce the law. You can't have anarchy. Whatever the social injustices of the time were, that wasn't the way to solve them." Landrieu pauses a moment as he deftly shifts his point of view. "I actually had a grudging respect for the Panthers—not for what they did, not for how they did it. But they were willing to put it on the line. I often thought if I had been black, I might have been a Black Panther myself. You had to respect the fact that however wrong they were, however misguided I thought they were, they were never just mouth. They were willing to put something on the line. They were willing to put their lives on the line for what they believed and what injustices they felt existed."[96]

For many, part of Landrieu's legacy is that of a liberal politician who opened up city hall's doors not only to blacks but also to women. One wonders, then, why he would stand pat while blacks were continually being mistreated by police officers, and why he allowed the police to run roughshod over the NCCF and the residents of Desire? Desire residents viewed his inaction as a slap in the face, especially since Landrieu enjoyed nearly unanimous support from them in the 1970 mayoral election.[97] Did making a record number of black appointments exempt the mayor of his responsibility as an officer of the law to ensure the safety and civil liberties of his citizens, no matter how much he may have disagreed with their politics? These questions will no doubt be forever debated but perhaps never resolved.[98]

Desire Heats Up

After the Piety Street shootout, tensions between the Panthers and the police seemed to subside, at least for a while. Rahim and several others were locked up in the Orleans Parish Prison. But Francois and a few other comrades returned to the Piety House after the shootout. They found "awful stuff." Francois recalls: "When we walked in, the sun was shining through the holes in the building. The tear gas was thick. The police had urinated in the refrigerator. We had no weapons. But we decided to sleep there anyway. We called central [headquarters] and told them we were still open."[99]

In the weeks that followed, the Panthers continued their activities, meanwhile polling residents as to whether they wanted them to stay. Claiming an overwhelming mandate from the people, the Panthers set up their headquarters in apartment 3315 in Desire on October 25, 1970. But city officials were determined that they could not stay, and the Housing Authority provided the rationale. The Panthers were not a family by definition, but a political group. This third eviction for the Panthers was shaping up to be a confrontation larger than the one on Piety Street. A small army, including a newly purchased "tank," had been sent into Desire to enforce a trespass law that carried a maximum $50 fine.

Mayor Landrieu was under increasing public pressure from the white community to exert control over Desire and evict the Panthers. But it was clear to Don Hubbard, Bob Tucker, Henry Faggen, Cecil Carter, and others that it would not be an easy thing to do. The Panthers were holed up in a fortified apartment with scores of Desire residents supporting them. In 2003 the first author interviewed the four of them at the splendid Hubbard Mansion Bed and Breakfast on St. Charles, and this is what they remembered:

Cecil Carter, one of the young black civil rights leaders who worked in the Landrieu administration, says: "Moon had asked us to go and see what we could do. So we had some conversations with residents and Panthers. The conversation went like this: [He quotes the Panthers.] 'We have occupied. We claim nesters' rights. We ain't movin.'" "Moon really got on our case," Bob Tucker, Landrieu's special assistant in 1970, recalls. "He thought we should have been able to talk them out of the Project."[100]

Don Hubbard, who ran antipoverty programs in Desire and twenty-seven years later built the mansion where he hosted us for the interview, says:

We just looked at the Panthers like they were another community organization. We weren't in awe of them or what they were doing. The Panthers came to
the Desire Community Center one day and announced that they were going to
liberate my office. And I didn't know what the hell they were talking about. So
I listened. I said, "Well, look. If you want to use the facility here it's no problem.
You can register just like the Better Young Men's Boys Club or whoever, get
a night, come in and have your meeting or your rally. I don't know what you
mean by 'liberate.' If 'liberate' means run me out of here, you've got a problem
because this is my job. You can't liberate my job."[101]

Hubbard continues:

We had been a part of CORE [Congress of Racial Equality]. We weren't in awe.
What they were doing—all that military stuff—was no problem, but certainly
they escalated it to another level. We had some differences with the Panthers.
Some of the smaller neighborhood grocery stores, mom-and-pop stores, complained about them demanding food for their breakfast program. We had a
meeting with the Panthers and suggested they not do that. We said, "Look. We
got a whole bunch of white folks round here y'all could shake down. We got
Schwegmann's, there was Canal Villere, Mackenzie's doughnuts." Without giving you all the details, it was just suggested that they do things differently.[102]

Ultimately, negotiations failed.

Henry Faggen, who had lived in Desire from the time it opened and was
affectionately christened its "mayor," recalls the conversation he and Hubbard
had with the Panthers: "They just talked crazy about revolutionary suicide. I
gotta wipe my hand off. [Faggen's way of distancing himself from Panther rhetoric.] You know I wasn't for that."[103]

As Hubbard and Carter were standing around talking to residents in Desire
that tense fall, a young man came over to them and said, "If they put that tank
on these kids [Panthers], we got something for 'em." "You got something—like
what?" inquired Hubbard. The man opened a Schwegmann's grocery bag, and
in it were half a dozen hand grenades.[104]

"At the point where the deal went down," says Tucker, "I think the pins on
those grenades were going to get pulled. A grenade has no conscience." He
points out that Desire had over 10,000 people living there, and many more
streaming in every day, with most of the people being children in this veritable
war zone; the leaders who were in a position of responsibility were concerned
about collateral damage. Tucker explained to Landrieu on the phone from
Faggen's house that when the people in Desire wanted the police, they never
could get them. They had to wait four or five hours for an ambulance. "There

are a lot of adults today," Tucker says, "who were babies born in ambulances trying to get out of Desire, locked in by bridges, a train track, and a canal. Now that the Panthers were there, organizing for black self-determination, though, the cops came swarming."[105]

Faggen adds: "They [the police] were there to hurt, not to help. The police would come into Desire and do like they wanted. You'd be sittin' on your porch and they'd tell you to go inside. All that resentment just built up. And when these guys [Panthers] confronted them [police], that brought people to them [Panthers]. The people were *willing* to protect the Panthers with their *lives*. But I didn't want to see that."[106]

Hubbard saw a kid sprinkling cayenne pepper, creating a perimeter, to deter the police dogs. And he saw Johnny Jackson (who later became a state legislator) come out of the Desire Community Center, sit down on the steps, put his head in his hands, and moan, "Man, I never thought it was going to come to this."[107]

The evictions from St. Thomas and from Piety Street had only hardened the Panthers' resolve. Their programs—protection for the elderly, breakfast for children, pest control, and education for self-determination—had continued without interruption after the shootout, and law enforcement's stance had strengthened support for the Panthers in Desire. Despite more than a dozen Panther arrests, a core group of armed Panthers living in a Desire apartment said they would fight to the last person to defend their "home" if the police interfered. Five clergymen decided to get involved.

In early November, fearing a racial Armageddon, Chief Giarrusso and Mayor Landrieu asked Jerome LeDoux and William London, both black, and three white clergy—William Barnwell, Harold Cohen, and Joe Putnam—to join the negotiating effort on November 16 to try to get the Panthers to leave peacefully.

Father LeDoux, S.V.D., pastored St. Augustine's Catholic Church in Treme, a historic treasure founded by free people of color during slavery, until the New Orleans archbishop reassigned him to a parish in Texas during Lent following Hurricane Katrina. Rev. William Barnwell, a retired Episcopal priest, teaches and consults nationally on church outreach work. In 1970 Father LeDoux had visited Desire many times. On at least one occasion he had scheduled the Panthers to speak at his theology class at Xavier University. On the other hand, for Barnwell, Desire was alien territory. "Will they take us hostage?' he asked himself on the drive to the development in mid-November 1970. "Of course not," he replied, as if trying to convince himself.[108]

Both priests remember Panther headquarters as a fortress. According to LeDoux, it had "window-high sandbagged walls, scores of grenades, dozens of assault rifles, and numerous bandoliers of ammunition on both floors of the residence."[109]

Barnwell, in his memoirs, quotes one of the Panthers as saying, "You've moved Black people with your urban renewal programs so you can build shiny new buildings we never see the insides of. You've taken us from our homes to beautify our city as though people don't matter. You moved us to build Interstates that we can't afford cars for. This time we ain't moving." According to Barnwell's memoirs, the mediation went like this: "Look," said a black priest, "if you will just leave this apartment for a few weeks and make formal application to the Housing Authority, I think we can arrange for you to have it legally. Already some people have agreed to pay the rent."[110]

Barnwell's amazingly detailed memoirs contain this dialogue: "Man," said George, a Panther spokesman who Barnwell recognized from coverage on television, "you haven't been getting the message. We don't have to make *no* formal application to *no* housing authority. This is our housing project, our community. We are here because the Desire residents want us here. Ask them, if you don't believe us. That's all the authority we need."

"The police are going to come in here and shoot up the whole place and kill every one of you. They mean business. I can promise you that," said LeDoux.

"It ain't no different from any other time," responded another Panther. "They're always coming in here and shooting up everything. The only difference is this time they are going to have to kill a whole lot of us. And for every one of us they kill there'll be ten more right from this project to take his place. It ain't no different."

"Will you listen to reason?" another member of the clergy pleaded.

"Your reason is white man's reason," said someone Barnwell does not identify. "Look at what your reason has got us: bad housing, rats, wall-to-wall roaches, schools that don't teach you nothing but how to smoke dope, and no decent jobs. If the pigs are so concerned with law and order, why don't they get the dope pusher who's ruining our children?"[111]

LeDoux recalls that a Panther by the name of Poison finally said, no more talk.[112] The mediation ended.

Barnwell remembers a young woman in an elegant long dress in the apartment saying, "You know what a panther is? A panther is an animal that attacks only when attacked." He wanted to wipe away the tear that crept down her cheek. He realized she was the tender age of the students he taught. He thought as he listened to her, "Tomorrow she'll probably be dead." He was struck by the contrast between the Panthers' tough political rhetoric and the gentleness with which they treated one another and the clergymen.[113]

In 2002 LeDoux made a similar observation about the Panthers' stance: "Ever careful to avoid being the aggressors, the Panthers always kept themselves in a protective mode only. Not very many whites believed them or trusted them, especially given their strident tone, their constant taunting and challenging of the white world, and their ominous flaunting of arms." He adds, "They were not racist baiters of whites and others, but staunch, fearless protectors of the poor, the abused, the disenfranchised, and the helpless."[114]

Barnwell's memoirs continue: "The Panthers repeated their refusal to move, repeated their Ten Demands, then shut the door. 'One: we demand that all political prisoners be freed. Two: we demand that all Black people be given jury trials by their peers.'" Notes Barnwell, "It looked as though the Panthers would be totally destroyed."[115]

At the Hubbard Mansion in 2003, former Desire resident Henry Faggen remembers the day this way:

Faggen ran a methadone clinic. He had seventy or eighty people to care for. Bob Tucker, who had just finished a staff meeting with Landrieu to plan the arrest of the Panthers, called Faggen about 3:00 a.m. in the morning and told him to get his people to the clinic and get them medicated. Hurriedly putting on his clothes while running down the stairs, he heard groaning. "I saw a guy lying there," Faggen says. "He was shot. I didn't know what to do with him. I definitely didn't want him hanging around, but I didn't want him to die. We got the boy to the hospital, and when we got to the hospital, to my surprise they had four or five other people who had been shot *in Desire!* But nobody had heard any shots. And that . . . surprised me."[116]

As Faggen finished tending to his methadone patients and the wounded man, the sun came up, and he returned home to meet Tucker. They, along with Don Hubbard and Charlie Elloie of the Division of Youth Services, huddled to decide their next move. Tucker stayed at Faggen's house in order to be in phone contact with the mayor and the police chief. Hubbard, Faggen, and Elloie walked the streets. Faggen says the police did not enter Desire like trained and disciplined troops. "They just came in running—running right past that building [where the Panthers were headquartered]. The police came in with tanks. The people had hand grenades. The [white] officer driving the tank, we called him Big Red. Big Red knew me, and he was a straight shooter. He said, 'Man, you better get these people off the street 'cause it's gonna be bad.'"[117]

Faggen remembers an old woman, about seventy, with one leg. "They [police] were throwing her down the steps. People saw that and they started hootin' and hollarin' and cursin'. Wasn't no leadership there until Bob and Don came out. When we got over to Pleasure Street we heard a loud scream. It was Geraldine, a friend of mine, and they [police] had jammed her in her house. She just screamed and screamed and when she saw me she said, 'Faggen, help me, please help me.' Then my adrenaline started running, and the police they got their guns crossed but that didn't move me. I just pushed the guns away and went up to the step to cool her down. The shouting stopped. We got out the back door some kind of way. As the day progressed, [the police] got real, real, agitated. And I'll never forget as long as I live. We were walking on Pleasure and Alvar, and they had police lining up everywhere. I was talking to the chief of police, and this cop was looking at me. And I saw he just wanted to shoot me. He had all the venom in his eyes. I said, 'Go ahead shoot me. That's what you want to do. Shoot, you coward! You're just taking over our community. Just shoot!' Clarence [Giarrusso] told me to cool it. I had a lot of respect for him.

"Whatever was happening, I'd go back to my house and I'd tell Bob. Bob would confer with the mayor. At one point Bob put me on the phone with the mayor. The only thing I could tell him was it was a bad situation, and if the police didn't get out of there by night, there was going to be some action. Those boys [Panthers] were playing. But the people were not playing. I don't want to downgrade those kids [Panthers]. They were just young kids doing a good job in the community, feeding the children, teaching them discipline. What got me was they were talking about revolutionary suicide. A lot of people fixin' to get hurt; hurt *bad*! Young kids with their own philosophy and an ideology that to me was not concerned about the *masses* of people."[118]

The mayor asked Bob Tucker to go from building to building with Giarrusso to inform the police it was time to leave.[119] When Landrieu and Giarrusso issued the order for the police to leave, the police were furious. Faggen remembers not one or two but many police officers calling Giarrusso a "nigger lover" on the way out. "He just took it," says Faggen. "After the police left and the sun went down, some Desire residents brought out food and beer. They carried the Panthers on their shoulders all the way to Florida Avenue. Folks partied all night long. The Panthers were the heroes, not us. But we prevented the killing. I don't like to pin no roses on myself, but it would have been a very tragic day had it not been for us."[120]

Roy Reed, one of Rev. Barnwell's parishioners at the Chapel of the Holy Spirit, was in Desire on Thursday, November 19. He sent this special report to the *New York Times*:

The New Orleans Police Superintendent called off an armed four-hour confrontation with a Black Panther group today to prevent what he saw as an impending "blood bath." Neither side fired a shot. The move, believed to be unprecedented in police-Panther relations, forestalled what could have been a serious clash between hundreds of tense policemen and an angry portion of the black community here. Three to four hundred emotionally charged young Negroes had stationed themselves between the police and the Panther group, which was garrisoned in an empty apartment building. It was concern for the young crowd, not for the Panthers, that caused him to withdraw his officers, Superintendent Clarence Giarrusso said afterward.[121]

The *Black Panther*, not necessarily known for its attention to detail or objectivity, published this seemingly embellished report:

On the morning of November 19th, approximately 600 pigs, in armored vehicles (new ones having been recently bought by the New Orleans Pig Department), moved in to assault the office in the projects. Three to five thousand Black people, men and women old and young, stood between the pigs and the office demanding that the fascists leave their community immediately. The fascists frustrated themselves trying to get the people to leave, but the people continued demanding they withdraw from the community. Finally, after four hours, they retreated. It was the only thing they could do in the face of the power of the People. And the People sang and danced in the streets.[122]

Dirty Pool

On the fifth and sixth days following the standoff, the police pulled what many considered to be two dirty tricks. Many New Orleanians remember the first one, probably because it involved a celebrity. But amazingly, very few remember the second, the final arrest of the Panthers. Even the man who ordered it has seemingly forgotten. On November 24, five days after the showdown, Jane Fonda arrived in New Orleans to protest HANO's efforts to evict the Panthers from their apartment in Desire. The actress had become increasingly political during the Vietnam War years. The *States-Item* reported: "The 33–year-old actress-turned-activist appeared at the HANO office at 542 Camp shortly before noon, dressed in a green turtle neck sweater, brown buckskin pants and Navy P-coat and announced she had come 'to help arouse the public consciousness as to what is happening to the black people.' Miss Fonda urged the audience to go to the Desire Project and 'find out for yourselves' what is happening there. 'Don't you believe what you read in the newspaper,' she said." Praising the NCCF's efforts in resisting the police attempt at eviction, Fonda said, "How can we smug white people say what black people should do? We have done nothing for centuries to stop the violence perpetrated against them." Fonda reported that she had been working with the Black Panthers nationally for about a year and a half, raising money for their causes. From there she went to Loyola University's Field House, where she told a large crowd that "Desire is a concentration camp where a reign of terror exists." She said that the terror was being perpetuated by the New Orleans police, not by members of the NCCF.[123]

The following day, November 25, Fonda rented four cars to transport the Panthers and their supporters to the Revolutionary Peoples' Constitutional

Convention in Washington, D.C. Before they were able to get out of town, however, they were stopped by members of the NOPD and arrested.

The *NOLA Express*, in a special edition on December 1, reported:

The pretense at legality was very thin. The police thought, or at least would have the public think, that they captured a gang of "militants," including the bulk of the NCCF chapter. In all, two members of the NCCF were in the caravan. The other 23 arrested, including a mother of two, seven juveniles, and six whites, were proclaimed guilty of walking into the NCCF headquarters earlier in the day to sign some papers. For this they were charged with two counts of criminal trespass and one count of criminal mischief each.[124]

Former intelligence officer Larry Williams recollects:

When Jane Fonda came to town, I was assigned to follow her around. She got nasty. She called me an Uncle Tom . . . pointed me out and called me a sell-out. She comes to town and she rents the automobiles. There are people who get into the automobiles. They are leaving New Orleans and going to Washington, D.C. We arrest them. They are leaving town. To this day, I have no idea why they are arrested. But I do know when I arrested a group, my English teacher from Xavier got out of the car. He and I chatted. I could not imagine what law they had violated. But, see, we would do stupid things like that. Everything is going good. They're not doing anything to anybody. We were in a position where if they did something serious we'd know it in advance, because we already had them infiltrated. And we do something damn stupid like arrest them for nothing. Bring them downtown. No charges. The District Attorney would never take the charges. There *are no charges* [Williams is laughing] for getting in a car and driving out of town. It's not illegal. But that's the kind of stuff we would do on a slow day.[125]

With the second underhanded move, the police accomplished the final arrest of the Panthers in Desire. Early Thanksgiving morning, police disguised as clergy and postal workers forced their way into the Panthers' Desire apartment, shooting Panther Betty Powell in the process when she tried to slam the door shut. The same morning Johnny Jackson, director of the Desire Community Center, was working late in his office when he heard a noise and went to investigate. He thought the noise had come from a group of kids preparing for a Thanksgiving party in the rear of the building. When he reached them, the kids told him they saw priests, police in disguise, leading members of the NCCF from their headquarters, which was next door to the Community Center.

Jackson stepped out onto the porch to see what was going on. Someone called to him from the shadows. As he stepped around the corner, he was thrown up against the wall by a police officer and had a shotgun stuck in his chest. "Get us out of here safely," he, Joseph Lewis, and John Cook were told, "or you won't be a shield, you'll be a target." When they refused to cooperate, they were hand-cuffed and placed in the squad car with NCCF members. Some residents began shouting, "Pigs in the community!" and "Power to the People!" As Jackson put it, "I belong to all these organizations and have these titles, but when you get down to it with the police—I'm just another nigger."[126] Jackson was later elected to the Louisiana state legislature and the New Orleans City Council.

Describing the early-morning raid, Jackson said:

The police department disguised themselves in many ways, from Public Service repairmen, mailmen to a priest. It was the police officer disguised as a priest offering a donation for the Breakfast Program (with the other policemen hidden in the hallway with all sorts of guns) that lured one of the occupants to open the door. At that point, they [the policemen] burst into the office and began shooting, wounding a young Black woman. Incidentally, many of this strike force were "COLORED" policemen who later were called "AMERICANS" by the Superintendent.[127]

Commenting on the chief's declarations, Jackson offered:

Some of these "instant Americans" have grown up with people of this Black community. Some have been to our schools, teaching our children about "Officer Friendly" and community relations in the day and raiding our community by night. Two other Black people of this community besides me were kidnapped from the Community Center and used as shields/hostages to get them out of this hostile community and booked firstly with a city charge and then a state charge of resisting arrest and interfering with police officers. More trumped up charges like these and others are just part of the systematic games run on Black people.[128]

In an open letter to "All Black People and Concerned People" printed in the *NOLA Express*, Jackson called the arrest of the people trying to go to the Panther convention a conspiracy and a "plot by the Housing Authority of New Orleans, City Hall, the Police Department, the News Media, the Courts, and Undercover colored people." He said, "This is happening every day to Black people who attempt to get out of their place. Things haven't changed since Black people came to this country."[129]

At the Hubbard Mansion interview, everyone remembers the Jane Fonda incident. Tucker, alluding to perks of privilege, says, "Jane Fonda was probably sittin' on a Delta airline in first class sipping on a martini, as they [the police] were taking the Panthers off to the slammer."[130] Curiously, Hubbard, Carter, and Tucker, however, did not know about (or had forgotten) the trick that led to the final arrest of the remaining Panthers in the Desire apartment. The real priests and the Panthers, however, remembered it well. In Rahim's words, "It took them to do a deed that is about the greatest betrayal of morality that I have ever witnessed to get us. They came and raided the office dressed as priests."[131]

Father LeDoux, who hardly ever says a bad word about anyone, still considers Sergeant Robert Frey, the policeman who wore the priest garb, "the scum of the earth."[132] In 1970 LeDoux told the *Louisiana Weekly*, "For the past two years and especially during the recent crisis in the Desire Housing Project, the clergy played an important role as mediators. This subterfuge seriously undermines future effectiveness of the clergy."[133]

The Escapees Meet the Panthers in the Orleans Parish Prison

In mid-September 1970 Robert King Wilkerson was watching a guard's television through the bars of his cell in the Orleans Parish Prison. What had landed him in that cell—this time—was a jailbreak from prison with twenty-five other prisoners. When he found out that he received a thirty-five–year sentence for an armed robbery of an Uptown supermarket, which he says he did not commit, he decided that "the slaves have a right to rebel." "Many of us felt we were unjustly confined," he told a group of students at Tulane University in 2003. "I began to see that I had no moral obligation to a system that oppressed me. To run from injustice did not mean that I was guilty of a crime."[134] He was at large for two weeks before he was recaptured.

On September 15, 1970, the announcer on the small prison television interrupted regular programming to inform viewers that a group of black militants had barricaded themselves in an apartment in the Ninth Ward and were "shooting it out with the police." King writes in his autobiography: "This caught my attention. It was something that was unprecedented in the city of New Orleans, and as each scene unfolded, and every word uttered by the commentator, the kinship I felt with the group—whoever it was, grew. And if it was possible that I could have undergone a transfiguration, I would have transfigured myself to that scene, into that house with whomever it was that was shooting it out with the police."[135]

King soon learned that those shooting it out with police near the Desire housing development were members of the BPP. The nine men who were arrested on Piety Street came to the Orleans Parish Prison, and the three women, Catherine ("Top Cat") Bourns, age nineteen; Leah Bernadette Hodges, age eighteen; and Elaine ("E-Baby") Young, age twenty-two, were sent to the detention center next door. The youngest one, at fourteen years of age, who had stood up as the shooting started and called out for his mama, was a juvenile, so he was not held with the others.

The Panthers at first were separated from other prisoners, but they nevertheless found a way to communicate. King writes: "It was through this prison communication system that I met the firebrand of a sister, Top Cat, as she was called . . . a source of inspiration to many of the prisoners, and she was my greatest inspiration. In her letters to me she uttered the Party's Doctrine . . . as if she had written it herself."[136]

Ron Ailsworth also figured prominently into King's introduction to the BPP. After the bank robbery on Jefferson, he was housed with the escapees rather than with the Panthers. "It was [Ron's] knowledge and revelation about the Party which ultimately tied me to the Party's concept. . . . It was from Ron that I was introduced to the Party's teaching and Platform. We began to hold political discussions, and it was through these discussions that I grasped the historical plight of Blacks and other poor people in America."[137]

After the two groups of so-called troublemakers had been separated for a while, prison officials came up with another idea. Rahim remembers the encounter this way: "The guards said, 'Y'all think you some bad niggers. We're gonna send down some real bad niggers and they gonna kill you and have sex with all y'all.'" The guards planned to put the two groups together and let them kill one another other.[138] That's how Orleans Parish Prison escapees Herman "Hooks" Wallace, Albert Woodfox, and King met the Panthers.

"Send 'em on down," Rahim told the guards. "We know how to deal with them." When Woodfox arrived, Rahim remembers it was "real tense at first." Woodfox raised his fist. "Power to the People," he hollered, expressing solidarity instead of the violence the guards had anticipated. "They sent [Herman] Hooks [Wallace] down," Rahim recalls. "He had no shoes." Rahim insisted on giving Hooks his shoes when Hooks went to court. And that began their friendship.[139]

King and Rahim were not strangers; they had both grown up in Algiers, their backyards adjoining. King recalls that he immediately felt "awe and respect" for Rahim and the other Panthers. "They would hold political education classes. I wasn't an official member at that time, but when they spoke, they spoke for me. I was just as eager as anyone to see conditions change." There was a prisoners' rights movement sweeping the country, and the Black Panthers, says King, brought that movement into the Orleans Parish Prison. "Guys who were eager to effect change weren't necessarily party sympathizers or members of the Black Panthers. But they knew that they were being treated badly. For me, the Black Panther Party members helped articulate issues that lent a sort of legitimacy to my feelings."[140]

In his autobiography, King recalls the horrible prison conditions they faced. "Tiers originally built to house only 48 prisoners were holding twice as many. Toilets ran all night, and water, infested with feces, would at times run into the hallways where prisoners had to sleep. . . . Huge rats coming up from the sewer competed with prisoners for their food. The food was poor in quality and quantity, having no nutritional value and prepared in an unsanitary manner."[141]

The one bright spot for King and the others surfaced when Marion, Mary, and Linda (who were Tulane students), Shirley, and Althea came to visit.[142] The women, three of whom would become Panthers, visited regularly. King especially looked forward to seeing Marion. He called her the "Tulane Babe."[143]

All of the Panthers arrested in and near Desire, except Ailsworth, stayed in the Orleans Parish Prison for nearly a year awaiting trial. Wallace, Woodfox, and Ailsworth were sent to Angola in 1971, before King. "They began teaching unity amongst the inmates, establishing, arguably the only prison chapter of the Black Panther Party in the nation at that time."[144] That precipitated a palpable change at Angola.

In late April 1972, when King was escorted back to Angola from the Orleans Parish Prison by the National Guard, he was immediately put in solitary confinement. "My record traveled with me, so they knew of my Black Panther involvement."[145] From solitary, King's human contact was limited; but human communication continued. He notes, "I felt as if I had entered a different Angola than the one I had entered years before, where prisoners were totally subservient. Absent was the submissive, sycophantic behavior of years gone by. In its place, I witnessed a quiet defiance among many of the prison's population. And I knew this was due mainly to the presence of Albert [Woodfox], Herman [Wallace], and Ron [Ailsworth]."[146]

Because of the brutal and political nature of their prolonged solitary confinement (over three decades), King, Woodfox, and Wallace became known internationally as the Angola 3. Eleven months seemed like an eternity for the group arrested on Piety Street. In November they were joined by the Panthers who were arrested on their way to the Revolutionary People's Constitutional Convention in Washington, D.C., as well as those who were apprehended by police in disguise. The Orleans Parish Prison was a hellhole according to King and Rahim. King says, "The sewerage was real bad. Rats and roaches were running around like they owned the place. Guys were sleeping on foam rubber mattresses on the floor, on tables, in the hallways. If you were lucky you got an old army blanket that had been used thousands of other times. And that was if you were lucky."[147]

Rahim remembers the constant tear gas on their tier so thick that the guards had to wear gas masks. "The guards had broken up the porcelain toilets and dumped trash in the cells. Then they tried to make the prisoners clean it up. The guards put mace on the end of fire hoses so the mace would go as far as the water would go."[148]

The Panther defense team comprised of Robert Glass, Ernest Jones, Lolis Elie, Charles Cotton, Alvin Bronstein, and George Strickler effectively argued that the Panthers had acted in self-defense. Assistant District Attorney Numa Bertel Jr. countered that "if it was the intention of the New Orleans Police Department to slaughter these people, they could have dropped a bomb on them."[149] Bertel's argument was not entirely without precedent. In the city of Philadelphia fourteen years later, Mayor Wilson Goode authorized the dropping of a bomb on MOVE, a black radical group that had set up operations in the Westside section of the city. Sixty houses were destroyed in the process, to say nothing of the loss of life. The backlash resulting from this drastic measure was far-reaching. Mayor Goode, the city's first African American mayor, witnessed his support among blacks quickly evaporate. In 1987 the voters tossed him out of office.

By all accounts, Panther attorney Ernest Jones's closing arguments were eloquent. "When in the history of New Orleans have 150 men gone down there with a tank to serve simple arrest warrants?" he asked. He reminded the mostly black jury that after the Panthers surrendered, the police took posters, typewriters, newspapers, and leaflets from the Panther headquarters. "Why?" Jones asked. "Because these things were doing what they [police] feared most. They were giving ideas to black people."[150]

The highly publicized trial culminated on August 7, 1971, when a jury of ten blacks and two whites returned a unanimous verdict of "not guilty" after barely half an hour of deliberation. The verdict was greeted with a single shout of joy from friends and sympathizers of the defendants who packed the courtroom. Supporters, loved ones, and friends slapped one another on the back and hugged. One of the defendants, Leah Bernadette Hodges, buried her face in the shoulder of defense attorney Robert Glass.

After Judge Israel Augustine quieted the courtroom, Assistant District Attorney Bertel asked that the jury be polled. As each of the jurors rose and pronounced the defendants "not guilty," Kenneth Weaver, a white juror, one of the first to be picked, stood and said to the surprise of many, "In the spirit of Martin Luther King, not guilty!" As the defense attorneys left, they were applauded and hugged by some of the sympathizers who lined the corridor. At one point, attorney Ernest Jones was engulfed by the crowd, which swarmed around him.

Judge Augustine said that the decision proved that "fair trials can be had by any black people in the South. If ever there was a fair trial in the community, this trial was it." As he emerged from the courtroom in a shirt and tie, the crowd in the corridor began chanting, "Here come de Judge!" Here come de Judge!" Several times he was stopped and kissed by spectators.[151]

The New Orleans Black Panthers Disperse

When Rahim left Orleans Parish Prison, he needed a safe house. Freed Panthers could become police targets at any moment. Knowing Marion Brown and her roommates lived in the Newcomb dorms, Rahim thought, "What better safe house than a women's dormitory at an exclusive college?" In those days, dorms were segregated by gender. It was the last place anybody would think to look for him. He had a maintenance man's uniform in case anyone ever asked any questions, but no one did. Students and faculty got accustomed to seeing him over the course of the next nine months. People assumed he was a student or that he worked there. So Rahim came and went from those staid halls unimpeded.[152]

Later that year (1971), Marion Brown joined the party, dropped out of Tulane, and with nine other New Orleans Panthers answered the call from the central office to come to Oakland. According to Rahim, the New Orleans chapter lasted a few more years, then faded away. The Oakland experience for most of the New Orleans Panthers was a shock and a disappointment. They did not see the same discipline and commitment that they had established in New Orleans. Several thought that when they decided to leave Oakland, they barely escaped with their lives.[153]

The New Orleans Panther women had a particularly difficult adjustment. The stated ideals of the party concerning women were high. Panther Linda Greene described the "new phenomenon" of the revolutionary black woman in a 1968 issue of the *Black Panther*. "She is a worker. She is a mother. She is a companion; intellectual, spiritual, mental, and physical. . . . She is the strength of the struggle. . . . She is militant, revolutionary, committed, strong, and warm, feminine, loving, and kind. These qualities are not the antithesis of each other; they must all be in her simultaneously."[154]

Point Seven of the party's Eight Points of Attention states, "Do not take liberties with women." But the party struggled constantly with disparities between party rhetoric and the realities of daily life, according to some women party members. Some claimed that it was sexual open season, with men demanding their right to the "revolutionary fuck."[155]

New Orleans, however, was different. In 2003 local Panther Leah Hodges addressed a gathering at a BPP photo exhibit in honor of the Angola 3 at the Community Book Center. Thirty-three years after her arrest on Piety Street when she was eighteen years old, she is still quite glamorous as she pursues her singing career. Recalling the discipline of working for the people from sunup until late into the night, she remembers the New Orleans brothers as respectful.[156]

Marion Brown adds that the Panthers attracted misfits, the "white sheep" of the family. "We were like a family, the odd ones, who finally found a place that made us feel at home. People could see the principles we were living day by day. Everybody was expected to pull their weight, male or female. It was not a sexist thing. We were ahead of our time." But in Oakland, Marion Brown and Betty Powell, who had taken the buckshot in the final arrest, were "stuck in the child care center" taking care of Panther children "24/7," which was not the reason they had gone to Oakland. Both were eventually reassigned to positions in the field. But after a series of severe health problems, Brown left Oakland in October 1972. Because she was shrewd, outspoken, and feisty, and careful to put her complaints in writing, she was the last to be allowed to go "without a hassle."[157]

Althea Francois's departure was unceremonious. She called the Central Committee to say that she would not be opening up at the Lamppost, the Panther coffee house, that evening. She felt bad about not doing what she had said she would do. She remembers riding stony-faced past headquarters on a bus out of town with her young daughter, Olga, on her lap.

Grits Not Guns

Stephanie Moore was a child in the Lafitte Housing Project near downtown New Orleans in 1970 when the Panthers fed and taught her. She remembers eating breakfast before school—not just cereal but grits and eggs, and toast and milk. The Panthers also provided motivational speeches, arts and crafts, modern dance lessons, and booster shots. She says these offerings made a lasting impression. "We were well on our way to becoming self-sufficient, but they [the establishment] had a different plan for us. That's the reason the Panther story was suppressed."[158]

Ernest Jones, one of the attorneys who defended the Panthers, says,

You had a bunch of folks with no particular resources, not even jobs in the traditional sense. They weren't participants in the economy, but they dared to say, "There are people in our community who are hungry and we will feed them.

They don't have to go to the welfare office. They don't have to go to any of the central institutions that America has set up. *We* will feed these hungry people."

I really believe that the intellectuals and theoreticians who understand political structure said that this is something that could not be permitted. It just can't happen. You can't do that. And that was the beginning of the war against the Black Panther Party. There was a war against this organization. Most people think it was because the Black Panther Party used the slogan "off the pigs." It wasn't that. It was about the survival programs.[159]

Speaking of the Panthers both in New Orleans and nationally, Jones says:

Many of those survival programs, free food for poor children, health clinics, clothing and shoe giveaways, today have been institutionalized by government and churches. Many times people do not have a full understanding of the effect of what they are doing on the larger community and on the world. A bunch of young kids, who knew that they wanted to do something, weren't real sure how to go about it, had some guidance, and gave it their best effort—that was the Panthers. Moon and Giarrusso—they too moved in ways that they didn't expect, didn't fully understand or comprehend. None of us can understand until we look back.[160]

Conclusion

A forum in New Orleans on a mild September evening thirty years after the shootout brought together former Black Panthers, former Desire residents, community activists, and former city officials, including Mayor Moon Landrieu. It was powerful to witness the strength and depth of the legacy of the BPP. The party's Ten Point Program and Platform had sustained the Panthers throughout the years. The bonds of courage and service that they had forged together in their youth nourished a connection and a loyalty that overcame imprisonment, love affairs, breakups, and geographical separation.

The ten or so former Panthers in attendance had never opted out of the struggle for self-determination and self-sufficiency. The same is true for the three—Woodfox, Wallace, and Ailsworth—serving life sentences in Angola State Penitentiary. Althea Francois read a statement from Wallace; Rahim and Landrieu shook hands; and Landrieu told a reporter from the *Times-Picayune* that, in retrospect, the city had used excessive force against the Panthers.

As New Orleans struggles to recover from the neglect exposed by Hurricane Katrina, Rahim, King, and others are developing new possibilities for productive race relations and prison activism. They are creating survival programs that have garnered attention worldwide with their organizations called Common Ground and Free the Angola Three.

Seeds of social transformation sometimes take a long time to sprout and grow. The war against these New Orleans revolutionaries, after all, did not kill the revolution. And therein lies our hope for the future.

Notes

1. Adam Fairclough, *Race and Democracy: The Civil Rights Struggle in Louisiana, 1915–1972* (Athens: University of Georgia Press, 1995), xx.
2. Malik Rahim, interview by Orissa Arend, tape recording, November 15, 2002, New Orleans. All tapes of Arend's interviews are in Arend's possession unless noted otherwise.
3. Ibid.
4. Curtis J. Austin, *Up Against the Wall: Violence in the Making and Unmaking of the Black Panther Party* (Fayetteville: University of Arkansas Press, 2006), 249.
5. Jonathan Eig, "Desire Pays Price for Shortcuts," *New Orleans Times-Picayune*, June 19, 1989, Vertical file, Howard-Tilton Library, Louisiana Collection, Tulane University.
6. Gene Bourg, "Desire Project Incubator for Crime, Report Says," *New Orleans States-Item*, September 15, 1970, Vertical file, Howard-Tilton Library, Louisiana Collection, Tulane University.
7. Ibid.
8. Ibid.
9. Ibid.
10. Silas Lee et al., "Ten Years After (Pro Bono Publico?) The Economic Status of Blacks and whites in New Orleans—1985" (unpublished report, 1985), 2.
11. Monte Piliawsky, "The Impact of Black Mayors on the Black Community: The Case of New Orleans Ernest Morial," *Review of Black Political Economy* (Spring 1985): 6.
12. Ibid.
13. Geronimo ji Jaga, Anti-Violence Coordinating Committee meeting, Ashe Cultural Arts Center, New Orleans, January 21, 2004.
14. Superintendent Joseph I. Giarrusso, Department of Police, confidential interoffice correspondence, July 17, August 20, 1970, Moon Landrieu Collection, New Orleans Public Library.
15. "Judge Bagert Recuses Self in Desire Shooting Incidents," *New Orleans Times-Picayune*, September 17, 1970, Vertical file, Howard-Tilton Library, Louisiana Collection, Tulane University. The bulldozing of the St. Thomas Housing Development occurred in 2002. Judge Bagert's grandson Brod Bagert Jr. wrote a dissertation for the London School of Economics entitled "HOPE VI and ST. THOMAS, Smoke, Mirrors and Urban Mercantilism" (2002) detailing the wrongheadedness of the endeavor and the injustice to residents.
16. J. Giarrusso memo to Landrieu, July 30, 1970, Moon Landrieu Collection, New Orleans Public Library.
17. Barbara Guyton, flyer distributed in Desire, Moon Landrieu Collection, New Orleans Public Library.
18. J. Giarrusso memo, August 20, 1970, Moon Landrieu Collection, New Orleans Public Library.
19. "Racial Violence Is Culmination of Events," *New Orleans Times-Picayune*, September 17, 1970, Vertical file, Howard-Tilton Library, Louisiana Collection, Tulane University.

20. *Black Panther*, November 14, 1970.
21. J. Giarrusso memo to Landrieu, August 5, 1970, Moon Landrieu Collection, New Orleans Public Library.
22. Rahim, interview.
23. Ibid.
24. Ibid.
25. Kim Lacy Rogers, *Righteous Lives: Narratives of the New Orleans Civil Rights Movement* (New York: New York University Press, 1993), 154.
26. *New Orleans Times-Picayune*, April 27, 1970; *NOLA Express*, vol. 69, 1.
27. Rahim, interview.
28. "Death Toll Reaches New Mark," *Louisiana Weekly*, October 24, 1970, 1.
29. WTUL interview with Malik Rahim and Ahmad Rahman, March 13, 2000, transcript.
30. Adapted from Larry Schroeder, Lee Madere, and Jerome Lomba, *Local Government Revenue and Expenditure Forecasting: New Orleans*, Occasional Paper No. 52 (Syracuse, N.Y.: Metropolitan Studies Program, Maxwell School of Citizenship and Public Affairs, Syracuse University, October 1981), 5.
31. "N.O. Employment Has Reached Critical Stage," *Louisiana Weekly*, April 25, 1970, 1.
32. James R. Bobo, *The New Orleans Economy: Pro Bono Publico?* (New Orleans: College Business Administration, University of New Orleans, 1975), 1–2.
33. Rahim, interview.
34. Ibid.
35. Larry Preston Williams Sr., interview by Orissa Arend, tape recording, April 19, 2005, New Orleans.
36. Ibid.
37. Ibid.
38. Ibid.
39. Ibid.
40. Ibid.
41. Ibid.
42. Ibid.
43. Charles Y. W. Choi, "Who Rules New Orleans: A Study of Community Power Structures," *Louisiana Business Survey* 2 (October 1970): 10.
44. Rogers, *Righteous Lives*.
45. Moon Landrieu, interview by Orissa Arend, tape recording, March 2003, New Orleans.
46. Clarence Giarrusso, interview by Orissa Arend, tape recording, January 2003, New Orleans.
47. Ibid.
48. Allen Johnson, "News and Views: The Heroes of Howard Johnson's," *Gambit Weekly*, January 7, 2003, 9.
49. Ibid.
50. Ibid.
51. Joseph Fichter and Brian Jordan, *Police Handling of Arrestees: A Research Study of Police Arrests in New Orleans* (New Orleans: Department of Sociology, Loyola University of the South, 1964).
52. Ibid.
53. Israel Fields, interview by Orissa Arend, May 31, 2005, New Orleans.
54. Ibid.
55. Ibid.
56. Rahim, interview.

57. Ibid.

58. Althea Francois, telephone interview by Orissa Arend, May 24, 2005.

59. Warren Brown, "Residents Defend Panthers," *New Orleans States-Item*, September 15, 1970, Vertical file, Howard-Tilton Library, Louisiana Collection, Tulane University.

60. Rahim, interview.

61. Ibid.

62. Ibid.

63. Ibid. The first author tried her best to interview both Howard and Fields in 2002 and 2003. Fields, who is employed as a constable, said he would talk to me. On May 31, 2005, he finally did. Howard, who is still on the police force, told me he did not want to rehash the past.

64. Roy Reed, "Panthers 'Tried' 2 Police Agents," *New York Times*, September 19, 1970, Vertical file, Howard-Tilton Library, Louisiana Collection, Tulane University.

65. Rahim, interview.

66. Gene Bourg, "N.O. Panthers—from 'Birth' to Violence," *New Orleans States-Item*, September 16, 1970, Clippings file of Ruth Asher, historian for the NOPD.

67. *NOLA Express*, September 1970, Vertical file, Howard-Tilton Library, Louisiana Collection, Tulane University. Dates on many of the publications of this "underground" newspaper are estimates because in the "be here now" mentality of 1970, many editions are marked "the present" rather than dated.

68. Bourg, "N.O. Panthers."

69. Althea Francois, telephone interview by Orissa Arend, May 31, 2005.

70. Francois, interview, May 24, 2005.

71. Ferrel Guillory, "Desire Gun Fight," *New Orleans States-Item*, September 15, 1970, Vertical file, Howard-Tilton Library, Louisiana Collection, Tulane University.

72. Rahim, interview.

73. *New York Times*, September 15, 1970, Vertical file, Howard-Tilton Library, Louisiana Collection, Tulane University.

74. Rahim, interview.

75. Marion Brown, interview by Orissa Arend, tape recording, November 15, 2002, New Orleans.

76. "Races: Death in Desire," *Time*, September 28, 1970, 13, 28.

77. Rahim, interview.

78. Ibid.

79. Ibid.

80. *New Orleans Times-Picayune*, November 21, 1995. Giarrusso would later be criticized in a report issued by the International Association of Chiefs of Police for his handling of the situation.

81. HRC Archives, transcript of September 15, 1970, press conference.

82. "Desire Quiet," *New Orleans States-Item*, September 16, 1970, Clippings file of Ruth Asher, historian for the NOPD.

83. Williams, interview.

84. Ibid.

85. Ibid.

86. Ibid.

87. Giarrusso and Landrieu press conference, September 15, 1970, Moon Landrieu Collection, New Orleans Public Library.

88. *New York Times*, September 15, 1970.

89. Paul Atkinson, "Desire Area Residents Nervous After Shootings," *New Orleans Times-Picayune*, September 16, 1970.

90. "13 Panthers Charged with 5 Murder Attempts," *New Orleans States- Item*, September 21, 1970.

91. Joe Putnam, text of speech, Moon Landrieu Collection, New Orleans Public Library.

92. Ibid.

93. Ibid.

94. Landrieu, interview.

95. Baodong Liu and James M. Vanderleeuw, *Race Rules: Electoral Politics in New Orleans, 1965–2006* (Lanham, Md.: Lexington Books, 2007).

96. Landrieu, interview.

97. Kent B. Germany, *New Orleans after the Promises: Poverty, Citizenship, and the Search for the Great Society* (Athens: University of Georgia Press, 2007), 273.

98. These questions were raised by Judson L. Jeffries and are not the sentiments of Orissa Arend.

99. Francois, interview, May 31, 2005.

100. Cecil Carter, interview by Orissa Arend, tape recording, April 2, 2003, Hubbard Mansion, New Orleans; Bob Tucker, interview by Orissa Arend, tape recording, April 2, 2003, Hubbard Mansion, New Orleans.

101. Don Hubbard, interview by Orissa Arend, tape recording, April 2, 2003, Hubbard Mansion, New Orleans.

102. Ibid.

103. Henry Faggen, interview by Orissa Arend, tape recording, April 2, 2003, Hubbard Mansion, New Orleans.

104. Ibid.

105. Tucker, interview.

106. Faggen, interview.

107. Hubbard, interview.

108. William Barnwell, unpublished memoirs.

109. Jerome LeDoux, interview by Orissa Arend, tape recording, 2003, New Orleans.

110. Barnwell memoirs.

111. Ibid.

112. LeDoux, interview.

113. Barnwell memoirs.

114. LeDoux, interview.

115. Barnwell memoirs.

116. Faggen, interview.

117. Ibid.

118. Ibid.

119. Tucker, interview.

120. Faggen, interview.

121. Reed, "Panthers 'Tried' 2 Police Agents."

122. *Black Panther.*

123. *New Orleans States-Item*, November 24, 1970, Vertical file, Howard Tilton Library, Louisiana Collection, Tulane University.

124. *NOLA Express*, December 1, 1970, Vertical file, Howard Tilton Library, Louisiana Collection, Tulane University.

125. Williams, interview.

126. *NOLA Express*, December 1, 1970.

127. Ibid.

128. Ibid.

129. Ibid.

130. Tucker, interview.

131. Rahim, interview.

132. LeDoux, interview.

133. Harold Bethune, "Widely Different Views Voiced on NCCF and Its Impact on N.O.," *Louisiana Weekly*, December 5, 1970.

134. Robert King Wilkerson talks to Students Organized against Racism, Tulane University, 2003.

135. Robert King Wilkerson autobiography, unpublished, 4.

136. Ibid., 5

137. Ibid., 7

138. Rahim, interview.

139. Ibid.

140. Katy Reckdahl, "Panther Sprung," *Gambit Weekly*, March 6, 2001.

141. King autobiography, 7.

142. First names have been used to protect anonymity.

143. King autobiography; Robert King Wilkerson, interview by Orissa Arend, tape recording, 2003, New Orleans.

144. King autobiography, 9.

145. Reckdahl, "Panther Sprung."

146. Ibid., 9

147. King, interview.

148. Rahim, interview.

149. *New Orleans Times-Picayune*, August 7, 1971.

150. Ernest Jones, interview by Orissa Arend, tape recording, June 23, 2003, New Orleans.

151. Ed Anderson and Bruce Nolan, "12 Black Panthers Found 'Not Guilty,'" *New Orleans Times-Picayune*, August 7, 1971, Vertical file, Howard-Tilton Library, Louisiana Collection, Tulane University.

152. Rahim, interview.

153. Francois, interview, May 24, 2005.

154. Quoted in Charles E. Jones, ed., *The Black Panther Party (Reconsidered)* (Baltimore: Black Classic Press, 1998), 287.

155. Ibid.

156. Leah Hodges, "It's About Time" photo exhibit, April 3, 2003, Community Book Center, New Orleans.

157. Brown, interview.

158. Stephanie Moore, Anti-Violence Coordinating Committee Meeting, January 21, 2004.

159. Jones, interview.

160. Ibid.

CONCLUSION

Nesting the Black Panther Party in the Zeitgeist of Uncertainty

Omari L. Dyson

Sheriff John Brown always hated me
For what, I don't know
Every time I plant a seed
He said kill it before it grow
He said kill them before they grow.
—BOB MARLEY, "I SHOT THE SHERIFF"

Without ridding yourself of White supremacy, you will have new battles to fight from now on and evermore because it will constantly grow a new battle for you. As a matter of fact, this society will become more supremely racist when it is apparently non-racist.
—AMOS WILSON, "THE THIRD RECONSTRUCTION"

A philosophy professor once asked me during my dissertation phase, "What are you researching?" "The Black Panther Party in Philadelphia," I replied. He smirked and replied, "Aahh, resurrecting the unresurrectable, huh?" I stood frozen—removed of tongue and movement—and at a point allowed my insecurities to seep in, as I pondered my future as a scholar-activist. As I looked at this professor, I asked myself, What exactly did he mean? Was I attempting to crawl up a downward spiral? Would I be jeopardizing my academic career by pursing this particular subject matter? These questions, of course, were the manifestation of fear. My fear, however, would *never* compare to that experienced by many of the warriors who sacrificed their lives so that I may have the opportunity to study the subject of my choosing. After months of reflection, I made the decision to "resurrect the unresurrectable." During that time, I was able to expand the parameters of my consciousness in order to fully appreciate the complexity, significance, struggles, and beauty of the Black Panther Party (BPP), one of the most maligned yet celebrated organizations of the twentieth century.

This text extends beyond a historicity of Panther literature to provide readers with a manual on how social transformation was attempted, accomplished, and thwarted across various U.S. cities during the late 1960s and 1970s. In order to capture the magnitude of this book, I am going to utilize an hourglass framework—first, by discussing the current economic crisis vis-à-vis African-descended people; second, by couching this discussion in the context of this volume; and finally, by broadening the dialogue around what the Panthers represented at the local, national, and international levels.

Currently, the United States is in the throes of an economic crisis that has threatened (and will continue to threaten) people's very humanity. This predicament, like many other national atrocities, was preventable; however, a few people in positions of power allowed the seductiveness of capitalism to guide their behavior, which ultimately has put the livelihood of many American citizens in peril. From severe budget cuts in education to major reductions in the workforce, the reality of a worldwide recession has finally hit home. While the country attempts to find some footing in this quagmire, in-depth analysis uncovers an even more dire situation where blacks are concerned. In June 2009 the nation's unemployment rate reached 9.5 percent, as approximately 467,000 jobs were lost that month—totaling 6.7 million since the "onset" of the recession in December 2007 (Table 3 highlights the unemployment rates of the states included in this book).[1] When race is injected into the dialogue, the data shows that black unemployment, at 14.7 percent, is nearly twice that of whites, at 8.7 percent, and greater than that of Latinos and Asians, which hovers around 8.0 percent.[2] When gender and race are intersected, black men lead with a rate of 16.4 percent, followed by black women (11.3 percent), white men (9.2 percent), and white women (6.8 percent).[3]

On an ethical level, this recession has revealed a moral crisis that is undoubtedly rooted in greed. More than twenty years after the movie *Wall Street*, for many, greed is still good. Certain governmental officials, banks, mortgage and lending companies, and so forth capitalized on a vulnerable populace, simply because they could do so without fear of recourse or reprisal. But on a deeper level, this event represents something much more sinister when people of color are factored into the equation. Historically, property (that is, homeownership) has been a prize that, until relatively recently, has only been within reach of affluent whites and was tantamount to cultural capital (that is, whiteness), wealth, exclusiveness, and access to resources (for example, education and the ability to shape policy). As Ladson-Billings and Tate submit, "the purpose of the

Table 3. The shift of unemployment numbers and rates between December 2007 and June 2009

State	December 2007	June 2009	Job losses
Iowa	64,361 (3.8%)	104,123 (6.2%)	-39,762 (-2.4%)
Louisiana	79,974 (3.9%)	140,857 (6.8%)	-60,883 (-2.9%)
Michigan	363,738 (7.3%)	740,067 (15.2%)	-376,329 (-7.9%)
Missouri	160,466 (5.3%)	278,278 (9.3%)	-117,812 (-4.0%)
Texas	506,950 (4.4%)	899,740 (7.5%)	-392,790 (-3.1%)
Washington	157,572 (4.6%)	330,769 (9.3%)	-173,197 (-4.7%)

Source: "United States Department of Labor," July 21, 2009, Bureau of Labor Statistics, http://www.bls.gov/lau/.

government was to protect the main object of society—property."[4] Specifically, property was not only a right but a commodity afforded only to rich white men, and seldom attained by others. And, on occasion, when this ideology was challenged, numerous methods (that is, redlining, inflation, racial cleansing, lynching, and repression) were used to stymie the efforts of those who dared to trifle with such sacrosanct mores and customs.

By examining various policies administered by the U.S. government, it can be argued that they functioned to reinforce hegemonic relations by legitimizing socioeconomic inequities. When we turn to the subprime mortgage crisis, a close examination reveals that banks deliberately targeted black and Latino people in order to profit. In *Cuomo v. Clearing House Association* (2009), information derived from mortgage lending data illustrates that "national banks had issued a significantly higher percentage of high-interest predatory loans to African American and Hispanic borrowers than to White borrowers."[5] This predatory lending went unregulated for years and helped fuel the housing bubble, which eventually burst, leaving a disproportionate number of black and Latino people in home foreclosure and thus undercutting any possibility to accrue wealth. As Omali Yeshitela opines: "The wealth loss is staggering, people of color have collectively lost between $164 billion to $213 billion over the last eight years with Latinos losing slightly more than African Americans. . . . Before the crisis hit, it was estimated that it would take 594 years for Blacks to catch up with Whites in household wealth. And now, it could take ten times as much, nearly 5000 years."[6]

Overall, a thorough analysis of today's social conditions leaves little to celebrate, especially when juxtaposed against the pressing issues of the 1960s and 1970s: unemployment, underemployment, poor housing, segregation, poor education, and crime. These factors, among others, contributed to the rise of the Black Panther Party (BPP) and its numerous branches, chapters, and affiliates across the nation and globe. After examining these facets of society, the question that emerges is: What has *really* changed, structurally, in this country? On the surface, some may say we have a "black face in a high place," but what does this mean in the context of (neo)colonialism (whether some want to acknowledge its impact or not)?[7] Despite some economic gains in the post–civil rights/Black Power era, many black people, among others, continually face challenges that hinder social mobility. We represent a class of de-humanized individuals who are forced to survive under very tenuous conditions.

Although not explicitly tackled in this text, we, as researchers, are shaped by the times. This, I believe, is the stark reality of this book; we, like our Panther predecessors, have sacrificed our time, lives, and families to tell a story that continues to face vilification, silencing, and misrepresentation with the general purpose of miseducating the public. As researchers, we usually find an intrinsic motivation to uncover documents and testimonies from our history because it is empowering, transformative, and liberating. The realities found are not to be quantified and reduced to the following statement: "65 percent of Panthers were repressed." Such an analysis lacks vivacity and does not capture the realness of an experience as expressed about the shoot-out between police and Panthers in New Orleans on September 15, 1970. Our duty is to share such experiences with the masses in order to inform, educate, and transform the reader.

Although rewarding, developing a sequel to *Comrades: A Local History of the Black Panther Party* is a challenging task, especially when trying to locate former Panthers after a span of four decades. And if one is fortunate enough to find them, the hope (from my experience) is that they share the "perfect testimony" that is accurate and errorless. Unfortunately, such thinking is flawed, especially since memory loss may threaten the veracity of stories/experiences. Furthermore, the Panthers' perspective is oftentimes limited to their tenure in a particular branch or chapter; whether they worked aboveground or were a member of the underground; or the responsibilities for which they were charged and their exposure to certain information, to name a few. Because of these potential threats, among others, it is vital that a methodological dialogue occurs across various sources (primary and secondary) in an effort to mitigate any such threats to dialogical validity.[8]

Again, the purpose of *On the Ground* is not to fix a Panther identity. Rather, it is to expand one's consciousness about the experiences of Panthers and the work they performed as well as the opposition they faced (by agents of the state) around the country. Our objective for this project was to establish particularization as we compared Panthers across time and context.[9] In so doing, some of the themes/stories gathered can be transferred to other branches and communities to compare, contrast, and guide future research, but others cannot. Therefore it is crucial to understand how a context such the Houston branch was characterized by three waves of activism (that is, a fledgling BPP formation, People's Party II, and a full-fledged branch of the BPP), but may not be representative of other locales. In addition, some of the authors highlighted the impact that the Newton-Cleaver split had on the organization. After this point, we witness a Detroit cadre focusing as much energy on urban guerrilla warfare as they were on the community survival programs, while Des Moines' conflict with national headquarters contributed to their severance and impetus to develop the Black Revolutionary Communist Youth, further extending their service offerings. Along the same lines, those in Seattle reorganized their group as a legitimate nonprofit organization by filing for 501 C 3 status. These nuances are just a few examples that this book exposes about the BPP and, like its precursor, this book attempts to capture the rich identity (identities) of the organization—reinforcing the fact that each chapter and branch had distinct characteristics relative to social context yet at the same time shared many interesting commonalities. Furthermore, when the dialogues of community members, police officers, and even children (impacted by the work of the Panthers) are incorporated, an even richer story emerges.

To further expound, I had a conversation with the Reverend Wesley Campbell, director of the Science Bound Program at Purdue University, who shared his experience with the Panthers in Chicago. He recalled that when he was a second grader, the Panthers took children from the projects and fed them breakfasts in the morning, snacks in the evening, and dinner when needed. "Not only did they nourish our bodies, but they tutored us after school, protected us from gangs, promoted the importance of exercise, taught us self-defense, and helped us to love ourselves." One evening Rev. Campbell's experience changed when he witnessed two Panthers (one of whom was bearing a rifle) resting on a porch after being chased by the police near DuSable High School. "I did not know what triggered this chain of events, but what I do know is the end results. I knew that the Panthers had guns and the police were trying to shut them down for some reason." He continued: "After the Panthers were shut down, I noticed how gangs such as the Blackstone Rangers and the Disciples took over. Before, the Panthers were able to prevent the spread of gangs, but now, there was no one left to regulate that."[10] This impromptu dialogue with Rev. Campbell is valuable to understanding how children (now adults) conceptualized Panther efforts. Although Rev. Campbell's story was isolated to Chicago, it is remarkable to see how this story transfers to other locales, illustrating that the Panthers successfully initiated programs to meet the needs of youth by providing them with nourishment (mind and body), security, self-image initiatives, and positive models that were proactive and self-governing.

As I argued in my work on the Philadelphia Panthers in *Comrades*, the organization, as a whole, was a metonym for education. Not only did the Panthers raise the consciousness of the public via critical thought (that is, "*conscientiçacão*"), observation, and participation, but they also instilled a sense of humanity in the lives of oppressed individuals/groups.[11] This is not an attempt to embellish, because even at moments of critique (for example, feminist, womanist, queer, and so forth), the Panthers fueled others to become fully human in their own right.

The Panthers, through their community survival programs, provided a form of education that exposed America's contradictions and its insatiable appetite for materialism at poor people's expense. As James Baldwin once commented,

To any citizen of this country who figures himself as responsible—and particularly those of you who deal with the minds and hearts of young people—we must be prepared to "go for broke." Or to put it another way, you must understand that in the attempt to correct so many generations of bad faith and cruelty, when it is operating not only in the classroom but in society, you will meet the most fantastic, the most brutal, and the most determined resistance. There is no point in pretending that this won't happen.[12]

The Panthers were able to transcend the dominant ideology and, as a result, found themselves face-to-face with the seamy side of American repression.[13] This reality helps to explain why some Panthers decided to engage law officials on the battlefront. In some cases, though, when some Panthers were unsuccessful in such clashes, they found themselves attacking members of their own group. This is how power and oppression work—one's inability to conquer his or her colonizer (that is, oppressor) will cause individuals to redirect their frustrations inward, hence destroying themselves and those closest to them.[14] Some clear examples of how this process manifests itself in oppressed communities are witnessed in cases of drug/alcohol abuse, child abuse, domestic violence, and black male–on–black male homicide. These, of course, are acts of reactionary suicide that can be attributed to oppression (for example, police misconduct, segregation, miseducation, and glass ceilings in the workplace).

As the Panthers performed numerous limit-acts to overcome their limit-situations,[15] they used lived experiences to develop consciousness and galvanize individuals to transform society. By controlling for repression, when Panther practices are theorized by way of Abraham Maslow's hierarchy of needs, we witness how they focused on meeting the basic needs of the community in order to foster growth. From Maslow's perspective, if an individual's deficiency needs (physiological, safety, belongingness and love, and esteem) are unmet, that person will not be able to maximize his or her growth needs (need to know and understand, aesthetic, and self-actualization).[16] If an individual's needs are unmet, he or she will be robbed of reaching higher points of spiritual growth and purpose and, in turn, will react negatively. The individual's frustrations and hostility will be directed against himself or herself and/or his or her family, partners, children, and/or community. The diagram below provides a pyramidic view of Maslow's hierarchy of needs and its application to the survival programs of the local branches and chapters of the BPP.[17] Through their community survival programs, the Panthers laid the foundation for self-actualization (or one's motivation to recognize his or her full capabilities). Internally, the Panthers also reached higher levels of awareness as their ideology advanced across four stages: black nationalism (1966–1968), revolutionary socialism (1969–1970), internationalism (1970–1971), and, finally, intercommunalism (1971–).[18] The development of the Panthers' revolutionary ideology is a testament to their ability to adopt and grow with the changing political landscape within the United States and throughout the world. Intercommunalism, specifically, was introduced at the Revolutionary People's Constitutional Convention in Philadelphia, on September 4–6, 1970. Here, the Panthers sought to fuse ties with all oppressed groups in order to rewrite a nonexclusionary constitution. Whether community members and/or those served actually achieved self-actualization is a subject for future research and not within the purview of this essay.

Throughout their existence, the Panthers were dialectical materialists; the theory behind their resistance was to respond to the present conditions of oppression. Rather than accept Marxist historical materialism, which strictly relies on history to determine future direction when it is applied rigidly, the Panthers assessed each event within its specific context. Huey P. Newton states, "as dialectal materialists we emphasize that we must analyze each set of conditions separately and make concrete analyses of concrete conditions in each instance."[19]

As this society continues to grapple with rising unemployment (especially in Michigan, a state that suffered huge job losses due to layoffs from Ford, Chrysler, and General Motors), home foreclosures, high student loans, poor housing, high interest rates from credit, and lack of health care, one wonders how these forces will (re)shape U.S. public education. Alan Greenspan states, "I have voiced concern about the state of our elementary and secondary education while lauding the world-class university system we have built over the generations. It should be clear, however, that unless the former can be brought up to world class, the latter will either have to depend on foreign students or sink into mediocrity."[20]

The current educational system is far removed from humanity, culture, history, and real-world applicability. As a result, we find poor students of color performing worse than their white counterparts in reading, writing, and math. Furthermore, research has shown that there remains a gap in overall academic achievement between black and white students.[21] The explanation for this is linked to generations of oppression, a lack of wealth, and increasing poverty.[22] As President Barack Obama expressed at the 100th convention of the National Association for the Advancement of Colored People (NAACP) on July 16, 2009: "The state of our schools is not an African American problem; it's an American problem. If black and brown children cannot compete, America cannot compete."[23]

Our duty (as researchers, academicians, and activists), as the Panthers demonstrated, is to work to enhance the life chances of not only children but also adults by reeducating them and meeting their basic needs. We have an obligation to attack policies that continue to disenfranchise and marginalize the oppressed. Our responsibility is to dig deep within ourselves and find a commitment and passion to love one another through service. If we fail to do so, our hopes of attaining liberation will be even more remote than it was over forty years ago when the BPP was founded.

Hierarchy of Needs and Panther Survival Programs

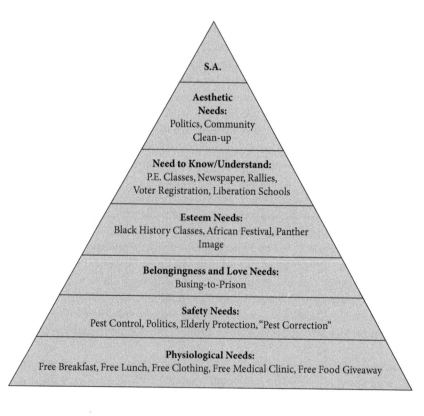

S.A.

Aesthetic Needs:
Politics, Community Clean-up

Need to Know/Understand:
P.E. Classes, Newspaper, Rallies, Voter Registration, Liberation Schools

Esteem Needs:
Black History Classes, African Festival, Panther Image

Belongingness and Love Needs:
Busing-to-Prison

Safety Needs:
Pest Control, Politics, Elderly Protection, "Pest Correction"

Physiological Needs:
Free Breakfast, Free Lunch, Free Clothing, Free Medical Clinic, Free Food Giveaway

Notes

1. Kelly Evans and Alex Frangos, "Rising Job Losses Damp Hopes of Recovery," *Wall Street Journal*, July 3, 2009.

2. U.S. Department of Labor, Bureau of Labor Statistics, July 2, 2009, http://www.bls.gov/news .release/empsit.to2.htm, accessed July 27, 2009; Brandon A. Perry, "Unemployment Alarming Trend among Blacks," *Indianapolis Recorder*, July 17, 2009.

3. U.S. Department of Labor, Bureau of Labor Statistics; Perry, "Unemployment Alarming Trend among Blacks."

4. Gloria Ladson-Billings and William F. Tate, "Toward a Critical Race Theory of Education," *Teachers College Record* (1995): 47–67.

5. "Supreme Court Ruling to Combat Predatory Lending," *Indianapolis Recorder*, July 17, 2009.

6. Omali Yeshitela, "The Economic Crisis of the United States, Part 1," *RBG Tube*, 2008, , accessed June 15, 2009.

7. Alex Spillius, "Barack Obama Tells Africa to Stop Blaming Colonialism for Problems," *Telegraph.co.uk*, July 9, 2009, dindianocean/5778804/Barack-Obama-tells-Africa-to-stop-blaming-colonialism-for-problems.html, accessed July 10, 2009.

8. Paula Saukko, *Doing Research in Cultural Studies: An Introduction to Classical and New Methodological Approaches* (Thousand Oaks, Calif.: Sage, 2003).

9. R. E. Stake, "Case Studies," in *Handbook of Qualitative Research*, ed. Norman K. Denzin and Yvonna S. Lincoln (Thousand Oaks, Calif.: Sage, 2000), 236–248.

10. Wesley Campbell, interview by Omari L. Dyson, July 29, 2009.

11. Paulo Freire, *Pedagogy of the Oppressed* (New York: Continuum International Publishing Group, 1970).

12. James Baldwin, "The Negro Child—His Self-Image," October 16, 1963, in *Sources: Notable Selections in Education*, ed. Fred Schultz (Guilford, Conn.: Dushink, 1998), 174–180.

13. Chela Sandoval, *Methodology of the Oppressed* (Minneapolis: University of Minnesota Press, 2000); Alan Wolfe, *The Seamy Side of Democracy: Repression in America* (New York: David McKay, 1973).

14. Amos Wilson, *Black-on-Black Violence* (Bronx, N.Y.: Afrikan World InfoSystems, 1990); Freire. *Pedagogy of the Oppressed*; Frantz Fanon, *The Wretched of the Earth* (New York: Grove Press, 1963).

15. "Limit-acts" are actions directed at negating and overcoming a social barrier, rather than passively accepting it. Freire, *Pedagogy of the Oppressed*.

16. Abraham Maslow, *The Farther Reaches of Human Nature* (New York: Viking Press, 1971); Abraham Maslow, *Motivation and Personality* (New York: Harper and Row, 1954).

17. On the pyramid, I used "pest correction" to refer to Panther use of survival-war tactics to contest any de-humanizing attacks on the part of local police (that is, pest). And, as Russell Shoatz (former member of the Black Unity Council [BUC] in Philadelphia and political prisoner) stated in *The Making of a Political Prisoner: The Autobiography of Russell "Maroon" Shoatz* (1999), "corrected" was a Panther euphemism for the assassination of a law official.

18. Judson L. Jeffries, *Huey P. Newton: The Radical Theorist* (Jackson: University Press of Mississippi, 2002); Maslow, *Farther Reaches of Human Nature*.

19. Erik H. Erikson and Huey P. Newton, *In Search of Common Ground: Conversations with Erik H. Erikson and Huey P. Newton* (New York: Norton, 1973), 26.

20. Alan Greenspan, *The Age of Turbulence: Adventures in a New World* (New York: Penguin Books, 2008).

21. Libby Quaid, "Achievement Gap Still Splits White, Black Students," *Yahoo News!* July 14, 2009, http://news.yahoo.com/s/ap/20090715/ap_on_re_us/us_black_white_achievement, accessed July 14, 2009.

22. Gloria Ladson-Billings, "From the Achievement Gap to the Education Debt: Understanding Achievement in U.S. Schools," paper presented at the Ninetieth Anniversary American Education Research Association Conference, Chicago, April 2006; Ladson-Billings and Tate, "Toward a Critical Race Theory of Education," 47–67; John U. Ogbu, *Cultural Models and Educational Strategies of Non-dominant Peoples* (New York: City College Workshop Center, 1989).

23. Martha T. Moore, "President Notes Racial Progress to NAACP," *USA Today*, July 17, 2009.

CONTRIBUTORS

Judson L. Jeffries is professor of African American and African studies at Ohio State University and director of the African American and African Studies Community Extension Center. Prior to that time he was an associate professor of political science, homeland security studies, and American studies at Purdue University. He earned his Ph.D. in political science at the University of Southern California in 1997. His research foci are radical formations of the 1960s, police-community relations, and African American politics. His work has appeared in such journals as *Ethnic and Racial Studies*, *Journal of Black Studies*, *PS: Political Science & Politics*, *Journal of Political Science*, *Western Journal of Black Studies*, *Caribbean Quarterly*, *Radical Philosophy Review*, *Journal of African American Studies*, and various other venues.

Reynaldo Anderson is an assistant professor of education at Harris-Stowe State University in St. Louis. He earned his Ph.D. at the University of Nebraska in the communications department. As an undergraduate he attended Jackson State University. His manuscript on the Black Panther Party in the Midwest is currently under review.

Orissa Arend, BCSW, LCSW, is a psychotherapist, mediator, community organizer, and freelance writer and journalist who lives in New Orleans. She holds a B.A. from Newcomb College in American studies and a master's of social work from Tulane University. She has been a contributing writer to the *Louisiana Weekly* (weekly columnist from 1999 to 2005), the *New Orleans Tribune*, and the *New Orleans Times-Picayune*. She convened a community forum on the Black Panthers in New Orleans in 2003. Her book *Showdown in Desire* has been published by the University of Arkansas Press.

Omari L. Dyson is an assistant professor in the Department of Teacher Education at South Carolina State University. He received his B.S. in experimental psychology at the University of South Carolina, his M.A. in child development and family studies, and his Ph.D. in curriculum instruction at Purdue University.

His previous publications include a chapter on the Philadelphia branch of the Black Panther Party in *Comrades: A Local History of the Black Panther Party* and several journal articles on African American males specifically and the black family in general.

Bruce Fehn is an associate professor in the Department of Social Studies Education at the University of Iowa. His has written articles and books on matters related to gender and race. He is the author of *Striking Women: Gender, Race and Class in the United Packinghouse Workers of America (UPWA) 1938–1968.*

Robert Jefferson is an associate professor of history at Xavier University in Cincinnati, Ohio. He earned his B.A. at Elon College, his M.A. at Old Dominion University, and his Ph.D. at the University of Michigan. His research focuses on African American GIs and military history. His seminal work is *Fighting for Hope: African American Troops of the 93rd Infantry Division in World War II and Postwar America.*

Charles E. Jones is an associate professor of African American studies and the founding chair of the Department of African American Studies at Georgia State University. Previously he was an associate professor of political science at Old Dominion University. He has published widely on the Black Panther Party and African American electoral politics. His seminal work is *The Black Panther Party (Reconsidered).* Jones earned his Ph.D. in political science at Washington State University in 1985.

Ryan Nissim-Sabat is a union organizer in Southern California. He earned an M.A. in black studies at Ohio State University in 1999. As an undergraduate, he attended Virginia Tech, where he majored in political science. His publications include a chapter on the Cleveland branch of the Black Panther Party in *Comrades: A Local History of the Black Panther Party.*

Joel P. Rhodes is an associate professor in the history department of Southeast Missouri State University. His teaching and research interests are in modern U.S. political and social history and Missouri. Rhodes's articles have appeared in the *Missouri Historical Review*, and he has written *The Voice of Violence: Performative Violence as Protest in the Vietnam Era* and *A Missouri Railroad Pioneer: The Life of Louis Houck.*

Jeff Zane earned his J.D. at New York University and his Ph.D. in history at the University of Notre Dame. Currently, he is an attorney at Diamond McCarthy LLP in Dallas, Texas.

INDEX

E 185.615 .O57 2010

On the ground

9 781617 032004